RANDALL JARRELL

A Descriptive Bibliography

1929–1983

RANDALL JARRELL

A Descriptive Bibliography

1929–1983

STUART WRIGHT

Published for the Bibliographical Society of
the University of Virginia by the
University Press of Virginia, Charlottesville

A Linton R. Massey Descriptive Bibliography

THE UNIVERSITY PRESS OF VIRGINIA
Copyright © 1986 by the Rector and Visitors
of the University of Virginia

First published 1986

Frontispiece: Randall Jarrell in 1964
(*Photograph by Pat Alspaugh, University of North Carolina
at Greensboro, courtesy of Mrs. Randall Jarrell*)

Library of Congress Cataloging in Publication Data

Wright, Stuart T.
    Randall Jarrell : a descriptive bibliography :
1929–1983.
    "A Linton R. Massey descriptive bibliography"—T.p.
verso.
    Includes index.
    1. Jarrell, Randall, 1914-1965—Bibliography.
I. Title.
Z8450.1.W74   1984   [PS3519.A86]   016.811'52   85-3132
ISBN 0-8139-1055-2

Printed in the United States of America

Unreservedly
for Mary
naturally

———————

Contents

Acknowledgments

My greatest debt in the preparation of this bibliography is to Mary von Schrader Jarrell, Randall Jarrell's widow. Without her encouragement, invaluable assistance, and friendship, my task would have been much greater.

The staffs of Randall Jarrell's publishers were enormously helpful in supplying information about his books. I am deeply indebted to Martin Weaver, of Farrar, Straus, and Giroux, and also to Michael Di Capua. Victoria Woods, of Alfred A. Knopf, deserves my sincere and continuing thanks for her efforts in securing the publication information I needed. At Macmillan Publishing Company, I would like to thank especially Phyllis Larkin, Alexia Dorszynski, and Barbara Gatson. Mary Flower, Copyright Manager at Atheneum Publishers, generously provided the necessary facts and figures for Jarrell's Atheneum publications. Harry Ford, also of Atheneum, deserves my thanks. Charlotte Holmes, of Ecco Press, kindly provided helpful information. Of Randall Jarrell's English publishers I would like to express my deepest thanks to Mavis E. Pindard, of Faber and Faber, and Anne Charvet, Senior Editor at Granada Publishing.

It is impossible for me to acknowledge everyone who has offered assistance and encouragement, so I must accept responsibility for omissions here. But those I would now acknowledge include: Emmy Mills, Curator of Special Collections at the Jackson Library, University of North Carolina at Greensboro, who repeatedly and generously supplied vital information from the extensive Jarrell Collection deposited there; Bert and DiDi Carpenter, of Greensboro, N.C.; Patricia Giles, of the Z. Smith Reynolds Library, Wake Forest University, Winston-Salem, N.C.; Marice Wolfe, Curator of the Fugitive Collection, Vanderbilt University, Nashville; Bruce Wilson, of Representative Steve Neal's Office, Washington, D.C.; Eugene R. Lehr, of the Reference and Bibliography Section, Library of Congress, Washington, D.C.; Evert Volkersz, Department of Special Collections, Melville Library, SUNY at Stony Brook; George G. Stewart, Reader Services Librarian, Oglethorpe University, Atlanta; J. M. Edelstein, Chief Librarian, National Gallery of Art, Washington, D.C.; Patrick G. Hager, Heritage Printers, Inc., Charlotte, N.C.; Maurice Sendak; Peter Taylor; and Robert Penn Warren. Finally, I would like to thank two specialist book dealers who assisted me by locating rare and out-of-print books, letters, and manuscripts by Jarrell: Henry Turlington, Resurrection Books, Pittsboro, N.C.; and J. Howard Woolmer, Revere, Pa.

For permission to quote from Randall Jarrell's letters I would like to extend grateful acknowledgment to Mary von Schrader Jarrell.

Bibliographical Method

This bibliography lists and describes the known publications of American poet, critic, and novelist Randall Jarrell. It owes much to the earlier work of Charles M. Adams, of Greensboro, N.C., whose *Randall Jarrell: A Bibliography* (Chapel Hill: Univ. of N.C. Press, 1958), and supplementary checklists, "A Supplement to Randall Jarrell: A Bibliography," *Analects*, 1 (Spring 1961), and "A Bibliographical Excursion with Some Bibliographical Footnotes on Randall Jarrell," *Bulletin of Bibliography*, 28 (July–September 1971), provided a solid foundation upon which to build and expand. I am deeply indebted, then, to the pioneering work of Mr. Adams.

Section A, which contains separate publications (books, pamphlets, and broadsides) by Randall Jarrell lists titles chronologically by edition and by country, American editions followed by English editions. For each of Jarrell's books there is a detailed description of the first American and first English edition. Subsequent editions are described in such detail as distinguishes them from earlier editions. A simple numbering system has been employed for entries in this section. **A6d**, for example, signifies the second edition, paperback (1980), of *Pictures from an Institution*: **A** refers to the section, **6** indicates that this is Jarrell's sixth separate publication, and **d** designates the proper chronological position within the sequence of published editions of that title. Advance proof copies, issued for review purposes, are described in the *Notes* paragraph (see below).

The descriptive formularies are taken from Fredson Bowers, *Principles of Bibliographical Description* (Princeton, N.J.: Princeton Univ. Press, 1949), with modifications by G. Thomas Tanselle, and further modifications by James L. W. West III. Descriptions for each book contain a paragraph for collation, contents, running titles (when present), typography, paper and binding, dust jacket, text contents, publication information, locations, and first appearance of new material (republication information relative to first appearance material is regularly noted in this paragraph). Leaf, board, and dust jacket measurements in descriptions of first printings are given in inches and millimeters; all other measurements are given in millimeters only.

Title Page: Title pages of first and subsequent reset editions (with the exception of **A3b**) have been photographically reproduced from the originals; unless otherwise indicated, all printing is in black ink.

Copyright Page: This page is also reproduced from the original, in compressed format, for first and subsequent reset editions (with the exception of **A3b**).

Collation: The standard Bowers formulary is used with two changes: there is no indication of format (8°, 16°), and dimensions of the leaves are given in the description of the paper below.

Contents: Standard Bowers formularies are again used.

Running Titles: The location of the running title (at head or foot) is first given. Then the printing is quasi-facsimiled from the left margin of the verso page across the gutter (indicated by a single vertical rule) to the right margin of the recto page.

Typography: Here the method is adapted from Tanselle's "The Identification of Type Faces in Bibliographical Description," *PBSA*, 60 (1966), 185–202.

Paper and Binding: Tanselle's "The Bibliographical Description of Paper," *SB*, 24 (1971), 26–67, serves as the guide here. Sheet size and bulking measurement are not given. Binding descriptions are based on Tanselle's "The Bibliographical Description of Patterns," *SB*, 23 (1970), 71–102. Cloth patterns are described verbally; stamping is quasi-facsimiled; edges, endpapers, and bands (when present) are also described.

Dust Jacket: Descriptions here are patterned after those in Tanselle's "Book-Jackets, Blurbs, and Bibliographers," *The Library*, 5th ser., 26 (June 1971), 91–134.

Text Contents: This paragraph lists the items included.

Publication: The date of publication and price are given first, followed by the number of copies printed (if known). Whenever possible the printer and binder are identified. Library of Congress registration information follows. The dates and size of subsequent printings complete this paragraph.

Locations: Although no fewer than ten copies of each book were scrupulously examined, only the following collections or institutional libraries have been noted.

DLC	Library of Congress
GU	University of Georgia, Athens
MJ	Mary Jarrell Collection, Greensboro, N.C.
NcGU	Randall Jarrell Collection, Jackson Library, Univ. of North Carolina at Greensboro
NcU	University of North Carolina, Chapel Hill
NcWsW	Wake Forest University, Winston-Salem, N.C.
NN	New York Public Library

STW	Stuart Wright Collection, Winston-Salem, N.C.
TxU	University of Texas, Austin
ViU	University of Virginia, Charlottesville

First Appearance: This paragraph identifies poetry and prose by Jarrell that appears in print for the first time; reprinted appearances of this material are regularly noted within this paragraph as well. Variants in subsequent printings of poems are also listed here.

Notes: These paragraphs contain descriptions of advance proof copies, oddities of manufacture, and miscellaneous supplemental information pertaining to the book or title described. They also include excerpts from the correspondence of Randall Jarrell with his publishers, colleagues, and friends that relate to the specific title. I have worked almost exclusively from typescripts prepared by Mary von Schrader Jarrell, who, with the compiler, is preparing for publication *Randall Jarrell's Letters* (Houghton Mifflin, 1985). These excerpts are printed here with the kind permission of Mrs. Jarrell. Excerpts appear also with specific poems, prose, or anthologies edited by Jarrell in sections B, C, and D.

Section B lists chronologically books edited by Jarrell and books containing first appearances of material by him. Subsequent variants are listed for those items that are appearing in print for the first time.

Section C lists chronologically first periodical appearances of works by Jarrell, including juvenilia, poems, translations, criticism, and fiction. Reprinted appearances of this material in books and periodicals, along with any variants in poems, are also listed.

Section D contains an annotated chronological listing of interviews with Randall Jarrell as well as published comments by him.

Section E contains three dust jacket blurbs by Jarrell, the first of which is actually an excerpt from his introduction to Eleanor Ross Taylor's *Wilderness of Ladies*. The third, which was published posthumously, was apparently the only one he contributed to a former student's work (Sylvia Wilkinson, *Moss on the North Side*). It is worth noting, however, that many excerpts from Jarrell's often-quoted book reviews were frequently used on the dust jackets of those of his contemporaries he seemed most to admire or champion—Robert Lowell, Elizabeth Bishop, and Wallace Stevens, most notably—and although several dozen such excerpts from reviews have been located, they do not qualify as original blurbs.

Section F lists four items that were mechanically reproduced by ditto process for stage use or for distribution, none of which was intended for general circulation.

Section G contains a chronological listing of sound recordings, disc and tape, of Jarrell reading from his work. Copies of the tape recordings prepared at the Recording Laboratory of the Library of Congress are identified by the numbering system used in *Literary Recordings: A*

Checklist of the Archive of Recorded Poetry and Literature in the Library of Congress, comp. Jennifer Whittington, rev. and enl. ed. (Washington, D.C.: Poetry Office, Manuscript Division, Research Services, Library of Congress, 1981).

Section H lists alphabetically by composer musical settings of poems by Randall Jarrell.

Section I contains a chronological listing of translations of Jarrell's writings, alphabetically arranged by country.

Section J lists a drawing by Jarrell that was published on the cover of the *Vanderbilt Masquerader* during his undergraduate years. It is possible, even likely, that he prepared other drawings for publication in this student humor magazine, but no other is signed or can be directly attributed to him.

Section K lists sound films devoted entirely to Jarrell and his work.

Abbreviations

WORKS

BFS	*Blood for a Stranger*
CP	*The Complete Poems*
KA	*Kipling, Auden & Co.*
LFLF	*Little Friend, Little Friend*
Los	*Losses*
LW	*The Lost World*
PA	*Poetry and the Age*
Pic	*Pictures from an Institution*
RFLP	"The Rage for the Lost Penny," in *Five Young American Poets* (1940)
SHS	*A Sad Heart at the Supermarket*
SLC	*The Seven-League Crutches*
SP2	*Selected Poems Including The Woman at the Washington Zoo* (1964)
SP55	*Selected Poems* (1955)
TBC	*The Third Book of Criticism*
WWZ	*The Woman at the Washington Zoo*

PUBLISHERS AND JOURNALS

AB	Anchor Books
AK	Alfred A. Knopf
AS	*American Scholar*
Ath	Atheneum
HB	Harcourt, Brace and Company
KR	*Kenyon Review*
Mac	Macmillan Company
Na	*Nation*
ND	New Directions
NR	*New Republic*
PB	Pantheon Books
Po	*Poetry*
PR	*Partisan Review*
PS	*Prairie Schooner*
SR	*Southern Review*
VQR	*Virginia Quarterly Review*

NAMES

AB	Amy Breyer
AE	Albert Erskine
AJR	Anna Jarrell Regan

AT	Allen Tate
CB	Cleanth Brooks
CC	Catherine Carver
CK	Charlotte Kohler
EB	Elizabeth Bishop
EE	Elisabeth Eisler
EW	Edmund Wilson
HA	Hannah Arendt
HF	Harry Ford
HH	Hiram Hayden
HR	Henry Rago
KS	Karl Shapiro
JC	John Ciardi
JCR	John Crowe Ransom
JE	Jason Epstein
JL	James Laughlin
LD	Lambert Davis
LU	Louis Untermeyer
MDC	Michael Di Capua
MJ	Mary Jarrell
MLJ	Mackie Langham Jarrell
MM	Margaret Marshall
MS	Maurice Sendak
PJ	Pyke Johnson
PRa	Philip Rahv
RG	Robert Giroux
RH	Rust Hills
RJ	Randall Jarrell
RL	Robert Lowell
RPW	Robert Penn Warren
SBQ	Sister Bernetta Quinn, O.S.F.

A

Separate Publications

A1 *BLOOD FOR A STRANGER*

First Edition (1942)

BLOOD FOR
A STRANGER

by

RANDALL JARRELL

Muss es sein?
Es muss sein!
Es muss sein!

HARCOURT, BRACE AND COMPANY, NEW YORK

Collation: [unsigned 1–6⁸]; 48 leaves; [2], [i–viii] ix–x, [1–2] 3–22 [23–24] 25–41 [42–44] 45–62 [63–64] 65–82 [83–84].

Contents: one blank leaf; p. i: half title: 'BLOOD FOR A | STRANGER'; p. ii: blank; p. iii: title page; p. iv: copyright page; p. v: dedication: 'TO | ALLEN TATE'; p. vi: blank; p. vii: acknowledgments, 5 lines in roman and ital; p. viii: blank; pp. ix–x: 'Contents'; pp. 1–82: text. *Note:* text is divided into four numbered sections.

Typography: text, 11/13 Janson; 33 lines per normal page; 154.5 (143.5) × 93 mm.; 20 lines = 92 mm.

Paper and Binding: leaf measures 8⁷⁄₁₆ × 5½ in. (214 × 140 mm.); yWhite (Centroid 92) wove, unwatermarked paper, uncoated smooth; v. R (Centroid 11) fine bead-cloth (202b) boards measure 8¹¹⁄₁₆ × 5⁷⁄₈ in. (221 × 148 mm.); front cover: unstamped; spine: vert., in d. B (Centroid 183), 'Randall Jarrell · Blood for a Stranger [at base, two lines] [right] Harcourt, Brace [left] And Company'; back: unstamped; top and bottom edges trimmed, fore-edge rough trimmed; yWhite (Centroid 92) wove, unwatermarked endpapers.

Dust Jacket: total measurement, 8¹¹⁄₁₆ × 19³⁄₈ in. (221 × 491 mm.); wove, unwatermarked paper; inner side white with flecks of red, outer side v. R (Centroid 11); both sides uncoated rough; lettered in white and vivid red; front: '[reversed out in white] BLOOD *for a* | STRANGER | *Poems by* | RANDALL JARRELL'; spine: in white, '[vert.] *Randall Jarrell · Blood for a Stranger* | [horiz.] HARCOURT | BRACE | AND | COMPANY'; back, in vivid red, 22 lines prin. in roman, blurb by Stephen Spender about W. R. Rodgers's *Awake!*; front flap: in vivid red, '$2.00 | BLOOD FOR A | STRANGER | By Randall Jarrell | [¶] BLOOD FOR A STRANGER is Randall | Jarrell's first book of poems. It in-|cludes, besides unpublished work, | verse which has appeared in

The | *Southern Review, Kenyon Review,* | *Partisan Review, New Republic,* | *Poetry, Atlantic Monthly, New* | *Yorker,* and in the 1940 New Di-|rections anthology of *Five Young American Poets.* | [¶] Mr. Jarrell, who is 28, grew up in Tennessee and California. He taught | for two years at Kenyon College and | has for the last three years lived in Austin, where he is on the faculty of | the University of Texas. | *Harcourt, Brace and Company* | 383 MADISON AVENUE, NEW YORK'; back flap, in vivid red, war bonds and stamps logo, 72 × 54 mm., and 9-line advertisement about war bonds and stamps.

Text Contents: 1. "On the Railway Platform," "London," "The Lost Love," "90 North," "A Story," "1938: Tales from the Vienna Woods," "A Little Poem," "Fat, Aging, the Child Clinging to Her hand . . . ," "Children Selecting Books in a Library," "A Poem for Someone Killed in Spain," "For an Emigrant"; 2. "The Iceberg," "Because of Me, Because of You . . . ," "The Bad Music," "The Blind Sheep," "1789–1939," "The Ways and the Peoples," "The Refugees," "Love, in Its Separate Being . . . ," "The Hanged Man on the Gallows . . . ," "A Picture in the Paper," "The Cow Wandering in the Bare Field . . . ," "When You and I Were All . . ."; 3. "For the Madrid Road," "The Automaton," "Over the Florid Capitals . . . ," "Kirilov on a Skyscraper," "Up in the Sky . . . ," "The Winter's Tale," "Jack," "Esthetic Theories: Art as Expression," "Dummies," "An Essay on the Human Will," "The See-er of Cities," "A Description of Some Confederate Soldiers"; 4. "The Head of Wisdom," "1938: The Spring Dances," "Fear," "The Machine-Gun," "The Memoirs of Glückel of Hameln," "Song: Not There," "The Long Vacation," "The Skaters," "The Christmas Roses," "Variations," "Che Faro Senza Euridice."

Publication: published 24 September 1942 at $2.00; 1,700 copies printed by Quinn and Boden Co., of Rahway, N.J. Copyright deposit copies received 16 September 1942. Registered in the name of Harcourt, Brace & Co., under A 167555. Registration renewed 20 November 1969, under A 47120, in the name of Mrs. Randall Jarrell.

Locations: DLC, GU, MJ, NcGU (2), NcU, NcWsW, NN, STW (3), TxU, ViU.

> *First Appearance:* "The Memoirs of Glückel of Hameln" SP55, SP2, CP.
> 4 almanac] ~, SP55+
> 20 They rather astonish than inform.] *omitted* SP55+
> 29–32 / 28–32 To marry and have children who get married | Is bad enough to do, and worse to hear: | In time, the amount of every dowry | Came to be, almost, more than I could bear.] One marries, one has children whom one marries; | One's husband dies; one mourns, remarries. | The reader reads, reads, and at last, grown

weary | With hearing the amount of every dowry, | He mumbles, Better to burn than marry . . . SP55⁺

38 please. . . ."] ~ . . ." SP55⁺

the last stanza is completely revised and rewritten in SP55⁺

Note: RJ originally submitted the manuscript of *Blood for a Stranger* to Scribner's, but the order and content differed somewhat from the published version: "An Interne in Pediatrics" (unpublished), "Children Selecting Books in a Library," "On the Railway Platform," "London," "A Little Poem," "Fat, Aging, the Child Clinging to Her Hand," "A Poem for Someone Killed in Spain," "Because of Me, Because of You . . . ," "The Bad Music," "1789–1939," "The Ways and the Peoples," "The Refugees," "Love, in Its Separate Being . . . ," "The Hanged Man on the Gallows . . . ," "When You and I Were All . . . ," "For the Madrid Road," "The Automaton," "The Winter's Tale," "Aesthetic Theories: Art as Expression," "The See-er of Cities" (which still included the note from RFLP), "A Description of Some Confederate Soldiers," "The Head of Wisdom," "The Machine-Gun," "The Christmas Roses," "Che Faro Senza Euridice," "A Story," "90 North," "The Tree" (in CP), "Variations," "The Blind Sheep," "The Skaters," "Eine Kleine Nachtmusik," "For an Emigrant."

RJ's friends at the *Southern Review*, Cleanth Brooks and Robert Penn Warren, had solicited a poetry manuscript for publication by the Louisiana State University Press, but things evidently were not running along smoothly or quickly enough to suit Jarrell. Allen Tate offered to do what he could to place this manuscript with a commercial house and, later on, with the University of North Carolina Press. Meanwhile, RJ received an invitation from James Laughlin of New Directions to submit a group of poems for inclusion in his Young Poets series (see below, B1). From the beginning, however, RJ regarded these projects as separate entities. *Blood for a Stranger* (the Brooks-Warren-Tate manuscript, basically, with occasional changes in contents), a book, and "The Rage for the Lost Penny," poems for an anthology appearance with four other poets. (Nevertheless, Laughlin advertised and promoted *Five Young American Poets*, in which RFLP was included, as "five books in one"). *Blood for a Stranger*, after going the rounds, was finally accepted by Harcourt, Brace in December 1941.

RJ to AT, February 1939: When I send the poems will you tell me whether you want any letters to go with them? I'm calling them *Blood for a Stranger*: a happily or unhappily characteristic title, I'm afraid.

RJ to SR (RPW), February 1939: Also, when do you want the poems for the book? Have you any idea when it will come through?

RJ to AT, February 1939: As for the North Carolina University Press, you're of course welcome to use my name in any way, and I'll give you if you want it, next spring, a book the size of this one. I've saved ⅔ as many as there are in this book, good ones, I mean,—I've lots of bad.

And I have good unfinished ones and I'll certainly be writing eight or ten before then: I'll have more than enough. Is that all right? Anyway, don't go to any trouble with Scribners or Random House, Allen; if they want it right away, OK, if not, Red [Robert Penn Warren] does.

RJ to AT, March 1939: Random House would be just as good as Scribners; you might try it first, if you think that better. I'll send you the stuff in a little.

RJ to AT, March 1939: I haven't answered yours because I'm so mixed up about that damn book. Red and the L. S. U. people wrote back that they want it badly, would print it immediately, etc. I haven't known what to do. Anyway, I'm sending you the manuscript.

RJ to AT, April 1939: I wrote Red a long time ago, asking him for . . . permission to give the poems to somebody else. . . . I've had no answer at all, and if I don't get one in three or four days I'm just writing him that I consider the absence of a reply a consent. I have the poems about half-typed; if, when you get them, you feel strongly that any should be left out, please tell me.

RJ to AT, January 1941: If you'll send back my manuscript, I'll add one or two poems to it that I can't bear leaving out (the *Poetry* one you liked ["The Ways and the Peoples"] and a couple of better ones, I hope) and change a few words in one; also, some more have been printed, so I have to change the acknowledgments a little. . . .[¶] Have you got any suggestions about leaving out ones, or are there parts that cry out to be changed, or anything like that? I wish you'd tell me about anything of the sort; probably, if you did, I'd just think, horrified, "How can he say *that* about *that*? that gem!"—people are fools, me too—but I might not.

RJ to AT, April 1941: This is just a note . . . thanks a lot for the suggestion about Scribners; I've typed another manuscript and am sending it to them.

RJ to HB (LD), December 1941: I'd like very much for you to publish the poems. I have no obligations anywhere else. We might write back and forth about when and what, and settle it finally when you come down. [¶] I've had about seventy poems published, and we could get most of the book from those; but there are plenty more to choose from. As for size, you know much more about that than I do. I remember Allen Tate's saying that more than forty or so poems bewilders everybody, especially reviewers. The sooner the better, so far as the time's concerned.

RJ to At, December 1941: Just as you told me to expect, Harcourt Brace wrote to say they'd print my poems. I'm sure you had a great deal to do with it, and I'm awfully grateful. I'd like to dedicate the book to you, if I may. You've certainly worked hard enough to get it printed.

RJ to AT, January 1942: Thanks a lot for helping select the poems. I told Lambert Davis I'd be delighted for you to, as I guess he told you. Select well, O Allen, or—but I can't think of a threat horrid enough; besides how'll I *know* whether you select well or not?

RJ to SR (CB), February 1942: Harcourt Brace is going to print a book of my poems in the fall; tell Red, won't you?

RJ to HB (LD), February 1942: I'm very sorry to be late with these poems; I've been so sick since Christmas that I've been unable to teach school or grade exams or do anything at all. The poems were in great confusion—I hadn't even copies of a good many—so I had to wait to do it myself; the only collection I could have made would have been a very feverish one, with drainage tubes stuck all over it. [¶] I've made no selection from these—probably any you select will suit me well enough; we can talk about it when we see each other. The only strong feeling I have is that we ought not to use too many—especially since so many of the poems are long or longish. [¶] If you want some more to choose from I'll add ten or fifteen unpublished ones. I haven't sent a good many published poems because I dislike them; and several I want to change.

RJ to HB (LD), March 1942: That's fine about Allen [Tate]; I wrote him expressing my delight—more or less. I'd rather have him do it [select the poems for inclusion]. If you'll send on all the suggestions, when they've been harvested, I'll read them and yell with pain or joy, and then we can finish the whole business when I'm there, as you suggest.

RJ to AT, March 1942: I can't tell you how I like the selections because Harcourt Brace hasn't sent them; but I will.

RJ to HB (LD), 5 May 1942: I wanted to do a good job of arranging, so I took the poems along on the train; I've worked out a good arrangement, I think—at least I worked a long time on it. I'm going to spend a day more on the punctuation, then I'll send them along, to get to you on Friday. Also I'll send the questionnaire for Mr. [Robert] Giroux.

RJ to HB (RG), May 1942: About quotations: I don't know any extremely usable ones. Allen [Tate] said in a *Partisan Review* article last spring, that I was "the white hope of American poetry"; but I needn't say that it would be highly inadvisable to use that. [John Crowe] Ransom (*Kenyon Review*) last summer said I used words like an angel; but I wouldn't use that either. Perhaps (I don't know whether this is ethical, or tactful or anything) you could ask Allen for a comment, the old one rephrased, say; or you might send Edmund Wilson the proofs and ask him for a quote—though I don't know whether this would be polite or justifiable. (I do know he's said he thinks me the most interesting young American poet, or something of the sort.) I know Ransom and Red Warren and Philip Blair Rice like my poetry; but probably it would be a bad idea to have more than one Agrarian say anything about it, or reviewers would be nastier than otherwise.

RJ to HB (LD), June 1942: The proofs just got to me yesterday, unbelievably enough—what with the censorship and the Mexican mails, the letters might as well walk. [RJ spent the summer of 1942 in Mexico.] I dislike just one thing: the way *for a* [in *Blood for a Stranger*] is printed on the title-page; having it in lower case and the rest in capitals gives a queer effect. If you could put it in capitals too I'd like it a lot better; it looks funny now.

RJ to HB (LD), September 1942: I was extremely delighted with the book, which has no typographical errors at all and which (especially the dust-jacket) is pretty as a picture. You are good publishers and I'm very grateful to you; I'll be more grateful if you'll send one more copy of the book at once—I especially need it.

RJ to HB (LD), November 1942: Thanks a lot for the reviews, advertisements, and letter. Advertisements! for poetry! I'm really overwhelmed.

RJ to EW, December 1942: Forgive me for not sending my book any sooner. . . . I started to write a touching inscription to you *qua* edition—you know, to the One who drew me from the sea of anonymity and exposed me, all dripping, to the world—or at least to the readers of the *New Republic*; but I couldn't bear to desert the Christmas-present formula (to——from——) I love.

A2 *LITTLE FRIEND, LITTLE FRIEND*

First Edition (1945)

LITTLE FRIEND, LITTLE FRIEND

By RANDALL JARRELL

....Then I heard the bomber call me in:

"Little Friend, Little Friend, I got two

engines on fire. Can you see me, Little

Friend?"

I said "I'm crossing right over you.

Let's go home."

DIAL PRESS · 1945 · NEW YORK

Title Page: 9¼ × 6 in. (234 × 152 mm.). Two rows of type ornaments printed in brill. B (Centroid 177).

Some of these poems have been published in Partisan Review, The Nation, The New Republic, The Kenyon Review, and Poetry.

This book is complete and unabridged in contents, and is manufactured in strict conformity with Government regulations for saving paper.

Printed in the United States of America by The Haddon Craftsmen, Inc., Scranton, Pa.

Collation: [unsigned 1–4⁸]; 32 leaves; [2], [1–10] 11–58 [59–62].

Contents: one unnumbered leaf; p. 1: half title: '*LITTLE FRIEND* | *LITTLE FRIEND*'; p. 2: blank; p. 3, title page; p. 4: copyright page; p. 5: dedication: 'TO | *SARA STARR*'; p. 6: blank; pp. 7–8: 'CONTENTS'; pp. 9–58: text; pp. 58–62: blank.

Typograpy: text, 14/17 Fairfield; 31 lines per normal page; 183 (170) × 105.5 mm.; 20 lines = 112 mm.

Paper and Binding: leaf measures 9¼ × 6 in. (234 × 152 mm.); yWhite (Centroid 92) wove, unwatermarked paper, uncoated smooth; gy. pB (Centroid 204) fine bead-cloth (202b) boards measure 9¹¹⁄₁₆ × 6³⁄₁₆ in. (240 × 157 mm.); stamping in black and v. OY (Centroid 66); front cover, in black: eleven solid five-point stars; spine: vertical, in black against a design in vivid orange yellow of an elongated pentagon attached by two interconnected hollow diamonds to an elongated hexagon, which in turn is connected by two hollow diamonds to an elongated pentagon like the first, all of which is framed top and bottom with triple rules: '[black] JARRELL [each vivid orange yellow diamond contains a black solid five-point star] *LITTLE FRIEND, LITTLE FRIEND* [two solid five-point stars within hollow diamond like first] DIAL'; back: contains publisher's device stamped in black in lower right corner; all edges trimmed; yWhite (Centroid 92) wove, unwatermarked endpapers, uncoated smooth.

Dust Jacket: total measurement, 9⁷⁄₁₆ × 22 in. (239 × 560 mm.); yWhite (Centroid 92) laid paper, vert. chainlines 30 mm. apart, watermarked '[open-face swash] *Ticonderoga | Text*'; front and spine are printed brO (Centroid 54), and front contains a solid black panel, 92 × 143 mm.; lettered in black and white; front: '[reversed out in white] POEMS | [row of type ornaments, 13 × 145 mm.] | [against solid black panel, within a frame of white rules] *Little Friend, | Little Friend* | [below black panel] [row of type ornaments in white, ident. to first] | [black] ". . . *THEN I HEARD THE BOMBER CALL ME IN: LITTLE | FRIEND, LITTLE FRIEND, I GOT TWO ENGINES ON FIRE. | CAN YOU SEE ME, LITTLE FRIEND?"* | [white] RANDALL JARRELL'; spine: vert., '[black] *JARRELL* [white, against a solid black panel, 92 × 7 mm.] *LITTLE FRIEND, LITTLE FRIEND* [at base, in black] *DIAL*'; back: in black, '[16 lines, prin. in roman, advertisement for Ezio Taddei's *The Pine Tree and the Mole*] | [swelled rule, 64 mm.] | [13 lines, prin. in roman, advertisement for *The Great Short Novels of Henry James* | [rule, 118 mm.] | THE DIAL PRESS, INC., 461 FOURTH AVE., NEW YORK 16'; front flap: in black, '[right] $2.00 | [left] LITTLE FRIEND, | LITTLE FRIEND | [swelled rule, 63 mm.] *By* RANDALL JARRELL | [swelled rule, 63 mm.] Randall Jarrell is one of the most | gifted of the new generation of | American poets. His new book of | verse, *Little Friend, Little Friend,* is | about war, about sorrow and about | guilt. Some of these poems are the | best record of the impact of the war | upon a truly modern sensibility. | They may also indicate certain of | the leading and the most creative | directions taken by writers during | the postwar period. | [¶] Jarrell is one of the best contem-|porary critics of poetry, and in one | of his recent reviews, speaking of | another poet's view of the war, he | said: "Most of the people in a war | never fight for even a minute. They | do not fight, but only starve, only | suffer, only die: the sum of all this | passive misery is that great activity, | War . . . The real war poets are | always war poets, peace or any time." | This new book of poems is full of | such insight, expressed in poetic | terms by a mind which is lively, | sensitive, original and learned.'; back flap: '*About the Author* | RANDALL JARRELL has lived | most of his life in Texas, Tennessee, | California, and the Army Air Force. | During peacetime he is an instructor | at the University of Texas. He en-|listed in the Air Force in 1942, and | was washed out as a pilot after a | month and a half's flying. When | the war ended he was a CNT oper-|ator at a field training B-29 crews, | with the rating of sergeant. | [¶] Mr. Jarrell writes regularly for | *Partisan Review,* the *Kenyon Re-|view,* the *Nation,* and other maga-|zines of the sort; his criticism is | known for its humor and severity. | Another book of his poems, *Blood | for a Stranger,* was published in | 1942. *Time* said about it that "some | of the lyrics in *Blood for a Stranger* | register the pain of human guilt as | it has seldom been registered in | American poetry."'

Text Contents: "2nd Air Force," "A Pilot from the Carrier," "The

Emancipators," "Losses," "The Dream of Waking," "Leave," "Siegfried," "Mother, Said the Child," "The Carnegie Library, Juvenile Division," "Soldier (T.P.)," "A Front," "The Learners," "Gunner," "Port of Embarkation," "Come to the Stone," "The Metamorphoses," "Absent with Official Leave," "Mail Call," "The Angels at Hamburg," "Protocols," "The Snow-Leopard," "The Boyg, Peer Gynt, the One Only One," "The Difficult Resolution," "1914," "The Soldier Walks under the Trees of the University," "A Lullaby," "The Soldier," "The Sick Nought," "Prisoners," "An Officers' Prison Camp Seen from a Troop Train," "The State," "The Wide Prospect, " "The Death of the Ball Turret Gunner."

Publication: published 23 October 1945 at $2.00; 2,000 copies printed by Haddon Craftsmen, Scranton, Pa. Registered in the name of Dial Press, Inc., under A 1973. Copyright deposit copies received 25 October 1945.

Locations: DLC, GU, MJ, NcGU, NcU, NcWsW, NN, STW(2), TxU, ViU.

> *Note:* The collection of RJ's war poems that became LFLF started out as a selection for James Laughlin's Poet of the Month series but was never published in that series.
>
> *RJ to ND (JL), March 1943:* About the invitation to be in the *Poets* series: I'd be interested in giving you my long Greek poem (the one in *Kenyon Review*) ["Orestes at Tauris"] and a few later ones, but only for a book in early 1944 and only if Harcourt Brace doesn't object.
>
> *RJ to MLJ, 14 April 1943:* I got a letter from [James] Laughlin saying the beginning of 1944 would be fine with him, and for me to write Harcourt Brace about it.... I'll write Lambert Davis and ask him whether Harcourt Brace minds my using *Orestes* and five or six poems for a New Directions book (they can reprint them in my second book with them). If they don't want me to presumably it'll only be because they want another [book] of mine fairly soon.
>
> *RJ to MLJ, 27 July 1943:* I believe I'll try to get Harcourt to publish a book of poems—all my army poems, *Orestes*, and a dozen or so others—next spring or so. I believe they'd have a real chance of selling more than usual. I put in (roughly): all the army poems and Orestes; the Difficult Resolution; Eine Kleine Nachtmusik; Scherzo; The Boyg, Peer Gynt; A Small Sonata; The Dialectic; Mother, said the Child; The Patient Leading the Patient; and three or four more—also any new army poems I write in the next few months. That would make an awfully good book, wouldn't it? You make any suggestions you can think of about the ones you'd like in.... I'd name the book, of course, *When the War Is Over We Will All Enlist Again*.

A3 *LOSSES*

A3a *First Edition (1948)*

LOSSES

RANDALL JARRELL

NEW YORK
HARCOURT, BRACE AND COMPANY

Title Page: $7^{15}/_{16} \times 5^{1}/_{4}$ in. (201×134 mm.).

Collation: [unsigned 1–5⁸]; 40 leaves; [i–x], [1–2] 3–63 [64] 65–68 [69–70].

Contents: p. i: half title: 'LOSSES'; p. ii: list of books '*By the same author*'; p. iii: title page; p. iv: copyright page; p. v: dedication: 'To | TOM MERCER'; p. vi: blank; p. vii: acknowledgments, 5 lines in roman and ital; pp. 1–63: text; p. 64: blank; pp. 65–68: RJ's '*Notes*' on the poems; pp. 69– 70: blank.

Typography: text, 11/13 Granjon; 34 lines per normal page; 163 (147) × 94 mm.; 20 lines = 92 mm.

Paper and Binding: leaf measures 7¹⁵⁄₁₆ × 5⁵⁄₁₆ in. (201 × 135 mm.); yWhite (Centroid 92) wove, unwatermarked paper, uncoated smooth; black fine bead-cloth (202b) cloth boards measure 8³⁄₁₆ × 5⁹⁄₁₆ in. (208 × 141 mm.); front cover: unstamped; spine: vert., in gold, 'LOSSES *Randall Jarrell* [two lines] [right] HARCOURT, BRACE [left] AND COMPANY'; all edges trimmed, unstained; yWhite (Centroid 92) wove, unwatermarked endpapers, uncoated smooth.

Dust Jacket: total measurement 8³⁄₁₆ × 18⁹⁄₁₆ in. (208 × 472 mm.); wove, unwatermarked paper, inner side coated smooth, outer side coated glossy; inner side, flaps, and back are white, front and spine are printed bGy (approx. Centroid 191); lettered in black and white; front: '[within a d. R (Centroid 16) oblong frame, the corners of which are rounded] [white] LOSSES | [horiz. propellorlike design in dark red] [black] POEMS BY | RANDALL | JARRELL'; spine: vert., '[in white] LOSSES [in black] *Randall Jarrell* [two lines] [top] HARCOURT, BRACE [bottom] AND COMPANY'; back: in black, '*Critical Comment | on Randall Jarrell's Poems* | [26 lines, prin. in roman, including blurbs or excerpts by Dudley Fitts (*Partisan Review*), Delmore Schwartz (*Nation*), Alan Swallow, *Time*, John Crowe Ransom, Theodore Spencer (*Saturday Review of Literature*), and Theodore Weiss (*Quarterly Review*, which is concluded on the back flap), and a black-and-white photograph of RJ, 70 × 76 mm., on the left side, opposite the first three excerpts ('RANDALL JARRELL' beneath)] | HARCOURT, BRACE AND COMPANY | 383 Madison Avenue, New York 17, N.Y.'; front flap: in black, '[upper right corner] $2.00 | [center] RANDALL JARRELL | LOSSES | [swelled rule, 38 mm.] | [11 lines, prin. in roman, including blurbs by Joseph Warren Beach (*Chimaera* [sic]) and Clement Greenberg (*Partisan Review*)] | [swelled rule, 38 mm.] | [5 lines, prin. in roman and ital, about the book] | *Harcourt, Brace and Company* | 383 Madison Avenue, New York 17'; back flap: in black, '*(Continued from back panel)* | [29 lines, prin. in roman, including conclusion of Weiss excerpt from the *Quarterly Review* and blurb-excerpts by W. T. Scott and Arthur Mizener (*Kenyon Review*)] | *Harcourt, Brace and Company* | 383 Madison Avenue, New York 17'.

Text Contents: "Lady Bates," "The Dead Wingman," "A Camp in the Prussian Forest," "Money," "Pilots, Man Your planes," "Stalag Luft," "The Place of Death," "O My Name It Is Sam Hall," "Eighth Air Force," "The Lines," "The Dead in Melanesia," "The Rising Sun," "A Country Life," "Burning the Letters," "The Breath of Night," "Sears Roebuck," "Jews at Haifa," "A Field Hospital," "When I Was Home Last Christmas," "New Georgia," "The Range in the Desert," "In the Camp There Was One Alive," "A Ward in the States," "The Märchen," "The Child of Courts," "The Subway from New Britain to the Bronx," "1945: The Death of the Gods," "Moving," "Loss," "In the Ward: The Sacred Wood," "Orestes at Tauris," "Notes."

Publication: published 17 March 1948 at $2.00; 1,000 copies printed and bound at Quinn and Boden Co., Rahway, N.J. Registered in the name of Harcourt, Brace and Co., Inc., under A16521; renewed 8 May 1975, under A 16521, by Mary von Schrader Jarrell.

Locations: DLC, GU, MJ, NcGU, NcU, NcWsW, NN, STW (3), TxU, ViU.

First Appearances:

"A Country Life" SP55, SP2, CP. Reprinted in *New York Times Book Review*, 2 May 1948, p. 2; *Modern American Poetry* (combined mid-century edition), ed. Louis Untermeyer (New York: Harcourt, Brace, 1950), pp. 683–84, and in the enlarged ed. (1962), pp. 649–50; *Mid-Century American Poets*, ed. John Ciardi (New York: Twayne, 1950), pp. 197–98; *North Carolina Poetry*, ed. Richard Walser (Richmond: Garrett & Massie, 1951), pp. 166–67.

"When I Was Home Last Christmas" SP55, SP2, CP. Reprinted in *As I Walked Out One Evening: A Book of Ballads*, ed. Helen Plotz (New York: Greenwillow Books, 1976).

"Moving" SP55, SP2, CP. Reprinted in *Don't Forget to Fly*, ed. Paul Janeczko (Scarsdale, N.Y.: Bradbury Press, 1981), pp. 79–81.

Note: In all copies examined, the "4" of "43" at the bottom of page 43 is broken.

Joseph Warren Beach's blurb on the front flap of the dust jacket is incorrectly attributed to "*Chimaera*" (*The Chimera*); it was in fact taken from Beach's review in *Accent*.

RJ to HB (RG), January 1947: I decided to put in some new poems, as you suggested. I'll send a few notes and some quotations from reviews in the next few days. The quotations from *Little Friend* are very favorable and ought to sell some copies of this book—I wish you'd use the back of the dust jacket for them, and perhaps put a couple on the inside of the front jacket? [¶] I include a new table of contents and some acknowledgments to magazines. By the way, will you put on the page opposite the title-page the names of my other books? [¶] This is as good an arrangement of the poems as I can think of—I'm sure the book shouldn't be split into war and non-war sections, since the effect would be much more monotonous.

RJ to HB (RG), October 1947: The jacket cover is very nice. I wish the red were less purpley-brown and more red-vermillion; but if you can't change it I can bear it very easily—it's very sober and classical, and makes me feel quietly contented. [¶] I'll look forward to seeing proofs of the jacket. As I understand it, those quotations from criticism that I sent will be on the back of the jacket, and the last two quotations (Joseph Warren Beach and [Clement] Greenburg [*sic*] will be inside the front jacket with whatever you cook up.

A3b *Second Edition (1954)*

All identical to **A3a** except for:

Title Page: 8 × 5³⁄₁₆ in. (203 × 132 mm.).

Copyright Page: omits '*first edition*'.

Contents: p. ii: includes *The Seven-League Crutches* in the list of books by RJ.

Dust Jacket: total measurement 8³⁄₁₆ × 18¹¹⁄₁₆ in. (208 × 475 mm.); wove, unwatermarked paper, both sides coated glossy; inner side, back, and flaps are white; front and spine are printed black; lettered in black, white, and m. YG (Centroid 120); front: '[contains a design of irregular interconnected ovular lines in white and moderate yellow green, which enclose six-and-a-half ovular solid panels in moderate yellow green, white, and black] [reversed out in white against a moderate yellow green panel] RANDALL JARRELL | [in moderate yellow green against a white panel] LOSSES | [against a black panel] POEMS | [reversed out in white against a black panel] "Certainly one of the two or three | most gifted of our contemporary poets." | JOSEPH WARREN BEACH'; spine: vert., '[reversed out in white] RANDALL JARRELL [moderate yellow green] LOSSES [white] Harcourt, Brace and Company'; back: in black, 'ALSO BY RANDALL JARRELL | The Seven-League Crutches | [30 lines prin. in roman, including excerpts from reviews by Robert Lowell (*N. Y. Times Book Review*), Fredrick Brantley (*Yale Review*), Paul Engle (*Chicago Tribune*), Winfield Townley Scott (*Virginia Quarterly Review*), and Lloyd Frankenberg (*Harper's Magazine*)]'; front flap: in black, '[upper right corner] $3.00 | [center] *Randall Jarrell* | LOSSES | [24 lines prin. in roman, including excerpts from reviews by Dudley Fitts (*N. Y. Times Book Review*), Robert Fitzgerald (*New Republic*, Hayden Carruth (*Poetry*), and *Time* | [center] (*Continued on back flap*)'; back flap: in black, '[center] (*Continued from front flap*) | [left] [4 lines in roman, conclusion of *Time* excerpt] | [15 lines in roman, blurb by Louis Untermeyer] | [center] HARCOURT, BRACE AND COMPANY | 383 Madison Avenue, New York 17, N.Y.'

Publication: 1,000 copies from a fresh setting of type were published in January 1954 at $3.00.

Locations: NcWsW, STW.

A4 *THE SEVEN-LEAGUE CRUTCHES*

First Edition (1951)

RANDALL JARRELL

The

SEVEN-LEAGUE
CRUTCHES

NEW YORK
HARCOURT, BRACE AND COMPANY

Title Page: 8 × 5¼ in. (203 × 133 mm.).

Collation: [unsigned 1–6⁸]; 48 leaves; [1–6] 7–47 [48] 49–69 [70]
71–94 [95–96].

Contents: p. 1: half title: 'THE SEVEN-LEAGUE CRUTCHES'; p. 2:
'*Books by Randall Jarrell* | [4 lines in roman]'; p. 3: title page; p. 4:
copyright page and dedication: 'To | MACKIE'; pp. 5–6: '*Contents*';
pp. 7–94: text; pp. 95–96: blank. Contents are divided into three
titled sections: "Europe," "Children," and "Once upon a Time."

Typography: text, 11/13 Granjon; 34 lines per normal page; 162
(147.5) × 96.5 mm.; 20 lines = 90 mm.

Paper and Binding: leaf measures 8 × 5¼ in. (203 × 133 mm.);
yWhite (Centroid 92) wove, unwatermarked paper, uncoated smooth;
black bead-cloth (202) boards measure 8¼ × 5½ in. (210 × 137
mm.); front: unstamped; spine: vert., in gold, 'THE SEVEN-LEAGUE
CRUTCHES *Randall Jarrell* [two lines at base] [top] HARCOURT,
BRACE [bottom] AND COMPANY'; back: unstamped; all edges
trimmed; yWhite (Centroid 92) wove, unwatermarked endpapers, uncoated smooth.

Dust Jacket: total measurement 8¼ × 13¾ in. (208 × 476 mm.);
wove, unwatermarked paper, both sides coated smooth; inner side,

flaps, and back are l. gY (Centroid 101), front and spine are gy. rO (Centroid 39); lettered in black, light grayish yellow, and grayish reddish orange; front: in light grayish yellow, 'The | Seven-|League | Crutches | [against a solid black panel, 29 × 165 mm., that crosses front and spine] RANDALL JARRELL | Twenty-eight new poems by "a poet with a | language of his own, a mind of first-rate in-|telligence, preoccupied with the question of | the nature of man."—STEPHEN SPENDER'; spine: vert., '[in black] The Seven-League Crutches [in light grayish yellow] RANDALL [against solid black panel] JARRELL [two lines, in black, at base] [top] *Harcourt, Brace* [bottom] *and Company*'; back: '[in grayish reddish orange] *Critical Comment on | Randall Jarrell's "Losses"* | [remainder in black] [32 lines prin. in roman, including excerpts from reviews by Dudley Fitts (*N.Y. Times Book Review*), Robert Fitzgerald (*New Republic*), Hayden Carruth (*Poetry*), and Louis Untermeyer)]'; front flap: '[upper right corner in black] $2.75 [left] *Randall Jarrell* | [right, in grayish reddish orange] The | Seven-|League | Crutches | [remainder left, in black] [18 lines prin. in roman, about the poet and his work] | [in grayish reddish orange] HARCOURT, BRACE AND COMPANY *383 Madison Avenue, New York 17, N.Y.*'; back flap: in black, '[29 lines prin. in roman, about the poet and his work, with publisher's name and address at bottom]'.

Text Contents: "Europe": "The Orient Express," "A Game at Salzburg," "A Soul," "Hohensalzburg: Fantastic Variations on a Theme of Romantic Character," "An English Garden in Austria," "The Face," "The Knight, Death, and the Devil," "Nollekens," "The Truth," "The Contrary Poet," "A Rhapsody on Irish Themes," "The Olive Garden," "A Conversation with the Devil"; "Children": "A Sick Child," "The Black Swan," "A Quilt-Pattern," "Afterwards," "The Night before the Night before Christmas"; "Once upon a Time": "A Girl in the Library," "The Sleeping Beauty: Variation of the Prince," "La Belle au Bois Dormant," "The Island," "Hope," "Good-bye, Wendover; Good-bye, Mountain Home," "Transient Barracks," "Terms," "Jonah," "The Venetian Blind," "Seele im Raum."

Publication: published 4 October 1951 at $2.75; 2,000 copies printed and bound by Quinn and Boden Company, Rahway, N.J. Registered in the name of Randall Jarrell, under A 59937; registration renewed under RE 19–783, 30 January 1979, by Mary von S. Jarrell.

Locations: DLC, GU, MJ, NcGU, NcU, NcWsW, NN, STW (4), TxU, ViU.

First Appearance: "A Rhapsody on Irish Themes" SP55, SP2, CP. An explanatory note by RJ concerning this poem is in SP55 and SP2 on p. xii and in CP on p. 7.
47 step] ~ SP55⁺

48–55 *[indented]* (And, as you say, the *Herr Geheimrath* | *[indented]*
Is the cut of a cast of Apollo; *Monseigneur* | *[indented]* An *emigre*
from a death in Saint-Simon | *[indented]* And Bishop of Maryland—
Baltimore, Maryland: | *[indented]* What counts is Religion *[right]* and
Politics. | *[indented]* I know, I know—they all say so at home; | *[in-
dented]* But at home they mean money—do you mean
money?] omitted SP55⁺

80–81 / 72 The red of dawn: | *[indented]* the capillaries are bro-
ken.] *all contained on line 72* SP55⁺

Note: Sets of "Advance Uncorrected Proofs" consisting of twenty-five
unbound leaves were sent out to special reviewers before publication.
One such set is in the Jarrell Collection at the Jackson Library, University of North Carolina at Greensboro.

   Although the front flap of the dust jacket indicates that this collection
contains twenty-eight poems, there are in fact twenty-nine.

RJ to RL, September-October 1949: I wrote a sort of longish curse on
Ireland—not too good, but fairly funny—earlier in the fall, but mostly
I've been finishing up older poems or translations.

RJ to SBQ, October 1949: I wrote another peom before this ["An English Garden in Austria"], a mocking, fairly funny, fairly long poem
about Ireland; I'll send it next letter.

RJ to ND (JL), January–February 1950: I'm not sending them [new
poems] to Harcourt because Harcourt always seemed so grudging and
dreary—they made me feel that publishing the poems was a minor cultural duty that they performed without the slightest enthusiasm. (Also,
they sold out *Losses* quickly, promised bookstores a new edition on
different definite dates, and never printed one.) What I want is a publisher with a Happy Smile—your ordinary advances and advertisements
will do, whatever they are, but I do want that look of joy, or mild
pleasure, or *something*—I got the feeling from Harcourt, that a win-
dow-dummy made out of ectoplasm was publishing those poor poems.

RJ to HB [RG], March-April 1951: Here is one of the books I wrote
you about, the verse one. If you want to publish it, please write me
about it as soon as you can; if you don't . . . I'll go ahead with the other
arrangements. I'd like to have it published in September—next fall,
anyway.

RJ to HB (RG), April-May 1951: I believe I'd like you to do the book
on those terms. I'd like to pick the type and such, but won't be in New
York until about the 20th of May. If that won't be soon enough tell me
and I'll just pick some recent Harcourt poetry book as a model. I'll send
you some quotations from critics to use on the dust-jacket and in your
fall catalogue.

RJ to HB (RG), April-May 1951: Here is a poem ["The Knight, Death,
and the Devil"] I'd like to have in my book—just after "The Face."

And I'd like very much to get all the arrangements made for the book; if you haven't time to go into details, will you just drop me a note about it?

RJ to HB (RG), May 1951: It's quite all right to go ahead with the 96-page version—I'd rather have more space and a page between sections, but if you can't you can't. The section-titles look nice.

RJ to HB (RG), 17 June 1951: Here's the proof, which seems notably correct. When I sent you proof of the *Acknowledgments* page I think I misspelled *Botteghe Oscure*—somebody's probably already caught it.

RJ to HB (RG), July 1951: Here are the galley proofs—sorry, I didn't realize they were used after the page proofs. [¶] I send biographical data for the back page; the Salzburg part of it ought to be useful for people who think "Why all of these poems about Europe?" [¶] The dustjacket is very pretty; I hope you will give my compliments to the chef.

RJ to HB (RG), late August 1951: Thanks ever so much for the book— I'm delighted with its looks; it couldn't be better as far as I'm concerned.

A5 *POETRY AND THE AGE*

A5a *First Edition (1953)*

Randall Jarrell

POETRY

AND

THE AGE

Alfred A. Knopf: New York

1953

Title Page: 8⅜ × 5½ in. (212 × 140 mm.).

Acknowledgment is hereby made for permission to quote from the following: LOUGH DERG, *copyright 1946 by Denis Devlin, used by permission of Harcourt, Brace & Co.* LORD WEARY'S CASTLE, *copyright 1944, 1946 by Robert Lowell, used by permission of Harcourt, Brace & Co.* THE MILLS OF THE KAVANAUGHS, *copyright 1946, 1947, 1948, 1950, 1951, by Robert Lowell, used by permission of Harcourt, Brace & Co.* CEREMONY AND OTHER POEMS, *copyright 1948, 1949, 1950 by Richard Wilbur, used by permission of Harcourt, Brace & Co.* SELECTED POEMS, *copyright 1938 by New Directions, used by permission of the publisher.* PATERSON, *copyright 1946, 1948 by William Carlos Williams, used by permission of New Directions.* THE GREEN WAVE, *copyright by Muriel Rukeyser, used by permission of the author.* COLLECTED POEMS, *copyright 1951 by Marianne Moore, used by permission of The Macmillan Company.* COMPLETE POEMS OF ROBERT FROST, *copyright 1930, 1947, 1949 by Henry Holt & Co., Inc. Copyright 1936, 1942 by Robert Frost. Used by permission of the publisher.* THE COLLECTED POEMS OF A. E. HOUSMAN, *copyright 1936 by Barclays Bank Ltd. Copyright 1940 by Henry Holt & Co., Inc. Used by permission of the publisher.* NORTH AND SOUTH, *copyright 1946 by Elizabeth Bishop, used by permission of Houghton Mifflin Co.* SELECTED POEMS *by John Crowe Ransom, copyright 1924, 1927, 1939, 1945 by Alfred A. Knopf, Inc., used by permission of the publisher.* HARMONIUM *by Wallace Stevens, copyright 1923, 1931 by Alfred A. Knopf, Inc., used by permission of the publisher.* THE AURORAS OF AUTUMN, *copyright 1947, 1948, 1949, 1950 by Wallace Stevens, used by permission of Alfred A. Knopf, Inc.*

L. C. catalog card number: 52-12173

THIS IS A BORZOI BOOK
PUBLISHED BY ALFRED·A·KNOPF, INC.

FIRST EDITION

Collation: [unsigned 1–5^{16} 6^8 7^{16} 8^8 9–10^{16}]; 144 leaves; [4], [i–vi] vii [viii] ix–x, [1–2] 3–271 [272–274].

Contents: two blank leaves; p. i: half title: 'POETRY | AND | THE AGE'; p. ii: blank; p. iii: title page; p. iv: copyright page; p. v: dedication page: 'TO | *Mary von Schrader*'; p. vi: blank; p. vii: preface and acknowledgments; p. viii: blank; pp. ix–x: contents; pp. 1–271: text; p. 272: 'A NOTE ON THE TYPE | [17 lines prin. in ital]'; pp. 273–274: blank.

Running Titles: head, 'POETRY AND THE AGE | [title of individual essay in all caps]'.

Typography: text, 10/16 Monotype Bodoni; 28 or 29 lines per normal page; pages with 28 lines measure 163 (168) × 97.5 mm., and pages with 29 lines measure 169 (174) × 97.5 mm.; 20 lines = 108 mm.

Paper and Binding: leaf measures 8⅜ × 5½ in. (212 × 139 mm.); yWhite (Centroid 92) wove, unwatermarked paper, uncoated smooth; black fine bead-cloth (202b) boards measure 8⁹⁄₁₆ × 5¾ in. (217 × 146 mm.); front cover: blindstamped, '[swelled rule, 86 mm.] | *Randall Jarrell*'; spine: horiz., in gold, '*Randall* | *Jarrell* | [swelled rule, 24 mm.] | POETRY | AND | THE AGE | [swelled rule, 24 mm.] | *Alfred A.* | *Knopf*'; back: Borzoi books logo blindstamped in lower right corner; top and bottom edges cut, fore-edge untrimmed; top edge stained p. gY (Centroid 104); yWhite (Centroid 92) wove, unwatermarked endpapers, uncoated smooth.

Dust Jacket: total measurement, 8⁹⁄₁₆ × 21 in. (217 × 533 mm.); wove, unwatermarked paper; inner side, back, and flaps are white; front and spine contain two panels in d. OlG (Centroid 126), which are separated by a third panel which is reversed out in white; lettered in white, v. R (Centroid 11), and dark olive green; both sides coated glossy; front: '[reversed out in white against dark olive green panel] *Randall Jarrell* | [against a white panel in vivid red] POETRY | [in dark olive green] AND | [in vivid red] THE AGE | [reversed out in white against a dark olive green panel] *A Brilliant Evaluation of* | *Poetry and Criticism of Our Time* | [in vivid red] ALFRED A. KNOPF: PUBLISHER: NEW YORK'; spine: '[horiz.] [reversed out in white against a dark olive green panel] *Randall* | *Jarrell* | [in vivid red against a white panel] POETRY | AND | THE AGE | [Borzoi books logo] | [reversed out in white against a dark olive green panel] *Alfred A.* | *Knopf*'; back: '[in vivid red] *Randall Jarrell* [remainder in dark olive green] [26 lines about the author]'; front flap: '[upper right corner in dark olive green] *$4.00 net* | *Randall Jarrell* | POETRY AND THE AGE | [in vivid red] *In a now famous essay,* | [remainder in dark olive green] "The Age of Criticism," reprinted in | this book, Mr. Jarrell describes a type | of criticism, increasingly rare these days, | which is both intelligent and useful and | which "sounds as if it had been written | by a reader for readers, by a human | being for human

beings," *not* as if it had | been written by "a syndicate of encyclo-
|pedias for an audience of International | Business Machines." *Poetry
and the Age* | is the author's first volume of criticism, | an extraordi-
narily intelligent and useful | book about poets and poetry in our time.
| Jarrell's range is as wide as his insights | and evaluations are pene-
trating. His | book contains (to use his own words) | "criticisms of a
good many of the best, | some of the better, and a few of the | [in vivid
red] *(continued on back flap)*'; back flap: '[in vivid red] (continued
from front flap) | [remainder in dark olive green] worse American
poets," and he gives us | besides his appraisals of several modern |
British and French poets. [¶] This is a book in which the poem is |
never an excuse for a display of critical | virtuosity intended for critics
only, but | is instead a statement by one human | being for other human
beings which is | always to be met and explored on its | own ground.
What does the poem say? | How does the poet say it? Apart from | his
steady concern for making himself | intelligible to the reader, Mr. Jar-
rell's | chief aim is to suggest answers to these | questions, and he does
so with his well-|known humor, learning, and sensibility. | Here is crit-
icism at its very best, criti-|cism that not only illuminates modern |
poetry and the age that has given birth | to it, but in a quite wonderful
way | awakens the reader to a more acute | awareness of his relation-
ship to both. | [in vivid red] *Printed in U.S.A.*'

Text Contents: "The Obscurity of the Poet," "Two Essays on Robert
Frost: 'The Other Frost' and 'To the Laodiceans,'" "The Age of Crit-
icism," "John Ransom's Poetry," "Some Lines from Whitman," "Re-
flections on Wallace Stevens," "A Verse Chronicle: I. Walter de la
Mare, II. Alex Comfort, III. Tristan Corbière, IV. Muriel Rukeyser, V.
R. P. Blackmur, VI. Anthologies, VII. Bad Poets," "Two Essays on
Marianne Moore: '*The Humble Animal*' and '*Her Shield*,'" "From the
Kingdom of Necessity," "Poets," "An Introduction to the *Selected Po-
etry of William Carlos Williams*," "Three Books," "The Situation of a
Poet."

Publication: published 23 August 1953 at $4.00; 2,000 copies printed
and bound by Kingsport Press, Inc., Kingsport, Tenn. Registered in
the name of Randall Jarrell, under A 100639. The publisher issued a
second printing of 1,750 copies in September 1953. The words 'FIRST
EDITION' were omitted from the copyright page, and the following
inserted: '*Published August 17, 1953* | *Second Printing, October
1953*'; remainder identical.

Locations: DLC, GU, MJ, NcU, NcWsW, NN, STW (4), TxU, ViU.

Note: Although the copyright page of the second printing lists the publication date of the first printing as 17 August 1953, Library of Congress records list the date as 23 August 1953.

RJ to ND (JL), January or February 1950: Delmore Schwartz told me—after I'd said that I wasn't going to send my next book to Harcourt—that he'd mentioned to you, and that you were interested in publishing it. I could send the book of poems to you immediately; and I could send in two or three months a critical book on modern poets that is finished except for the last thirty or forty pages.

RJ to HB (RG), February or March 1950: As you know I wrote James Laughlin about his publishing a new book of poems and one of criticism. He talked to you about it, and asked me to think it over for a while, in order to "avoid anything that might smack of any taint of stealing authors" and he goes on to say that "I don't want to have false hopes that we would be able to do much better than Harcourt, Brace. They do a very fine job at all times." He really quite leaned over backwards, as you see.

RJ to AK (HF), January or February 1953: One of the type-faces I liked best, in looking at Knopf books, was one by Durggius named Caledonia. It seemed to me particularly clear and easy to read. I know nothing about such things, though: I don't like a pale elegant page that one notices too much, but there're many different sorts of looks that I like.

RJ to AK (HF), May 1953: I got the proofs Friday and read them over and over all the weekend; it sounds disloyal to say it, but I'm sick of reading most of those essays. The proof seemed very correct. [¶] I'd rather have smooth black cloth than rough, other things being equal. But this is just because I liked the look of my last books; if you've got some pretty color or clever idea go ahead. I'm eager to see the binding and dustjacket—as I've said before, the book seems beautifully printed to me, as firm and readable as can be.

RJ to KR (JCR), 12 May 1953: I just sent page proofs of my criticism book to Knopf; it's named *Poetry and the Age* and is going to come out August 17th. They're going to print *Pictures* next spring.

A5b *Second Edition (1955)*

Randall Jarrell

POETRY

AND

THE AGE

New York: Vintage Books

1955

Title Page: 7¼ × 4⅛ in. (184 × 105 mm.).

Copyright Page: 'FIRST VINTAGE EDITION'.

Collation: perfect bound; 128 leaves; [i–vii] viii, [1–3] 4–25 [26] 27–33 [34] 35–62 [63] 64–86 [87] 88–100 [101] 102–120 [121] 122–

134 [135] 136–161 [162] 163–166 [167] 168–187 [188] 189–199 [200] 201–214 [215] 216–226 [227] 228–240 [241] 242–246 [247–248].

Contents: p. i: half title: 'POETRY | AND | THE AGE'; p. ii: blank; p. iii: title page; p. iv: copyright page; p. v: dedication page: 'TO | *Mary von Schrader*'; p. vi: preface and acknowledgments; pp. vii–viii: contents; pp. 1–246: text; p. 247: '[11 lines about the author, prin. in ital] | [8 lines about the type, prin. in ital]'; p. 248: '*Vintage Books* | [rule, 69 mm.] | [18 lines in small caps and ital listing 14 authors and titles in the Vintage Series (*Poetry and the Age* is listed as K–12)]'.

Running Titles: head, 'POETRY AND THE AGE | [individual essay titles in all caps]'.

Typography: text, 10/12 Linotype Janson; 36 lines per normal page; 152 (158) × 84.5 mm.; 20 lines = 84 mm.

Paper: leaf measures 7¼ × 4¼ in. (184 × 108 mm.); yWhite (Centroid 92) wove, unwatermarked paper, uncoated smooth.

Paper Binding: thick, wove, unwatermarked wrapper; inner side white, outer side printed black; both sides coated smooth; lettered in black, white, v. R (Centroid 11), and s. OY (Centroid 68); front: '[within a med. Gy (approx. Centroid 265) frame] [against a strong orange yellow panel in black] *Randall Jarrell* | [against a vivid red elongated rectangular panel that connects the two vertical sides of the octagonal frame] [letters reversed out in white and highlighted in black] POETRY | [against strong orange yellow frame in black] *and* | [against a vivid red panel like first in white letters highlighted in black] THE AGE | [against a strong orange yellow panel in black] A *Vintage Book* | [at bottom, below octagonal frame, in strong orange yellow] *Originally published by Alfred A. Knopf, Inc. 95¢ In Canada $1.00 K–12*'; spine: '[vert.] [in vivid red] *Randall Jarrell* [in strong orange yellow] POETRY AND THE AGE [in vivid red] *Vintage* [reversed out in white] *K–12*'; back: '[within a vertically elongated octagonal frame in medium gray] [against a strong orange yellow vertically elongated octagonal panel in black] *In a now famous essay,* | [25 lines prin. in roman taken from dust jacket flaps of A5a] | [below octagonal frame in vivid red] A *Vintage Book* | *Originally published by Alfred A. Knopf, Inc.*'

Text Contents: identical to A5a.

Publication: published 24 January 1955 at 95¢; 17,750 copies printed. A second printing of 7,500 copies was issued in October 1955. Copies are identical to the first printing except for the copyright

page: 'VINTAGE EDITION PUBLISHED JANUARY 24, 1955 | SEC-
OND PRINTING, OCTOBER 1955'. A third printing was issued in
November 1959 at $1.25; the copyright page contains: '*Vintage edi-
tion published January 24, 1955; second printing,* | *October 1955;*|
third printing, November 1959.' After the third printing, the publisher
reissued *Poetry and the Age* as Vintage Book V–12 in a number of
printings, but no record of dates or number of copies printed could be
located. There is no indication of the particular printing on the copyright page, which does, however, contain this notice below the ac-
knowledgments on all copies examined: 'VINTAGE BOOKS | are
published by ALFRED A. KNOPF, INC. | and RANDOM HOUSE, INC. |
Copyright, 1953, by RANDALL JARRELL | All rights are reserved under
International and Pan-American | Copyright Conventions. Published
in New York by Random | House, Inc., and in Toronto, Canada, by
Random House of | Canada, Limited. | Reprinted by arrangement
with ALFRED A. KNOPF, INC. | Manufactured in the United States of
America'.

Locations: STW(2),TxU,ViU.

A5c *First Octagon Books Impression (photo-offset from A5a)*
(1972)

All identical to **A5a** except for:

Randall Jarrell | [rule, 93 mm.] | POETRY | AND | THE AGE | [pub-
lisher's device] | [swelled rule, 62.5 mm.] | 1972 | *Octagon Books* |
New York

Title Page: 8 × 5⁵⁄16 in. (202 × 135 mm.).

Copyright Page: 'First Octagon edition, 1972'.

Collation: [unsigned 1–9¹⁶]; 144 leaves, [4].

Contents: the verso of the first unnumbered leaf and the recto of the
second unnumbered leaf contain a list of books by RJ; the verso of the
second unnumbered leaf is blank; p. 272 omits 'A NOTE ON THE
TYPE'.

Binding: d. R (approx. Centroid 16) fine bead-cloth (202b); cover
measures 8⁵⁄16 × 5⁷⁄8 in. (211 × 146 mm.); front cover stamped in
gold with Octagon Books device; spine: in gold, '[horiz.] Randall |
Jarrell | [rule, 26 mm.] | POETRY | AND | THE AGE | [at base] [Oc-
tagon Books device]'; all edges cut, unstained; cloth head and tail
bands have alternating yellow and red stripes.

Dust Jacket: issued without a dust jacket.

Publication: published in 1972 at $10.00; 500 copies printed.

Locations: MJ, STW.

A5d *First Noonday Press Paperback Impression (photo-offset from A5a) (1972)*

All identical to **A5a** except for:

Randall Jarrell | [rule, 93 mm.] | POETRY | AND | THE AGE | [publisher's device] | [swelled rule, 63 mm.] | *The Noonday Press* | A DIVISION OF | *Farrar, Straus and Giroux* | NEW YORK

Title Page: 7¹⁵/₁₆ × 5¼ in. (202 × 134 mm.).

Copyright Page: 'First Noonday edition, 1972'.

Collation: perfect bound; 144 leaves.

Paper Binding: thick, wove, unwatermarked paper wrapper; inner side is white, outer side is printed black; inner side coated smooth, outer side coated glossy; front and back covers contain an octagonal design similar to **A5b** in d. gy. Br (Centroid 62), s. OY (Centroid 68), and deep yPk (Centroid 27); lettered in black, white, and deep yellowish pink; front: '[within a dark grayish brown octagonal frame, against a strong orange yellow panel in black] *Randall Jarrell* | [against a deep yellowish pink panel in black ornamental block type outlined in white] POETRY | [against a strong orange yellow panel in black] *and* | [against a deep yellowish pink panel in black and white ornamental type like first] THE AGE | [against strong orange yellow panel in black] *Noonday N419 $2.85*'; spine: '[vert.] [in strong orange yellow] *Randall Jarrell* [in deep yellowish pink outlined in white ornamental type like front] POETRY [in strong orange yellow] *and* [in deep yellowish pink and white ornamental type like first] THE AGE [publisher's device in strong orange yellow] [horiz., reversed out in white] *N419*'; back: '[in deep yellowish pink] [left] *N 419 Literary Criticism* | ISBN 0–374–50972–7 | [right] $2.85 | [within a dark grayish brown octagonal frame, against a strong orange yellow panel, in black] [25 lines prin. in roman, including blurbs or quotations from reviews by Delmore Schwartz, John Berryman, John Crowe Ransom, and Leslie Fiedler] | [below octagonal frame, reversed out in white] COVER DESIGN BY RONALD CLYNE | THE NOONDAY PRESS *19 Union Square West, New York 10003*'.

Publication: published 15 March 1972 at $2.85; 5,078 copies printed.

A second printing was issued in August 1972, but publisher's records do not indicate the number of copies.

Locations: MJ, STW.

A5e   *First Ecco Press Paperback Impression (photo-offset from* **Afd***)* *(1980)*

All identical to **A5d** except for:

Randall Jarrell | [rule, 94 mm.] | POETRY | AND | THE AGE | [publisher's device] | [swelled rule, 63 mm.] | The Ecco Press | NEW YORK

Title Page: 8 × 5⅛ in. (201 × 130 mm.)

Copyright Page: 'This edition first published in 1980 by The Ecco Press, Ltd.'

Collation: perfect bound; 144 leaves.

Contents: p. 3: lists 'OTHER ECCO BOOKS OF RELATED INTEREST'; pp. 4–5: in the list of other books by RJ, '*Kipling, Auden and Co. 1979*' has replaced '*The Complete Essays and Criticism edition in preparation*', and '*edition in preparation*' has been omitted after *Fly by Night* and *Faust Part I*, with the publication date, 1976, inserted after each of these entries.

Paper Binding: heavy, wove, unwatermarked paper wrapper; inner side white, outer side printed v. yG (Centroid 129); inner side coated smooth, outer side coated glossy; front contains a black-and-white photograph of RJ, 95 × 117 mm.; lettered in black and white; front: '[above photograph of RJ, in black] RANDALL | JARRELL | [below photograph] POETRY & | THE AGE'; spine: '[vert.] [two lines, top line reversed out in white] RANDALL JARRELL [bottom line in black] POETRY & THE AGE [at base, centered between the two lines] Ecco'; back: '[right side in black] $6.95 | [remainder left] [29 lines prin. in roman, including blurbs by Schwartz, Berryman, Ransom, and Fiedler (from **A5d**)] | *Cover design by Loretta Li* | Photo by Ted Russell | [left, publisher's device the height of the last four lines] [reversed out in white] THE ECCO PRESS | [black] 1 West 30th Street, New York 10001 | Distributed by the Viking Press | 625 Madison Avenue, New York 10022 **SBN: 912–94670–9**'.

Publication: published March 1980 at $6.95; 3,000 copies printed.

Locations: MJ(5), STW(2).

A5f *First English Edition (1955)*

RANDALL JARRELL

Poetry and the Age

FABER AND FABER LIMITED
24 Russell Square
London

Title Page: 8⁹⁄₁₆ × 5³⁄₈ in. (211 × 136 mm.).

Copyright Page: 'First published in mcmlv'.

Collation: [unsigned A⁸] B-P⁸; 120 leaves; [1–8] 9–11 [12] 13 [14] 15–240.

Contents: pp. 1–2: blank; p. 3: half title: 'Poetry and the Age'; p. 4: list of other Faber books by RJ; p. 5: title page; p. 6: copyright page; p. 7: dedication page: 'To | MARY VON SCHRADER'; p. 8: blank; pp. 9–10: contents; p. 11: acknowledgments; p. 12: blank; p. 13: preface (ident. to **A5a**); p. 14: blank; p. 15: text.

Running Titles: head, '[essay or review title in all caps] | [essay or review title in all caps (ident. to verso page)]'.

Typography: text, 12/13 Walbaum; 36 lines per normal page; 169 (174) × 101 mm.; 10 lines = 90 mm.

Paper and Binding: leaf measures 8½ × 5⁵⁄₁₆ in. (218 × 137 mm.); yWhite (Centroid 92) wove, unwatermarked paper, uncoated smooth; s. R (Centroid 12) linen-cloth (304) boards measure 8¹³⁄₁₆ × 5¾ in. (224 × 146 mm.); front cover: unstamped; spine: in gold, '[horiz.] [ornamental type] *Poetry* & | *the Age* | *Randall* | *Jarrell* | [at base] *Faber*'; back: unstamped.

Dust Jacket: total measurement, 8¹³⁄₁₆ × 18⅛ in. (224 × 454 mm.); wove, unwatermarked paper; both sides uncoated smooth; both sides l. gY (approx. Centroid 101); front and spine contain three panels in gGy (Centroid 155); lettered in black; front: '[against upper greenish gray panel in black] POETRY | and the | AGE | [against center greenish gray panel] RANDALL | JARRELL | [against bottom greenish gray panel] Faber and Faber'; spine: '[horiz.] [against upper panel] PO-ETRY | and the | AGE | [against center panel] Randall | JARRELL | [against bottom panel] [vert. from top to bottom] Poetry & the Age | [horiz.] FABER'; back: 'SOME FABER POETRY | [swelled rule, 100 mm.] | [28 lines prin. in roman, including a list of 20 books by eight poets] | [swelled rule, 99 mm.] | FABER & FABER LIMITED 24 Russell Square London WC1'; front flap: 'Poetry and the Age | by RANDALL JARRELL | [¶] There could be no more lively | or helpful introduction to modern | American poetry than this exhilarating | volume. In it Mr Jarrell—one of the | most distinguished of the younger | American poets and critics—has col-|lected 'criticisms of a good many of | the best, some of the better, and a | few of the worse American poets'; | and for good measure there are | appraisals of several British and French | poets as well. | [¶] There is nothing heavy or pedantic | about Mr Jarrell's writing; it is un-|defiled by cliches or critical jargon. | Illuminated with intelligence and sen-|sibility, adorned with it, it is a | constant delight to read. Most impor-|tant of all, it is criticism which sends | its readers to the poems themselves | with new or reawakened interest. | [¶] Recently in this country there has | been a marked revival of interest in | American literature. *Poetry and the Age,* | both as an example of modern Ameri-|can criticism at its best and as a guide | to the American poetic scene, is | assured of a warm welcome. | [lower right corner] 18s'; back flap: '*Also by Randall Jarrell* | SELECTED POEMS | *12s 6d net* | ★ | PICTURES FROM AN | INSTITUTION | [34 lines prin. in roman, including excerpts from reviews of PI by John Metcalf, the *Manchester Guardian, Birmingham Post, Vogue, Punch, Sunday Times,* and *Queen*] | *12s 6d net*'; all edges cut, unstained; yWhite (Centroid 92) wove, unwatermarked endpapers.

Text Contents: identical to A5a.

Publication: published 7 April 1955 at 12s. 6d.; 2,000 copies printed.

Locations: MJ, NcGU, STW.

A5g *First English Paperback Impression (photo-offset from **A5f**)* *(1973)*

all identical to **A5f** except for:

RANDALL JARRELL | *Poetry and the Age* | FABER AND FABER LIMITED | LONDON'

Title Page: 7¾ × 4⅞ in. (196 × 124 mm.).

Copyright Page: '*First published in this edition in 1973*'.

Collation: [unsigned A-F¹⁶ G⁸ H¹⁶]; 120 leaves; [1–8] 9–11 [12] 13 [14] 15–240.

Paper Binding: heavy wove, unwatermarked white paper wrapper; inner side coated smooth, outer side coated glossy; lettered in s. B (Centroid 178), s. OY (Centroid 68), and white; front: '[left side in strong blue] *Poetry* | *& the* | *Age* | [rule, 100 mm.] | [in black] *Randall Jarrell* | [rule in strong blue, 100 mm.] | [right side, vert. from top to bottom, in strong orange yellow] [rule, 196 mm.] Faber paper covered editions'; spine: '[vert., from top to bottom] [in black] *Poetry & the Age* [strong blue] *Randall Jarrell* [reversed out in white against a strong orange yellow panel] Faber'; back: '[left side in strong orange yellow, vert. from bottom to top] [rule, 196 mm.] Faber paper covered editions | [right] [remainder in black] *Faber and Faber* | *publish books by the following poets* | [left column, list of twenty names in all caps] [right column, list of twenty names] | [center] RICHARD WILBUR | *Please write to* | Faber & Faber Limited 3 Queen Square London WC1N 3AU | *for a complete list of Faber Paper Covered Editions*'; inside front cover: '[in black] Poetry and the Age | by | Randall Jarrell | [9 lines prin. in roman, including a quote from David Daiches in the *Manchester Guardian*] | £1·20 | *net* | [rule, 80 mm.] | Faber paper covered editions | [rule, 80 mm.]'; inside back cover: '[in black] The Complete Poems | RANDALL JARRELL | [32 lines prin. in roman, including a quote from Robert Lowell, a description of the book, and excerpts from reviews by Ian Hamilton (*Observer*) and Alan Brownjohn (*New Statesman*)]'

Publication: published in 1973 at £1.20; publisher's records do not give the date and number of copies printed.

Locations: MJ, STW.

Pictures

from an

Institution

A Comedy by

Randall Jarrell

NEW YORK ALFRED A. KNOPF 1954

Title Pages: each page measures 8¼ × 5⅜ in. (207 × 137 mm.).

A6 PICTURES FROM AN INSTITUTION

A6a *First Edition (1954)*

Collation: [unsigned 1–2¹⁶ 3⁸ 4–7¹⁶ 8⁸ 9–10¹⁶]; 144 leaves; [2], [i–vi] vii [viii], [1–2] 3–31 [32–34] 35–75 [76–78] 79–128 [129–130] 131–183 [184–186] 187–222 [223–224] 225–248 [249–250] 251–277 [278].

Contents: one unnumbered leaf, the verso of which contains a list of books by RJ; p. i: half title: '[script] *Pictures* FROM AN | [script] *Institution*'; pp. ii–iii: title pages; p. iv: copyright page and disclaimer by RJ; p. v: dedication page: 'TO [script] *Mary* AND [script] *Hannah*'; p. vi: blank; p. vii: contents; p. viii: blank; pp. 1–277: text; p. 278: 'A NOTE ON THE TYPE | [14 lines in ital] | [publisher's device] | [3 lines in roman and ital]'.

Running Titles: head, '*Pictures* FROM AN *Institution* | [individual chapter titles in ital and small caps]'.

Typography: text, 11/14 Linotype Janson; 32 lines per normal page; 164.5 (170) × 97 mm.; 20 lines = 98 mm.

Paper and Binding: leaf measures 8¹⁄₁₆ × 5⁵⁄₁₆ in. (206 × 134 mm.); yWhite (Centroid 92) wove, unwatermarked paper, uncoated smooth; bluish green (no Centroid equivalent) fine bead-cloth (202b) boards measure 8³⁄₈ × 5³⁄₄ in. (212 × 143 mm.); front blindstamped: '[swelled rule, 86 mm.] | [script] *Randall Jarrell* | [swelled rule, 86 mm.]'; spine: in gold, '[horiz., in script] *Randall Jarrell* | [vert.] *Pictures* FROM AN [script] *Institution* | [horiz.] *Alfred A.* | *Knopf*'; back: publisher's device blindstamped in lower right corner; top and bottom edges cut, fore-edge untrimmed; top edges stained s. Pk (Centroid 2); yWhite (Centroid 92) wove, unwatermarked endpapers, uncoated smooth.

Dust Jacket: total measurement, 8³⁄₈ × 20⁵⁄₈ in. (212 × 517 mm.); wove, unwatermarked paper; inner side, flaps, and back are white; both sides coated smooth; front and spine are divided into two large panels, the top of which is printed in black, and the bottom in m. OlG (Centroid 125); front contains a design consisting of five horiz. jagged panels (three against the upper black panel and two against the lower moderate olive green panel), in m. rO (Centroid 37), moderate olive green, and black, with corresponding regular panels in ident. colors on the spine; lettered in white, black, and moderate reddish orange; front: '[in white: all lettering against irregular panels except fourth line] PICTURES | FROM AN | INSTITUTION | [script] *A Comedy* | [in moderate reddish orange] *BY RANDALL* | *JARRELL*'; spine: '[horiz.] [in black] PICTURES | [reversed out in white] FROM AN | [in black] INSTITU-|TION | [in white] A COMEDY | [in black] RAN-DALL | JARRELL | [publisher's device in black against a small moderate reddish orange panel] | [in white] ALFRED A. | KNOPF'; back: '[in black] PRAISE FOR [in moderate olive green] *Pictures From an Institution* | [28 lines in black, prin. in roman, including blurbs by Marianne Moore, David Daiches, Eric Bentley, Richard P. Bissell, Stanley Edgar Hyman, James Agee, Louis Untermeyer, Mark Schorer, and William Carlos Williams]'; front flap: '[upper right corner in moderate olive green] $3.50 net | [remainder left] [in black, four lines in roman, blurb by Wallace Stevens] | [in moderate olive green, 17 lines in roman, about the book] | [in black, eight lines in roman, blurb by Jean Stafford] | [in moderate olive green] Jacket design: HARRY FORD'; back flap: '[black-and-white photograph of RJ, 94 × 66 mm., at top] | [below photograph in moderate olive green] Photograph by R. THORNE MCKENNA | [in black, 20 lines about the author] | [in moderate olive green] *Printed in U.S.A.*'

Text Contents: 1. "The President, Mrs., and Derek Robbins"; 2. "The Whittakers and Gertrude"; 3. "Miss Batterson and Benton"; 4. "Constance and the Rosenbaums"; 5. "Gertrude and Sidney"; 6. "Art Night"; 7. "They All Go."

Publication: published 3 May 1954 at $3.50; 6,000 copies printed and bound by Kingsport Press, Inc., Kingsport, Tenn. Registered in the name of Randall Jarrell, under A 124769. The publisher issued three subsequent printings in cloth; the words 'FIRST EDITION' were dropped from the copyright page, and the printing was indicated: 2d printing, 1,500 copies in June 1954; 3d printing, 1,500 copies in August 1954; and a 4th printing, 2,000 copies, in January 1955.

Locations: DLC, MJ, NcGU, NcU, NcWsW, NN, STW (4), ViU.

First Appearances:

"The Whittakers and Gertrude."

"Art Night" Reprinted in *The Greensboro Reader*, ed. Robert Watson and Gibbons Ruark (Chapel Hill: Univ. of North Carolina Press, 1968), pp. 3–23.

"They All Go."

Note: Advance copies in printed wrappers were issued to selected reviewers before publication. They are identical to **A6a** except for the wrappers of pale grayish blue (no Centroid equivalent) wove, unwatermarked paper: front: '[in black] [publisher's device] *Advance Copy* | PICTURES | FROM | AN | INSTITUTION | *a comedy by* | *Randall Jarrell* | *Alfred A. Knopf* | PUBLISHER | *New York*'; spine: two lines, '[vert., in black] [top line] *Randall Jarrell* [publisher's device] [bottom line] *Advance Copy* PICTURES FROM AN INSTITUTION *Alfred A. Knopf*'.

Before publication, as part of its promotion campaign, the publisher mailed out to bookdealers a broadside consisting of a single yellow leaf, 303 × 228 mm., containing the **A6a** jacket blurbs by Marianne Moore, David Daiches (in part), Wallace Stevens, and Louis Untermeyer. The blurbs by Bentley, Bissell, Hyman, Agee, and Schorer were not included; however, this promotional flyer did contain blurbs that were not used on the jacket by Jean Stafford, Robert Penn Warren, Gerald Warner Brace, Robie Macauley, Henri M. Peyre, Granville Hicks, Leslie Fiedler, and Irving Howe.

RJ to HA, August 1951: Did I tell you that I've written fifty more pages for *Pictures from an Institution?* Lovely pages, many about Art—tell your husband; if he isn't crazy about *Art Night at Benton* I'll die of chagrin.

RJ to MJ, 30 August 1951: I've been reading *Pictures from an Institution* and thinking about changes and additions; 'speck I'll do quite a few things to it this fall. I liked some of the narrative parts well enough to think, "No, Homer, and everybody since was right—it *is* better to have narrative with digressions rather than digressions without narrative": I'll remember next time. Man is the animal that likes narrative.

RJ to KR (JCR), September 1952: I was really much flattered to be asked for part of my prose book—a comedy, I call it, since it's hardly a novel. I've copied out for you, and send, the first book, which I think does pretty well by itself; there are two parts which would do as well or better: one, a little shortened, is a general treatment of Benton College in (quite particular) terms of an old teacher of Creative Writing named Camille Turner Batterson (this part's almost like a short story); the other part is the story of Gertrude at Art Night, a yearly event at which the painting and sculpture and drama departments [have an exhibition and a] writer makes a speech. One is considerably more serious than Book I and the other is considerably funnier (Peter's [Taylor] read both and can give you an idea of them.) I tell you about them because I don't want to print the first book by itself unless you think you'd have room for them later on, *if* you liked them of course. You see why this is: as long as I have the first book for an introduction I can arrange some of the other parts and print them in a magazine, but without the first part I'd be rather at a loss. [¶] I have the whole book done except for thirty or forty pages here and there. I'll have it entirely finished by the first or second week of January, I think. . . . [¶] I don't want the sight-unseen part of this *Pictures from an Institution* deal to be in any way troublesome to you: if you feel it would be a lot better to see them now, the other two parts, I could send one of them complete and the other ⁹⁄₁₀ done.

RJ to KR (JCR), November 1952: As for the relation of Dwight Robbins [president of Benton College in PI] and Harold Taylor [then-president of Sarah Lawrence College], I'd better talk at length. *My* President is a Molière-esque type, the type of all such presidents, and is pretty different from Taylor, but he's also like him in some notable way. The real trouble here is this: *any* character who's a curly-haired young president of a progressive college will seem (to people in the world of colleges) to be Harold Taylor because there's only one curly-haired young president of a progressive college, Harold Taylor. I'll talk some about the differences and similarities. Mrs. Taylor is an ordinarily unpleasant Englishwoman, not within a million miles of my fabulous South African; the Taylors have two ordinary children, no growling Derek; they have an ordinary English sheepdog, no Afghan twins; Taylor himself is a Canadian; a philosopher not a sociologist; was never an Olympic diver or anything of the sort; didn't hire lots of Rhodes Scholars; isn't a sort of *idiot savant* of Success like Robbins, but is much shrewder, more pretentious and hypocritical, more intelligent, etc., was an Assistant Professor metamorphosed into a President, not a professional educator like Robbins. He didn't come from the Lower Depths à la Gatsby, and has perfectly ordinary manners. But my Dwight Robbins' appearance, perpetual youngness, perfect adjustment to his sur-roundings, are modelled on Taylor's (Taylor's conversation is quite un-like Robbins', Robbins talks ordinary President banalities, Taylor likes to sound as cultivated as possible, as versatile as possible, like Renais-sance Man being pals with Stephen Spender.) [¶] In other words, I think Taylor is like my Dwight Robbins (except for a few particulars like curly hair, ingenuous sincerity) only insofar as he's like the general type of such Boy Wonder executives, he was mostly a point of departure for me, but I did take several steps before departing. [¶] But this is all dif-ferent from the question: *will* this part of the book get me or *Kenyon* [*Review*] into trouble as being too like Taylor? I just don't have the knowledge or training to judge. Knopf seems sure it wants to publish the finished book, and no fears about libel have occurred to it, but the *New Yorker*, when Peter [Taylor] showed it to them, was afraid. . . . I couldn't make essential changes like having Pamela Robbins come from Independence, but I could, with tears, change smaller things. . . . [¶] I've taken it for granted that all this will delay the piece to the next issue . . . probably I'll have the new parts of the book finished by then, and you can look at it in its completed form and pick whatever parts you like. [¶] Benton College is completely synthetic, fanciful, typical; its education is like the education at Sarah Lawrence, but there is no teacher or student at Sarah Lawrence with *any* resemblence to my people at Benton—Dwight Robbins is the only human resemblence. My Dwight Robbins is so different from Taylor that I . . . think about him, "Poor creature, if he could only become human!" But Taylor seems to me a smarter, more disingenuous, more unpleasant man, a real differ-entiated individual—Robbins is just a type, inhuman because he's no more than a type. [¶] I do hope this hasn't been a trouble to you; what-ever you think best, I'd even sacrifice the curly hair, though as many tears as a princess in a fairy tale.

RJ to PR (PRa), August 1953: Gertrude is so large and real to me (I can make up in my sleep a sentence for her to say about anything) that it seems funny to have her confused with Mary McCarthy, whom I know slightly and don't know too much about; but she *is* the same general type as Mary McCarthy, her books are like [hers], and I got five or six happenings or pictures from M. M. But the readers who know Jean Stafford best think she is Gertrude, and the ones who know—but I won't go on with this list of Lady Writers. I hope (this is said in a grandiloquent tone) that Gertrude will survive when all of them are forgotten. One of the other characters says about her, "She is one of the principles of things—a naked one," and I hope this is right too. [¶] If you should want to cut Book II in two [for publication in PR], at the end of the party at Gertrude's, that would be all right with me. Let me know as soon as you conveniently can, will you? I've promised to get a part to Accent. I believe these two books are the best for you to pick from; Book IV is a long serious, sympathetic, more or less, section about the Rosenbaums and Constance, and Book VII, the last, is full of Happy Endings, endings, and wouldn't do to print by itself.

RJ to AK (HF), 10 November 1953: The sample pages are *extremely* good looking, I think—almost better than *Poetry and the Age.* The print's beautiful and plain, the proportions of the page nice, the chapter numerals and page numerals unusually nice, and so on; and the big *Constance and the Rosenbaums* somehow makes the book look beguiling and easy, as if it were Angela Thirkell or a box of candy . . . [¶] Doing it just from page proof will be fine. . . . I don't think any biggish changes will occur to me.

RJ to HA, January 1954: Although the Rosenbaums aren't too like you and Heinrich as individuals, I hardly could, hardly would have made them up without knowing you. I think I made them very like you in some of the very big general things—in most of the medium-sized things they're quite different. I first got the idea for Gottfried from a man different in almost every way from Gottfried, with whom I spent some summer weeks at the beach house of a family I used to be friendly with—he was Freud's friend and disciple [of] Hans Sachs. Then I used a lot of things from myself for him, just as I did for Gertrude. After I'd written a little about Gottfried he seemed real and wrote himself; Irene was a vaguer, non-romantic, partly contradictory idea, and I had to think a lot about her, work and change, before she got to seem real. I think she's a little more like you than Gottfried's like Heinrich—but it's only part of her that's like part of you, and there's almost nothing in her that corresponds to the historian-philosopher part of you. But the Rosenbaum's relation to this country is very much understood in terms of you and your husband—and the sentence about Gottfried and Irene "quarreling" fiercely about Goethe and Hölderlin, etc., applies even better to you two than to the Rosenbaums.

RJ to EB, September 1956: I've got worse and worse about writing real letters, and I got started not writing to you when (I blush to say it) I was vexed at your letter about *Pictures,* which to me is a serious book not about Mary McCarthy. But I soon got over that, and after that not writing was just ordinary or extraordinary neurotic behavior.

A6b *First Meridian Paperback Impression (photo-offset from* **A6a***) (1960)*

All identical to **A6a** except for:

[left, in script] *A Comedy by* | *Randall Jarrell* | [in roman and ital] MERIDIAN FICTION *New York*   [right, in script] *Pictures* | [in roman] FROM AN | [script] *Institution*

Title Pages: each page measures 7¹¹⁄₁₆ × 4¹⁵⁄₁₆ in. (196 × 126 mm.).

Copyright Page: 'First printing January 1960'.

Collation: perfect bound; 144 leaves.

Paper Binding: thick, wove, unwatermarked dark yellowish white paper wrapper; both sides coated smooth; lettered in black and S. OY (Centroid 68); front: '[in black] [hollow type which reveals photographic image within] PICTURES FROM AN INSTITUTION | [in strong orange yellow] a comedy | RANDALL | JARRELL | [in black, photographic close-up of an eye and forehead on the left and a vertical row of three photographic close-ups of eyes, the middle of which is framed by horn-rimmed glasses] [right of bottom eye, vert. from bottom to top] RAMIREZ | [horiz., left] Meridian Fiction MF 2 [right] $1.35 / Canada $1.45'; spine: '[vert., in black hollow type like front] PICTURES FROM AN INSTITUTION | [horiz. at base] M F 2'; back: '[in strong orange yellow] PICTURES FROM AN INSTITUTION | [25 lines in roman all caps, with names in boldface, including blurbs by Robert Penn Warren, James Agee, Jean Stafford, Granville Hicks, Orville Prescott, Eric Bentley, and Wallace Stevens] | [left, in black, publisher's device] [right, in strong orange yellow, 3 lines concerning Meridian Fiction publications] | MERIDIAN FICTION IS DISTRIBUTED BY MERIDIAN BOOKS, INC.'

Publication: published in 1960 at $1.35; number of copies is not known.

Locations: MJ, NcGU, STW.

A6c *First Farrar, Straus & Giroux Impression (photo-offset from* **A6a**) *(1968)*

All identical to **A6a** except for:

[left, in script] *A Comedy by* | *Randall Jarrell* | [in roman] FARRAR, STRAUS AND GIROUX   NEW YORK   [right, in script] *Pictures* | [in roman] FROM AN | [in script] *Institution* | [publisher's device]

Title Pages: each page measures 7^{15}/₁₆ × 5^{5}/₁₆ in. (202 × 135 mm.).

Copyright Page: 'First Farrar, Straus and Giroux edition, 1968'.

Collation: [unsigned 1–9^{16}]; 144 leaves; [i–x], [1–2] 3–31 [32–34] 35–75 [76–78] 79–128 [129–130] 131–183·[184–186] 187–222 [223–224] 225–248 [249–250] 251–277 [278].

Binding: s. bG (approx. Centroid 160) fine bead-cloth (202b) boards measure 8³⁄₁₆ × 5½ in. (209 × 142 mm.); front cover blindstamped: '[script] *Randall Jarrell* | [decorative rule, 112 mm.]'; spine: in gold, '[vert., two lines] [top line, in script] *Pictures from an Institution* [bottom line, in script] *Randall Jarrell*; | [horiz. at base] [publisher's device] *FARRAR* | *STRAUS* | *GIROUX*'; back cover: unstamped; wove, unwatermarked brO (Centroid 54) endpapers, uncoated rough.

Dust Jacket: total measurement, 8¼ × 19⅝ in. (209 × 498 mm.); wove, unwatermarked paper; both sides are white; inner side coated smooth, outer side coated glossy; front contains four panels, three rectangular and one circular, each containing within it a solid black panel, one ovular, two rectangular, and one circular; lettered in white, black, and s. gB (Centroid 169); front: '[left side, within a rectangular panel in brill. YG (Centroid 116), against a solid ovular panel] [reversed out in white] Pictures [right side, within a strong greenish blue rectangular panel, against a black rectangular panel] from | an | [within a s. G (Centroid 141) rectangular panel, against an elongated black rectangular panel] Institution [within a brilliant yellow green solid circle, against a solid black circle] A COMEDY | [brilliant yellow green rule, 25 mm.] | BY *Randall* | *Jarrell*'; spine: '[two lines, vert., in black] [top] Pictures from an Institution [bottom] *Randall Jarrell* FARRAR, STRAUS & GIROUX | [horiz. at base, in strong greenish blue, publisher's device]'; back: '[in strong greenish blue] *(continued from back flap)* [in black] achievement, our only way of | [29 lines prin. in roman, including blurbs by Paul Pickrel (continued from back flap), Robert Penn Warren, Wallace Stevens, Paul Engle, William Carlos Williams, Harvey Curtis Webster, Marianne Moore, Joseph Henry Jackson, Orville Prescott, and Eric Bentley; text in black, names in strong greenish blue] | [in black] FARRAR, STRAUS & GIROUX'; front flap: '[upper right corner, in black] $5.95 | [first 3 lines bold] "*Pictures from an Institution* just | might be Randall Jarrell's great | masterpiece." | [30 lines prin. in roman, about the book, including a comment by John Crowe Ransom and blurbs by Jean Stafford and James Agee (which is concluded on back flap); text in black, names in strong greenish blue] | [in strong greenish blue] *(continued on back flap)*'; back flap: '[in strong greenish blue] *(continued from front flap)* | [28 lines, including conclusion of Agee blurb and blurbs by Sylvia Angus, Granville Hicks, and Paul Pickrel (which is concluded on back of jacket)] | [in strong greenish blue] *(continued on back of jacket)* | [in black] *Jacket design by Janet Halverson* | FARRAR, STRAUS AND GIROUX | 19 UNION SQUARE WEST | NEW YORK 10003'.

Publication: published 15 April 1968; 5,500 copies printed, of which 1,500 were issued in cloth at $5.95 and 4,000 copies in printed paper wrappers. A second printing of 3,000 copies was issued in January 1970, 1,000 in cloth and 2,000 in paper wrappers; and a third printing of 2,500 copies in paper wrappers was issued in March 1970.

Susbsequent printings are so identified on the copyright page, '*Second Printing 1969*' [sic], '*Third Printing 1970*', although the first edition notice was not dropped.

Locations: MJ, NcGU, STW.

> *Note:* Although the copyright page indicates that a Canadian edition by Ambassador Books, Ltd. was published simultaneously, no copy has been located.
>
> The list of books by RJ on pp. i–ii includes as "editions in preparation": *The Complete Poems of Randall Jarrell; The Essays and Criticism of Randall Jarrell; Fly by Night; The Three Sisters; Faust, Part I;* and *Modern Poetry: An Anthology.*

A6d *Second Edition (1980)*

PICTURES FROM AN INSTITUTION

A Comedy by
RANDALL JARRELL

 A BARD BOOK/PUBLISHED BY AVON BOOKS

Copyright Page: 'First Bard Printing, October, 1980'.

Collation: perfect bound; 120 leaves; [1–10] 11–34 [35–36] 37–69 [70–72] 73–113 [114–116] 117–159 [160–162] 163–191 [192–194] 195–214 [215–216] 217–238 [239–240].

Contents: p. 1: '[27 lines all in roman within a frame of single rules which are rounded at the corners, about the author]'; p. 2: blank; p. 3: title page; p. 4: copyright page; p. 5: dedication page; p. 6: blank; p. 7: contents; p. 8: blank; pp. 9–238: text; p. 239: blank; p. 240: list of other Bard fiction titles.

Running Titles: head, '[page number in arabic numerals] Pictures FROM AN Institution | [chapter title in ital and small caps] [page number in arabic numerals]'.

Typography: text, 9/10 Century Schoolbook; 43 lines per normal page; 151 (157) × 84 mm.; 20 lines = 80 mm.

Paper Binding: thick, wove, unwatermarked paper wrapper; inner side and back are white; front and spine are imprintd with an illustration of a typewriter, books, a pen and pencil, and characters from the novel, prin. in white, V. p. B (Centroid 184), gy. B (approx. Centroid 186), l. Br (Centroid 42), and brill. OY (Centroid 67); illustration signed 'Blumrich' in grayish blue on front below pen; back contains at the bottom the character grouping from the front in ident. colors; printed in black and white; front: '[left, in black] [first 5 lines slightly taller than 'PICTURES'] [publisher's device] | AVON | BARD | 49650 | $2.95 | [right] PICTURES | FROM AN INSTITUTION | A Comedy by Randall Jarrell | [left] *"One of | the wittiest | books | of modern | times"* | The New York Times'; spine: '[horiz., in black] [publisher's device] | BARD | [vert.] PICTURES FROM AN INSTITUTION · RANDALL JARRELL | [horiz., reversed out in white] AVON | 0·380 | 49650·X | 295'; back: '[in black] THE ART OF | INTELLIGENT | LIVING | [17 lines in roman, about the book] | [9 lines, blurbs by Robert Penn Warren and James Agee] | [across bottom] [color illustration from front the height of other elements] [area for marking with price tape; 'o' to left, '71001 00295' below, and '49650' above] ISBN 0–380–49650–X | A BARD BOOK / PUBLISHED BY AVON BOOKS | [right side, vert. from bottom to top] Printed in U.S.A.'

Text Contents: identical to A6a.

Publication: published in October 1980 at $2.95; number of copies printed is not known.

Locations: MJ(5), NcGU, STW(2).

A6e *First English Edition (1954)*

PICTURES
FROM AN INSTITUTION

A COMEDY BY

RANDALL JARRELL

FABER AND FABER LIMITED

24 Russell Square

London

Title Page: 7⁵⁄₁₆ × 4¾ in. (185 × 119 mm.).

Copyright Page: 'First published in Great Britain in mcmliv'.

Collation: [unsigned A⁸] B–R⁸ S + S* ⁸⁺²; 146 leaves; [1–8] 9 [10] 11–290 [291–292].

Contents: pp. 1–2: blank; p. 3: half title; p. 4: blank; p. 5: title page; p. 6: copyright page; p. 7: dedication page: 'TO | MARY | AND | HANNAH'; p. 8: blank; p. 9: contents; p. 10: blank; pp. 11–290: text; pp. 291–292, blank.

Running Titles: '[chapter title in all ital] | [chapter title in all ital]'.

Typography: text, 11/13 Walbaum; 31 lines per normal page; 146 (152) × 89 mm.; 20 lines = 90 mm.

Paper and Binding: leaf measures 7¼ × 4¾ in. (183 × 120 mm.); yWhite (Centroid 92) wove, unwatermarked paper, uncoated smooth; all edges cut, unstained; yWhite (Centroid 92) wove, unwatermarked endpapers, uncoated smooth; two bindings, priority as follows: *binding 1:* medium grayish blue (no Centroid equivalent) coarse bead-cloth (202) boards measure 7½ × 5 in. (190 × 127 mm.); front cover: unstamped; spine: '[horiz., in black] Pictures | from an | Institution | BY | Randall | Jarrell | Faber'; back: unstamped; *binding 2:* moderate green (between Centroid 141 and 145) fine bead-cloth (202b) cover measures 7⁹⁄₁₆ × 5⅛ (192 × 130 mm.); front: unstamped; spine: '[horiz., in white] Pictures | from an | Institution | BY | Randall | Jarrell | Faber'; back: unstamped.

Dust Jacket: total measurement, 7⁹⁄₁₆ × 18¹⁄₁₆ in. (192 × 459 mm.); p. Y (approx. Centroid 89) wove, unwatermarked paper; both sides uncoated smooth; front and spine contain thick horiz. rules, 7 mm. tall, in s. R (Centroid 12), and thin horiz. rules, 3 mm. tall, in s. G (Centroid 141), two of which cross both front and spine; front also contains a frame of quadruple strong red thick rules (7 mm.) at the bottom, the lowest of which extends across the spine; within the quadruple-rules frame is a solid rectangular strong green panel surrounded by a frame of single black rules; lettered in black and strong red; front: '[in black] Pictures | from an | Institution | A COMEDY BY | [against solid strong green panel, within a single-rules frame] Randall | Jarrell | [below panel] *Recommended by the Book Society*'; spine: '[horiz., in black] Pictures | from | an | Institu|tion | A | Comedy | by | [strong red] Randall | Jarrell | [in black] Faber | and | Faber'; back: '[in black] PICTURES FROM AN INSTITUTION | *by Randall Jarrell* | [¶] The American publication of *Pictures from an Institution*, in | May, 1954, was a literary event. Here are some of the things that people say about it: — | [27 lines prin. in roman, including blurbs or comment from the *Chicago Tribune*, by Orville Prescott (*New York*

Times), *Saturday Review of Literature*, David Daiches, Louis Unter-meyer, and Jean Stafford] | [rule, 101 mm.] | FABER AND FABER LIMITED 24 Russell Square London WC1'; front flap: '[in black] *Pictures from an* | *Institution* | RANDALL JARRELL | [40 lines prin. in roman, about the book] | *Recommended by* | *the Book Society* | [lower right corner] 12s 6d | *net*'; back flap: '[black-and-white photograph of RJ at top, 87 × 57 mm.] | *Also by Randall Jarrell* | POETRY AND THE AGE | A Brilliant Evaluation of | Poetry and Criticism in our time | 18s *net* | SELECTED POEMS | 12s 6d *net* | *(For publication in 1955)*'.

Text Contents: identical to **A6a**.

Publication: published 1 October 1954 at 12S. 6d.; 4,944 copies printed (the publisher no longer has a record of the number of copies in each of the two bindings).

Locations: NcGU (binding 2), STW (bindings 1 and 2), TxU (binding 2).

A6f   *Second English Edition (1959)*

PICTURES
FROM AN INSTITUTION

BY
Randall Jarrell

PENGUIN BOOKS
IN ASSOCIATION WITH
FABER AND FABER

Title Page: 7⅛ × 4¼ in. (182 × 108 mm.).

Copyright Page: 'Published in Penguin Books 1959'.

Collation: perfect bound; 104 leaves; [1–8] 9–206 [207–208].

Contents: p. 1: half title; p. 2: blank; p. 3: title page; p. 4: copyright page; p. 5: contents; p. 6: dedication page; pp. 7–207: text; p. 208: blank.

Running Titles: head, '*Pictures from an Institution* | [chapter titles in all ital]'.

Typography: text, 9/11 Times Roman; 39 lines per normal page; 151 (157) × 88 mm.; 20 lines = 82 mm.

Paper: leaf measures 7⅛ × 4¼ in. (182 × 108 mm.); yWhite (Centroid 92) wove, unwatermarked paper, uncoated smooth.

Paper Binding: thick, wove, unwatermarked cream-colored paper wrapper (no Centroid equivalent); front contains two vertically elongated panels in v. rO (Centroid 34), one on either side; the top and bottom of the spine are printed vivid reddish orange, but the central portion is cream; the back contains two elongated vertical panels in vivid reddish orange ident. to front; lettered in black and vivid reddish orange; front: '[in vivid reddish orange] PENGUIN BOOKS | [in black, rule, 111 mm., that extends across the front, spine, and back] | [in black] PICTURES | FROM AN | INSTITUTION | [in vivid reddish orange, rule, 11 mm.] | [in black] 'A wonderful blend of | wickedness and sheer fun . . . it | combines the quick play of the wit, | the imagination of the poet, and | the spell-binding charm of the | half-ironic, half-whimsical, and | wholly detached story-teller.' | *Louis Untermeyer* | [in vivid reddish orange, rule, 11 mm.] [in black] RANDALL | JARRELL | [rule, 111 mm., that extends across front, spine, and back] | COMPLETE [in vivid reddish orange] 2/6 [in black] UNABRIDGED | [in black, right side, centered, publisher's device]'; spine: '[vert. from top to bottom, in black, against central panel] Randall Jarrell [in vivid reddish orange, publisher's device] [in black] Pictures from an Institution | [horiz., in black] 1249'; back: '[flanked on either side by elongated panels in vivid reddish orange, like front] [in vivid reddish orange] PENGUIN BOOKS | [in black, rule, 111 mm., that crosses front, spine, and back] | [black-and-white photograph of RJ, 50 × 48 mm.] | [in black, 19 lines about the author] | [rule ident. to first] | NOT FOR SALE IN THE U.S.A. OR CANADA | [in black, left side, publisher's device against a tan oval]'; inside of front jacket: '[in black, 3½ lines prin. in roman, including a description of the book ident. to that printed on the front flap of A6e] | [4 lines in ital, advertisement]'; inside back cover: '[in black, 20 lines prin. in roman, advertisement for C. P. Snow, THE MASTERS] | NOT FOR SALE IN THE U.S.A. | [publisher's device]'.

Text Contents: identical to **A6a**.

Publication: published in February 1959 at 2/6; the publisher declined to reveal the number of copies in the first printing or the number of subsequent printings and the copies printed.

Locations: NcGU, STW.

A6g *First English Edition, Second Impression (photo-offset from* **A6e***) (1974)*

All identical to **A6e** except for:

PICTURES | FROM AN INSTITUTION | [ornamental rule, 66.5 mm.] | A COMEDY BY | RANDALL JARRELL | FABER AND FA-BER LIMITED

Title Page: 7¹¹⁄₁₆ × 4⅞ in. (195 × 124 mm.).

Copyright Page: 'First published in Great Britain in 1954 | Reissued in 1974'.

Collation: [unsigned A–Q⁸] R⁸ [unsigned S⁸]; 146 leaves; [1–8] 9 [10] 11–290 [291–292].

Binding: m. gB (approx. Centroid 173) paper-covered boards (imitation bead-cloth, 202) measure 8 × 5⁵⁄₁₆ in. (202 × 133 mm.); front cover: unstamped; spine: '[in gold, horiz.] [within a box of ornamental rules] Pictures | from an | Institution | [below box] Randall | Jarrell | Faber | and Faber'; back: unstamped.

Dust Jacket: 8¹⁄₁₆ × 18⅜ in. (204 × 467 mm.); inner side and flaps are white; front contains two vertically elongated panels which cover it, the left one in deep G (Centroid 142) and the right one in brill. YG (Centroid 116); entire back of jacket contains a black-and-white photograph of RJ; lettered in white, s. gB (Centroid 169), and deep green; front: '[left side, against deep green panel, reversed out in white] *Pictures | from an | Institution* | [in strong greenish blue] *Randall | Jarrell* | [right side, against brilliant yellow green panel, in deep green] [vert. from top to bottom] *Randall Jarrell*'; spine: '[two lines, vert. from top to bottom] [top line, in strong greenish blue] *Pictures from an Institution* [bottom line, reversed out in white] *Randall Jarrell* [at base, in strong greenish blue] *Faber*'; back: contains a black-and-white photograph of RJ; front flap: '[in black] *Pictures from an | Institution | by Randall Jarrell* | [30 lines prin. in roman] | [lower right corner] £2.50 net'; back flap: '[in black] *Randall Jarrell* | [13 lines in roman, about the author] | Faber & Faber also publish *The Com-|plete Poems of Randall Jarrell*'.

Publication: published in 1974 at £2.50; number of copies printed is not known.

Locations: MJ, NcGU, STW.

A7 *SELECTED POEMS*

A7a *First Edition (1955)*

SELECTED POEMS

RANDALL JARRELL

NEW YORK ALFRED A KNOPF *1955*

Collation: [unsigned 1–2^{16} 3^8 4–5^{16} 6^{12} 7–8^{16}]; 116 leaves; [2], [i–iv] vii–xvii [xviii] xix–xxii, [1–2] 3–81 [82] 83–119 [120] 121–132 [133–134] 135–153 [154] 155–205 [206–208].

Contents: one unnumbered leaf, the verso of which contains a list of books by RJ; p. i: half title; p. ii: blank; p. iii: title page; p. iv: copyright page; p. v: dedication page: 'TO | *Mary,* | *Alleyne,* | AND | *Beatrice*'; p. vi: blank; pp. vii–xvii: introduction and notes about the poems by RJ; p. xviii: blank; pp. xix–xxii: contents; pp. 1–205: text; p. 206: 'A NOTE ON THE TYPE | [24 lines prin. in ital]'; pp. 207–208: blank. Contents are divided into two numbered sections, the first of which contains six titled subsections, and the second, seven titled subsections.

Typography: text, 11/14 Linotype Janson; 33 lines per normal page; 170.5 × 101 mm.; 20 lines = 97 mm.

Paper and Binding: leaf measures 8⅜ × 5⁹⁄₁₆ (212 × 141 mm.); yWhite (Centroid 92) wove, unwatermarked paper, uncoated smooth; gy. B (approx. Centroid 186) fine bead-cloth (202b) boards measure

8⁹⁄₁₆ × 5½ in. (217 × 146 mm.); front: blindstamped, 'SELECTED |
POEMS | [rule, 63 mm.] | RANDALL | JARRELL'; spine: '[in gold,
vert.] SELECTED POEMS | [horiz., rule, 19 mm.] | [reversed out in
grayish blue against a gold panel, 16.5 × 20 mm.] *Alfred A.* | *Knopf*
| [in gold, rule, 19 mm.] | [vert.] RANDALL JARRELL'; back: Borzoi
books device blindstamped in lower right corner]'; top and bottom
edges cut, fore-edge untrimmed; top edges stained brill. Y (Centroid
83); yWhite (Centroid 92) wove, unwatermarked endpapers, uncoated smooth.

Dust Jacket: total measurement, 8⁵⁄₈ × 20⁹⁄₁₆ in. (219 × 521 mm.);
wove, unwatermarked paper; inner side, flaps, and back are white;
front and spine are printed black; inner side coated smooth, outer side
coated glossy; lettered in black, white, and s. Y (Centroid 84); front:
'[in strong yellow] SELECTED | [ornamental type in strong yellow
and white] POEMS | [in strong yellow, roman] RANDALL | JARRELL
| AUTHOR OF *PICTURES FROM AN INSTITUTION* | AND PO-
ETRY AND THE AGE'; spine: '[vert., in strong yellow] SELECTED
POEMS [diag. rule reversed out in white] [in strong yellow] RAN-
DALL JARRELL [diag. rule reversed out in white like first] [in strong
yellow, two lines] [top line] ALFRED A. [bottom line] KNOPF'; back:
'[black-and-white photograph of RJ, 93 × 67 mm.] | [below photo-
graph, in black] *R. Thorne McKenna* | [17 lines prin. in roman, about
the author] | ALFRED A. KNOPF, PUBLISHER, NEW YORK [pub-
lisher's device]'; front flap: '[upper right corner, in black] $4.00 *net* |
[21 lines prin. in roman, about RJ's work, including quotes from Delmore Schwartz, Theodore Spencer, Dudley Fitts, and Robert Lowell]
| *(continued on back flap)* | [left] *Jacket design: Harry Ford*'; back flap:
'*(continued from front flap)* | [21 lines prin. In roman, about SP55] |
Printed in U. S. A.'

Text Contents: introduction and notes on the poems by RJ; I. "Lives":
"A Girl in the Library," "A Country Life," "The Knight, Death, and
the Devil," "The Face," "Lady Bates," "When I Was Home Last
Christmas . . . ," "A Conversation with the Devil," "Nollekens,"
"Seele im Raum," "The Night Before the Night before Christmas";
"Dream-Work": "A Sick Child," "The Black Swan," "The Venetian
Blind," "A Quilt-Pattern," "The Island," "In the Ward: the Sacred
Wood"; "The Wide Prospect": "The Orient Express," "A Game at
Salzburg," "An English Garden in Austria," "A Soul," "A Rhapsody
on Irish Themes," "The Memoirs of Glückel of Hameln," "To the
New World," "The Märchen," "Hohensalzburg: Fantastic Variations
on a Theme of Romantic Character"; "Once upon a Time": "Mov-
ing," "The Sleeping Beauty: Variation of the Prince," "The Prince,"
"The Carnegie Library, Juvenile Division," "The Blind Sheep," "The
Skaters," "Jonah," "Song: Not There," "Children Selecting Books in
a Library"; "The World Is Everything That Is The Case": "Sears Roe-

buck," "A Utopian Journey," "Hope," "90 North," "The Snow-Leopard," "The Boyg, Peer Gynt, the One Only One," "Money," "The Emancipators," "Variations," "Le Poète Contumace"; "The Graves in the Forest": "LaBelle au Bois Dormant," "A Story," "Loss," "The Breath of Night," "Afterwards," "The Place of Death"; II. "Bombers": "Eighth Air Force," "The Death of the Ball Turret Gunner," "Losses," "Transient Barracks," "Siegfried"; "The Carriers": "A Pilot from the Carrier," "Pilots, Man Your Planes," "The Dead Wingman," "Burning the Letters"; "Prisoners": "Stalag Luft," "Jews at Haifa," "Prisoners," "O My Name It Is Sam Hall," "A Camp in the Prussian Forest"; "Camps and Fields": "A Lullaby," "Mail Call," "Absent with Official Leave," "A Front," "The Sick Nought," "Leave," "The Range in the Desert," "Second Air Force"; "The Traders": "The Rising Sun," "New Georgia," "The Subway from New Britain to the Bronx," "1945: The Death of the Gods," "A Ward in the States," "The Wide Prospect," "The Dead in Melanesia"; "Children and Civilians": "The State," "Coming to the Stone . . . ," "The Angels at Hamburg," "Protocols," "The Metamorphoses," "The Truth"; "Soldiers": "Port of Embarcation," "The Lines," "A Field Hospital," "1914," "Gunner," "Good-bye, Wendover; Good-bye Mountain Home," "The Survivor among Graves," "A War," "Terms."

Publication: published 21 February 1955 at $4.00; 2,000 copies printed and bound by the Kingsport Press, Inc., Kingsport, Tenn. Registered in the name of Randall Jarrell, under A 176702.

Locations: DLC, GU, MJ, NcGU, NcU, NcWsW, NN, STW (5), TxU, ViU.

> *Note:* RJ deleted his explanatory "A Jill is a Japanese torpedo-plane" from "Pilots, Man Your Planes" but restored it in A7b.
>
> Galley proofs containing RJ's holograph corrections, with the Knopf receipt stamp dated 13 December 1954, are located in the Jarrell Collection at the University of North Carolina at Greensboro. Second galleys, also in the Jarrell Collection, are dated 4 January 1955.
>
> Two trial cases with stamping identical to A7a are also contained in the Jarrell Collection at the University of North Carolina at Greensboro; one is covered in black cloth, and the other in d. B (approx. Centroid 183).
>
> *RJ to AK (HF), April-May 1953:* When I get done with *Pictures* August 1 I'm going to do the last work on a Selected Poems—I've rewritten some of the early ones, though with a lot of the poems in my first book leaving out's the only thing to do; and I've thought up an arrangement, and notes or remarks about technical things in the war ones, and so on.
>
> *RJ to AK (HF), 6 October 1954:* Do just send page proofs without galleys—we haven't had a typographical error in the last two books,

and I imagine the poetry one'll be even easier. . . . The title page sounds swell. Send me a couple of sample pages as soon as you get that far, will you?

RJ to AK (HF), Jauary 1955: I'm crazy about the pages and the dust-jacket—so is Mary [Jarrell]. The dustjacket's almost too good for a dustjacket and ought to be on my tomb. I've always been crazy about grey and yellow. I think you're right, that the page numbers are too bold and would be better thicker and blacker than the type. And I like the idea of having the *Poems* the only thing in white. . . . [¶] How beautiful the double page part of *Girl in Library* looks! And the part title is beautiful—is that what you're using for the title page?

RJ to AK (HF), late January 1955: I'm really quite overwhelmed with how beautiful you've made this book—I was crazy about *Poetry* and *Pictures*, but this beats them. The Introduction is printed so delightfully that you almost hate to get to the poems, and you can't believe that some poetry books don't have introductions. . . . The proof were pretty correct, though I found a few errors and a few spaces omitted; I went over it several times carefully, though it was hard after just having finished the English proof of *Poetry and the Age.* Some of *it* I could barely make myself read; and when I compare something in it with something in the American edition I'd look up with resigned distaste at the English. [¶] I like the write-ups on the dustjacket very much and don't want to add any other quotations—I didn't realize what it was going to be like, but thought it was going to be a collection of quotations.

A7b   *First English Edition (1956)*

SELECTED POEMS

✴

RANDALL JARRELL

FABER AND FABER LIMITED

24 Russell Square

London

Title Page: 8 × 4¹⁵⁄₁₆ in. (203 × 127 mm.).

Copyright Page: 'This selection first published in mcmlvi'.

Collation: [unsigned A⁸] B–O⁸; 112 leaves; [1–6] 7–11 [12] 13–23 [24–26] 27–154 [155–156] 157–223 [224].

Contents: p. 1: half title; p. 2: list of books by RJ; p. 3: title page; p. 4: copyright page; p. 5: dedication page: 'To | MARY, | ALLEYNE, | and | BEATRICE'; p. 6: blank, pp. 7–10: contents; p. 11: acknowledgments; p. 12: blank; pp. 13–23: introduction and notes on the poems by RJ (ident. to A7a); p. 24: blank; pp. 25–223: text; p. 224: blank. Text divided into two numbered sections like A7a but contains no subsections.

Typography: text, 11/13 Perpetua; 33 lines per normal page; 154 × 92.5 mm.; 20 lines = 90 mm.

Paper and Binding: leaf measures 7⁹⁄₁₆ × 5⅛ in. (200 × 129 mm.); yWhite (Centroid 92) wove, unwatermarked paper, uncoated smooth; all edges cut, unstained; yWhite (Centroid 92) wove, unwatermarked endpapers, uncoated smooth; two bindings, no priority; *binding 1:* d. rP (approx. Centroid 242) coarse linen-cloth (304c) boards measure 8³⁄₁₆ × 5⁵⁄₁₆ in. (209 × 137 mm.); front: unstamped; spine: [in gold, horiz.] *Selected | Poems |* ★ *| Randall Jarrell |* [at base] *| Faber*; back: unstamped; *binding 2:* reddish purple (but lighter in hue than binding 1; approx. Centroid 238) linen-cloth (304); remainder identical to binding 1.

Dust Jacket: total measurement, 18 × 8³⁄₁₆ in (208 × 454 mm.); v. l. gB (approx. Centroid 171) laid, unwatermarked paper, chainlines 25 mm. apart; both sides uncoated rough; lettered in black; front: [in d. b (Centroid 183), row of thick vertical rules, 11.5 mm. high, that extend across front and spine] | [in black] *Selected | POEMS |* [row of vert. rules in dark blue like first] | *Randall | Jarrell |* [row of vert. rules in dark blue like first] | FABER'; spine: '[row of vert. rules in dark blue] | [horiz., in black] Selected | Poems | ★ | Randall | Jarrell | [row of vert. rules in dark blue] | [in black, vert., in two lines] [top line] *RANDALL* [bottom line] *JARRELL* | [row of vert. rules in dark blue] | [in black, horiz. at base] Faber'; back: '[in black] *by Randall Jarrell* | POETRY AND THE AGE | [32 lines prin. in roman, including blurbs from *New Statesman* and *Nation*, Philip Toynbee (*Observer*), Louis MacNeice (*London Magazine*), David Daiches (*Manchester Guardian*), and John Wain (*Spectator*) | 18s *net* | FABER & FABER LIMITED 24 Russell Square London WC1'; front flap: '[in black] Selected | POEMS | Randall Jarrell | [31 lines prin. In roman, about RJ's work] lower right corner] 15s | *net*'; back flap: '[in black] by Randall Jarrell | PICTURES FROM | AN INSTITUTION | [34 lines prin. in roman, including blurbs by John Metcalf (*Spectator*), and from the *Birming-ham Post*, *Punch*, *Sunday Times*, and *Queen*] | 12*s* 6*d net*'.

Text Contents: identical to **A7a**. The first two full paragraphs on p. xvi of **A7a** have been moved to p. 21 in **A7b**.

Publication: published 27 January 1956 at 15s.; 1,735 copies printed.

Locations: MJ (binding 1), NcGU (binding 1), STW (bindings 1 and 2).

A8 THE APPALLING TASTE OF THE AGE

First Separate Edition (reprint from **C314***)(1960)*

Cover Title: FROM THE SATURDAY EVENING POST | AD-VENTURES | OF | THE | MIND | 8. | [rule, 269 mm.] | The Appalling | Taste of the Age | *By RANDALL JARRELL* | © The Curtis Publishing Company

Collation: one leaf, 13⁹⁄₁₆ × 31⅞ in. (345 × 810 mm.), folded twice toward center, first, right to left, then left to right, forming an accordion-style format consisting of three unnumbered leaves, each 13¼ × 10⅝ in. (338 × 270 mm.); [1–6].

Contents: p. 1: cover title; p. 2: 'ADVENTURES OF THE MIND 8. | [remainder ident. to **C314**; text and 'About the Author']'; p. 3: full-page photograph of RJ by Philippe Halsman; pp. 4–5: text, ident. to **C314**, except for last eleven lines, which contain a list of books for further reading, the first of which is RJ's *Poetry and the Age* (**A5b**); p. 6: blank.

Paper: yWhite (Centroid 92) wove, unwatermarked paper.

Text Contents: "The Appalling Taste of the Age" (**C314**).

Publication: unknown number of copies prepared for distribution by the *Saturday Evening Post* in March 1960; not for sale.

A9 *THE WOMAN AT THE WASHINGTON ZOO*

First Edition (1960)

THE WOMAN AT THE WASHINGTON ZOO

POEMS & TRANSLATIONS

RANDALL JARRELL

NEW YORK ATHENEUM PUBLISHERS
1960

Collation: [unsigned 1–5⁸]; 40 leaves; [4], [i–vi] vii–viii [1] 2–65 [66–68].

Contents: two unnumbered leaves, the verso of the second of which contains a list of books by RJ; p. i: half title; p. ii: blank; p. iii: title page; p. iv: copyright page; p. v: dedication page: 'To Mary'; p. vi: blank; pp. vii–viii: contents; pp. 1–65: text; p. 66: blank; p. 67: 'Randall Jarrell | [18 lines prin. in roman, about the author] | [swelled rule, 51 mm.]'; p. 68: blank.

Typography: text, 11/14 Janson; 33 lines per normal page; 171 × 96 mm.; 20 lines = 98 mm.

Paper and Binding: leaf measures 8⅜ × 5⅜ in. (212 × 136 mm.); white wove, unwatermarked paper, uncoated smooth; bluish black (no Centroid equivalent) coarse bead-cloth (202) boards measure 8⁹⁄₁₆ × 5⁹⁄₁₆ in. (218 × 142 mm.); front: unstamped; spine: in gold, '[vert.] THE WOMAN AT THE WASHINGTON ZOO RANDALL JARRELL ATHENEUM'; back: unstamped; all edges cut; top edges stained deep yPk (Centroid 27); d. rO (Centroid 38) wove, unwatermarked endpapers, uncoated rough.

Dust Jacket: total measurement, 8½ × 20 in. (216 × 508 mm.); wove, unwatermarked paper; inner side, flaps, and back are white; front and spine are printed black; inner side is coated smooth, outer side, glossy; lettered in black, v. R (Centroid 11), s. O (Centroid 50), and brill. Y (Centroid 83); front: '[in vivid red] RANDALL | JAR-RELL | [in strong orange] THE WOMAN | AT THE | WASHING-TON | ZOO | [in brilliant yellow] POEMS & TRANSLATIONS'; spine: '[vert.] [in strong orange] THE WOMAN AT THE WASHING-TON ZOO [in vivid red] RANDALL JARRELL [in brilliant yellow] ATHENEUM'; back: '[in vivid red] *The Poetry of Randall Jarrell:* | [in black, 31 lines, prin. in roman, including blurbs by Karl Shapiro, Stephen Spender, and Robert Lowell]'; front flap: '[in vivid red, in upper right corner] $3.75 | [in black, 27 lines prin. in roman, about RJ's work and this book] | [in vivid red] *Jacket design: Harry Ford*'; back flap: '[black-and-white photograph of RJ, 74 × 63mm.] | [remainder in vivid red, 25 lines prin. in roman, about the author]'.

Text Contents: "The Woman at the Washington Zoo," "Cinderella," "The End of the Rainbow," "In Those Days," "The Elementary Scene," "Windows," "Aging," "Nestus Gurley," "The Great Night" (Rilke), "The Grown-up" (Rilke), "Washing the Corpse" (Rilke), "Evening" (Rilke), "Childhood" (Rilke), "Lament" (Rilke), "The Child" (Rilke), "Death" (Rilke), "Requiem for the Death of a Boy" (Rilke), "The Winter's Tale" (Radauskas), "The Archangel's Song" (Goethe), "Forest Murmurs" (Mörike), "Jamestown," "The Lonely Man," "The Traveller," "A Ghost, a Real Ghost," "The Meteorite," "Charles Dodgson's Song," "Deutsch durch Freud," "The Girl Dreams That She Is Giselle," "Jerome," "The Bronze David of Donatello."

Publication: published 7 September 1960 at $3.75; 3,500 copies printed and bound at the Kingsport Press, Inc., Kingsport, Tenn. Registered in the name of Randall Jarrell, under A 462536. Copyright deposit copies received 12 September 1960.

Locations: DLC, MJ, NcGU, NcU, NcWsW, NN, STW (3), TxU, ViU.

First Appearances:

"Forest Murmurs" *SP2, CP.*

"Evening" *SP2, CP.*

Note: RJ's corrected galleys, in the Jarrell Collection at the University of North Carolina at Greensboro, were received by Atheneum on 6 June 1960 and are so stamped.

RJ to Ath (HF), 12 October 1959: I was able to get the whole manuscript done so fast that I didn't send you the table of contents first.

Having the book pretty much like the *Selected Poems* but with a slightly narrower page would be fine. Maybe you might use straight up-and-down titles instead of slanted ones, and dead white paper instead of cream. I'll certainly enjoy getting to see the sample pages and jacket—I've just been looking at all the books of mine you've designed, and thinking how beautiful they are.

A10 *A SAD HEART AT THE SUPERMARKET*

A10a *First Edition (1962)*

Randall Jarrell

A SAD HEART
AT THE
SUPERMARKET

Essays & Fables

Atheneum : New York
1962

8 × 4¹⁵/₁₆ in. (203 × 125 mm.). A10a

Collation: [unsigned 1–7¹⁶]; 112 leaves; [2], [i–vi] vii [viii], [1–2] 3–211 [212–214].

Contents: one unnumbered leaf, the verso of which contains a list of books by RJ; p. i: half title; p. ii: blank; p. iii: title page; p. iv: copyright page; p. v: dedication page: 'To Mary'; p. vi: 'The Author to the Reader | I've read that Luther said (it's come to me | So often that I've made it into meter): | *And even if the world should end tomorrow | I still would plant my little apple-tree.* | Here, reader, is my little apple-tree.'; p. vii: contents; p. viii: blank; pp. 1–211: text; p. 212: blank; p. 213: 'Randall Jarrell | [25 lines prin. in roman, about the author]'; p. 214: blank.

Running Titles: head, '[chapter title in all ital] | [chapter title in all in ital, page number in arabic numerals]'.

Typography: text, 11/14 Janson; 31 lines per normal page; 153 (159) × 84 mm.; 20 lines = 98 mm.

Paper and Binding: leaf measures 8 × 5 in. (202 × 124 mm.); yWhite (Centroid 92) wove, unwatermarked paper, uncoated smooth; gy. B (Centroid 186) linen-cloth (304) boards measure 8¼ × 5¼ in. (209 × 133 mm.); front: blindstamped, 'RANDALL JARRELL'; spine: in gold, '[vert.] A SAD HEART AT THE SUPERMAR-KET RANDALL JARRELL ATHENEUM'; back: unstamped; all edges cut, top edges stained m. R (Centroid 15); l. OlBr (Centroid 94) wove, unwatermarked endpapers, uncoated smooth.

Dust Jacket: total measurement, 8¼ × 19⅜ in. (209 × 491 mm.); wove, unwatermarked paper; inner side, back, and flaps are white; front and spine are printed black; inner side coated smooth, outer side coated glossy; lettered in black, white, v. R (Centroid 11), and l. B (Centroid 181); front: '[in vivid red] *RANDALL JARRELL* | [in light blue] a ʂad | [in vivid red] ʜeart | [in light blue] at ᴛhe ʂuper | mₐrket | *ESSAYS AND FABLES*'; spine: '[in vivid red, two lines, vert.] [top line] *RANDALL [bottom line] JARRELL* [in light blue] A Sad [in vivid red] Heart [in light blue] at the Supermarket [reversed out in white] Atheneum'; back: '[black-and-white photograph of RJ, 122 × 113 mm.] | [right side, in light blue] *Photograph by Ted Russell* | [left side, in vivid red] *RANDALL JARRELL*'; front flap: '[upper right corner, in light blue] *$4.50* | [left, in black, 8 lines prin. in roman, blurb by Robert Lowell] | [in vivid red] *Robert Lowell* | [in black, 20 lines prin. in roman, about the book] | [in light blue] *Jacket design: Harry Ford*'; back flap: '[in vivid red] *RANDALL JARRELL* | [in black, 20 lines prin. in roman, about the author] | [in light blue] *Atheneum*'.

Text Contents: "The Intellectual in America," "The Taste of the Age," "The Schools of Yesteryear," "A Sad Heart at the Supermarket," "Poets, Critics, and Readers," "On Preparing to Read Kipling," "Stories," "The Woman at the Washington Zoo," "Malraux and the Statues at Bamberg," "A Wilderness of Ladies."

Publication: published 28 March 1962 at $4.50; 4,500 copies printed and bound by the Kingsport Press, Inc., Kingsport, Tenn. Registered in the name of Randall Jarrell, under A 556995. Copyright deposit copies received 9 April 1962.

Locations: DLC, GU, MJ, NcGU, NcWsW, NN, STW(3), TxU, ViU.

A1ob *First English Edition (1965)*

RANDALL JARRELL

*A Sad Heart
at the Supermarket*

ESSAYS & FABLES

1965
Eyre & Spottiswoode

Copyright Page: 'First published in Great Britain in 1965 by | Eyre & Spottiswoode (Publishers) Ltd'.

Collation: [unsigned A⁸] B–P⁸; 120 leaves; [2], [1–8] 9–234 [235–238].

Contents: one unnumbered blank leaf; p. 1: half title; p. 2: list of books by RJ publ. by Faber & Faber; p. 3: title page; p. 4: copyright page; p. 5: dedication; p. 6: acknowledgments; p. 7: contents; p. 8: blank; pp. 9–234: text.

Running Titles: 'A SAD HEART AT THE SUPERMARKET | [essay or review title in all caps]'.

Typography: text, 11/13 Intertype Baskerville; 33 lines per normal page; 159 (164.5) × 93 mm.; 20 lines = 90 mm.

Paper and Binding: leaf measures 7⅞ × 5³⁄₁₆ (200 × 132 mm.); yWhite (Centroid 92) wove, unwatermarked paper, uncoated smooth; m. O (Centroid 53) paper-covered boards (imitation bead-cloth) measure 8⅛ × 5½ in. (207 × 140 mm.); spine stamped in gold: '[horiz.] [heavy rule, 21 mm.] | A SAD | HEART | AT THE | SUPER-|MARKET | [thin rule, 21 mm.] | Randall | Jarrell | [heavy rule, 21 mm.]'; all edges cut, unstained; grayish white (no Centroid equivalent) wove, unwatermarked endpapers, uncoated smooth.

Dust Jacket: total measurement, 8⅛ × 19³⁄₁₆ in. (206 × 483 mm.); wove, unwatermarked paper, both sides coated smooth; inner side, back, and flaps are white; front and spine are printed in m. P (approx. Centroid 223); lettered in black and white; front: '[against a frame reversed out in white, heavier at top than sides and bottom, within a frame of single black rules, 191 × 121 mm.] [in black] RANDALL JARRELL | [rule, 121 mm., that connects the two sides of the frame] | [against moderate purple panel that fills out the page; reversed out in white] *a sad* | *heart* | [in black] at the | super-|market | [reversed out in white] | EYRE & SPOTTISWOODE'; spine: '[against a panel reversed out in white, within a frame of black single rules, 191 × 22 mm.] [vert. from top to bottom, in two lines, in black] [top] RANDALL [bottom] JARRELL [reversed out in white] *a sad heart* [in black] at the supermarket | [horiz.] E & S'; back: '[within a frame of moderate purple single rules, 190 × 109 mm., in black] [19 lines in roman, about RJ and the book] | [moderate purple rule, 110 mm., that connects the vertical frame rules, in black] EYRE & SPOTTISWOODE · Publishers · Ltd | 22 HENRIETTA STREET · LONDON WC2'; front flap: '[moderate purple rule, 63 mm.] [in black, 10-line blurb, signed "Robert Lowell"] | A description of this book is given on the | back of the jacket. | [moderate purple rule, 63 mm.] | [right corner, in black] PRICE | 25s net | IN U.K. ONLY'; back flap: '[centered at bottom, in black] PRINTED IN GREAT BRITAIN'.

Text Contents: identical to **A10a**.

Publication: published in 1965 at 25s. Number of copies printed is not known.

Locations: MJ, NcGU, STW (2).

A11 *THE RABBIT CATCHER AND OTHER FAIRY TALES OF LUDWIG BECHSTEIN*, translated by RJ

First Edition (1962)

The Rabbit Catcher

AND OTHER FAIRY TALES OF
LUDWIG BECHSTEIN

TRANSLATED AND INTRODUCED BY
RANDALL JARRELL

ILLUSTRATED BY UGO FONTANA

THE MACMILLAN COMPANY, NEW YORK / MACMILLAN NEW YORK, LONDON / 1962

Title Page: 13 × 9⁹⁄16 in. (330 × 243 mm.); 'The Rabbit Catcher' in v. pR (Centroid 254).

To Mary

THE MACMILLAN COMPANY, NEW YORK
A Division of The Crowell-Collier Publishing Company

MACMILLAN NEW YORK, LONDON
BRETT-MACMILLAN LTD., GALT, ONTARIO

PRINTED IN ITALY
FABBRISTAMPA · MILANO

Collation: two bindings: *binding 1* (library issue): [unsigned 1–3⁸]; 24 leaves; [4], [i–ii] iii–v [vi], [1] 2–5 [6] 7 [8] 9 [10–12] 13–14 [15–19] 20 [21] 22 [23–24] 25–26 [27–31] 32 [33–38]; *binding 2* (trade issue): identical except for: [2] (first and last leaves serve as pastedowns).

Contents: binding 1: two blank unnumbered leaves; p. i: title page; p. ii: copyright page and dedication: 'To Mary'; pp. iii–v: introduction by RJ and 'ABOUT RANDALL JARRELL' (bottom of p. v); p. vi: blank; p. 1: contents, pp. 2–34, text; pp. 35–38: blank; *binding 2:* one blank unnumbered leaf, remainder identical.

Typography: text, 18/24 Granjon; 28 lines per normal page; 243 × 160 mm.; 20 lines = 82 mm.

Paper and Binding: leaf measures 13 × 9⁹⁄₁₆ in. (330 × 243 mm.); white wove, unwatermarked paper, uncoated smooth; *binding 1 (library issue):* s. OY (Centroid 68) linen-cloth (304) pictorial cloth boards measure 13¼ × 10 in. (33 × 250 mm.); front: '[illustration of jester from p. iii reproduced in deep Pk (Centroid 3) and gy. OlG (Centroid 127)] | '[in deep pink] The Rabbit Catcher | [in grayish olive green] AND OTHER FAIRY TALES | [in deep pink] LUDWIG BECHSTEIN'; spine: '[vert.] [in deep pink] BECHSTEIN THE RABBIT CATCHER [in grayish olive green] AND OTHER FAIRY TALES [in deep pink] MACMILLAN'; back: '[in upper left corner, in grayish olive green] MACMILLAN | MASTER LIBRARY | EDITION'; all edges cut; *binding 2 (trade issue)*: pictorial paper-covered boards (ident. to jacket of library issue, except that the flap material has been omitted) measure 13⅜ × 9¹³⁄₁₆ (339 × 249 mm.); first and final unnumbered leaves serve as pastedowns; remainder identical to binding 1.

Dust Jacket: for binding 1 (library issue only): total measurement 13¼ × 25⁵⁄₁₆ in. (337 × 693 mm.); wove, unwatermarked paper; inner side white, outer side printed m. R (approx. Centroid 15); inner side coated smooth, outer side coated glossy; lettered in black and white; front contains an illustration from "The Rabbit Catcher" (p. 6), prin. in d. gB (Centroid 174), l. yPk (Centroid 28), d. yPk (Centroid 30), deep Br (Centroid 56), brill. Y (Centroid 83), v. R (Centroid 11), l. O (Centroid 52), and shades of greenish yellow; front: above illustration, '[reversed out in white] THE Rabbit Catcher | [in black] AND OTHER FAIRY TALES OF LUDWIG BECHSTEIN | TRANSLATED AND INTRODUCED BY [reversed out in white] RANDALL JARRELL'; spine: '[vert.] [reversed out in white] BECHSTEIN [in black] THE RABBIT CATCHER AND OTHER FAIRY TALES [white] MAC-MILLAN; back: '[16 lines in black or reversed out in white advertising 'More Marvelous Tales,' including Ruskin, Wilde, Andersen, *The Arabian Nights*, and *The Golden Bird and Other Fairy Tales of the Brothers Grimm*, also trans. by RJ; titles are reversed out in white, remainder in black; each title separated by a black ornament]'; front flap: '[in black] The Rabbit | Catcher *And Other* | *Fairy Tales of* | LUDWIG BECHSTEIN | [44 lines in roman, about the book]'; back flap: '[in black] [photographic reproduction of a painting of Bechstein, 59 × 47 mm.] | INTER NATIONES | LUDWIG BECHSTEIN | [11 lines, about the author] | [photograph of RJ, 60 × 47 mm.] | RANDALL JARRELL | [13 lines in roman, about RJ] | *Jacket design by Ursula Suess* | THE MACMILLAN COMPANY | 60 Fifth Avenue, New York 11, N.Y.'.

Text Contents: introduction by RJ; "The Rabbit Catcher," "The Brave Flute-Player," and "The Man and the Wife in the Vinegar Jug."

Publication: published in September 1962 at $3.09 (library binding) and $1.95 (trade edition); number of copies not available; printed at Fabbristampa in Milan, Italy.

Locations: MJ (both bindings), NcGU (both bindings), STW (2 copies in each binding).

Note: All copies examined of the jacket of the library binding have a gold metallic label across the spine: '[in black] [left, vert.] LIBRARY EDITION LIBRARY EDITION LIBRARY EDITION LIBRARY

EDITION [right, horiz.] MACMILLAN MASTER LIBRARY EDITION'.

RJ's translations for this title and the one that follows, *The Golden Bird*, were prepared for the simultaneous publication of the two books; therefore, the annotations that follow are relevant to both and are not repeated in **A12**.

RJ to Mac (MDC), 20 January 1962: I'll be delighted to do the translations—they're some of my favorite stories, and I've even written a Hansel and Gretel poem myself ["A Quilt-Pattern"]. I'd enjoy choosing the additional story or stories myself. I have the German text, but if you can get me one in Roman type I'd be pleased; mine looks as if a monk had done it with a paint-brush. I believe that I'll be able to finish the work by April 1. [¶] And I'll think about the brief introductory comments for young readers—perhaps something will come to me. I'm eager to see the illustrations; I'm sure they will be beautiful books.

RJ to Mac (MDC), early February 1962: The other story is *The Fisherman and His Wife*; I've already started to work on it and on *Hänsel and Gretel*. My *Hänsel and Gretel* poem is named *A Quilt-Pattern* in my *Selected Poems*. For that matter, I've written a couple of Sleeping Beauty poems and a poem about Grimms' Tales named *The Märchen*. [¶] I'll be delighted to have the Grimm in modern type and to see the illustrations. . . . [¶] *The Fisherman and His Wife* did select itself automatically; I imagine that by serious literary standards it's the best of all Grimms' Tales—certainly one of the best.

MJ to Mac (MDC), 22 February 1962: To date he [RJ] has finished: I. *The Fisherman and His Wife*, II and III, *Hänsel and Gretel* and *Snowwhite* are practically in a finished state: a final going-over as they are typed will be enough. IV. *The Golden Bird* is in "good" rough form. V. *Snowwhite and Rosered* has not been started. [¶] He says the byline should read "Translated by" as they are truly translations and not retellings.

A12 *THE GOLDEN BIRD AND OTHER FAIRY TALES OF THE BROTHERS GRIMM*, translated by RJ

First Edition (1962)

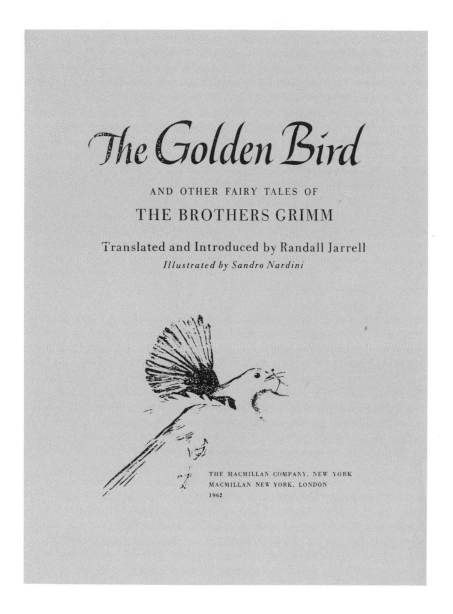

The Golden Bird

AND OTHER FAIRY TALES OF

THE BROTHERS GRIMM

Translated and Introduced by Randall Jarrell

Illustrated by Sandro Nardini

THE MACMILLAN COMPANY, NEW YORK
MACMILLAN NEW YORK, LONDON
1962

Title Page: 13 × 9⁹/₁₆ in. (330 × 242 mm.).

For Marie Irene Boyette

THE MACMILLAN COMPANY, NEW YORK
A Division of The Crowell-Collier Publishing Company

COLLIER-MACMILLAN LTD., LONDON
BRETT-MACMILLAN LTD., GALT, ONTARIO

PRINTED IN ITALY
FABBRISTAMPA - MILANO

Collation: [1–4⁸]; 32 leaves; [4], [i–ii] iii–vi, [1–2] 3 [4] 5–6 [7–8] 9 [10] 11 [12] 13–14 [15] 16 [17–18] 19–20 [21–22] 23–26 [27] 28 [29–30] 31 [32] 33–34 [35] 36 [37–38] 39 [40] 41–44 [45–47] 48 [49–50], [4].

Contents: two unnumbered blank leaves, the first of which serves as the front pastedown; p. i: title page; p. ii: copyright page and dedication: '*For Marie Irene Boyette*'; pp. iii–vi: introduction by RJ; p. 1: contents; pp. 2–50: text; two blank unnumbered leaves, the second of which serves as the rear pastedown.

Typography: text, 14/18 Granjon; 37 lines per normal page: 243 × 259 mm.; 20 lines = 124 mm.

Paper and Binding: leaf measures 13 × 9⁹⁄₁₆ in. (330 × 242 mm.); white wove, unwatermarked paper, uncoated smooth; m. yG (Centroid 136) pictorial paper-covered boards, coated glossy, measure 13⁵⁄₁₆ × 9¹³⁄₁₆ in. (339 × 248 mm.); front contains an illustration from "The Golden Bird" (p. 22), principally in d. gy. OlG (Centroid 128), p. YG (Centroid 121), l. yPk (Centroid 28), l. P (Centroid 222), l. Gy (Centroid 264), and gold; front: '[ornamental type, in black] The Golden Bird | [remainder in roman] AND OTHER FAIRY TALES OF

THE BROTHERS GRIMM | TRANSLATED AND INTRODUCED BY [reversed out in white] RANDALL JARRELL'; spine: '[vert., revsered out in white] GRIMM [in black] **THE GOLDEN BIRD** AND OTHER FAIRY TALES [in white] MACMILLAN'; back: '[in black and white (titles)] [16 lines prin. in roman, including a list of "More Marvelous Tales" in the Master Library Editions by Andersen, *The Arabian Nights*, Bechstein (*The Rabbit Catcher*, trans. by RJ), Ruskin, and Wilde]'.

Text Contents: introduction by RJ; "Snow-White and the Seven Dwarfs," "Hänsel and Gretel," "The Golden Bird," "Snow-White and Rose-Red," and "The Fisherman and His Wife."

Publication: published 3 September 1962 at $1.95; number of copies unknown; printed by Fabbristampi in Milan, Italy. Registered in the name of Fratelli Fabbri Editori, under A 0–37618; deposit copies received 5 November 1962.

Locations: DLC, MJ, NcGU, STW (3).

> *First Appearances:* Of the translations in this volume, four were reprinted in *The Juniper Tree and Other Tales from Grimm*, 2 vol., sel. by Lore Segal and Maurice Sendak (New York: Farrar, Straus & Giroux, 1973): in v. I: "The Fisherman and His Wife," pp. 94–112, and "Hänsel and Gretel," pp. 152–68; in v. II, "The Golden Bird," pp. 201–16, and "Snow-White and the Seven Dwarfs," pp. 256–74. Two of the translations were later published separately: *Snow-White and the Seven Dwarfs* (**A26**), and *The Fisherman and His Wife* (**A30**).

Note: For annotations, see above, **A11**.

This title was apparently issued in the trade binding only; the publisher has no records of a library binding, and *Publisher's Weekly* lists only the trade issue.

A13 *THE GINGERBREAD RABBIT*

A13a *First Edition (1964)*

Title Pages: 8³⁄₈ × 6¹⁵⁄₁₆ in. (213 × 151 mm.).

The Gingerbread Rabbit

By RANDALL JARRELL

Pictures by Garth Williams

THE MACMILLAN COMPANY, NEW YORK
COLLIER-MACMILLAN LIMITED, LONDON

Collation: [unsigned 1–4⁸]; 32 leaves; [i–vi], 1–2 [3] 4–8 [9] 10–13 [14] 15 [16] 17–20 [21–22] 23–24 [25] 26–28 [29] 30–36 [37] 38–39 [40–41] 42–43 [44] 45–48 [49] 50–51 [52–54] 55 [56–58].

Contents: p. i: half title; p. ii–iii: title pages; p. iv: copyright page; p. v: dedication page: '[illustration of a squirrel resting ona pile of leaves] | to my little Mary'; p. vi: illustration; pp. 1–55: text; pp. 56–58: blank.

Typography: text, 14/20 Caslon; 22 lines per normal page: 162 × 101 mm.; 20 lines = 138 mm.

Paper and Binding: leaf measures 8⅜ × 5¹⁵⁄₁₆ (213 × 150 mm.); white wove, unwatermarked paper, uncoated smooth; m. Br (Centroid 58) pictorial paper-covered boards measure 8⁹⁄₁₆ × 6⅜ in. (223 × 157 mm.); front contains an illustration of the gingerbread rabbit, the fox, and the big brown rabbit, ident. to dust jacket, prin. in l. YG (Centroid 119), d. OY (Centroid 72), black, white, and tan; lettered in brill. Y (Centroid 83), deep OY (Centroid 69), and black; front: '[above illustration, in brilliant yellow] THE GINGERBREAD | RABBIT [in deep orange yellow] by Randall Jarrell | [below illustration] PICTURES BY GARTH WILLIAMS'; spine: '[vert.] [in deep orange yellow] Randall Jarrell [in brilliant yellow] THE GINGER-BREAD RABBIT [in deep orange yellow] Macmillan'; back: '[in black, illustration of the gingerbread rabbit with the big brown rabbit and the silvery gray rabbit, ident. to back of dust jacket]'; all edges cut, unstained; brill. Y (Centroid 83) wove, unwatermarked endpapers, uncoated rough.

Dust Jacket: total measurement, 8¾ × 21⅞ in. (221 × 544 mm.); wove, unwatermarked paper; inner side and flaps are white; front, spine, and back are printed m. Br (Centroid 58); both sides uncoated smooth; lettered in brill. Y (Centroid 83) and deep OY (Centroid 69); front: all ident. to front board; spine: all ident. to spine of binding;

back: ident. to back board; front flap: '[in black, upper right corner] $2.95 | [type reprod. from orig. design by Garth Williams] The | Gingerbread Rabbit | [remainder in roman] by RANDALL JARRELL | pictures by GARTH WILLIAMS | [26 lines prin. in roman, about the book; left of lines 9–14 is an illustration of a fox, and right of lines 16–20 is an illustration of two rabbits] | [lower right corner] 74756'; back flap: '[upper left corner] 05/08 | About RANDALL JARRELL | [18 lines prin. in roman, about the author] | About GARTH WILLIAMS | [8 lines prin. in roman, about the illustrator] | THE MACMILLAN COMPANY | 60 Fifth Avenue, New York 11, New York'.

Text Contents: The Gingerbread Rabbit.

Publication: published 9 March 1964 at $2.95; 15,900 copies printed by the Halliday Lithograph Corp. of West Hanover, Mass., and bound by the Sendor Bindery of New York City. Registerd in the name of Randall Jarrell, under A 681092 (copyright is claimed on text); registered in the name of Garth Williams, under A 681093 (copyright is claimed on illustrations). Copyright deposit copies received 16 March 1964. There were two subsequent hardcover printings: a second of 4,325 copies in October 1965 at $3.95, and a third of 5,275 copies in December 1966. All identical except the words "First Edition" have been dropped from the copyright page; the back flap of the jacket of the third printing contains a notice of RJ's death in October 1965.

Locations: DLC, MJ, NcGU, NcWsW, STW (2).

First Appearance: The Gingerbread Rabbit.

RJ to Mac (MDC), June 1963: Suppose we substitute for that sentence in *The Gingerbread Rabbit*: "He smiled and leaned closer to the rabbit."

RJ to Mac (MDC), c. January–February 1962: I'll write out a few things about the characters in *The Gingerbread Rabbit* and the most likely things to illustrate. The rabbit himself ought to be very sincere and naive and ingenuous, so that his whole body and face express whatever he feels. The big rabbit ought to be handsome, secure, and competent-looking; the mother rabbit should be delicate and demure and beautiful. The fox should be very smooth and flashy, like Valentino playing W. C. Fields. The little girl's mother should be young (28 or so) and beautiful and *kind*, just the mother a little girl would want. The little girl should be something any little girl can identify easily with. [¶] These are some of the better scenes to illustrate, I think: 1. Mother and big rabbit as the rabbit sneezes. 2. Mother making the gingerbread rabbit. 3. Perhaps the vegetable man, perhaps not. 4. The gingerbread rabbit sneezes and comes to life, surrounded by the mixing bowl, paring knife, and rolling pin—these with faces and characteristic expressions. 5. The rabbit looks at his reflection—background of mixing bowl, paring knife, and rolling pin. 6. Mother enters kitchen with arms full of sacks—she's seen from below looking up as a giant, the way the rabbit sees her. 7. The rabbit wriggles out of her grasp—mother still as giant. 8. The rabbit at top speed as a somewhat blurred wheel with six spokes. 9. The squirrel catches hold of the rabbit and they fall from the bough. 10. Perhaps a picture showing the mother crying and talking to the squirrel. 11. The conversation between the rabbit and the fox. 12. The big rabbit cries *Fox! fox!* and they run off with the fox two steps behind. 13. The two rabbits come to the hole by the willow tree on the back of the stream—perhaps. 14. Lunch at the rabbits'. 15. The rabbits take their nap. 16. The conversation between the mother and the fox. 17. Perhaps the conversation between the mother and the squirrel, when she squeals with joy. 18. The mothr makes the rabbit. 19. The little girl finds the rabbit hidden behind the door. 20. The three rabbits look at the house in the moonlight. [¶] Perhaps there'll be other scenes the illustrator will want to do and perhaps he'll want to leave out some of these—These are just suggestions. If you'd like me to write any more about the book or the characters or the scenes, just tell me and I will.

RJ to Mac (MDC), September 1963: I was enchanted with the drawings for the *Gingerbread Rabbit*—making the rabbit so small, in the walking-into-the-moon pictures, was a wonderful idea.

RJ to AJR, June 1963: They'll publish my children's book . . . this fall. I've seen two of the illustrations for it; they're drawn by Garth Williams, the artist who illustrated *Stuart Little* and *Charlotte's Web*. It will be fun to have an illustrated book.

A13b *First Collier Books Paperback Impression (photo-offset from* **A13a***) (1972)*

All identical to **A13a** except for:

[left, contains Garth Williams illustration, which is continued on right]   [right] [fancy type] The | Gingerbread | Rabbit | [in roman] By RANDALL JARRELL | Pictures by Garth Williams | [publisher's device] | COLLIER BOOKS, NEW YORK, NEW YORK | COLLIER-MACMILLAN LTD., LONDON

Title Pages: each page measures $7^{11}/_{16} \times 5^{1}/_{8}$ in. (196×130 mm.).

Copyright Page: 'First Collier Books Edition 1972 | 10 9 8 7 6 5 4 3 2 1'.

Typography: 158.5×99 mm.; 10 lines = 138 mm.

Paper Binding: thick, wove, unwatermarked pictorial paper wrapper; white inner side uncoated, printed outer side coated smooth; front is identical to the jacket of **A12a** except the price, '95¢', is reversed out in white in the upper right corner; spine and back are s. O (Centroid 50); lettered in black; spine: '[vert., in black] JARRELL / WILLIAMS **THE GINGERBREAD RABBIT** Collier Books 04390'; back: '[in black] An easy-to-read modern fairy tale | by the author of | *The Animal Family* and *The Bat-Poet* | [left, reprod. from Garth Williams's letter design] The | Gingerbread | Rabbit [right, slightly taller than the three lines to the left, illustration of the old brown rabbit and the gingerbread rabbit] | by RANDALL JARRELL | Pictures by Garth Williams | [8 lines in roman, about the book] | [left, illustration of squirrel in leaves ident. to dedication page] [right] 04390 | For a complete list of Collier editions for young people write to | [publisher's device centered between last two lines] COLLIER BOOKS, Juvenile Paperbacks | 866 Third Avenue, New York, N.Y. 10022'.

Publication: published in June 1972 at 95¢; 18,523 copies printed. The publisher has issued four subsequent printings, all of which retain 'First Collier Books Edition 1972' on the copyright page. The printing, however, is identified as the lowest number in the sequence '10 9 8 7 6 5 4 3 2 1'; for example, the fifth, and most recent printing, contains the legend: '10 9 8 7 6 5'. Printings are as follows: 2d printing of 52,480 copies in August 1972; 3d printing of 27,975 copies in May 1974; 4th printing of 10,750 copies in December 1979; and 5th printing of 10,750 copies in June 1980.

Locations: MJ (2), NcGU, STW (2).

A14 *THE BAT-POET*

A14a *First Edition (1964)*

Title Page: 8¹³/₁₆ × 6⅛ in. (224 × 155 mm.).

THE BAT-POET

By RANDALL JARRELL

Pictures by Maurice Sendak

THE MACMILLAN COMPANY, NEW YORK
COLLIER-MACMILLAN LIMITED, LONDON

Collation: [unsigned 1–3⁸]; 24 leaves; [i–iv], 1–12 [13] 14–20 [21] 22–28 [29] 30–37 [38–41] 42 [43–44].

Contents: p. i: half title and dedication: 'THE BAT-POET [design by Sendak] | to Mary'; p. ii: full-page illustration of a bat in flight over a wooded landscape; p. iii: title page; p. iv: copyright page; pp. 1–43: text; pp. 44: blank.

Typography: text, 14/17 Bell; 29 lines per normal page; 168 × 101 mm.; 20 lines = 110mm.

Paper and Binding: leaf measures 8¹³⁄₁₆ × 6⅛ in. (224 × 155 mm.); heavy, white, wove, unwatermarked paper, uncoated smooth; gy. yBr (Centroid 80) fine bead-cloth (202b) boards measure 9¼ × 6⅜ in. (232 × 163 mm.); front: blindstamped, '[Sendak illustration within a double-rule frame, the outer of which is thick, the inner, thin]'; spine: '[in gold, vert.] Jarrell / Sendak THE BAT-POET [at base] Macmillan'; back: contains blindstamped double-rule frame ident. to front; all edges cut; top edges stained l. Pk (Centroid 4); deep yellowish white (no Centroid equivalent) laid endpapers, vert. chainlines 21 mm. apart, watermarked 'TWEEDWEAVE', uncoated rough.

Dust Jacket: total measurement, 9⅛ × 20¹⁵⁄₁₆ in. (231 × 532 mm.); deep yellowish white laid paper (ident. to endpapers), vert. chainlines 21 mm. apart, watermarked 'TWEEDWEAVE', uncoated rough; lettered in black and deep G (Centroid 142); front: '[within a frame of double rules, the outer of which is thick and in deep green, the inner one thin in black] [illustration of a bat flying through a forest] | [in deep green highlighted in black] THE BAT-POET | [in black] By Randall Jarrell | Pictures by Maurice Sendak | [illustration of five fernlike leaves in black and l. yG (approx. Centroid 135)]'; spine: '[horiz., double rules in deep green and black, like frame on front] [vert., in black] Jarrell / Sendak [in deep green highlighted in black like front] THE BAT-POET [at base, in black] Macmillan'; back: contains double-rule frame in deep green and black like front, but unlettered; front flap: '[upper right corner, in black] $2.75 | [in deep green highlighted in black] THE BAT-POET | [in black] By Randall Jarrell | Pictures by Maurice Sendak | [initial 'T' in deep green highlighted in black, remainder in black, 24 lines prin. in roman, about the book] | [lower right corner, in black] 74762'; back flap: '[in black, 20 lines prin. in roman, about RJ and his work] | [20 lines prin. in roman, about Sendak and his work] | THE MACMILLAN COMPANY | 60 Fifth Avenue, New York, N.Y. 10011'.

Text Contents: The Bat-Poet.

Publication: published 4 May 1964 at $2.75; 22,900 copies printed by Affiliated Lithographers, Inc., of New York City, and bound by Economy Book Binders, also of New York City. Copyright copies received 12 May 1964. Registered in the name of the Macmillan Company, under A 691323. The publisher has issued six additional cloth printings: 2d printing, 6,200 copies in January 1965; 3d printing, 6,300 copies in November 1965; 4th printing, 13,380 copies in February 1966; 5th printing, 8,730 copies in May 1966; 6th printing, 22,500 copies in April 1967; 7th printing, 6,000 copies in April 1976. The earliest of these are identical to the first printing; later printings may be identified by the number scheme on the copyright page. For example, the most recent (7th) printing is identified by the scheme '7 8 9 10'.

Locations: DLC, MJ (2), NcGU, NcWsW, NN, STW (5).

> *First Appearance: The Bat-Poet.* A long excerpt from *The Bat-Poet*, with Sendak illustrations, was reprinted in *Alumni News* (Univ. of N.C. at Greensboro), 54 (Spring 1966), 34–38. In addition, the following republications have been noted.
>
> "The Chipmunk's Day" Reprinted in *Piping Down the Valleys Wild*, ed. Nancy Larrick (New York: Delacorte, 1968), p. 142; record sleeve of Bill Crofut, *Poetry in Song*, Crofut Productions, 1973; William Crofut, *The Moon on the One Hand* (New York: Atheneum, 1973), p. 29, with Crofut's musical setting on pp. 30–32; *A Book of Animal Poems*, ed. William Cole (New York: Viking, 1973), p.133 (as "In and out of the Bushes"); *New Coasts and Strange Harbors: Discovering Poems*, ed. Helen Hill and Agnes Perkins (New York: Crowell, 1974).
>
> "The Bat Baby" Reprinted in *Wonders and Surprises*, ed. Phyllis McGinley (Philadelphia: Lippincott: 1968), p. 50.
>
> *Note:* Before publication the publisher sent to select reviewers and readers advance copies composed of three unbound signatures (all ident. to A14a) laid in the jacket of A14a.
>
> *RJ to Mac (MDC), October 1963:* I was enchanted with the news about the Bat-Poet pictures—since it's going ahead so well and the [*Gingerbread*] *Rabbit* is stuck in the wilds of Mexico, why don't we just bring out *The Bat-Poet* first? Probably it's the best to start with the best of the children's books anyway. Tell Maurice [Sendak] I can't wait to see the cover.

RJ to Mac (MDC), September 1963: The Bat-Poet manuscript looks splendid—The type size for the poems is quite all right. I return it with this letter.

RJ to Mac (MDC), November 1963: I herewith return *The Bat-Poet* manuscript—I didn't realize they wanted it back.

RJ to Mac (MDC), March 1964: The book looks wonderful—Mary and I were crazy about it. It was particularly clever of you to fix the *to my little Mary* page as you did—the squirrel and nest are even prettier than they are larger-sized later on. We've looked at and looked at it, and I've even read it a couple of times. May all the little children and their mothers love it!. . . . Thanks so much for thе book; it's wonderful. When you send me my ten [copies] I'd like to buy fifteen more.

RJ to Mac (MDC), July 1964: I (Mary too) was really *enchanted* with the look of the *Bat-Poet*—it's exactly right, I think; it even has a sort of serious elevated look, as if it were a classic as much for grown-ups as children. I think that Maurice [Sendak] did it wonderfully, the printing and paper are perfect. I'm crazy about the small bat-drawings at the side, the ones he did last; some of them are the most accomplished drawings of bats I've ever seen.

A14b *First Collier Books Paperback Impression (photo-offset from* **A14a**) *(1977)*

All identical to **A14a** except for:

THE BAT-POET | BY RANDALL JARRELL | [bat decoration by Sendak] | MACMILLAN PUBLISHING CO., INC. | NEW YORK

Title Page: 8⅞ × 6¹⁄₁₆ in. (225 × 153 mm.).

Copyright Page: 'First Collier Books Edition 1977 | 10 9 8 7 6 5 4 3 2 1'.

Collation: perfect bound; 24 leaves.

Paper Binding: thick, wove, unwatermarked deep tan (no Centroid equivalent) paper wrapper, uncoated rough; green lettering is deeper than **A14a**; front: all ident. to jacket of **A14a** except the price, '$1.95', is printed in the upper right corner (within the double-rule frame); spine: '[vert., in black] JARRELL / SENDAK **THE BAT-POET** Collier Books ISBN 0–02–043910–5'; back: '[upper left corner, within double-rule frame in deep G (Centroid 142) and black, like **A14a**, in black] FICTION | *"The trouble isn't making poems, the trouble's | finding somebody that will listen to them."* | [open-face type] THE BAT-POET | [roman] by Randall Jarrell | Pictures by Maurice Sendak | [8 lines in roman, about the book] | [9 lines prin. in roman, including quotes from Gene Shalit (*McCall's*) and *School Library Journal*] | For a complete list of Collier editions for young people write to | [publisher's device] COLLIER BOOKS, Juvenile Paperbacks | 866 Third Avenue, New York, N.Y. 10022 | [lower right corner, within double-rule frame] ISBN 0–02–043910–5'.

Publication: published in January 1977 at $1.95; 22,629 copies printed. The publisher has issued one additional printing, 10,344 copies in May 1978.

Locations: MJ (3), NcGU, STW (5).

A14c *First English Edition (photo-offset from* A14a*) (1977)*

All identical to A14a except for:

[bat ornament by Sendak] | THE BAT-POET | By RANDALL JARRELL | Pictures by Maurice Sendak | KESTREL BOOKS

Title Page: 9⅛ × 6 in. (232 × 153 mm.).

Copyright Page: 'First Published in Great Britain 1977'.

Paper and Binding: leaf measures 9⅛ × 6 in. (233 × 152 mm.); yWhite (Centroid 92) wove, unwatermarked paper, uncoated smooth; yG (approx. Centroid 136) paper-covered boards (imitation beadcloth) measure 9½ × 6¼ in. (240 × 158 mm.); front: unstamped; spine: '[vert. from top to bottom, in gold] Jarrell / Sendak THE BAT-POET KESTRELL BOOKS'; back: unstamped; all edges cut, unstained; laid, deep grayish tan endpapers (no Centroid equivalent), vert. chainlines 23 mm. apart.

Dust Jacket: total measurement 9⁷⁄₁₆ × 20⅝ in. (240 × 525 mm.); deep grayish tan laid paper ident. to endpapers; lettered in black and v. d. G (Centroid 147); front: ident. to A14a; spine: all ident. to A14a except 'KESTREL BOOKS' at base; back: ident. to A14a; front flap: '[in black] THE BAT-POET | By Randall Jarrell | *Pictures by Maurice Sendak* | [21 lines prin. in roman, about the book] | 008⁺ | I S B N o 7226 5358 1 £2.50 net'; back flap: '[in black] *Another Kestrel Book* | *by Randall Jarrell* | THE ANIMAL FAMILY | *with decorations by Maurice Sendak* | [32 lines prin. in roman, about the book] | KESTREL BOOKS | Printed in Great Britain'.

Publication: published 13 October 1977 at £2.50; 4,500 copies printed.

Locations: MJ, NcGU, STW (2).

A15 *SELECTED POEMS INCLUDING THE WOMAN AT THE WASHINGTON ZOO*

*First Edition (photo-offset from **A7a** and **A9** (1964)*

RANDALL JARRELL

SELECTED POEMS

INCLUDING

THE WOMAN AT
THE WASHINGTON ZOO

NEW YORK ATHENEUM *1964*

Title Page: 8¼ × 5¼ in. (209 × 133 mm.).

Collation: perfect bound; 152 leaves; in two titled sections: 'SELECTED POEMS': [2], [i–vi] vii–xvii [xviii] xix–xxii, [1–21] 3–81 83–119 [120] 121–132 [133–134] 135–153 [154] 155–205 [206]; 'THE WOMAN AT | THE WASHINGTON ZOO | POEMS & TRANSLATIONS': [2], vii–viii, [1] 2–65 [66–70].

Contents: one unnumbered blank leaf; p. i: half title: 'RANDALL JARRELL | [swelled rule, 76 mm.] | SELECTED POEMS [swelled rule, 76 mm.] | THE WOMAN AT | THE WASHINGTON ZOO'; p. ii: blank; p. iii: title page; p. iv: copyright page; p. v: part title; p. vi: dedication page (ident. to A7a); pp. vii–xvii: introduction and notes on the poems by RJ (ident to A7a); p. xviii: blank; pp. xix–xxii: contents (ident to A7a); pp. 1–205: text (ident. to A7a); one unnumbered leaf that contains the half title on the recto: 'THE WOMAN AT | THE WASHINGTON ZOO | POEMS & TRANSLATIONS | [swelled rule, 63 mm.] | RANDALL JARRELL', and the dedication on the verso: '*To Mary*' (ident. to A9); pp. vii–viii: contents (ident. to A9); pp. 1–65: text (ident. to A9); p. 66: blank; p. 67: 'RANDALL JARRELL | [24 lines prin. in roman, about the author]' (ident. to A9); pp. 68–70: list of Atheneum paperbacks (45 lines on p. 68, 47 lines on p. 69, including this title as number 66, and 42 lines on p. 70).

Typography: identical to **A7a** and **A9**.

Paper and Paper Binding: leaf measures 8¼ × 5¼ in. (209 ∴ 133 mm.); yWhite (Centroid 92) wove, unwatermarked paper, uncoated smooth; thick, wove, unwatermarked printed paper wrapper; inner side white, outer side printed in s. R (approx. Centroid 12), s. OY (approx. Centroid 68), v. Y (Centroid 82), black, and white; front: '[divided by a strong red H-shaped frame formed by two thick vert. rules, one on either side, that are bisected by a thick horiz. rule which separates two panels, the upper of which is black, and the lower, strong orange yellow] [all against upper black panel, reversed out in white] [left] *Atheneum 66* [right] *$2.75* | [in vivid yellow] RANDALL JARRELL | [in strong orange yellow] SELECTED POEMS | [in strong red] INCLUDING | [in vivid yellow] THE WOMAN AT | THE WASHINGTON ZOO'; spine: '[vert.] [in two lines, top] [in vivid yellow] RANDALL JARRELL [in strong orange yellow] SELECTED POEMS [bottom, in strong red] INCLUDING [in vivid yellow] THE WOMAN AT THE WASHINGTON ZOO [at base, centered between the two lines, reversed out in white] *Atheneum 66*'; back: all ident. to front, except: '[below thick strong red horiz. rule, against strong orange yellow panel, in black] [17 lines prin. in roman, about RJ and his work]'.

Text Contents: identical to **A7a** and **A9**.

Publication: published 21 September 1964 at $2.75; 5,000 copies printed. The publisher has issued an additional five printings but no longer has a record of the number of copies printed; each retains the notation '*First Atheneum Edition August 1964* [sic]' but also includes the month and year of the latest printing: 2d printing, October 1966; 3d printing, September 1968; 4th printing, March 1969; 5th printing, March 1974; 6th printing, March 1980.

Locations: DLC, MJ (2), NcGU, NcU, STW (3).

A16 *THE LOST WORLD*

A16a *First Edition (1965)*

THE
LOST
WORLD

RANDALL
JARRELL

THE MACMILLAN COMPANY, NEW YORK
COLLIER-MACMILLAN LIMITED, LONDON

Title Page: 8⁵⁄₁₆ × 5¼ in. (211 × 133 mm.).

Collation: [unsigned 1–5⁸]; 40 leaves; [i–x], [1–2] 3–7 [8] 9–19 [20] 21–69 [70].

Contents: p. i: half title; p. ii: blank; p. iii: list of books by RJ; p. iv: blank; p. v: title page; p. vi: copyright and acknowledgments; p. vii: dedication page: 'To Michael | FROM RANDALL AND MARY'; p. viii: blank; p. ix: contents; p. x: blank; pp. 1–69: text; p. 70: 'ABOUT THE AUTHOR | [15 lines in roman and ital.]'.

Typography: text, 11/13 Janson; 33 lines per normal page; 159 × 97 mm.; 20 lines = 95 mm.

Paper and Binding: leaf measures 8⁵/₁₆ × 5¼ in. (211 × 135 mm.); yWhite (Centroid 92) wove, unwatermarked paper, uncoated smooth; gy. rBr (Centroid 46) bead-cloth (202) boards measure 8⁹/₁₆ × 5⁹/₁₆ in. (218 × 140 mm.); front: unstamped, spine: '[vert., in gold] THE

LOST WORLD · RANDALL JARRELL [at base] MACMILLAN';
back: '[lower right corner, in gold] 55898'; all edges cut; top edges
stained s. Pk (Centroid 2); m. O (Centroid 53) wove, unwatermarked
endpapers, uncoated rough.

Dust Jacket: total measurement, 8½ × 19¹³⁄₁₆ in. (216 × 503 mm.);
both sides are white; inner side coated smooth, outer side coated
glossy; lettered in v. R (Centroid 11) and black; front: '[in black]
RANDALL JARRELL | [in vivid red, thick rule, 98 mm.] | The | Lost
| World | [in vivid red, thick rule, 98 mm.] | [in black] NEW POEMS';
spine: '[vert., in black] JARRELL [in vivid red] The Lost World [in
black] MACMILLAN'; back: '[in black] THE POETRY OF RAN-
DALL JARRELL | [27 lines prin. in roman, including blurbs by Karl
Shapiro, Stephen Spender, and Robert Lowell] | The Macmillan Com-
pany, 60 Fifth Avenue, New York, N.Y. 10011'; front flap: '[upper
right corner, in black] $3.95 | [28 lines prin. in roman, about RJ and
his work] | *(Continued on back flap)* | Jacket design / Dick Adelson';
back flap: '[black-and-white photograph of RJ, 129 × 98 mm.] | [in
black] Philippe Halsman | *(Continued from front flap)* | [13 lines prin.
in roman, about RJ]'.

Text Contents: "Next Day," "The Mockingbird," "In Montecito,"
"The Lost World," "A Well-to-Do Invalid," "The X-Ray Waiting
Room in the Hospital," "In Galleries," "Well Water," "The Lost Chil-
dren," "Three Bills," "Hope," "The Bird of Night," "Bats," "The One
Who Was Different," "A Hunt in the Black Forest," "The House in
the Wood," "Woman," "Washing," "In Nature There Is Neither Right
nor Left nor Wrong," "The Old and the New Masters," "Field and
Forest," "Thinking of the Lost World."

Publication: published 1 February 1965 at $3.95; 4,000 copies
printed and bound by Hadden Craftsmen, Inc., Scranton, Pa. Registered in the name of Randall Jarrell, under A 773383. Copyright de-
posit copies received 22 June 1965. The publisher issued four additional cloth printings: 2d printing, 1,500 copies in April 1965; 3d
printing, 2,000 copies in February 1966; 4th printing, 1,500 copies in
August 1966; 5th printing, 3,000 copies in August 1967.

Locations: DLC, GU, MJ (2), NcGU, NcU, NcWsW, NN, STW (3),
TxU, ViU.

First Appearances:

"In Nature There is Neither Right nor Left nor Wrong"   CP.

"The Old and the New Masters"   CP; reprinted in *Exploring
Poetry*, ed. M. L. Rosenthal and A. J. M. Smith, 2d ed. (New

York: Macmillan, 1973); *The Modern Age (Literature)*, ed. Leonard Lief and James F. Light, 2d ed. (New York: Holt, Rinehart, and Winston, 1972), pp. 627–28, and 3d ed. (1976), pp. 670–71.

RJ to Mac (MDC), June 1963: About the last two poems I sent you: would you put "The Sign" after "Bats" and "X-Ray Waiting Room" after "Woman"? ["The Sign" was not included in this selection.]

RJ to Mac (MDC), June 1963: I was delighted that you liked "Gleaning" that much. Here is the whole *Lost World*. Two of the poems I'd just written and meant to save for *Woman* [*at the Washington Zoo*], I decided to put in this book—they're "A Well-to-Do Invalid" and "The Lost Children."

RJ to Mac (MDC), June 1963: If you want to ask Maurice Sendak to try a dust-jacket for *The Lost World* it's fine with me; it might turn out awfully good. I'd be enchanted at the prospect.

RJ to AJR, 29 June 1963: I just finished a new poetry book that Macmillan will print early next spring; it's called *The Lost World*.

RJ to Mac (MDC), December 1963: In a day or two I'll send you that poem I read you ["In Galleries"] to take the place of "A Well-to-Do Invalid" in *The Lost World*. I think I want to make some changes or additions sometime, whereas "In Galleries" is the way I want it. I'd send you "In Galleries" now but I'm not certain that you spell *bellissima* that way, none of the Italian dictionaries at the library *have* the word, and I need to call up the head of the Romance Languages department.

RJ to Mac (MDC), 8 January 1964: Here's the dust jacket [material] and, oh joy!, here's *The Well-to-Do Invalid* all finished. Let's put it just before *In Galleries*.

RJ to SBQ, 4 February 1964: I've been writing a lot of poems, a whole new bookful—it will be named *The Lost World*.

RJ to Mac (MDC), April 1964: There's one thing Mary and I would like to do to show our gratitude for all you did to help me write it—we'd like to dedicate the book to you.

A16b *First Collier Books Paperback Impression (photo-offset from A16a) (1966)*

All identical to **A16a** except for:

THE | LOST | WORLD | [swelled rule, 63 mm.] | RANDALL JAR-

RELL | *with an appreciation by* | *ROBERT LOWELL* | [Collier Books device] | COLLIER BOOKS, *NEW YORK*

Title Page: 7¹⁵⁄₁₆ × 5¼ in. (201 × 132 mm.).

Copyright Page: 'FIRST COLLIER BOOKS EDITION 1966'.

Collation: perfect bound; 44 leaves.

Contents: p. 70: '*About the Author* | [18 lines in roman and ital]'; pp. 71–80: '*Randall Jarrell, 1914–1965:* | *An Appreciation* | ROBERT LOWELL'.

Paper Binding: wove, unwatermarked printed paper wrapper; inner side uncoated, outer side coated glossy; front: adds two lines, '[in black] WITH AN APPRECIATION BY | ROBERT LOWELL'; spine: '[vert., in black] [Collier Books device] JARRELL [in vivid red] The Lost World [in black, at base] 06975'; back: '[upper left corner, in black] POETRY | RANDALL JARRELL [vivid red] The Lost World | [in black, thick rule, 78 mm.] | With an Appreciation by Robert Lowell | [30 lines prin. in roman, including blurbs or excerpts from reviews by Robert Penn Warren, Robert Lowell (*New York Review of Books*), Marianne Moore, William Meredith (*Book Week*), and Philip Booth (*Christian Science Monitor*) | [Collier Books device in vivid red] | [in black] COLLIER BOOKS | 866 THIRD AVENUE, NEW YORK, NEW YORK 10022 06975'.

Text Contents: Lowell's appreciation added at end.

Publication: published in 1966 at $1.50; 5,000 copies printed. A second printing of 5,000 copies was issued in 1967.

Locations: MJ (3), NcGU, STW (2).

A16c *First English Edition (1966)*

RANDALL JARRELL

The Lost World

WITH AN APPRECIATION OF
RANDALL JARRELL
BY ROBERT LOWELL

EYRE *&* SPOTTISWOODE
LONDON

Title Page: 8½ × 5⅜ in. (215 × 137 mm.)

Copyright Page: 'First published in 1966 by | Eyre and Spottiswoode (Publishers) Ltd'.

Collation: [unsigned A⁸] B–E⁸; 40 leaves; [1–8] 9–69 [70–71] 72–80.

Contents: p. 1: half title; p. 2: blank; p. 3: title page; p. 4: copyright page and acknowledgments; p. 5: dedication page; p. 6: blank; p. 7: contents; p. 8: blank; pp. 9–69: text; p. 70: blank; p. 71: 'Randall Jarrell, 1914–1965: | An Appreciation | [ornamental rule, 50 mm.] | Robert Lowell'; pp. 72–80: Lowell's appreciation.

Running Titles: 'THE LOST WORLD | [title of individual poem in all caps, or] RANDALL JARRELL, 1914–1965'.

Typography: text, 11/13 English Monotype Garamond 156; 36 lines per normal page; 169 (176) × 92.5 mm.; 20 lines = 90 mm.

Paper and Binding: leaf measures 8½ × 5⅜ in. (215 × 135 mm.); yWhite (Centroid 92) wove, unwatermarked paper; d. gy. Br (Centroid 62) paper-covered boards (imitation bead-cloth) measure 8¾ × 5⅝ in. (233 × 143 mm.); front: unstamped; spine: '[vert. from top to bottom, in gold] The Lost World RANDALL JARRELL [at base] E & S'; back: unstamped; all edges cut, unstained; l. gy pR (Centroid 261) laid endpapers, vert. chainlines 25 mm. apart, watermarked in ornamental type 'Greenfield' or 'Abbey Mills' with a crown ornament.

Dust Jacket: total measurement, 8¾ × 18¾ in. (222 × 477 mm.); paper identical to endpapers, uncoated rough; front, spine, and back contain an illustration in black of a row of buildings, a tree, and children at play, signed on back by artist 'BREN DAWKEY'; lettered in black and d. R (Centroid 16); front: '[above illustration, in black] The Lost World | [in dark red] RANDALL JARRELL'; spine: '[vert. from top to bottom, above illustration in black] THE LOST WORLD [in dark red] · RANDALL JARRELL [at base, below illustration] E & S'; back: unlettered but contains a portion of Dawkey's drawing; front flap: '[in black] The Lost World by | Randall Jarrell | WITH A CRITICAL APPRECIATION | By ROBERT LOWELL | [33 lines prin. in roman, about RJ and his work] | *continued on back flap* | PRICE IN U.K. | 18s net'; back flap: '[in black, 16 lines prin. in roman, including blurbs by Marianne Moore, Robert Penn Warren, and Alan Pryce-Jones] | [at bottom] PRINTED IN GREAT BRITAIN'.

Text Contents: identical to **A16a** except this edition includes Robert Lowell's appreciation.

Publication: published in 1966 at 18s.; the date of publication and number of copies printed are not available.

Locations: MJ, NcGU, STW (2).

A17 *THE ANIMAL FAMILY*

A17a *First Edition: Trade Issue (1965)*

The Animal Family
by Randall Jarrell

DECORATIONS BY
Maurice Sendak

PANTHEON BOOKS

Title Page: 6⅝ × 5⅛ in. (167 × 129 mm.).

Collation: [unsigned 1–12⁸]; 96 leaves; [i–x], [1–4] 5–27 [28–32] 33–54 [55–58] 59–66 [67–70] 71–95 [96–100] 101–126 [127–130] 131–145 [146–150] 151–179 [180–182].

Contents: p. i: half title; p. ii: unlettered but contains decorations by Sendak; p. iii: title page; p. iv: copyright page; p. v: dedication: 'To Elfi | From Randall and Mary'; p. vi: blank; p. vii: 'Say what you like but such things do | happen—not often, but they do happen. | [decoration by Sendak]'; p. viii: blank; p. ix: contents; p. x: blank; p. 1: second half title; p. 2: blank; pp. 3–180: text; pp. 181–182: blank. Contents are divided into seven titled chapters.

Running Titles: head: 'THE ANIMAL FAMILY | [unlettered]'.

Typography: text, 14/16 Cloister; 17 lines per normal page; 94 (105) × 66 mm. (verso pages); 20 lines = 104 mm.

Paper and Binding: leaf measures 6¹¹/₁₆ × 5¼ in. (169 × 133 mm.); yWhite (Centroid 92) laid paper, vert. chainlines 22 mm. apart, unwatermarked, uncoated smooth; gy. B (approx. Centroid 186) coarse bead-cloth (202) boards measure 6⅞ × 5½ in. (174 × 138 mm.); front: in silver, '[three blossoming vine plants reversed out in grayish blue against a solid silver panel which measures 83 × 62 mm.]'; spine: '[in silver, horiz.] RANDALL | JARRELL | THE | ANIMAL | FAMILY | [at base] PANTHEON'; back: unstamped; all edges cut, unstained; tan (no Centroid equivalent) laid endpapers, vert. chainlines 21 mm. apart, unwatermarked, uncoated rough.

Dust Jacket: total measurement, 6¹³/₁₆ × 19⁵/₁₆ in. (173 × 490 mm.); wove, unwatermarked paper; inner side white, outer side p. Y (Centroid 89); both sides uncoated rough; lettered in black and d. rO (Centroid 38); front: '[all within a solid black frame containing a plantlike design reversed out in white] [within a frame of black double rules separated by a border that is reversed out in white, Sendak illustration of a wooded scene] | [in dark reddish orange] THE ANIMAL FAMILY | BY RANDALL JARRELL | DECORATIONS BY | MAURICE SEN-DAK | PANTHEON BOOKS | [decoration by Sendak, in black]'; spine: '[in dark reddish orange, horiz.] RANDALL | JARRELL | THE | ANIMAL | FAMILY | [at base] PANTHEON'; back: '[decoation by Sendak, in black; unlettered]'; front flap: '[in black] $3.50 | T.A.F. | PAN. | [25 lines prin. in roman, about the book] | *all ages*'; back: '[in black] [31 lines, prin, in roman, about RJ, including quotes from Robert Penn Warren and Robert Lowell] | [9 lines prin. in roman, about Sendak] | PANTHEON BOOKS | A DIVISION OF RANDOM HOUSE | Printed in the U.S.A.'

Text Contents: The Animal Family .

Publication: published in 16 November 1965 at $3.50; number of copies unknown. Printed by Reehl Litho Co. of New York City. Registered in the name of Maurice Sendak, under A 894885, then in the name of Random House, under A 894886, following publication. See below, Note, for information concerning subsequent printings.

Locations: DLC, GU, MJ (2), NcGU, NcU, NcWsW, NN, STW (5), TxU, ViU.

> *First Appearance: The Animal Family.* Of the contents of this volume, the following republication has been noted.
>
> *"The Mermaid"* Reprinted in *Anthology of Children's Literature*, ed. Edna Johnson et al., 4th rev. ed. (Boston: Houghton Mifflin, 1970), pp. 696–700.
>
> Note: Although the publisher was unable to provide any information concerning the subsequent printing history of *The Animal Family*, later printings of the trade issue may be identified as follows:
>
> *All identical to* **A17a** except for:
>
> *Title Page:* 168 × 131 mm.
>
> *Copyright Page:* contains Library of Congress and ISBN information.
>
> *Paper and Binding:* leaf measures 6⅝ × 5⅛ in. (168 × 130 mm.); p. Y (approx. Centroid 89) laid paper, vert. chainlines 21 mm. apart, unwatermarked, uncoated smooth; m. G (approx. Centroid 145) paper-covered boards measure 6¹³⁄₁₆ × 5⁷⁄₁₆ in. (173 × 138 mm.); stamped in silver; front: design ident. to **A17a** reversed out in moderate green against a solid silver panel, 83 × 62 mm.; spine: '[horiz.] RANDALL | JARRELL | THE | ANIMAL | FAMILY | [at base] PANTHEON'; back: unstamped.
>
> *RJ to PB (MDC), April 1964:* I've roughly finished the *Animal Family*, and haven't been working on it for a few days.

RJ to PB (MDC), July 1964: I've been writing a *lot* on *The Animal Family*, and have it two-thirds done; it will be at least 2½ times the length of *The Bat-Poet*. I hope to get it roughly finished in a month, and then mean to go over and over it adding little things and trying to get it exactly right. I'm going to wait till it's finished to show it to you; I think you'll enjoy it more.

RJ to PB (MDC), 15 October 1964: The Animal Family's going to be seven chapters long (I. The Hunter. II. The Mermaid. III. The Hunter Brings Home a Baby. IV. The Bear. V. The Lynx. VI. The Lynx and the Bear Bring Home a Boy. I got *baby* and *boy* backwards—sorry. VII. The Boy. And I have the first four and all of the sixth done.) The whole thing gets more realistic all the time—the animals don't steal the baby, now.

RJ to PB (MDC), December 1964: How about my coming to Pantheon at 4 that afternoon [December 22], talking about the anthology and everything else, and seeing Maurice [Sendak] at dinner; we could talk about designing *The Animal Family* then. (I've got it pretty smooth, almost finished, and have typed some pages.)

RJ to PB (MDC), February 1965: I think it might be a good idea to show *Red Book* the *Animal Family*: show them surreptitiously or informally, so to speak. It was bad luck that *McCall's* had just bought an animal fantasy, wasn't it?

RJ to PB (MDC), early March 1965: Any time you can come down [to North Carolina] I'd love to see you; and if you could bring cloth samples for the cover of the book (especially beautiful intense blue buckram ones, like the sky or sea) I could pick one. Page samples of the type and paper would be good, too. I can decide things like that. . . . [¶] Probably it ought to be brought out primarily as a children's book; the other's too risky and too much of a change. I'd have the best quotations about *The Bat-Poet* on the back jacket. The front jacket ought to read, I think: [within a frame of hand-drawn single rules] THE | ANIMAL FAMILY | RANDALL JARRELL | A STORY FOR CHILDREN | AND GROWN UPS [below frame]   I think it would be good to give it to read to a lot of the people who liked *Bat-Poet* best and get quotations for the dust jacket and advertisements.

RJ to PB (MDC), April 1965: Just a note to say that I know you're right about the children *and grownups* on the jacket—cut out *and grownups* entirely. I went over to the library and found nothing photographically interesting . . . back in the stacks under Washington, Oregon, and California. You'll have to find some good ones for me to pick from. But I'm not worried about the photographs; if we have to do without them I know you'll have a perfect book just the same.

RJ to PB (MDC), 24 May 1965: All your plans and news sound splendid. That size book, with Maurice's decorations, ought to be beautiful.

I'm sure I'll be as delighted with the looks of the *Animal Family* as I was with the looks of the *Bat-Poet*. With this book I'll just leave everything to you—next book I'll be well and help myself out.

RJ to RPW, August 1965: The last book I wrote ... was one about a hunter and his family living all alone in the forest at the edge of the sea. As soon as I get some copies I'll send you one and the children one too—it's another of these books half for children and half for grown ups.

RJ to MS, 11 September 1965: I feel so lucky to have had your pictures for both the *Animal Family* and *The Bat-Poet. The Animal Family* was harder for you, since you couldn't make the pictures direct illustrations and since drawing came right in the middle of such a hard time in your life—and I'm *so* grateful to you for working so hard on them and making them so beautiful. It's hard for me to pick the ones I like best—the one of the moonlight on the sea [on page 31] and the dust-jacket itself are my favorites, almost. It will make so much difference to readers having your decorations rather than a book without drawings—the book will feel rich and full to them in a way it couldn't possibly without what you've done. They really are some of your most original and profound drawings—not only will the readers of *The Animal Family* love them, but there are all the people who get any book you make drawings for, just because they are your drawings. [¶] What you say about *The Animal Family* makes me feel awfully good. I'd like to have it a good book, and when people like you like it as you do—people with so much understanding and remembrance of childhood, so much magic and imagination of their own—it makes me hope that the book really is what it ought to be.

A17b   *First Edition, Library Issue (1966)*

All identical to **A17a** except for:

Title Page: 7⅝ × 4⅝ in. (193 × 118 mm.).

Paper and Binding: leaf measures 7⅝ × 4⁹⁄₁₆ in. (193 × 116 mm.); yWhite (Centroid 92) wove, unwatermarked paper, uncoated smooth; p. gY (Centroid 104) paper-covered boards measure 7⅞ × 5³⁄₁₆ in. (201 × 131 mm.); all edges cut, stained p. Y (Centroid 89); white endpapers, uncoated smooth.

Publication: published in March 1966 at $3.84.

Locations: MJ, STW

Note: Subsequent printings identical except for:

Collation: [unsigned 1–6¹⁶].

Title Page: 6⁹⁄₁₆ × 5¼ in. (167 × 133 mm.).

Copyright Page: contains Library of Congress and ISBN cataloging information.

Paper and Binding: leaf measures 6⅝ × 5¹⁄₁₆ in. (162 × 130 mm.); tan (no Centroid equivalent) laid paper, vert. chainlines 21 mm. apart, unwatermarked; uncoated smooth; glossy coated paper::covered boards measure 6¹⁵⁄₁₆ × 5⅜ in. (175 × 137 mm.); floral border and Sendak illustration and decoration on front, Sendak decoration, price, and ISBN ident. number on back are printed in d. gy. yBr (Centroid 81) instead of black; all edges cut, unstained; yWhite (Centroid 92) wove endpapers coated smooth.

A17c *First English Edition (photo-offset from A17a) (1967)*

All identical to **A17a** except for:

The Animal Family | by Randall Jarrell | [decoration by Maurice Sendak] | DECORATIONS BY | Maurice Sendak | RUPERT HART-DAVIS | LONDON | 1967

Title Page: 6⁷⁄₁₆ × 5 in. (164 × 127 mm.).

Copyright Page: 'First published in Great Britain 1967'.

Collation: [unsigned 1–6¹⁶].

Paper and Binding: leaf measures 6½ × 5 in. (164 × 127 mm.); grayish white (no Centroid equivalent) laid paper, vert. chainlines 28 mm. apart, unwatermarked, uncoated smooth; d. rO (approx. Centroid 38) paper-covered boards (imitation bead-cloth) measure 6¹³⁄₁₆ × 5⅜ in. (173 × 139 mm.); front: unstamped; spine: in gold, '[horiz.] The | Animal | Family | [decoration by Sendak] | Randall | Jarrell | [at base] Rupert | Hart-Davis'; back: unstamped; all edges cut, unstained; grayish tan (no Centroid equivalent) laid endpapers, vert. chainlines 26 mm. apart, watermarked '[crown device] | [open-face] *Abbey Mills | Green Field*'.

Dust Jacket: total measurement, 6¾ × 17¹⁵⁄₁₆ in. (172 × 457 mm.); uncoated paper ident. to endpapers; printed in black and d. rO (approx. Centroid 38); front: '[thick rule, 4 × 129 mm., in dark reddish orange] | [left side, in dark reddish orange] the | animal | family | [right side, in dark reddish orange] Randall | Jarrell | [thick rule ident. to first, broken on right side by Sendak illustration in black]'; spine: '[horiz.] [heavy rule, 3 × 14 mm., in dark reddish orange] | [in black] the | animial | family | Randall | Jarrell | [rule in dark reddish orange, ident. to first] [at base, in black] Rupert | Hart-|Davis'; back: contains Sendak decoration in black; front flap: '[in black, 16 lines prin. in roman, about the book] | [lower right corner] 12s 6d *net*'; back flap: '[in black] [14 lines in roman, about RJ] | [4 lines prin. in roman, about Sendak] | [publisher's device] | Rupert Hart-Davis Ltd | 3 Upper James Street | Golden Square London W1 | Printed in Great Britain'.

Publication: published in 1967 at 12s. 6d.; number of copies unknown.

Locations: NcGU, STW (2).

A18 *THE BIRD OF NIGHT*

First Separate Edition (1966)

Collation: broadside, 10¼ × 8 in. (280 × 204 mm.).

Contents: "The Bird of Night" and '[rule, 98 mm.] | FIVE COPIES REPRINTED HORS COMMERCE FOR THE HOUSE & FRIENDS BY THE BROOK | RANDALL JARRELL'; verso: blank.

Paper: 10¼ × 8 in. (280 × 204 mm.); gray wove paper, unwatermarked; all edges deckled; rough.

Text Contents: "The Bird of the Night" (C347).

Publication: five copies printed for private distribution by Walter Hamady in 1966. No copyright clearance was obtained for this printing, nor was permission granted by the Estate of Randall Jarrell. Not for sale.

> *Note:* Evert Volkersz, head of the Department of Special Collections, Melville Memorial Library, at the State University of New York at Stony Brook, who kindly provided information concerning this item, wrote that he "vaguely" recalled "a humorous story Walter [Hamady] tells about his plumber and daughter" and the printing of this broadside. Letter to SW, 17 September 1982.

A19 *BAMBERG*

First Edition (1966)

BAMBERG *a poem by Randall Jarrell*

Collation: broadside, 16⅜ × 4¾ in. (414 × 120 mm.).

Contents: recto: "Bamberg" and statement of limitation; verso: blank.

Paper and Typography: single leaf measures 16⅜ × 4¾ in. (414 × 120 mm.), folded horizontally six times to measure 2⁷⁄₁₆ × 4¾ in. (61 × 120 mm.); light grayish white (no Centroid equivalent) laid paper, vert. chainlines 23 mm. apart, unwatermarked; top and side edges trimmed, bottom edge deckled; text, 18/18 Garamond.

Envelope: laid into an open-sided envelope of black heavy, wove, unwatermarked paper, folded twice horizontally to 2½ × 5¼ in. (63 × 133 mm.); paper label: front contains a printed paper label, 1⁹⁄₁₆ × 2⅜ in. (40 × 60 mm.): '[in black] [within a frame of irregular double rules, the outer of which are thin, the inner ones, thick] BAMBERG | RANDALL JARRELL'.

Statement of Limitation: '50 copies printed at the Gehenna Press by A. Troxler, | with the permission of Mrs. Randall Jarrell. July 1966'.

Publication: published in July 1966; 50 copies printed; not for sale.

Locations: MJ, STW.

> *First Appearance:* "Bamberg"   CP.

A20 *THE SIGN*

First Edition (1966)

THE SIGN

Collation: broadside, 13¹⁵⁄₁₆ × 9⁹⁄₁₆ in. (355 × 243 mm.).

Contents: recto: "The Sign" and colophon; verso: blank.

Paper and Typography: two papers noted, no priority: *paper 1:* yWhite (Centroid 92) laid, vert. chainlines 25 mm. apart, water-marked '*Linweave Text*' ('*L*' superimposed against '*T*'); left, top and bottom edges trimmed, right edge deckled; *paper 2:* pale gray (no Centroid equivalent) laid, horiz. chainlines 23 mm. apart. watermark ident. to paper 1; side and bottom edges trimmed, top edge deckled; text, 18/24 Caslon.

Colophon: '*A Keepsake for Friends of the Library of the University of North Carolina* | *at Greensboro, April 20, 1966: courtesy of Mrs. Randall Jarrell;* | [right side, Bert Carpenter's logo the height of the last two lines] | *drawing by Bert Carpenter; printed at the Chapman Press.*'

Publication: published 20 April 1966; approx. 100 copies printed; not for sale.

Locations: MJ, NcGU, STW (both papers and proof copies).

> *First Appearance:* "The Sign" CP.
>
> *Note:* A few copies printed on yellowish white proofing paper, 393 × 268 mm., were distributed before 20 April 1966.
>
> The printer was originally supplied a text that was supposed to have been an unpublished poem of Jarrell's. It was in fact Walter de la Mare's "Comfort," which RJ had copied out on a blank leaf in his review copy of de la Mare's *The Burning-Glass*. A few proof copies of "As I Mused by the Hearthside" (by RJ!) were struck, but the error was discovered before the edition was printed. Mrs. Jarrell then supplied the text of "The Sign," and Carpenter prepared another illustration.

A21 *THE COMPLETE POEMS*

A21a *First Edition (1969)*

Randall Jarrell

THE

COMPLETE

POEMS

Farrar, Straus & Giroux

NEW YORK

Title Page: 9³⁄₁₆ × 6¹⁄₁₆ in. (233 × 153 mm.).

Collation: [unsigned 1–15¹⁶ 16⁸ 17¹⁶]; 264 leaves; [2], [i–iv] v–xvi
[xvii–xviii], [1–2] 3–11 [12–14] 15–51 [-2] 53–63 [64] 65–91 [92]
93–107 [108] 109–139 [140–142] 143–151 [152] 153–187 [188]
189–199 [200] 201–211 [212–214] 215–275 [276–278] 279–338

[339–342] 343–355 [356] 357–403 [404] 405–415 [416] 417–459 [460] 461–491 [492] 493–497 [498] 499–507 [508].

Contents: one blank, unnumbered leaf; p. i: half title; p. ii: blank; p. iii: title page; p. iv: copyright page and acknowledgments; pp. v–xvi: contnts; pp. xvii–xviii: blank; pp. 1–491: text; p. 492: blank; pp. 493–497: index of titles; p. 498: blank; pp. 499–507j: index of first lines; p. 508: blank. Contents are divided into eleven titled sections: RJ's individual book titles, "New Poems," and "Unpublished Poems."

Running Titles: foot, '[page number in Arabic numerals] *Randall Jarrell* / *The Complete Poems* | [individual section title in roman all caps] [page number in Arabic numerals]'.

Typography: text, 12/14 Granjon; 37 lines per normal page; 167 (192) × 110 mm.; 20 lines = 98 mm.

Paper and Binding: leaf measures 9³⁄₁₆ × 6¹⁄₁₆ in. (233 × 153 mm.); yWhite (Centroid 92) laid paper, vert. chainlines 20 mm. a part, un-watermarked, uncoated smooth; s. bG (approx. Centroid 160) fine bead-cloth (202b) boards measure 9⁷⁄₁₆ × 6⁵⁄₁₆ in. (240 × 161 mm.); front: unstamped; spine: '[horiz., in gold] *Randall* | *Jarrell* | [ornament in silver] | [in silver] *The* | *Complete* | *Poems* | [gold rule, 38 mm.] | [in silver] *Farrar, Straus & Giroux*; back: unstamped; top and bottom edges cut, fore-edges untrimmed; top edges stained l. Y (Centroid 86); black wove, unwatermarked endpapers; cloth head and tail bands have alternating green and yellow stripes.

Dust Jacket: total measurement, 9⁷⁄₁₆ × 22½ in. (240 × 571 mm.); wove, unwatermarked paper, uncoated rough; inner side and flaps are white; front and spine contain two printed panels in s. bG (approx. Centroid 160) and s. YG (Centroid 117) that run horiz. on the front and vert. down the spine; lettered in strong yellow green, strong bluish green, and white; front: '[in strong yellow green, against a strong bluish green horiz. panel] [ornament] *Randall Jarrell* | [reversed out in white against a strong yellow green panel] THE COMPLETE POEMS | [below panel, black-and-white photograph of RJ, 178 × 162 mm.]'; spine: '[vert., against a vert. elongated strong bluish green panel, in strong yellow green] RANDALL JARRELL [reversed out in white against a vert. elongated strong yellow green panel] *The Complete Poems* | [horiz., in strong bluish green] *Farrar,* | *Straus & | Giroux*'; back: '[against strong yellow green, in black] [10 lines prin. in roman, blurb by Robert Lowell] | [11 lines in roman, blurb by Karl Shapiro] | [7 lines in roman, blurb by James Dickey] [5 lines prin. in roman, blurb by Marianne Moore]'; front flap: '[upper right corner, in black] $10 | [in strong bluish green] RANDALL JARRELL | [in strong yellow green] *The Complete Poems* | [in black, 4 lines in roman, excerpt from

John Berryman] | [remainder in black, 21 lines prin. in roman, about RJ and his work]'; back flap: '[in black, 18 lines prin. in roman, about RJ and his work] | *Jacket photograph by Philippe Halsman* | *Jacket design by Guy Fleming* | FARRAR, STRAUS AND GIROUX | 19 UNION SQUARE WEST | NEW YORK 10003'.

Text Contents: "Introduction" (RJ's explanatory notes from SP55); *Selected Poems:* "Lives": "A Girl in the Library," "A Country Life," "The Knight, Death, and the Devil," "The Face," "Lady Bates," "When I Was Home Last Christmas . . . ," "A Conversation with the Devil," "Nollekens," "Seele im Raum," "The Night before the Night before Christmas"; "Dream-Work": "A Sick Child," "The Black Swan," "The Venetian Blind," "A Quilt-Pattern," "The Island," "In the Ward: The Sacred Wood"; "The Wide Prospect": "The Orient Express," "A Game at Salzburg," "An English Garden in Austria," "A Soul," "A Rhapsody on Irish Themes," "The Memoirs of Glückel of Hameln," "To the New World," "The Märchen" "Hohensalzburg: Fantastic Variations on a Theme of Romantic Character"; "Once Upon a Time": "Moving," "The Sleeping Beauty: Variation of the Prince," "The Prince," "The Carnegie Library, Juvenile Division," "The Blind Sheep," "The Skaters," "Jonah," "Song: Not There," "Children Selecting Books in a Library"; "The World Is Everything That Is the Case": "Sears Roebuck," "A Utopian Journey," "Hope," "90 North," "The Snow-Leopard," "The Boyg, Peer Gynt, the One Only One," "Money," "The Emancipators," "Variations," "Le Poète Contumace"; "The Graves in the Forest": "La Belle au Bois Dormant," "A Story," "Loss," "The Breath of Night," "Afterwards," "The Place of Death"; "Bombers": "Eighth Air Force," "The Death of the Ball Turret Gunner," "Losses," "Transient Barracks," "Siegfried"; "The Carriers": "A Pilot from the Carrier," "Pilots, Man Your Planes," "The Dead Wingman," "Burning the Letters"; "Prisoners": "Stalag Luft," "Jews at Haifa," "Prisoners," "O My Name It Is Sam Hall," "A Camp in the Prussian Forest"; "Camps and Fields": "A Lullaby," "Mail Call," "Absent with Official Leave," "A Front," "The Sick Nought," "Leave," "The Range in the Desert," "Second Air Force"; "The Traces": "The Rising Sun," "New Georgia," "The Subway from New Britain to the Bronx," "1945: The Death of the Gods," "A Ward in the States," "The Wide Prospect," "The Dead in Melanesia"; "Children and Civilians": "The State," "Come to the Stone . . . ," "The Angels of Hamburg," "Protocols," "The Metamorphoses," "The Truth"; "Soldiers": "Port of Embarkation," "The Lines," "A Field Hospital," "1914," "Gunner," "Good-bye, Wendover; Good-bye, Mountain Home," "The Survivor among Graves," "A War," "Terms"; *The Woman at the Washington Zoo:* "The Woman at the Washington Zoo," "Cinderella," "The End of the Rainbow," "In Those Days," "The Elementary Scene," "Windows," "Aging," "Nestus Gurley," "The Great Night" (Rilke), "The Grown-Up"

(Rilke), "Washing the Corpse" (Rilke), "Evening" (Rilke), "Child-hood" (Rilke), "Lament" (Rilke), "The Child" (Rilke), "Death" (Rilke), "Requiem for the Death of a Boy" (Rilke), "The Winter's Tale" (Radauskas), "The Archangels' Song" (Goethe), "Forest Murmurs" (Mörike), "Jamestown," "The Lonely Man," "The Traveler," "A Ghost, a Real Ghost," "The Meteorite," "Charles Dodgson's Song," "Deutsch Durch Freud," "The Girl Dreams That She Is Giselle," "The Sphinx's Riddle to Oedipus," "Jerome," "The Bronze David of Donatello"; *The Lost World*: "Next Day," "The Mockingbird," "In Montecito," "The Lost World" (three parts), "A Well-to-Do Invalid," "The X-Ray Waiting Room in the Hospital," "In Galleries," "Well Water," "The Lost Children," "Three Bills," "Hope," "The Bird of Night," "Bats," "The One Who Was Different," "A Hunt in the Black Forest," "The House in the Wood," "Woman," "Washing," "In Nature There Is Neither Right nor Left nor Wrong," "The Old and the New Masters," "Field and Forest," "Thinking of the Lost World"; "New Poems": "Gleaning," "Say Good-bye to Big Daddy," "The Blind Man's Song" (Rilke), "The Augsburg Adoration," "The Owl's Bedtime Story," "A Man Meets a Woman in the Street," "The Player Piano"; From *The Rage for the Lost Penny*: "Eine Kleine Nachtmusik"; From *Blood for a Stranger*: "On the Railway Platform," "London," "The Lost Love," "1938: Tales from the Vienna Woods," "A Little Poem," "Fat, aging, the child clinging to her hand," "A Poem for Someone Killed in Spain," "The Iceburg," "Because of me, because of you," "The Bad Music," "1789–1939," "The Ways and the Peoples," "The Refugees," "Love, in its separate being," "The hanged man on the gallows," "A Picture in the Paper," "The cow wandering in the bare field," "When you and I were all," "For the Madrid Road," "The Automaton," "Over the florid capitals," "Kirilov on a Skyscraper," "Up in the sky the star is waiting," "The Winter's Tale," "Jack," "Esthetic Theories: Art as Expression," "Dummies," "An Essay on the Human Will," "The See-er of Cities," "A Description of Some Confederate Soldiers," "The Head of Wisdom," "1938: The Spring Dances," "Fear," "The Machine-Gun," "The Christmas Roses," "Che Farò Senza Euridice"; From *Little Friend, Little Friend*: "The Dream of Waking," "Mother, Siad the Child," "Soldier [T.P.]," "The Learners," "The Difficult Resolution," "The Soldier Walks under the Trees of the University," "The Soldier," "An Officers' Prison Camp Seen from a Troop-Train"; from *Losses*: "In the Camp There Was One Alive," "Orestes at Tauris"; from *The Seven-League Crutches*: "The Olive Garden" (Rilke). "Uncollected Poems": "O weary mariners, here shaded, fed," "The man with the axe stands profound and termless," "Above the waters in their toil," "Zeno," "And did she dwell in innocence and joy," "The Indian," "Old Poems," "An Old Song," "When Achilles fought and fell," "Falling in love is never as simple," "A Dialogue between Soul and Body," "Enormous Love, it's no good asking," "A Nursery Rhyme," "January 1938," "The Country Was,"

"Time and Thing-in-Itself in a Textbook," "Man," "The Islands," "The November Ghosts," "The Laboratory," "Scherzo," "An Indian Market in Mexico," "The Miller," "To the New World," "The Street Has Changed," "News," "'The Germans Are Lunatics'," "The Dead," "A Ghost Story," "The Clock in the Tower of the Church," "Overture: The Hostages," "Lament of the Children of Israel in Rome" (Gregorovius), "A Perfectly Free Association," "The Princess Wakes in the Wood," "All or None," "The Tower," "The Forsaken Girl" (Mörike), "The Author to the Reader," "The Chipmunk's Day," "The Fire at the Waxworks" (Radauskas), "In a Hospital Garden" (Radauskas); "Unpublished Poems": "My aunt kept turnips in a flock," "A Summer Night," "He," "Randall Jarrell, Office Hours 10–11," "The Tree," "The Dream," "The Northern Snows," "I love you, too. There was no use, I had no time," "The Trees in Spring," "The Happy Cat," "Today is almost over," "Prologue to Wiley on November 17, 1941," "The rabbit hurries to the brim of its wood," "To Be Dead," "The Farewell Symphony," "The Times Worsen," "The lot is vacant still," "There Was Glass and There Are Stars," "'Do such, wait so,' you said; I waited. Did you wait?," "City, City!," "The Romance of Science," "The Birth of Venus," "Dreams," "The School of Summer," "Perfect Love Casteth Out Everything," "Fairy Song," "Faded" (Rilke), "A Lady on a Balcony" (Rilke), "A Variation on 'To Say to Go to Sleep'" (Rilke), "The Unicorn" (Rilke), "The Widow's Song" (Rilke), "The Reader" (Rilke), "The Evening Star" (Rilke), "The Love for One Orange," "(A Seductive Piece of Business)," "The Sign," "The Wild Birds," "Man in Majesty," "Women on a Bus," "What was longed for and, once, certain," "A Prayer at Morning," "Bamberg," "Let's love each other for what we are," "The old orchard in the middle of the forest," "What's the Riddle. . . ."

Publication: published 24 January 1969 at $10.00; 6,250 copies printed by American Stratford Press, New York City. Registered in the name of Mrs. Randall Jarrell, under A 47120; copyright deposit copies received 3 February 1969. The publisher issued three additional printings between June 1969 (2,000 copies) and 1975; with the exception of the second printing, no further information is available.

Locations: DLC, GU, MJ (2), NcGU, NcU, NrWsW, NN, STW (3), TxU, ViU.

> *First Appearances:* See above, *Contents* section, "Unpublished Poems," excepting "My aunt kept turnips in a flock" (B43), "The Birth of Venus" (C364), "The Sign" (A20), and "Bamberg" (A19). Of the poems first published in this volume, the following republications have been noted.

> "A Prayer at Morning"   Reprinted in C. E. Main and Peter J. Seng,

Poems (Wadsworth Handbook and Anthology), 3d ed. (Belmont, Calif.: Wadsworth Publishing Co., 1973), p. 366.

"The Happy Cat"   Reprinted in *A Celebration of Cats*, ed. Jean Burden (New York: Paul S. Eriksson, 1974), p. 12.

"A Variation on 'To Say to Go to Sleep'"   Reprinted in *I Like You and Other Poems for Valentine's Day*, sel. and illustrated by Yaroslava (New York: Scribner's, 1976), p. 20.

A21b   *First Sunburst Books Paperback Impression (photo-offset from* **A21a** *(1969)*

All identical to **A21a** except for:

Title Page: 8³⁄₁₆ × 5¼ in. (208 × 133 mm.).

Copyright Page: contains an additional line in the acknowledgments, after line 18: '[ll. 18–19] published here by permission of W. W. Norton & Company, Inc., | and Insel-Verlag, Frankfurt-am-Main'.

Collation: sidestitched in printed paper wrappers.

Paper and Paper Binding: leaf measures 8³⁄₁₆ × 5¼ in. (208 × 133 mm.); yWhite (Centroid 92) wove, unwatermarked paper (but cheaper quality than **A21a**), uncoated smooth; white wove, unwatermarked paper wrapper; inner side coated smooth, outer side coated glossy; printed in black, v. R (Centroid 11) and v. YG (Centroid 115); front: '[in black] RANDALL | JARRELL | [Sunburst Books device in black and vivid red, with eight vivid yellow green dots between the rays] | [in black] THE | COMPLETE | POEMS | [lower right corner in vivid yellow green] $2.95'; spine: '[two lines, vert., in black] [top] RANDALL JARRELL [bottom] The Complete Poems | [Sunburst Books device in vivid yellow green] [horiz., in black] S4'; back: '[13 lines in ital, all in black except first two words, which are in vivid yellow green, about the Sunburst Books series] | [in black, 14 lines in ital, including a list of the first seven titles in the Sunburst Books series] | SUNBURST COVER DESIGNS BY PATRICIA DE GROOT | [in vivid yellow green] SUNBURST BOOKS | [in black] A division of FARRAR, STRAUS & GIROUX | 19 Union Square West | New York, N.Y. 10003'.

Publication: published as Sunburst Books 4 on 17 April 1969 at $2.95; number of copies printed is not known; a second printing was also issued in 1969, and is so identified on the copyright page.

Locations: MJ, NcGU, STW.

A21c *First Noonday Books Paperback Impression (photo-offset from* **A21a***) (1981)*

All identical to **A21a** except for:

Title Page: 9⅜ × 6 in. (233 × 151 mm.).

Copyright Page: 'Fifth printing, 1981'.

Collation: perfect bound; 264 leaves.

Paper and Paper Binding: leaf measures 9⅜ × 6 in. (233 × 151 mm.); yWhite (Centroid 92) wove, unwatermarked paper, uncoated smooth; thick, wove paper wrapper, inner side white, coated smooth; outer side coated glossy; front and spine are ident. to dust jacket of **A21a** except for Noonday Books device and 'N518' at base of spine; back: '[in black] [left] N518 [right] $12.95 | ISBN 0–374–51305–8'; [center, reversed out in white] *Randall Jarrell / The Complete Poems* | [in black, 8 lines in ital, including Robert Lowell's blurb from jacket of **A21a**, except for first sentence, which has been omitted] | —ROBERT LOWELL | [7 lines in ital, including James Dickey's blurb from jacket of **A21a**] | —JAMES DICKEY | [in s. bG (Centroid 160)] [ornament] | [in black] [10 lines prin. in roman, including lines 12–28 of front flap of jacket of **A21a**] | *Cover photography by Philippe Halsman / Cover design by Guy Fleming* | FARRAR · STRAUS · GIROUX | *19 Union Square West New York 10003*'.

Publication: published 12 April 1981 at Noonday Paperbooks N518 at $12.95; number of copies printed is not known.

Locations: MJ (3), NcGU, STW (2).

A21d *First English Edition (photo-offset from* **A21***) (1971)*

All identical to **A21a** except for:

Randall Jarrell | THE | COMPLETE | POEMS | FABER AND FABER | 3 Queen Square | London

Title Page: 8⁷⁄₁₆ × 5¼ in. (215 × 133 mm.).

Copyright Page: '*First published in England in 1971*'.

Collation: [unsigned 1-33⁸]; 264 leaves.

Paper and Binding: leaf measures 8½ × 5⅜ in. (214 × 136 mm.);

white wove, unwatermarked paper, uncoated smooth; m. rBr (approx. Centroid 43) coarse bead-cloth (202) boards measure 8¹³⁄₁₆ × 5½ in. (222 × 140 mm.); front: unstamped; spine, in gold: '[horiz.] The | Complete | Poems | [rule, 21 mm.] | RANDALL | JARRELL | [at base] Faber'; back: unstamped; all edges cut, unstained; white wove, unwatermarked endpapers, uncoated smooth.

Dust Jacket: total measurement, 8¾ × 19⅜ in. (222 × 490 mm.); inner side and back are white; both sides coated smooth; front and spine are printed in deep O (approx. Centroid 51) and l. gB (between Centroid 171 and 172); lettered in black; front: '[against a deep orange panel that extends across the front in spine, in black] RANDALL | JARRELL | [thick rule reversed out in white that extends across front and spine] | [against a light greenish blue panel that extends across front and spine, in black] The | Complete | POEMS | [white rule ident. to first] | [against a deep orange panel, in black] FABER'; spine: '[against a deep orange panel, horiz., in black] Randall | Jarrell | [rule, 38 mm.] | The | Complete | Poems | [heavy rule reversed out in white] | [against a light greenish blue panel, in two lines, in black] [top] RANDALL [bottom] JARRELL | [white rule like first] | [against a deep orange panel, horiz., in black] Faber | & Faber'; back: '[in black] FABER & FABER | publish books by the following poets | [two columns of nineteen names each, in all caps] | *All prices shown are net and are subject to alteration*'; front flap: '[in black] The Complete Poems | RANDALL JARRELL | [16 lines prin. in roman, including Robert Lowell's blurb from dust jacket of **A21a**] | [17 lines prin. in roman, about the book, from front jacket of **A21a**] | [lower right corner] £4.00 | *net*'; back flap: '[in black] *Also by Randall Jarrell* | SELECTED POEMS | [7 lines prin. in roman, excerpt from *TLS*] | [2 lines prin. in roman, excerpt from *Observer*, and price] | POETRY AND THE AGE | [6 lines prin. in roman, excerpt from John Wain in the *Spectator*, and price] | *By Robert Lowell* | [16 lines prin. in all caps, including a list of 11 titles and prices] | *Please write for a poetry catalogue to* | *Faber and Faber Limited* | London WC1).

Publication: published in 1971 at £4.00; the publisher declined to reveal the date of publication and number of copies printed.

Locations: MJ, NcGU, STW (2).

> *Note:* Before publication the publisher issued advance proof copies to selected reviewers. These are bound in plain unprinted yellowish white paper wrappers (the compiler's copy has written on the spine in black ink, vert. from top to bottom, '*Randall Jarrell—Complete Poems*'), 8½ × 5½ in. (216 × 145 mm.); white wove, unwatermarked paper.

A21e *First Faber and Faber Paperback Impression (photo-offset from **A21d**) (1981)*

All identical to **A21d** except for:

Randall Jarrell |THE | COMPLETE | POEMS | *Faber and Faber* | LONDON BOSTON

Title Page: 9³⁄₁₆ × 6 in. (233 × 152 mm.).

Copyright Page: 'First published in Faber Paperbacks in 1981'.

Paper Binding: ident. to **A21c** except for spine: '[in s. bG (Centroid 160) at base] FABER'; back: '[in black] [upper right corner] £5.50 | net | [center, reversed out in white] *Randall Jarrell / The Complete Poems* | [9 lines prin. in ital, blurb by Robert Lowell from back of dust jacket of **A21a**] | [ornament in strong bluish green] | [remainder in black] [9 lines prin. in roman, about RJ and his work, from front flap of dust jacket of **A21a**] | [3 lines prin. in roman, excerpt from Ian Hamilton in the *Observer*] | [2 lines prin. in roman, excerpt from Alan Brownjohn in the *New Statesman*] | *Cover photograph by Philippe Halsman / Cover design by Guy Fleming*'.

Publication: published in 1981 at £5.50; the publisher declined to reveal the exact date of publication and number of copies printed.

Locations: MJ, NcGU, STW.

> *Note:* One copy examined contained a white gummed label attached to the upper left corner of the back flap imprinted in black with the ISBN number.

A22 *THE THREE SISTERS,* by Anton Chekhov, translated by RJ

First Edition (1969)

ANTON CHEKHOV

The Three Sisters

English Translation and Notes by

RANDALL JARRELL

The Macmillan Company

Collier-Macmillan Limited / London

Title Page: 8⁵⁄₁₆ × 5⁹⁄₁₆ in. (212 × 141 mm.).

Collation: [unsigned 1–3^{16} 4^8 5–6^{16}]; 93 leaves; [i-xii], [1–2], [2], [3] 4–6, [2], 7–27 [28–29] 30, [2], 31–53 [54–55] 56, [2], 57–74 [75] 76–96, [2], 97 [98–99] 100 [101–103] 104–113 [114] 115 [116] 117–155 [156] 157–160 [161–164]. *Note:* The unnumbered leaves bound between pp. 2–3, 6–7, 30–31, 56–57, and 96–97 are black-and-white photographs of scenes from the 1964 Actors Studio production of RJ's translation of *The Three Sisters.*

Contents: p. i: blank; p. ii: list of books by RJ; p. iii: half title; p. iv: blank; p. v: title page; p. vi: copyright page and acknowledgments; p. vii: further acknowledgments; p. viii: blank; p. ix: second half title; p. x: blank; p. xi: contents; p. xii: blank; pp. 1–97: text; p. 98: blank; pp. 99–100: afterword by Mary Jarrell; pp. 101–160: 'About THE THREE SISTERS | NOTES' by RJ; pp. 161–164: blank.

Running Titles: head: '[act number in roman numerals within brackets] [page number in arabic numerals] CHEKHOV / *Jarrell* THE THREE SISTERS [act number in roman numerals within brackets] [page number in arabic numerals]', or '[page number in arabic numerals] CHEKHOV /*Jarrell* | THE THREE SISTERS [page number in arabic numerals]'.

Typography: text, 11/13 Janson; text and afterword, 32 lines; 164 (169.5) × 97 mm.; 20 lines = 98 mm.; 'NOTES' section, 36 or 37 lines; pages with 36 lines measure 157 (166) × 97 mm.; 20

lines = 82 mm.; pages with 37 lines measure 157 (166) × 97 mm.; 20 lines = 92 mm.

Paper and Binding: leaf measures 8⅜ × 5⁹⁄₁₆ in. (212 × 142 mm.); yWhite (Centroid 92) wove, unwatermarked paper, uncoated smooth; black-and-white photographs reproduced on thick, wove, tan (no Centroid equivalent) unwatermarked paper, uncoated rough, 8⅜ × 5½ in. (212 × 140 mm.); m. Br (approx. Centroid 58) bead-cloth (202) covered boards measure 8⁹⁄₁₆ × 5¹³⁄₁₆ in. (217 × 147 mm.); front: '[blindstamped with a design by Guy Fleming]'; spine: in gold, '[vert.] *Jarrell* CHEKHOV: *The Three Sisters Macmillan*'; back: in gold in lower right corner, '55900'; top edges cut, bottom and fore-edges untrimmed; top edge stained s. V (Centroid 207), bottom and fore-edges unstained; l. OY (approx. Centroid 70) wove, unwatermarked endpapers, uncoated rough; cloth head and tail bands have alternating red and yellow stripes.

Dust Jacket: total measurement, 8⁹⁄₁₆ × 20⅝ in. (217 × 525 mm.); wove, unwatermarked paper, uncoated rough; inner side and flaps are white; front, spine, and back are printed d. OY (Centroid 72); front and spine contain an elaborate Russian-like design in v. rO (Centroid 34); lettered in black, white, and m. V (Centroid 211); front: '[in black] *Anton Chekhov* | [reversed out in white] THE | THREE | SISTERS | [swelled rule, 101.5 mm.] | [in black] *New English Translation & Notes by* | [reversed out in white] *Randall Jarrell*'; spine: '[horiz.] *Chekhov* / | *Jarrell* | [reversed out in white] [rule, 24 mm.] | *The* | *Three* | *Sisters* | [rule, 24 mm.] | [in black] *Macmillan*'; back: '[in black] [3 lines in ital, blurb by Stanley Kauffman] | [2 lines prin. in roman, blurb by Kenneth Tynan] | [10 lines prin. in roman, blurb by Howard Taubman (*New York Times*)] | THE MACMILLAN COMPANY | [lower right corner] 55900'; front flap: '[in moderate violet] [upper right corner] $5.95 [3 lines prin. in roman, excerpt from Taubman blurb on back] | [30 lines in roman, about RJ's translation] | *(Continued on back flap)*'; back flap: '[in moderate violet] *(Continued from front flap)* | [7 lines in roman, about the translation] | [photograph of RJ, 68 × 66 mm.] | [3 lines prin. in roman, advertisement for *The Lost World* and *The Bat-Poet*] | Jacket design / Guy Fleming | Author's photo / Ted Russell | THE MACMILLAN COMPANY | 866 THIRD AVENUE, NEW YORK, N.Y. 10022'.

Text Contents: RJ's translation of *The Three Sisters.*

Publication: published 31 March 1969 at $5.95; 3,500 copies printed by Maryland Linotype Co., Baltimore, and bound by Haddon-Craftsmen, Inc. Registered in the name of the Estate of Randall Jarrell, under A 119567. Copyright deposit copies received 6 January 1970.

Locations: DLC, MJ (2), NcGU, NcWsW, STW (2), ViU.

Note: The back flap of the dust jacket states that eight photographs of the Actors Studio production are contained in this volume; actually, there are only five photographs of the production, and one of a poster advertising it (on the verso of the first unnumbered leaf, between pp. 2–3).

The first acting version of RJ's translation of *The Three Sisters* was produced at Aycock Auditorium of the University of North Carolina at Greensboro (then Woman's College) on 12–13 March 1954. Acting scripts were prepared by ditto process from RJ's typescript; see below, F2.

RJ to AAK (HF), 12 May 1953: I'm at present translating *The Three Sisters*. Not from Russian, which I don't know a word of, but from Constance Garnettese, a grammatical, organized, shapely tongue, into speech, an altogether different affair and some Russians are translating literally for me anything that she didn't.

RJ to MDC, July 1963: I've been working on *The Three Sisters* a good deal. I think any additional changes are going to be rather easy, but I'm very much looking forward to going over the whole thing with quite a literal translation.

RJ to MDC, July 1963: It would be strange to make a lot of money out of something you did entirely for love. The more I've read the manuscript [of *The Three Sisters*] the fewer changes I've thought to make; but the last changes make such a difference in anything, and the word-for-word translation will be extremely valuable to me.

RJ to MDC, September 1963: I really am feeling the force of destiny about that literal *Three Sisters*—"Maledictione!" as they kept saying in the Macht of Schicksal, our second night here.

Randall Jarrell

THE THIRD BOOK
OF CRITICISM

Farrar, Straus & Giroux

NEW YORK

Title Page: 7^{15}⁄$_{16}$ × 5^5⁄$_{16}$ in. (202 × 135 mm.).

A23 THE THIRD BOOK OF CRITICISM

A23a   *First Edition, Clothbound Issue (1969)*

Collation: [unsigned 1–11¹⁶]; 176 leaves; [2], [i-vi] vii-viii [ix-x], [1–2] 3–51 [52–54] 55–73 [74–76] 77–112 [113–114] 115–150 [151–152] 153–187 [188–190] 191–231 [232–234] 235–275 [276–278] 279–292 [293–294] 295–333 [334–340].

Contents: one blank, unnumbered leaf; pp. i-ii: list of books by RJ; p. iii: half title; p. iv: contains a design by Guy Fleming; p. v: title page; p. vi: copyright page and acknowledgments; pp. vii-viii: *'Note'* about this collection and further acknowledgments; p. ix: contents; p. x: blank; pp. 1–334: text; pp. 335–340: blank.

Running Titles: head, 'RANDALL JARRELL | [individual essay title in ital]'.

Typography: text, 12/14 Walbaum; 30 or 31 lines; pages with 30 lines measure 158 (166) × 92 mm., 20 lines = 102 mm.; and pages with 31 lines also measure 158 (166) × 92 mm., 20 lines = 98 mm.

Paper and Binding: leaf measures 7¹⁵⁄₁₆ × 5⅜ in. (202 × 137 mm.); yWhite (Centroid 92) wove, unwatermarked paper, uncoated smooth; yWhite (Centroid) linen-cloth (304) covered boards measure 8³⁄₁₆ × 5⅝ in. (209 × 145 mm.); front: blindstamped with a design by Guy Fleming (from p. iv); spine: '[in deep R (Centroid 13), design by Guy Fleming] | [in black] [horiz.] *Randall | Jarrell* | [in deep red, rule, 26 mm.] | [in black] *The | Third Book | of | Criticism* | [in deep red, rule, 26 mm.] | [in black] *Farrar, Straus | & Giroux* | [in deep red, design by Fleming ident. to first]'; back: unstamped; all edges cut; top edges stained brill. OY (Centroid 67); black wove, unwatermarked endpapers, uncoated smooth.

Dust Jacket: total measurement, 8³⁄₁₆ × 19¹³⁄₁₆ in. (208 × 503 mm); inner side and flaps are white; back contains a black-and-white photograph of RJ; front is printed brill. gB (Centroid 168) and contains a design of gull-like birds by Guy Fleming printed in d. pB (Centroid 201); spine is printed d. B (Centroid 183); lettered in black, white, v. OY (Centroid 66), and brill. V (Centroid 206); front: '[in vivid orange yellow] *Randall Jarrell* | [reversed out in white] *The Third Book of Criticism* | [in vivid orange yellow, a lyrelike design surrounding a flower]'; spine: [vert.] [in vivid orange yellow] *Randall Jarrell* [in brilliant violet] / [two lines, top line reversed out in white] *The Third Book of Criticism* [bottom line in brilliant violet] *Farrar, Straus & Giroux*'; back: contains a black-and-white photograph of RJ, unlettered; front flap: '[upper right corner, in black] $7.50 | RANDALL JARRELL | [in brilliant violet] *The Third Book of | Criticism* | [in black, 23 lines prin. in roman, about RJ and his criticism] | [in brilliant violet] *(continued on back flap)*'; back flap: '[in brilliant violet] *(continued from front flap)* | [in black, 15 lines, about RJ's criticism and this book] | JACKET DESIGN BY GUY FLEMING | *Photograph of Randall Jarrell* | *copyright © 1967 by Philippe Halsman* | [in brilliant violet] FARRAR, STRAUS AND GIROUX | 19 UNION SQUARE WEST | NEW YORK 10003'.

Text Contents: "An Unread Book," "The Collected Poems of Wallace Stevens," "Graves and the White Goddess," "Changes of Attitude and Rhetoric in Auden's Poetry," "Freud to Paul: The Stages of Auden's Ideology," "Robert Frost's 'Home Burial,'" "Six Russian Short Novels," "The English in England," "Fifty Years of American Poetry."

Publication: published 1 December 1969; 8,139 copies printed of which 5,974 were bound in cloth ($7.50), and 1,165 were perfect bound in printed wrappers ident. to dust jacket of clothbound issue and issued as Noonday N 398 ($3.45). A second clothbound printing of 2,987 copies was issued in January 1971.

Locations: DLC, GU, MJ (3), NcGU, NcWsW, NN, STW (2), TxU, ViU.

> *Note:* Spiral-bound proof copies were prepared for selected reviewers before publication: 137 hand-numbered leaves; leaf measures 8½ × 5½ in. (215 × 140 mm.); yWhite (Centroid 92) wove, unwatermarked, uncoated paper; all edges trimmed; v.p.B (approx. Centroid 184) thick, coated, wove, unwatermarked paper wrapper measures 8½ × 6 in. (215 × 152 mm.); front: '[in black] UNCORRECTED PROOF | *Randall Jarrell* | [rule, 76 mm.] | THE THIRD BOOK | OF CRITICISM | [rule, 64 mm.] | *Farrar, Straus & Giroux* | NEW YORK | [17 lines prin. in roman, excerpted from flaps of dust jacket of cloth issue]'; inside the front of the wrapper of the compiler's copy is a printed blue label that lists the publication date as October 1969 and the price, $6.95; white plastic ring binding.
>
> Some copies of the clothbound issue sent out to reviewers before publication contain an early state of the dust jacket. The front and spine are identical to the dust jacket of A23a, but the flaps and back are unlettered.

First Edition, Paperbound Issue (1969)

All identical to clothbound issue except for:

Randall Jarrell | [rule, 30 mm.] | THE THIRD BOOK | OF CRITICISM | [rule, 30 mm.] | *Farrar, Straus & Giroux* | NEW YORK

Title Page: 8 × 5⅜ in. (203 × 132 mm.).

Copyright Page: 'First printing, 1969'.

Collation: perfect bound; 176 leaves.

Paper Binding: printed paper wrapper measures 8 × 5⅜ in.

(203 × 132 mm.); spine: '*Farrar, Straus & Giroux*' deleted, with 'N 398' in v. OY (Centroid 66) at base; back: printed vivid orange yellow and lettered in black: '[left] N 398—Literary Criticism | SBN 374.5.0892.5 [right] $3.45 | *Randall Jarrell / The Third Book of Criticism* | [14 lines, prin. in roman, about RJ and his work, including a quote from Robert Lowell] | [rule, 63 mm.] | [15 lines, prin. in roman, including excerpts from reviews in *Kirkus, Saturday Review* (Robert Scholes), and *New York Times* (John Leonard)] | *Cover design by Guy Fleming* | THE NOONDAY PRESS | 19 UNION SQUARE WEST | NEW YORK 10003'; material from dust jacket flaps of clothbound issue has been deleted; black wove, unwatermarked endpapers.

Locations: MJ, STW.

A23b   *Second Noonday Press Paperback Impression (photo-offset from A23a) (1971)*

All ident. to **A23a** (paperbound issue) except for:

Copyright Page: 'First Noonday Press printing, 1971'.

Paper and Paper Binding: no endpapers.

Publication: published in April 1971 at $3.45.

A23c   *First English Edition (photo-offset from A23a) (1975)*

All identical to **A23a** except for:

Randall Jarrell | [rule, 77 mm.] | THE THIRD BOOK | OF CRITICISM | [rule, 77 mm.] | *Faber & Faber Limited* | LONDON

Title Page: 8⁹⁄₁₆ × 5⁵⁄₁₆ in. (217 × 135 mm.).

Copyright Page: "First published in Great Britain in 1975'.

Collation: [unsigned A-R⁸]; 176 leaves; [i-viii] ix-x [xi-xii], [1–2] 3–51 [52–54] 53–73 [74–76] 77–112 [113–114] 115–150 [151–152] 153–187 [188–190] 191–231 [232–234] 235–275 [276–278] 279–292 [293–294] 295–333 [333–340].

Contents: pp. i-ii: blank; p. iii: half title; pp. iv-v: list of books by RJ; p. vi: contains a design by Guy Fleming, but unlettered; p. vii: title page; p. viii: copyright page and acknowledgments; pp. ix-x: '*Note*'

and further acknowledgments; p. xi: contents; p. xii: blank; pp. 1–334: text; pp. 335–340: blank.

Paper and Binding: leaf measures 8⁹⁄₁₆ × 5³⁄₈ in. (216 × 136 mm.); yWhite (Centroid 92) wove, unwatermarked paper, uncoated smooth; deep OY (approx. Centroid 69) bead-cloth (202) boards measure 8¹³⁄₁₆ × 5½ in. (223 × 139 mm.); front: unstamped; spine: '[horiz., in d. gy. Br (Centroid 62)] RANDALL | JARRELL | [rule, 21 mm.] | [vert. from top to bottom] The Third Book of Criticism | [horiz.] [rule, 21 mm.] | FABER | & FABER'; back: unstamped; all edges cut, unstained; white wove, unwatermarked endpapers, uncoated smooth.

Dust Jacket: total measurement, 8¾ × 19⁷⁄₁₆ in. (222 × 493 mm.); wove, unwatermarked paper; both sides coated smooth; inner side and flaps are white; front, spine, and back are printed l. OY (approx. Centroid 70); front contains a solid panel, 193 × 119 mm., and a double-rule frame (outer thick, inner thin) in d. Br (Centroid 59); lettered in white, light orange yellow and dark brown; front: '[within a double-rule frame, against a solid panel, all in dark brown] [reversed out in white] The | Third Book | of | Criticism | [ornament reversed out in light orange yellow] | RANDALL JARRELL'; spine: '[horiz.] [in dark brown] RANDALL | JARRELL | [rule, 23 mm.] | [vert. from top to bottom] The Third Book of Criticism | [horiz.] [rule, 23 mm.] | FABER | & FABER'; back: '[in dark brown] The Complete Poems | RANDALL JARRELL | [10 lines prin. in roman, blurb by Robert Lowell] | [11 lines prin. in roman, about RJ's *The Complete Poems*] | [4 lines prin. in roman, blurb by Ian Hamilton (*Observer*)] | [3 lines prin. in roman, blurb by Alan Brownjohn (*New Statesman*), and at right, '*hard covers*']'; front flap: '[in dark brown] The Third Book of Criticism | RANDALL JARRELL | [20 lines prin. in roman, about RJ and his work] | [lower right corner] £4.50 | *net*'; back flap: '[in dark brown] *ALSO BY RANDALL JARRELL* | POERTY AND THE AGE | [11 lines prin. in roman, excerpt from David Daiches's review in *Manchester Guardian*] | *Faber Paperbacks* | PICTURES FROM AN | INSTITUTION | [9 lines prin. in roman, excerpt from Julian Symons in *Sunday Times*] | [6 lines prin. in roman, excerpt from Paul Theroux in *New Statesman* and, at right, '*hard covers*'] | [at base, 5 lines in ital, advertisement for Faber & Faber books]'.

Publication: published in 1975 at £4.50; the publisher declined to reveal the exact date of publication and number of copies printed.

Locations: NcGU, STW.

A24 *THE DEATH OF THE BALL TURRET GUNNER*

First Separate Edition (1969)

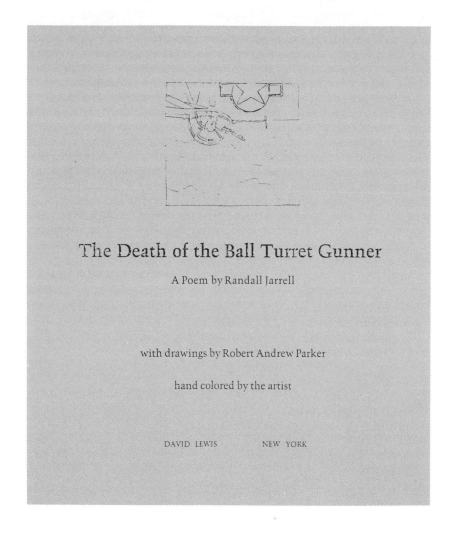

The Death of the Ball Turret Gunner

A Poem by Randall Jarrell

with drawings by Robert Andrew Parker

hand colored by the artist

DAVID LEWIS   NEW YORK

Title Page: 12¹⁵⁄₁₆ × 10¹⁵⁄₁₆ in. (334 × 278 mm.); hand-colored illustration above title, title printed in v. pB (Centroid 194); remainder in black.

Collation: [unsigned 1^2 s–3^6 4^2]; 16 leaves; [1–32].

Contents: pp. 1–4: blank; p. 5: title page; p. 6: copyright page; p. 7: text of poem; p. 8: blank; pp. 9, 11, 13, 15, 17, 19, and 21 contain hand-colored illustrations by Robert Andrew Parker; pp. 10, 12, 14, 16, 18, 20, and 22 are blank; p. 23: contains a hand-colored illustration by Parker and the text of the poem, signed 'Randall Jarrell', reproduced from holograph (not RJ's); p. 24: blank; p. 25: illustration; pp. 26–27: blank; p. 28: statement of limitation; pp. 29–32: blank.

Typography: text, 14/21 Trajanus.

Paper and Binding: leaf measures 13 × 10⅞ in. (329 × 278 mm.); white wove, watermarked 'C. M. FABRIANO—100 / 100 COTONE'; uncoated rough; deep pB (approx. Centroid 197) coarse bead-cloth (202) boards measure 13⅜ × 11¼ in. (342 × 286 mm.); unstamped; top and bottom edges cut, fore-edges are deckled; cloth head and tail bands are blackish B (Centroid 188).

Slipcase: open-faced slipcase of deep pB (Centroid 197) coarse bead-cloth covered boards ident. to binding measures 13¹³⁄₁₆ × 11½ in. (353 × 292 mm.); deep purplish blue cloth tape attached within slipcase to facilitate removal of book; front contains a white paper label, 77 × 132 mm., printed in v. pB (Centroid 194) and black: '[within a black double-rule frame] [in vivid purplish blue] THE DEATH OF THE | BALL TURRET GUNNER | [in black] A Poem by Randall Jarrell | *With Pictures by Robert Andrew Parker* | DAVID LEWIS NEW YORK'.

Statement of Limitation: p. 28: 'THIS EDITION IS LIMITED TO ONE HUNDRED AND FIFTY COPIES HAND COLORED AND SIGNED BY | THE ARTIST. THE TEXT HAS BEEN PRINTED BY MANHATTAN ART PRESS AND HAND BOUND IN THE | STUDIO OF LAURA S. YOUNG. BINDING AND TYPOGRAPHY HAS BEEN DESIGNED BY EDWARD AHO. | [remainder supplied by Parker in black ink] *No* [arabic number] | *Robert Andrew Parker*'.

Text Contents: "The Death of the Ball Turret Gunner" (C134).

Publication: published in June 1969 at $100.00; 150 copies printed.

Locations: MJ, NcGU, STW.

A25 *JEROME: THE BIOGRAPHY OF A POEM*

First Separate Edition (1971)

The Biography of a Poem
Jerome
Randall Jarrell,
with
Woodcuts and Engravings
by
Albrecht Dürer

Grossman Publishers New York 1971

Title Page: 11 × 8⁷⁄₁₆ in. (278 × 214 mm.); 'Jerome' in black, remainder in light grayish yellowish brown (no Centroid equivalent).

Collation: [unsigned 1–5⁸]; 40 leaves; [i-ii], [1–6] 7 [8] 9–75 [76–78].

Contents: pp. i-ii: blank; p. 1: half title: '[in black] Jerome | [in l. gr. yBr (approx. Centroid 79), reproduction of a Dürer medallion depicting St. Jerome] | [at base, ornament]'; p. 2: blank; p. 3: title page; p. 4: copyright page and acknowledgments; p. 5: contents; p. 6: blank; p. 7: reproduction of Dürer's *St. Jerome in His Study*; p. 8: blank; pp. 9–18: "Reflections on Jerome" by Mary von S. Jarrell; p. 19: reproduction of Dürer's *St. Jerome by the Pollard Window*; p. 20: reproduction of Dürer's *St. Jerome in His Cell*; pp. 21–70: RJ's worksheets for "Jerome"; p. 71: reproduction of Dürer's *St. Jerome in Penitence*; p. 72: reproduction of Dürer's *St. Jerome Curing the Lion*; p. 73: printed text of the final version of "Jerome"; p. 74: reproduction of Dürer's *St. Jerome in a Cave*; p. 76: colophon; pp. 77–78: blank.

Typography: text, 12/15 Baskerville; number of lines per page irregular, but p. 14: 219 × 143 mm.; 20 lines = 106.5 mm.

Paper and Binding: leaf measures 11¹⁵⁄₁₆ × 8⁷⁄₁₆ in. (279 × 214 mm.); white wove, unwatermarked paper, uncoated smooth; m. rBr (approx. Centroid 43) fine bead-cloth (202b) boards measure

11³⁄₁₆ × 8¾ in. (283 × 221 mm.); front: unstamped; spine: in copper, '[printed downward] JEROME [at base, ornament]'; back: unstamped; all edges cut, unstained; yGr (approx. Centroid 93) wove, unwatermarked endpapers, uncoated rough.

Dust Jacket: total measurement, 11¼ × 25¹¹⁄₁₆ in (285 × 653 mm.); wove, unwatermarked paper; inner side and flaps are white; outer side contains a black-and-white photographic design of a worksheet of the poem with a pen (front and spine), and a 16th-century printed leaf containing Dürer's *St. Jerome Curing the Lion* and a woodcutter's graver; lettered in black and white; front: '[in black] The Biography of a Poem | JEROME | Randall Jarrell Albrecht Dürer'; spine: '[printed downward, in black] JEROME | [vert.] Jarrell | [ornament]'; back: '[reversed out in white in lower right corner] SBN: 670–59847–X'; front flap: '[in black] [upper right corner] $10.00 | Jerome | The Biography of a Poem | [34 lines prin. in roman, about the book] | [lower left corner] 0971'; back flap: '[in black] [24 lines prin. in roman, about RJ] | [8 lines prin. in roman, about Dürer] | *Grossman Publishers* | 44 *West 56th Street* | *New York, N.Y. 10019* | *Jacket and book designed by* | *Antupit & Others.* | *Printed in the U. S. A.*'

Text Contents: "Jerome" (C323) and RJ's worksheets for this poem.

Publication: published 8 November 1971 at $10.00; 5,000 copies printed. Registered in the name of Mary von S. Jarrell, under A 291182; deposit copies received 15 December 1971.

Locations: DLC, MJ (5), NcGU, STW (2).

A26 *SNOW-WHITE AND THE SEVEN DWARFS,* by the Brothers Grimm, translated by RJ

First Separate Edition (1972)

Snow-White and the Seven Dwarfs

A TALE FROM THE BROTHERS GRIMM TRANSLATED BY

RANDALL JARRELL · PICTURES BY NANCY EKHOLM BURKERT

◆ FARRAR, STRAUS AND GIROUX · NEW YORK ◆

Title Page: 12 × 8¹⁵/₁₆ in. (305 × 226 mm.); lettering in black, quadruple-rule frame in s. B (Centroid 178), and illustration and ornaments prin. in brilliant yellow, gold, light grayish blue, and deep red.

Collation: [unsigned 1–4⁴]; 16 leaves; [1–32].

Contents: p. 1: half title (in medium gray); p. 2: blank; p. 3: title page; p. 4: copyright page; p. 5: dedication: 'For CLAIRE | *Together we are walking in the Forest | while the rhythms of light and shadow play.* | N.E.B.'; pp. 6–31: text and illustrations (text on pp. 7–9, 12–13, 16–17, 20–21, 24–25, 28–29); p. 32: blank.

Typography: text, 18/20 Bembo; number of lines per page irregular throughout, but p. 27: 172.5 × 155 mm.; 20 lines = 136 mm.

Paper and Binding: leaf measures 12 × 8¾ in. (305 × 224 mm.); white wove, unwatermarked paper, uncoated smooth; black bead-cloth (202) boards measure 12¼ × 9¼ in. (312 × 233 mm.); front: contains blindstamped design by Burkert; spine: in copper, '[vert.] GRIMM · SNOW-WHITE AND THE SEVEN DWARFS · BURK-ERT FSG'; back: unstamped; all edges cut, unstained; wove, unwa-termarked endpapers, one side of which is imprinted with a design by Burkert of interconnected diamonds which contain Russian crosses, fleur-de-lis-like designs, and clover leaves, all surrounded by an orna-mental frame, prin. in s. yPk (Centroid 26), deep rO (Centroid 36), deep yBr (Centroid 75), m.OY (Centroid 71), and B. (Centroid 181).

Dust Jacket: total measurement, 12³⁄₁₆ × 26¹⁄₁₆ in. (311 × 675 mm.); wove, unwatermarked paper; both sides coated smooth; inner side is white, outer side is printed deep rO (Centroid 36); front contains a color illustration by Burkert (enlarged from p. 10), against a panel that is reversed out in white, within a frame of black single rule, 256 × 221 mm., prin. in d. yWhite (approx. Centroid 92), gy. ol (Centroid 110), m. YG (Centroid 120), and l. B (approx. Centroid 181); front: below illustration and black single-rule frame, '[reversed out in white] Snow-White and the Seven Dwarfs | [in black] A TALE FROM THE BROTHERS GRIMM TRANSLATED BY | RANDALL JARRELL · PICTURES BY NANCY EKHOLM BURKERT'; spine: '[vert.] [in black] GRIMM · [reversed out in white] SNOW-WHITE AND THE SEVEN DWARFS [in black] · BURKERT · FARRAR, STRAUS AND GIROUX, back: unlettered; front flap: '[all within a black single-rule frame, 299 × 79 mm., in black except for initial "C" of "Considering"] [upper right corner] $5.95 | [23 lines prin. in roman, about the book]'; back flap: '[all within a black single-rule frame, 299 × 79 mm.] NANCY EKHOLM BURKERT | [9 lines prin. in roman, about the illustrator] | RANDALL JARRELL (1914–1965), | [5 lines in roman and ital, about the translator] | [publisher's device reversed out in white] | [in black] Farrar, Straus and Giroux | 19 Union Square West | New York 10003 | ISBN 0–374–37099–0'.

Text Contents: slightly revised version of RJ's translation that first appeared in A12.

Publication: published 22 December 1972 at $5.95; 15,000 copies printed by A. Horowitz & Son, Clifton, N.J., and Pearl Pressman Liberty Printing and Litho. Co., Philadelphia, Pa. Registered in the name of Nancy Ekholm Burkert, under A 395976. Copyright deposit copies received 8 January 1973. The publisher has issued five more printings: second printing, 15,000 copies on 28 February 1973; third printing, 33,520 copies on 30 March 1973; fourth printing, 32,000 copies on 3 May 1973; fifth printing, 11,000 copies in November 1975; and sixth printing, 27,000 copies in November 1978, each so identified.

Locations: DLC, MJ (3), NcGU, STW (3).

Note: The illustrations for printings after the first were printed from new plates. Martin Weaver (Farrar, Straus and Giroux) to SW, 6 January 1982.

Subsequent printings contain a round silver foil label attached to the upper right corner of the dust jacket indicating that this title was named a Caldecott Honor Book.

FLY BY NIGHT

Randall Jarrell

PICTURES BY
MAURICE SENDAK

Farrar, Straus & Giroux
New York

A27 *Title Page:* 7⅞ × 5⅛ in. (200 × 130 mm.).

A27 *FLY BY NIGHT*

First Edition (1976)

Collation: [unsigned 1⁶ 2⁸ 3⁶]; 20 leaves [i–viii], [1–2] 3–6 [7–8] 9–10 [11–12] 13–14 [15–16] 17–24 [25–28] 29–30 [31–32].

Contents: p. i: half title; p. ii–iii: blank; p. iv: Sendak illustration; p.v: title page; p. vi: copyright page; p. vii: dedication: 'To Mary'; p. viii: blank; pp. 1–30: text; p. 31: Sendak illustration; p. 32: blank.

Typography: text, 12/20 Monticello; 21 lines; 150 × 86 mm.; 20 lines = 130 mm.

Paper and Binding: leaf measures 7⅞ × 5⅛ in. (200 × 130 mm.); white wove, unwatermarked paper, uncoated smooth; d. Gy (approx. Centroid 266) paper-covered boards (imitation bead-cloth) measure 8³⁄₁₆ × 5⁷⁄₁₆ in. (208 × 138 mm.); front: contains a leaflike design by Sendak stamped in silver; spine: in silver, '[vert.] Jarrell / Sendak FLY BY NIGHT   FSG"; back: unstamped; all edges cut, unstained; light grayish tan (no Centroid equivalent) wove, unwatermarked endpapers, uncoated rough.

Dust Jacket: total measurement, 8⅛ × 18⅝ in. (206 × 472 mm.); wove, unwatermarked paper; inner side is white, outer side is printed light grayish blue (no Centroid equivalent); both sides coated smooth;

'[reversed out in white against a light grayish blue panel, 72 × 95 mm., within a frame of thick white rules also reversed out in white, all of which is against a gray-and-white illustration of Sendak of David, the little boy in the story, flying over a garden] FLY BY NIGHT | [in black, ornamental rule, 38 mm.] | [reversed out in white] Randall Jarrell [in black] PICTURES BY | [reversed out in white] MAURICE SENDAK'; spine: '[vert., reversed out in white] FLY BY NIGHT Jarrell [in black] / [in white] Sendak [in black] FSG' back: contains a black-and-white illustration by Sendak of a fish, 36 × 29 mm., within a frame of thick rules reversed out in white; front flap: '[in black] [upper right corner] $5.95 | [23 lines prin. in roman about RJ, Sendak, and this book; the first word contains the initial 'N']'; back flap: '[in black] [15 lines in roman and ital, about RJ] | [9 lines in roman and ital, about Sendak] | *Farrar, Straus and Giroux* | *19 Union Square West* | *New York 10003*'.

Text Contents: Fly by Night.

Publication: published 29 October 1976 at $5.95; 26,699 copies printed of which 20,209 were bound; the remaining sheets are as yet unbound.

Locations: DLC, MJ, NcGU, STW (3).

> *First Appearance: Fly by Night.*
>
> *Note:* The dust jackets of some copies examined contain one or more irregular circles or ovals that have been (presumably accidentally) reversed out in white.
>
> *RJ to MS, April 1963:* I've finished my next children's book, *Fly By Night*, and I'll make an extra carbon for you when I type it out. It ought to be as easy to illustrate as *The Bat-Poet* is hard—if *The Bat-Poet*'s hard, that is.
>
> *RJ to Mac (MDC), 4 May 1963:* Thanks so much for your letter about FLY BY NIGHT—it was kind of you to write. I'm delighted that you liked it that much; I feel just as you do about it being a picture book.
>
> *RJ to Mac (MDC), October 1964:* I had ... great luck in redoing *Fly By Night*, now that that great big black thing in the sky, *The Bat-Poet*, isn't overshadowing it. I believe I've got it all smooth now, and what you learn in the beginning about David awake makes David's dream what it is. I'm pretty sure that *Fly By Night* ought to be my next children's book. *The Animal Family* is so long and different that *Fly By Night*, coming after it, would suffer terribly. Coming after *The Bat-Poet*, *Fly by Night* suffers a *little* from not being an allegory or parable, but it's similar in length, has poems in it too (poems which are a continuation of the prose more than those in *Bat-Poet*), has the same talking-

animal world, etc. *Animal Family* is realistic, the lynx and the bear never say a word. I think the readers of *Bat-Poet* who like the poems will be quite fond of having a *big* poem like Owl's *Bedtime Story* the climax of the book. Also, Maurice [Sendak] ought to be able to do wonderful illustrations for it. I doubt very much *Animal Family* can take illustrations.

RJ to MS, 9 October 1964: I did get *Fly By Night* typed, and here it is; sending it airmail special delivery is a bit excessive, but I was sending it that way to Michael [di Capua], and continued with yours. Tell me how you like it, and whether it seems as thoroughly designed for your illustrations as it does to me.

A28 *FAUST, PART I,* by Johann W. von Goethe, translated by RJ

First Edition, Clothbound Issue (1976)

GOETHE'S

———

F A U S T

———————————

P A R T I

An English translation by

Randall Jarrell

Farrar, Straus & Giroux

N E W   Y O R K

Title Page: $8^{15}/_{16} \times 5^{5}/_{8}$ in. (227×143 mm.).

Collation: 152 leaves, Smyth sewn; [i-viii], [1–2] 3–18 [19–20] 21–
277 [278–280] 281–295 [296].

Contents: p. i: half title; p. ii: list of books by RJ; p. iii: title page; p.
iv: copyright page and 'CAUTION' to actors from publisher; p.v: RJ's
note on "But why translate *Faust*?"; p. vi: acknowledgments; pp. vii-
viii: contents; pp. 1–277: text of RJ's translation; p. 279: part title; p.
280: blank; pp. 281–296: afterword by Mary Jarrell.

Running Titles: foot, '[page number in arabic numerals] / FAUST PART

I | [floral ornament] [scene title in ital] / [page number in arabic numerals]', or '[page number in arabic numerals] / AFTERWORD | [floral ornament] *Afterword* / [page number in arabic numerals]'.

Typography: text, 11/14 Janson; 31 lines; 172 (181) × 89.5 mm.; 20 lines = 110 mm.; "Afterword," 35 lines; 172 (181) × 92 mm.; 20 lines = 86 mm.

Paper and Binding: leaf measures 8¹⁵⁄₁₆ × 5¾ in. (226 × 146 mm.); white wove, unwatermarked paper, uncoated smooth; m. yG (Centroid 136) bead-cloth (202) boards measure 9¼ × 6¹⁄₁₆ in. (230 × 154 mm.); front: unstamped; spine: '[against a black panel, 63 × 24 mm., within a gold double-rule frame] [horiz., in gold] *Goethe's* | *Faust* | [rule, 17 mm.] | *Part One* | Randall | Jarrell | [below panel, at base] *Farrar* | *Straus* | *Giroux*'; back: unstamped; all edges cut, unstained; yWhite (Centroid 92) wove, unwatermarked endpapers, uncoated smooth; cloth head and tail bands have alternating green and yellow stripes.

Dust Jacket: total measurement, 9⅛ × 20⁹⁄₁₆ in. (232 × 530 mm.); inner side coated smooth, outer side coated glossy; inner side, flaps, and back are white; front and spine are printed black; lettered in black, white, and v. Y (Centroid 82); front: '[against a s. G (Centroid 141) multileafed plant design] [reversed out in white] RANDALL JARRELL | [in vivid yellow, bold Gothic type] Goethe's | Faust | Part One | [reversed out in white, roman] A TRANSLATION'; spine: '[horiz., reversed out in white] JARRELL | [vivid yellow] [rule, 27 mm.] | [vert., in Gothic type like front] Goethe's Faust: | [horiz. rule, 22 mm.] | [vert.] Part One | [horiz.] [rule, 27 mm.] [reversed out in white] FARRAR | STRAUS | GIROUX'; back: '[black-and-white photograph of RJ, 193 × 152 mm.] | [below photograph, right] *Photo by Ted Russell* | [center] RANDALL JARRELL'; front flap: '[in black] $15.00 | RANDALL JARRELL | GOETHE'S FAUST | Part One | [26 lines prin. in roman, about RJ's translation] | *(continued on back flap)*'; back: flap: '*(continued from front flap)* | [13 lines prin. in roman, about the book] | *Jacket design by Guy Fleming* | FARRAR, STRAUS AND GIROUX | 19 UNION SQUARE WEST | NEW YORK 10003'.

Text Contents: RJ's translation except "Gretchen's Spinning Song," pp. 195–96, which was translated by Robert Lowell, and Mary Jarrell's "Afterword."

Publication: published 22 November 1976; 6,700 copies printed, 2,700 in cloth ($15.00) and 4,000 in paper wrappers as Noonday 412 ($6.95) (see below).

Locations: DLC, GU, MJ (5), NcGU, NcU, NcWsW, NN, STW (3), TxU, ViU.

> *Note:* Before publication the publisher issued paperbound proof copies to selected reviewers. These are identical to **A28** except for: 151 leaves perfect bound in printed wrapper; corrections have been reproduced from typescript or holograph on the verso of the first leaf (copyright page) and in Mary Jarrell's "Afterword," pp. 283, 284, 285, and 294; p. Y (Centroid 89) wove, unwatermarked paper wrapper measures 8¼ × 5⅜ in (210 × 131 mm.), printed in black on front, 'UNCOR-RECTED PAGE PROOF | *GOETHE'S* | [rule, 42 mm.] | FAUST | [swelled rule, 93 mm.] | PART I | *An English translation by* | Randall Jarrell | [publisher's device] *Farrar, Straus & Giroux* | NEW YORK'. The compiler's copy contains a blue-and-white paper label pasted to the recto of the first leaf giving publication information; the price for the paperback issue is given as $7.95.
> In the compiler's collection is a trial dust jacket which is lettered on the front and spine only and is printed in v. Y (Centroid 82), white, deep Br (approx. Centroid 56), and d. rO (approx. Centroid 38).

First Edition, Paperbound Issue (1976)

All identical to clothbound issue except for:

Title Page: 8⁹⁄₁₆ × 5¹³⁄₁₆ in. (227 × 149 mm.).

Collation: perfect bound; 152 leaves.

Paper Binding: printed paper wrapper measures 8⁹⁄₁₆ × 5¹³⁄₁₆ in. (227 × 149 mm.); front: reversed out in white at bottom, 'NOON-DAY 412 | $6.95'; spine: '[at base, publisher's device reversed out in white] | [v. Y (Centroid 82) rule, 15 mm.] | [reversed out in white] N 412'; back: in black, '[left] N 412—Literature ISBN 0–374–50942–5 [right] $6.95 | [center] RANDALL JARRELL | GOETHE'S FAUST | Part One | [25 lines prin. in roman, including material from dust jacket of clothbound issue, a list of other books by RJ in the Noonday paperback series, and the publisher's address]'.

Locations: MJ, NcGU, STW.

First Edition, English Clothbound issue (1976)

An unspecified number of copies of the clothbound issue was distrib-uted in England by Faber and Faber Ltd. These are identified by a printed paper label pasted to the base of the front flap of the dust jacket, in black: 'FABER | £8.25 NET'.

RJ to AB (PJ), 16 February 1959: I'd just begun on *Faust* when Jason [Epstein] talked to me about it; since then I've been working constantly on it, and have it about a third done. He suggested that it first be brought out in hard-cover, more or less deluxe edition . . . and then come out as an Anchor book; and he said that he could give me enough of an advance on it so that I could afford not to write anything else for a couple of years, and could spend all my writing time on it. I believe that the translation really will be quite different from any of the others—more natural, more like real English poetry, and more like Goethe; the people who have read or heard some of it all say this. Shall I send you several scenes or parts of scenes—fifty pages or so—to give you an idea of what it's like?

RJ to HF, September 1961: I certainly am glad to have the Prologue in the Theater done—though after I got used to it I really enjoyed it; how I wish I could get the squirrels or blue-jays or turnips around here to do the Intermezzo at the end of Walpurgisnacht.

RJ to SBQ, 8 November 1962: I'm about 9/10 done with *Faust.* . . .

RJ to Mac (MDC), June 1963: I'm going to give that *New York Book Review* [*New York Review of Books*] some translations of *Faust* lyrics and I'll make carbons for you.

RJ to RL, January 1965: Yes, I'd love to have a fellowship myself to finish *Faust.*

A29 *A BAT IS BORN*

First Separate Edition (1978)

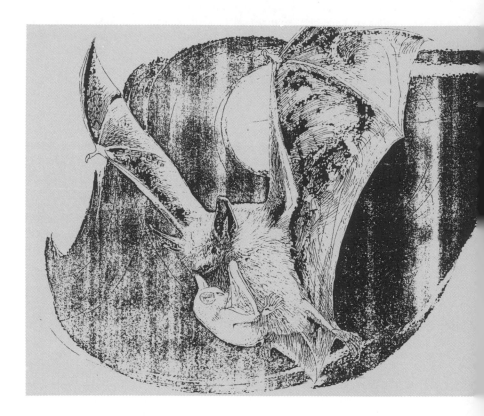

Title Pages: each page measures 7¹⁵⁄₁₆ × 10⁵⁄₁₆ in. (201 × 262 mm.);
illustration in deep B (approx. Centroid 179), black, and white.

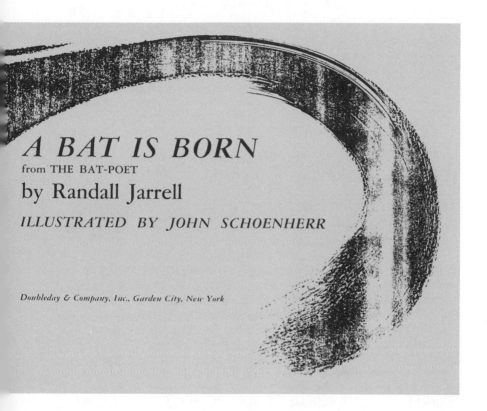

A BAT IS BORN
from THE BAT-POET
by Randall Jarrell
ILLUSTRATED BY JOHN SCHOENHERR

Doubleday & Company, Inc., Garden City, New York

Collation: [unsigned 1^{16}]; 16 leaves; [1–32].

Contents: p. 1: half title; pp. 2–3: title pages; p. 4: copyright page; p. 5: complete text of "A Bat Is Born"; pp. 6–31: text and illustrations; p. 32: blank.

Typography: text, 24/37 Garamond Bold; number of lines per page irregular throughout, but p. 5 contains two columns of text, left side, 18 lines, right side, 17 lines.

Paper and Binding: leaf measures $7^{15}/_{16}$ × $10^{5}/_{16}$ in. (201 × 262 mm.); white wove, unwatermarked paper, coated smooth; pictorial paper-covered boards (imitation linen) measure $8^{5}/_{16}$ × $10^{11}/_{16}$ in. (210 × 271 mm.); lettered in white and v. OY (Centroid 66); front: '[against Schoenherr illustration of a bat flying across the moon, prin. in black, deep B (Centroid 179), pale grayish blue (no Centroid equivalent), brill. OY (Centroid 67)] [in vivid orange yellow] A Bat Is Born | [reversed out in white] From THE BAT-POET by Randall Jarrell | Illustrated by John Schoenherr'; spine: '[vert., reversed out in white] JARRELL / SCHOENHERR A BAT IS BORN DOUBLEDAY'; back: unlettered; all edges cut, unstained; brill. pB (Centroid 195) wove, unwatermarked endpapers, coated smooth.

Dust Jacket: total measurement, $8^{1}/_{4}$ × 29 in. (209 × 737 mm.); wove, unwatermarked paper; inner side coated smooth, outer side coated glossy; inner side and flaps are white, outer side printed identical to pictorial boards; front flap: '[in black] [right side] A.B.I.B. | $5.95 | A BAT | IS BORN | by Randall Jarrell | [5 lines in ital, excerpt from "A Bat Is Born"] | [21 lines prin. in roman, about the book]'; back flap: '[in black] [12 lines prin. in roman, about RJ] | [21 lines prin. in roman, about the illustrator] | JACKET ILLUSTRATION BY JOHN SCHOENHERR | JACKET TYPOGRAPHY BY PETER SCHAEFER | ISBN: 0–385–12223–3 TRADE | 0–385–12224–1 PREBOUND | *Printed in the U.S.A.*'

Text Contents: "A Bat Is Born," first published in *The Bat-Poet* (A14)

Publication: published 6 January 1978 at $5.95; number of copies printed is unknown. Printed by Capital City Press of Montpelier, Vermont, and bound by Economy Bookbinding Corp. of Kearny, N.J. Registered in the name of the illustrator, John Schoenherr, effective 12 January 1978, under TX 39. Library of Congress deposit copies received 12 January 1978.

Locations: DLC, MJ (5), NcGU, STW (5).

Note: There are two errors of fact in the material contained on the flaps of the dust jacket. The first one is on the front flap and states that RJ's children's book *The Bat-Poet* is a novel; the second error is on the back flap and states that RJ received a National Book Award for fiction in 1962 (he received only the one NBA for poetry in 1960).

The publisher could provide no information concerning the "PRE-BOUND" issue of *A Bat Is Born* advertised on the back flap of the dust jacket; the compiler has seen only copies in illustrated paper-covered boards and identical dust jacket.

A30 *THE FISHERMAN AND HIS WIFE,* by the Brothers Grimm, translated by RJ

First Separate Edition (1980)

Title Pages: each page measures 12 × 8¾ in. (305 × 224 mm.); two-page illustration in color; 142 mm. rule at top is in l. B (approx. Centroid 181); bottom rule, also 142 mm., and square ornaments are in med. Gy (Centroid 265).

he Fisherman and His Wife

A TALE FROM THE BROTHERS GRIMM

TRANSLATED BY RANDALL JARRELL

PICTURES BY Margot Zemach

FARRAR · STRAUS · GIROUX NEW YORK

Collation: [unsigned 1–2⁸]; 16 leaves; [1–32].

Contents: p. 1: half title; p. 2–3: title pages; p. 4: copyright page and dedication: 'For Charles and Iva   M. Z."; pp. 5–32: text.

Typography: text 18/21 Perpetua; number of lines per page irregular throughout; 20 lines = 148 mm.

Paper and Binding: leaf measures 12 × 8¾ in. (305 × 224 mm.); white wove, unwatermarked paper, coated smooth; m. bG (Centroid 164) fine bead-cloth (202) boards measure 12⁵/₁₆ × 9¼ in. (311 × 235 mm.); front: '[in silver, rule, 117 mm.] | [in gold] The Fisherman and His Wife'; spine: '[vert.] [in gold] GRIMM [in silver] The Fisherman and His Wife [in gold] ZEMACH [at base] F S G'; back: unstamped; all edges cut, unstained; brill. B (approx. Centroid 177) wove, unwatermarked endpapers, uncoated rough.

Dust Jacket: total measurement, 12¼ × 26½ in. (312 × 673 mm.); inner side and flaps are white; front, spine, and flaps are printed l. bG (approx. Centroid 163); both sides coated smooth; front, spine, and back contain an illustration by Zemach prin. in v. rO (Centroid 34), v. l. gB (Centroid 171), light bluish green, v. G (Centroid 139), tan, black, v. l. yG (Centroid 134), d. gy. Y (Centroid 91), and m. OlBr (approx. Centroid 95); lettered in black, white, d. Gy (Centroid 266), and l. B (approx. Centroid 181); front: '[in black, below illustration] The Fisherman and His Wife | A TALE FROM THE BROTHERS GRIMM TRANSLATED BY | RANDALL JARRELL [square ornament] PICTURES BY Margot Zemach'; spine: '[vert., in black] GRIMM The Fisherman and His Wife ZEMACH [at base] F S G'; back: contains a portion of the illustration but unlettered; front flap: [in black] [upper right corner] $10.95 | The Fisherman | and His Wife | [in light blue, thin rule, 67 mm.] | [in black, 25 lines prin. in roman, about the book] | [in dark gray, thick rule, 67 mm.]'; back flap: '[in light blue, thin rule, 67 mm.] | [in black, 15 lines prin. in roman, about the artist] | [in light blue, thin rule, 67 mm.] | [in black, 5 lines in roman and ital, about RJ] | [in dark gray, thick rule, 67 mm.] | *Farrar, Straus and Giroux* | *19 Union Square West* | *New York 10003* | ISBN 0–374–32340–2'.

Text Contents: RJ's translation of "The Fisherman and His Wife," first published in **A12**.

Publication: published 25 April 1980 at $10.95; 31,500 copies printed, of which 12,075 were bound and distributed; the remaining unbound sheets are as yet listed in the publisher's inventory. Printed by A. Horowitz & Son, Clifton, N.J. Registered in the name of Margot Zemach, effective 17 June 1980, under TX 487–214 and creation in 1980. Library of Congress deposit copies received 17 June 1980.

Locations: DLC, MJ (5), NcGU, STW (3).

A31 *KIPLING, AUDEN & CO.*

A31a *First Edition (1980)*

Randall Jarrell

KIPLING,

AUDEN & CO.

Essays and Reviews

1935–1964

· ❀ ·

FARRAR, STRAUS AND GIROUX

NEW YORK

Title Page: 8⅞ × 5⅞ in. (226 × 150 mm.).

Collation: [unsigned 1–11¹⁶ 12⁸ 13¹⁶]; 200 leaves; [4], [i-iv] v [vi] vii-xii, [1–2] 3–368 [369–370] 371–381 [382–386].

Contents: two unnumbered leaves, the first of which is blank, the second contains a list of books by RJ on the recto and verso; p. i: half title; p. ii: blank; p. iii: title page; p. iv: copyright page; p. v: '*Note*' about this collection; p. vi: blank; pp. vii-xii: contents; pp. 1–368: text; p. 369: part title: '*Index*'; p. 370: blank; pp. 371–381: index; pp. 382–383: blank. Contents are divided into sections by year of publication.

Running Titles: head, '[page number in arabic numerals] [year of publication of individual essay or review in ital, within brackets] | [title of essay or review in ital] [page number in arabic numerals]'.

Typography: text, 10/12 Garamond no. 3; 39, 40, or 41 lines; pages with 39 lines measure 171 (176) × 107.5 mm.; 20 lines = 88 mm.; pages with 40 lines measure 171 (177) × 107.5 mm.; 20 lines = 94 mm.; pages with 41 lines measure 175 (181) × 107.5 mm.; 20 lines = 84 mm.

Paper and Binding: leaf measures 8¹⁵⁄₁₆ × 5¹⁵⁄₁₆ in. (227 × 151 mm.); yWhite (Centroid 92) wove, unwatermarked paper, uncoated smooth; m. yG (Centroid 136) fine bead-cloth (202) on spine and 19 mm. of front and back boards, brill. Y (approx. Centroid 83) paper on remainder; total measurement 9³⁄₁₆ × 6¼ in. (234 × 160 mm.); front: unstamped; spine: in gold, '[horiz.] [thick rule, 39 mm.] | RANDALL | JARRELL | · | Kipling, | Auden | & Co. | · | FARRAR | STRAUS |

GIROUX | [thick rule, 39 mm.]'; back: unstamped; all edges cut, unstained; yWhite (Centroid 92) wove, unwatermarked endpapers, uncoated smooth.

Dust Jacket: total measurement, 9³⁄₁₆ × 21³⁄₈ in. (232 × 542 mm.); wove, unwatermarked paper; inner side coated smooth, outer side coated glossy; inner side and flaps are white; borders of front, all of spine and back are printed deep YG (Centroid 118); front contains a black-and-white photograph of RJ; lettered in black, white, and l. OlBr (approx. Centroid 94); front: '[in black] RANDALL JARRELL | [in light olive brown] *Kipling, Auden & Co.* | [within ornamental brackets] ESSAYS AND REVIEWS 1935 – 1964]'; spine: '[horiz.] [in black, rule, 33 mm.] | [reversed out in white] RANDALL | JARRELL | [in light olive brown] · | [reversed out in white] *Kipling,* | *Auden* | *&* | *Co.* | [in light olive brown] · | [reversed out in white] FARRAR | STRAUS | GIROUX | [in black, rule, 33 mm.]'; back: unlettered; front flap: '[in black] [upper right corner] $17.95 | [22 lines in ital, quote about RJ by Robert Lowell] | ROBERT LOWELL | [22 lines prin. in roman, about the book] | *(continued on back flap)*'; back flap: '[in black] *(continued from front flap)* | [29 lines prin. in roman, conclusion of material about the book] *Jacket photograph by Ted Russell* | *Jacket design by Constance Fogler* | FARRAR, STRAUS AND GIROUX | 19 UNION SQUARE WEST | NEW YORK 10003 | [lower right corner] ISBN 0–374–18153–5'.

Text Contents: "Ten Books," "The Morality of Mr. Winters," "Texts from Housman," "From That Island," "Poetry in a Dry Season," "A Job Lot of Poetry," "Poets: Old, New, and Aging," "A Note on Poetry" (from B1), "The Rhetoriticians," "New Year Letter," "Contemporary Poetry Criticism," "Tate versus History," "Town Mouse, Country Mouse," "Kafka's Tragi-Comedy," "The End of the Line," "In All Directions," "The Development of Yeats's Sense of Reality," "The Fall of the City," "Ernie Pyle," These Are Not Psalms," "Poetry in War and Peace," "['H. D.'] from Verse Chronicle" (C163), "['Marsden Harley'] from Verse Chronicle" (C167), "['Oscar Williams, Arnold Stein, Stanton A. Coblentz, Ruth Pitter'] from Verse Chronicle" (C174), "Tenderness and Passive Sadness," "Corrective for Critics," "['W. H. Auden'] from Verse Chronicle" (C196), "Verse Chronicle" (C204), "['Jean Garrigue and Conrad Aiken'] from Verse Chronicle" (C206), "Verse Chronicle" (C209), "B. H. Haggin," "Poetry Unlimited," "The Profession of Poetry," "Answers to Questions" (from B15), "No Hope for Eliot," "To Fill a Wilderness," "On the Underside of the Stone," "Malraux and the Statues at Bamberg" (first published as "Malraux's Thunder of Silence"; also publ. in SHS), "Aristotle Alive!", "The Poet's Store of Grave and Gay," "The Little Cars," "A Poet's Own Way," "Very Graceful Are the Uses of Culture" (first published as "The New Books . . ."), "A Literary Tornado," "A Matter of Opinion," "Speaking of Books," "Recent Poetry" (C287), "Recent Poetry" (C291), "The Year in Poetry," "Love and Poetry," "With Berlioz, Once upon a Time . . .", "Harmony, Discord, and Taste," "Recent Poetry" (C298), "Five Poets," "Songs of Rapture, Songs of Death," "In Pursuit of Beauty," "Go, Man, Go!", "Against Abstract Expressionism" (first published as "The Age of the Chimpanzee . . ."), "The Taste of the Age" (first published as "The Appalling Taste of the Age"), "Poets, Critics, and Readers," "The Woman at the Washington Zoo" (first published in B25), "Four Shakespeare Plays," "On Preparing to Read Kipling," "In the Vernacular," "The English in England," "Good Fences Make Good Poets."

Publication: published 28 July 1980 at $17.95; 5,500 copies printed by Vail Ballou Press, Inc., of Binghamton, N.Y. Registered in the name of Mrs. Randall Jarrell, effective 8 August 1980, under TX 585–357 and creation in 1980. Copyright deposit copies received 8 August 1980.

Locations: DLC, GU, MJ (5), NcGU, NCU, NcWsW, NN, STW (3), TxU, ViU.

> *Note:* Before publication, the publisher issued advance proof copies to selected reviewers: 200 leaves perfect bound in printed wrapper; white wove, unwatermarked paper (of poorer quality than A31a), uncoated smooth; d. yPk (approx. Centroid 30) wove, unwatermarked paper wrapper, printed in black: 'UNCORRECTED PAGE PROOF | *Randall Jarrell* | [swelled rule, 93 mm.] | KIPLING, | AUDEN & CO. | *Essays and Reviews* | *1935–1964* | [ornament] | FARRAR, STRAUS AND GIROUX | NEW YORK'; total measurement, 8⅜ × 5⁵⁄₁₆ in. (213 × 134 mm.). Some copies were issued in a dust jacket identical to that of A31a except for: total measurement, 223 × 520 mm.; both sides uncoated rough; inner side and flaps are yWhite (Centroid 92); black, spine, and borders of front are printed d. yG (approx. Centroid 137); lettered in black, white, and d. Y (Centroid 88); flaps are unlettered.

A31b *First Paperback Impression (photo-offset from A31a) (1982)*

All identical to A31a except for:

Title Page: 9 × 5⅞ in. (228 × 150 mm.).

Copyright Page: 'Second printing, 1981' [*sic*].

Collation: perfect bound; 200 leaves.

Paper Binding: thick, wove unwatermarked paper wrapper, inner side coated smooth, outer side coated glossy; inner side white, outer side printed ident. to dust jacket of A31a except for back; deep yellow green ink is slightly darker than A31a (but no Centroid equivalent); back: "[in black] [left] N 682 | ISBN 0–374–51668–5 [right] $9.95 | [32 lines prin. in roman, including excerpts from reviews by Michael Dirda (*Washington Post Book World*), Christopher Lehmann-Haupt (*New York Times*), Larry McMurtry (*Washington Star*), Mark Taylor (*Commonweal*) and Ann Hulbert (*New Republic*)] | *Cover photograph by Ted Russell / Cover design by Constance Fogler* | FARRAR, STRAUS AND GIROUX / 19 UNION SQUARE WEST / NEW YORK 10003'.

Publication: published in January 1982 at $9.95; 4,500 copies printed.

Locations: MJ, NcGU, STW.

A31c   *First English Edition (photo-offset from A31a) (1981)*

All identical to A31a except for:

Randall Jarrell | [swelled rule, 89 mm.] | KIPLING, | AUDEN & CO. | *Essays and Reviews* | *1935–1964* | [ornament] | CARCANET NEW PRESS LIMITED | MANCHESTER

Title Page: 8⁷⁄₁₆ × 5¼ in. (214 × 134 mm.).

Copyright Page: 'First published in Great Britain in 1981 by | CAR-CANET NEW PRESS LIMITED | . . .'.

Collation: [unsigned 1–25⁸].

Paper and Binding: leaf measures 8⁷⁄₁₆ × 5¼ in. (214 × 134 mm.); yWhite (Centroid 92) wove, unwatermarked paper, uncoated smooth; d. B (Centroid 183) paper-covered boards (imitation coarse linen) measure 8¹³⁄₁₆ × 5⅝ in. (224 × 142 mm.); front: unstamped; spine: in gold, '[vert. from top to bottom] [in fancy type] *Randall Jarrell* [two lines, in roman] [top] Kipling, [bottom] Auden & Co. [at base] [publisher's device]'; back: unstamped; all edges cut, unstained; yWhite (Centroid 92) wove, unwatermarked endpapers, uncoated smooth.

Dust Jacket: total measurement, 8¹³⁄₁₆ × 18¾ in. (224 × 481 mm.); wove, unwatermarked paper; both sides coated glossy; inner side and flaps are white; front, spine, and back are printed v. p. B (Centroid 184); letter in d. B (Centroid 183) and white; front: '[all within a quadruple-rule frame which is reversed out in white, 208 × 126 mm.]

[in dark blue] Kipling, Auden & Co. | [reversed out in white] ESSAYS AND REVIEWS 1935–64 | [horiz. single rule that connects the two vert. sides of the frame] | [at bottom in dark blue fancy type] *Randall* ['*J*' of *Jarrell* crosses lower horiz. rule] *Jarrell*'; spine: '[vert. from top to bottom] [fancy type in dark blue] *Randall Jarrell* [reversed out in white, in roman] [two lines, top] Kipling, [bottom] Auden & Co. [publisher's device in dark blue at base]'; back: all in dark blue, '*Carcanet prose titles include:* | [two columns in roman] [right, 28 lines, including 10 authors and titles] [left, 28 lines, including 10 authors and 11 titles] | [5 lines in roman, including advertisement with publisher's address]'; front flap: all in dark blue, '[11 lines in ital, tribute to RJ by Robert Lowell] | ROBERT LOWELL | [26 lines prin. in roman, about the book (from dust jacket of A31a)] | *(continued on the back flap)* | *SBN 85635 346 9–£9.95*'; back flap: '[15 lines prin. in roman, about the book (based on the dust jacket of A31a)] | *Cover design by Sue Richards* | [at base] CARCANET NEW PRESS LIMITED | 330 Corn Exchange Buildings | Manchester M4 3BG'.

Publication: published in 1981 at £9.95; number of copies is not known.

Location: STW.

A32   *THE LOST CHILDREN*

A32a   *First Separate Edition, First Printing (Suppressed) (1980)*

The Lost Children

Collation: broadside, 19 × 8 in. (477.5 × 203 mm.).

Contents: recto: '[in v. R (Centroid 11)] The Lost Children | [in black, 77 lines prin. in roman] | Randall Jarrrell [*sic*] | Forty copies have been privately printed for distribution | by Mary Jarrell and Stuart Wright'; verso: blank.

Typography: text, 10/12 Baskerville; 378 (402.5) × 97 mm.; 20 lines = 85 mm.

Paper: white wove, unwatermarked paper, uncoated rough.

Text Contents: "The Lost Children" (C354).

Publication: forty copies privately printed in December 1980 for Stuart Wright by Heritage Printers, Inc., Charlotte, N.C.; not for sale.

Locations: MJ, STW.

> *Note:* After the edition had been printed, Mrs. Jarrell noticed two errors which had not been corrected in proof: (1) a stanza break between lines 43–44, and (2) Jarrell was misspelled "Jarrrell." All but eight or ten copies were destroyed, and a second printing was ordered.
> Mrs. Jarrell's account of the genesis of this poem was published in *Parnassus*, 5 (Fall-Winter 1976), 223–29.

A32b   *First Separate Edition, Second Printing (1980)*

All identical to **A32a** except for:

Contents: no stanza break between lines 43–44; 'Jarrell' spelled correctly.

Topography: 375 (399) × 97 mm.

Paper: yWhite (Centroid 92) wove, watermarked '*Arches*', uncoated smooth.

Publication: published in late December 1980; not for sale.

Locations: MJ, NcGU, STW.

A33 *ABOUT POPULAR CULTURE*

First Edition (1981)

ABOUT POPULAR
CULTURE

by RANDALL JARRELL

PALAEMON PRESS LIMITED / 1981

Title Page: 9⅞ × 5⅞ in. (251 × 151 mm.).

Copyright 1981 by Mrs. Randall Jarrell

Collation: [unsigned 1¹⁰]; 10 leaves; [1–20].

Contents: pp. 1–2: blank; p. 3: title page; p. 4: copyright page; p. 5: unsigned 'NOTE' about the text by Stuart Wright; p. 6: blank; pp. 7–17: text; p. 18: statement of limitation; pp. 19–20: blank.

Typography: text, 12/15 Caslon Old Face; 176 × 97 mm.; 20 lines = 96 mm.

Paper and Paper Binding: leaf measures 9⅞ × 5⅞ in. (251 × 151 mm.); yWhite (Centroid 92) wove paper, watermarked '[open-face] RIVES [infinity symbol]', uncoated smooth; handsewn with yellowish white cord in black wove, unwatermarked wrapper, 10¹⁄₁₆ × 6⁵⁄₁₆ in. (257 × 159 mm.), uncoated rough; unlettered.

Dust Jacket: total measurement, 10⅛ × 20¹⁄₁₆ (257 × 512 mm.); English Cockerell marbled paper no. 4, in bouquetlike design; wove, unwatermarked; inner side deep yellowish brown (no Centroid equivalent); outer side and flaps in d. yBr (approx. Centroid 78), brBlack (Centroid 65), and l. gy. YBr (Centroid 79); paper label: pasted to the front is a white paper label, 33 × 72 mm., printed in brO (approx. Centroid 54): '[all within a single-rule frame, 23 × 63 mm.] ABOUT | POPULAR CULTURE | *by* RANDALL JARRELL'.

Text Contents: address by RJ delivered at the National Book Awards ceremonies in New York City, 11 March 1958 (see below, F5).

Statement of Limitation: p. 18: '[in black] This first edition is limited to 175 [*sic*] copies | of which 100, numbered 1–125 [*sic*], are for | public sale; 50 copies, numbered *i-l*, are | for distribution. This is copy [arabic or roman numeral supplied in brownish orange ink]'.

Publication: published 6 May 1981 at $15.00; 163 copies printed by Heritage Printers, Inc., of Charlotte, N.C.

Locations: MJ, NcGU, STW.

> *Note:* The printer failed to make certain changes in the statement of limitation on p. 18, as indicated in the page proof, e.g., 150 copies instead of 175, with the numbering scheme 1–100, and *i–l*.
>
> The thirteen overrun copies were used for review purposes; all identical to A33 except for the wrapper: m. rBr (approx. Centroid 43) wove, unwatermarked paper, 10¹⁄₁₆ × 19⅞ in. (256 × 505 mm.), uncoated rough; front: in black, 'ABOUT POPULAR | CULTURE | by RANDALL JARRELL | *Review Copy*'.

A34 *LETTERS*

First Edition (1983)

LETTERS

Collation: broadside, 12 × 9 in. (305 × 230 mm.).

Contents: recto: '[in brill. B (Centroid 177)] [open-face type] LET-TERS | [in black; text, 23 lines in roman] | [in brilliant blue] RAN-DALL JARRELL | [in l. Gy (Centroid 264)] NUMBER [press number 'ONE', 'TWO', and so on] OF FIVE COPIES PRIVATELY PRINTED | FOR MARY JARRELL [ornament] FEBRUARY [ornament] 1983 | [blind-stamped] *Shadowy Waters Press*'; verso: blank.

Typography: 12/16 Caslon; 142 (157) × 99 mm.; 20 lines = 108 mm.

Paper: yWhite (Centroid 92) antique paper, uncoated rough; laid, with four identical watermarks (not in Briquet), two over two, 60 and 80 mm. apart, each of which contains a monogram T crossed by a monogram M or W, affixed by an eye, within a broken circle, all of which is within a complete circle, 1 [23 | 22] 2 mm.

Publication: five copies printed from handset type at the Shadowy Waters Press, Winston-Salem, N.C., in late January and early February 1983; not for sale.

Locations: MJ, STW.

First Appearance: "Letters."

B

*Contributions
to Books*

[within a triple-rule frame broken at base by triple-rule oval containing publisher's device] [open-face type] FIVE YOUNG | AMERICAN | POETS | [roman] MARY BARNARD ■ RANDALL JARRELL | JOHN BERRYMAN ■ W. R. MOSES | GEORGE MARION O'DONNELL | [below triple-rule frame, left of publisher's device] NEW DIRECTIONS [right of publisher's device] NORFOLK, CONN.

Copyright Page: 'COPYRIGHT 1940 BY NEW DIRECTIONS'.

Binding and Dust Jacket: coarse grayish blue cloth boards measure 8⅞ × 5¾ in. (225 × 145 mm.). Spine stamped in gold: '[within a double-rule frame] FIVE | YOUNG | AMERICAN | POETS | [double rule] | NEW | DIRECTIONS'; all edges trimmed; yellowish white wove endpapers. Grayish tan dust jacket printed in dark blue against light bluish gray panel.

Contains: poems by Mary Barnard, John Berryman, RJ, W. R. Moses, and George Marion O'Donnell. RJ's "The Rage for the Lost Penny," pp. 81–123: includes reproduction of holograph of "For the Madrid Road" (untitled here), p. 84; RJ, "A Note on Poetry," pp. 85–90; and "On the Railway Platform" (**C53**), "The Ways and the Peoples" (**C65**), "Love, in Its Separate Being" (**C44**), "The See-er of Cities," "When You and I Were All . . ." (**C57**), "The Automaton" (**C42**), "The Winter's Tale" (**C52**), "A Poem for Someone Killed in Spain," "The Refugees" (**C68**), "A Story" (**C63**), "The Machine-Gun" (**C49**), "Eine Kleine Nachtmusik," "1789–1939" (**C33**), "Because of Me, Because of You . . ." (**C40**), "The Bad Music," "A Little Poem" (**C34**), "For the Madrid Road" (**C94**), "Che Faro Senza Euridice," "For an Emigrant" (**C70**).

Publication: published 19 November 1940 at $2.50; 800 copies printed and bound by J. J. Little Ives and Company of New York City. Registered under A 147602 in the name of New Directions, Norfolk, Conn. Renewed under R 434648 on 27 March 1968, by New Directions, New York, N.Y., as proprietor of the work.

First Appearances:

"A Note on Poetry"   KA

"The See-er of Cities"   BFS, CP
    14   Goethe* *note at bottom of text:* '*Or Carlyle, perhaps; I should worry.']   *note omitted*   BFS+

"A Poem for Someone Killed in Spain" BFS, CP
    5 joy"—]   ~—"   BFS+

"Eine Kleine Nachtmusik" CP

"The Bad Music" BFS, CP
  19 hear . . .] ~. . . BFS +

"A Little Poem" BFS, CP
  1   stories,] ~. BFS +
  7   brother:] ~, BFS +
  12 I . . .] ~ . . . . BFS +
  32 corn . . .] ~. . . . BFS +

"For the Madrid Road" BFS, CP
  4   blood . . .] ~. . . . BFS +
  11 died . . .] ~. . . . BFS +

"Che Faro Senza Euridice" BFS, CP

Note: Much of the early publishing history of *The Rage for the Lost Penny* is closely intertwined with that of *Blood for a Stranger*. See above, **A1**.

RJ to ND (JL), May 1939: I was pleased to get your letter; I waited a little while for *New Directions* [1939] and the details, but decided I'd better send a note saying that I'm interested. Allen [Tate] probably told you that I would be; if he thought it a good plan, I'm sure I'll think so too.

RJ to ND (JL), July 1939: I've just received *New Directions* you were kind enough to send me, and I see that I quite misunderstood the nature of the plan you mentioned in your letter: I had thought that you were talking about publishing several books of poetry, mine among them. That I should have been interested in; unfortunately, I am not at all interested in having fifteen or twenty poems published along with equal amounts from five or six others, since I can't, in the circumstances in which I find myself, see that this would do my poems, or me, or anybody else, any good whatsoever. You see, I've been writing poems for almost ten years, and I've quite a big bunch, more nearly enough for two books than for one; and they're fairly homogeneous, that is, if there's any point in printing the rest. I didn't know that it was so difficult to get first books published; the LSU press has asked me to give them a book, and I hadn't settled things with them just because Allen [Tate] had asked me for mine when he believed that he was bringing out that series of books at North Carolina. However, if all these circumstances were different, the proposal you make would be a good thing; since they are as they are, I want to thank you for asking me, and to say that I'm sorry that I can't. [¶] I think your plan is a good idea; and the book ought to sell well and create interest in the poets it uses. I don't know anyone good to suggest for it whom you wouldn't know already; I thought George [Marion] O'Donnell and Harry Brown, and I'm sure they've occurred to you.

RJ to ND (JL), October 1939: I want to thank you for the last two letters I've gotten from you, the one written before and the one written after I wrote my last letter. All the details about the anthology make it look quite different; to tell you the truth, what you said about it in *New Directions* did it no justice. Also, I'm very grateful for the arguments that, naturally, come from a sort of knowledge and experience I am naked of; what I know about publishing and selling books could be put in a vacuum tube without materially impairing it. I'll write in a week or two and tell you definitely about the anthology—when Allen [Tate] wrote a couple of weeks ago he said he was giving the manuscript to Scribner's, and I'd better hear about that before saying anything. [¶] I guess your main duty to your poems is to get them read by as many people as possible. (When you told me about the sale of books by a university press I knew; I guess my attitude was completely pessimistic. I thought every first book of poetry—unless, of course, you're a *good* writer, like Paul Engle or Millay—sold so.) So I will think hard about having two or three times as many readers.

RJ to ND (JL), November 1939: I'll be glad to be in the anthology. When I last wrote you I hadn't seen your letter or heard from Allen [Tate]; I was amused at your letter, and sympathetic, too (I shouldn't like to have to get along with poets; they—always excepting me and thee. . . .) [¶] You said there were to be five poets and forty pages for each, didn't you? Incidentally, the prose preface space (for what we think about poetry, etc.) I am going to . . . put an extra poem in. I think I'll wait until I can get a few hundred pages before I tell the world what I think about poetry. [¶] Tell me when you want me to send you the poems. (Shall I count thirty lines for a page and assume that large spaces aren't going to be left—i.e., a four-line poem won't use up a page?)

RJ to AT, November 1939: I was amused and rather pleased with Laughlin's letter. I had written him several days before saying that I was interested in his anthology now that he'd sent me the details, and that when I heard from you about Scribners I'd be able to tell him definitely. I'd gotten quite a bad impression of it from the account in *New Directions* (that's all I knew of it, and Laughlin's preface style in *N.D.* is, as you know, not too prepossessing: rather like God giving a rough account of what he would have done during the six days if he'd had a free hand); from what you say, and from the new letters he's written me, I think I'd better do it. . . . [¶] Laughlin's notion of what we thought the world would do when it saw our poems (bray and yell with joy) is so exactly and perfectly wrong, so far as I am concerned, that it's funny. *I* had the notion that any first and about any last poems, except [Paul] Engle's or Millay's sold next to nothing. Publishing poetry has always seemed to me like throwing it down a well: mostly nothing, a few echoes if you're lucky. [¶] You understand, I still don't *like* the anthology, but my personal preferences seem to me irrelevant: so far as I have any duty to poems, it's to get them read by as many people as possible, I suppose; and this seems to be the best thing for that. Anyway, the whole question of how my poems get published seems to me so beautifully important.

RJ to ND (JL), February 1940: Yes, I'd be very glad to have Allen advise me on dividing the material for the two books or anything else. I'm pretty clear now on how to do it, I think; I'll write him and see what he thinks of the way.

RJ to ND (JL), April 1940: Here is one of the contracts—they were forwarded to me from Texas, rather belatedly. About the poems of that last girl: they were awful. [¶] I have one picture only, which I'll send you. I dislike it but you may not ... if you do, tell me what other arrangements to make. [¶] Since Scribners may not do my book at all, and certainly won't for a long time, I've no great problem of selection: I'll simply take most of the best poems I have, mostly disregarding very late ones. [¶] I'd like to get my preface there a couple of days later, if I may; if you really need it on the 10th, tell me by return mail and I'll try to have it there by then. I can by rushing. I hadn't realized you'd need anything until August or so. [¶] Are you really going to have a biographical note about each of us? If you are, I'd like to see (or, better, write) mine: I'd hate awfully to have anything but the most colorless details—born so-and-so, educated at such-and-such, and so forth. [¶] My preface will be short, poor and refractory, I'm afraid; but its existence is all that matters, isn't it? I know some of the others will have elaborate ones to make up for it. Do you want a poem written out? Or are you still going to have a facsimile of a short poem?

RJ to ND (JL), June 1940: Here are the poems. I never found exactly how many you wanted, whether they were supposed to be printed solid or not: so I've sent what will, I suppose, be a lot too many—what to take away first, second, and so on, when you have to take away.

[poems enclosed]
"Fat, aging, the child clinging to her hand"
"The Loves of the Magician"
"Up in the sky ..."
"Beheading"
"London"
"Fear"
"To Play Hard-to-Get ..."
"The Hanged Man on the Gallows ..."
"February 1938"
"1789–1939"
"The Bad Music"
"Because of me, because of you ..."
"The Refugees"
"Love, in its separate being ..."
"Eine Kleine Nachtmusik"

But the more you use the better, so far as I am concerned. [¶] You can arrange them as you please, except for the first and last; I'd like "On the Railway Platform" to be the first poem, and I'd like "A Little Poem," "For the Madrid Road," "Che Faro Senza Euridice," and "For an Emigrant" in that order, to be the last four poems, or as nearly that as possible. [¶] I put in a title-page; I didn't want to use the name I have for a book, so I borrowed [from Beethoven] *The Rage for the Lost Penny. . . .* [¶] I wrote out "For the Madrid Road"; leaving the title off was deliberate; I thought it spoiled the looks. [¶] The photograph is enclosed; I don't like it much, but it's literally the only one I have in the last four or five years. Outside of one making a smash [in tennis]. [¶] I enclose as little biographical data as possible. You *will* keep it strictly statistical, won't you? At least, please do for mine; or else use it as it's written. This is just a sweet request, I don't mean to sound demanding. [¶] I hope I've put in everything. I'm quite sorry to have been late with it; my circumstances were such that it was difficult for me to write my article ["A Note on Poetry"]. [¶] After the biographical data, pictures, and handwriting I started to go on to a finger-print and lock of hair.

["Biographical Data"]

I was born in 1914, and grew up in Tennessee and California, and went to school at Vanderbilt. There I studied psychology; but after I had to learn radiophysics I went over into English where I belonged. [*scored through*: (I remember getting to the point of thinking it would be better for everybody if I lay down on the table, and let the cat set up the cathode ray oscillograph.)] I taught English for two years at Kenyon College, and teach it now at the University of Texas. [*scored through*: This exhausts me.]

RJ to ND (JL), July 1940: I'm sending back the proof on the day I got it, as you ask; air-mail, too. In your little biographical note, would you change *belong* (which I used ironically, but which looks metaphysical almost, out of context) to *got along better*, as I've put it in the proof? [¶] Everything looks very nice; I was pleased you'd used so many [poems]; God give us luck, may everybody buy one. . . . [P.S.] I noticed in the proof "Confederate Soldiers" and "Automaton" are together; this is unfortunate, as they're both descriptions of battlefields. Could they be separated conveniently?

RJ to AT, January 1941: To talk about the anthology: I'm sure you're right about some of my lines being limp (though I do think that in the future when people are thoroughly used to reading accentual verse some of them will seem a lot stiffer); and I hope I can improve; but it's an occupational risk, a defect of a quality. In other words, I'd rather seem limp and prosaic than false or rhetorical, I want to be rather like speech—rather I did want all that; I've gone so far in that direction I'm interested in the opposite now. But you know what I mean; suppose somebody had said to you in 1925, "Mr. Tate, you tend to over-write."

I suppose you'd have answered, "I'll take the risk." But I'll think it over—I assure you I've thought it over plenty. (I've been moaning to myself all this fall about being too prosy, and when, lately, I did some that weren't at all, I felt wonderful.) [¶] I agree with you *exactly* about [W. R.] Moses [*Arteries of Morning*]: it's just a complete Bore. (The capital *b* is a nice example of a Freudian error—it was quite unconscious.) I don't think anything in the world would help Mrs. [Mary] Barnard [*Cool Country*] sufficiently. As for [George Marion] O'Donnell [*Prayer against the Furies*], prompted by love of Beethoven, not dislike of O'Donnell, my nasty remark about the Op. 111 piece gave you the wrong impression: I *don't* think all of his's that bad. He has real talents; for instance, he has a better feel for phrase, often, than [John] Berryman; but he's so much pure fake, so much posing and pretentiousness and imitation and romantic forcing, that the good qualities are pretty well vitiated. I think if we went over his poems line for line we'd agree almost always. I say this much on an unimportant subject because I don't want you to think my critical judgment weak enough to be overturned by my personal feelings. Doesn't that sound vain? but we have our little vanities, and that's a nice big one of mine. [¶] I thought Berryman [*Twenty Poems*] much better than O'Donnell so far as the negative virtues are concerned; as for positive ones, there the difference is smaller. I think Berryman has a pretty inferior feel for language for one thing; and to talk about your old favorite, the poetic subject, he's obviously not really found his. . . . [¶] Whether Laughlin will do a book [of my poems] I've no idea. I hope all my New Republic stuff (they're printing three poems and another review—[Edmund] Wilson's really an angel) will impress him; but I'm afraid he'll be so badly annoyed at the nasty things I say about his idol Pound that all the New Republics in the world wouldn't help. Maybe if I get some good reviews it'll help.

RJ to AB, November 1942: The Bad Music is certainly your private poem. So is *Che Faro* [*Senza Euridice*]; so are so many others. . . . I know I've so often exaggerated or said many things I only half meant, in poems, that I don't trust them as truth—except as the way things [are] felt.

B2 NEW POEMS 1942

[Within a frame of double rules, reversed out in white against a red panel, within a single rule frame in white] NEW | POEMS | 1942 | [below panel, in black] An Anthology of | British and | American Verse | *EDITED BY* | Oscar Williams | [below double-rule frame] *PETER PAUPER PRESS · MOUNT VERNON · N.Y.*

Copyright Page: "COPYRIGHT 1942 BY THE PETER PAUPER PRESS'.

Binding and Dust Jacket: Regular Issue: dark blue cloth boards with orangish red paper labels in front and spine printed in white measure 8⅜ × 6¼ in. (214 × 160 mm.). All edges cut, top edges stained light red; yellowish white wove endpapers. Red, white, and blue dust jacket printed in black and white. *Autographed Issue:* Contains four additional leaves with the contributors' signature (RJ's signature on the first of these). French marbled-paper boards with ivory linen spine and corners measure 9⁷⁄₁₆ × 6⅜ in. (241 × 160 mm.); green paper spine label printed in ivory. All edges trimmed, top edges gold; white wove endpapers. Glassine jacket. Dark green board slipcase.

Contains: "The Difficult Resolution" (C93), pp. 120–22; "A Poem" ("There I was, here I am . . .") (C55), p. 116; "90 North" (C79), pp. 117–18; and "The Long Vacation" (C96), pp. 119–20.

Publication: published 17 April 1942 at $3.00 (trade issue) and $25.00 (limited signed issue). Twenty-six lettered copies of the limited signed ("autographed") issue were for sale, and at least thirty-three additional copies were presented to the contributors (each containing the recipient's name on the limitation page). RJ's signature is contained on the first of the signed leaves.

> *Note:* The compiler has letter Q of the limited signed issue. Of the contributors' copies RJ's could not be located, but Wallace Stevens's copy (with "Wallace Stevens" supplied on the limitation page instead of a letter) is with his books at the Huntington Library, San Marino, California.

B3   *AN AMERICAN ANTHOLOGY* (1942)

[Open-face type, in blue] AN | AMERICAN | ANTHOLOGY | [roman, in black] *67 Poems now in anthology form | for the first time | Edited by | Tom Boggs | The world is, after all, served only by | what is out of the ordinary.* | GOETHE | THE PRESS OF JAMES A. DECKER | *Prairie City, Illinois*

Copyright Page: 'Copyright, 1942, by T. K. Boggs'.

Binding and Dust Jacket: two noted, no priority. *Binding 1:* Blue cloth boards measure 8⅛ × 5⅛ in. (208 × 131 mm.). All edges trimmed; white wove endpapers. Greenish blue dust jacket is printed in rust and black. *Binding 2:* Brown cloth boards measure 8¼ × 5½ in. (210 × 135 mm.). All edges trimmed; yellowish white wove endpapers. Dust jacket printed in gold and black. Both bindings stamped identically, in gold; front: 'AN | AMERICAN | ANTHOLOGY';

spine: '[vert.] AN AMERICAN ANTHOLOGY BOGGSDEC-KER'.

Contains: "The Head of Wisdom" (C88), pp. 49–50.

Publication: published in July 1942 at $2.00.

Colophon: p. 96, 'AN AMERICAN ANTHOLOGY, set in Inter-|type Waverly, was printed in April | and May, 1942, at the Press of James A. Decker.'

Note: In the table of contents Jarrell is misspelled "Jarell."

B4 *AMERICAN WRITING 1942*

AMERICAN | WRITING | *1942* | THE ANTHOLOGY AND YEAR-BOOK | OF THE | AMERICAN NON-COMMERCIAL MAGA-ZINE | *edited by ALAN SWALLOW* | *THE PRESS OF JAMES A. DECKER* | *Prairie City, Illinois*

Copyright Page: 'Copyright 1942 by Alan Swallow'.

Binding and Dust Jacket: black pebble-pattern cloth-covered boards measure 9 × 6 in. (229 × 152 mm.). Stamped in gold; front: '*American Writing 1942*'; spine: '[vert.] AMERICAN WRITING 1942 *Swallow* DECKER'. All edges trimmed, unstained; yellowish white wove endpapers. Dust jacket not seen.

Contains: "The Iceberg" (C81), pp. 98–99, and "January 1938" (C82), pp. 100–101.

Publication: publication information unknown.

B5 *NEW POEMS 1943*

NEW POEMS | 1943 An Anthology of | British and American Verse | *Edited by* OSCAR WILLIAMS | [rule, 92 mm.] | HOWELL, SOSKIN, PUBLISHERS

Copyright Page: 'COPYRIGHT, 1943, BY OSCAR WILLIAMS'.

Binding and Dust Jacket: light gray cloth boards measure 8³⁄₁₆ × 5½ in. (208 × 140 mm.) Spine stamped in black; '[vert.] *New Poems* 1943 | [horiz. at base] HOWELL, | SOSKIN'. All edges cut, unstained; yellowish white wove endpapers. Light olive green and black dust jacket is printed in black and white.

Contains: "Pictures from a World (Orestes at Tauris)" (C109), pp. 109–21.

Publication: published 17 August 1943 at $2.75.

B6 *NEW POEMS 1944*

['N' and 'P' in script] NEW POEMS 1944 | AN ANTHOLOGY OF AMERICAN AND | BRITISH VERSE, WITH A SELECTION | OF POEMS FROM THE ARMED FORCES | Edited By OSCAR WILLIAMS [three ornaments] | *New York* | HOWELL, SOSKIN, PUBLISHERS

Copyright Page: 'COPYRIGHT, 1944, BY OSCAR WILLIAMS'.

Binding and Dust Jacket: light orangish brown cloth boards measure 7¹¹⁄₁₆ × 5⅜ in. (196 × 136 mm.). Spine stamped in black: '[vert.] New Poems 1944 | [horiz. at base] HOWELL, SOSKIN'. All edges cut, untrimmed; yellowish white wove endpapers. Brownish orange and black dust jacket is printed in black, white, and orange.

Contains: "The Soldier Walks under the Trees of the University" (C118), pp. 237–38.

Publication: published 15 August 1944 at $3.00.

B7 *THE WAR POETS* (1945)

The War Poets | *An Anthology of the War Poetry* | *of the 20th Century* | *Edited with an Introduction by* | Oscar Williams | The John Day Company · New York

Copyright Page: 'COPYRIGHT, 1945, BY OSCAR WILLIAMS'.

Binding and Dust Jacket: tan cloth boards measure 7⅝ × 6 in. (195 × 154 mm.). Stamped in red and gold; front: '[against a red panel, within a frame of gold single rules] THE War | Poets'; spine: '[against a red panel above and below which are gold single rules] THE War | Poets | *edited by* | OSCAR WILLIAMS', and at base '[against a red panel above and below which are gold single rules] *JOHN DAY*'. Fore and bottom edges trimmed; top edges stained light red; yellowish white wove endpapers. Reddish pink dust jacket printed in black and white.

Contains: first book appearance of "The Emancipators" (C117), p. 157; "The Death of the Ball Turret Gunner" (C134), p. 157; "Prisoners" (C130), p. 158; "2nd Air Force" (C133), pp. 158–59; "An Officers' Prison Camp Seen from a Troop-Train" (C129), p. 160; "Soldier (T. P.)" (C119), p. 162; "Losses" (C126), p. 163. "The Soldier Walks under the Trees of the University" is reprinted on p. 161.

Publication: published 19 June 1945 at $5.00.

B8   *THE PARTISAN READER* (1946)

[Printed downward] THE | PARTISAN | [printed downward] READER | TEN YEARS OF THE PARTISAN REVIEW | 1934–1944: | AN ANTHOLOGY | EDITED BY | WILLIAM PHILLIPS AND PHILIP RAHV | INTRODUCTION BY | LIONEL TRILLING | THE DIAL PRESS, NEW YORK, 1946

Copyright Page: 'COPYRIGHT, 1946, BY DIAL PRESS, INC.'

Binding and Dust Jacket: yellow cloth boards measure $8^{7}/_{16}$ × $5^{5}/_{8}$ in. (215 × 142 mm.). Stamped in black; front: '[printed downward] THE | [horiz.] PARTISAN | [printed downward] READER'; spine: '[vert.] THE PARTISAN READER | [horiz., at base] DIAL'. All edges trimmed, unstained; yellowish white endpapers. Gray and white dust jacket printed in yellow, black, white, and red.

Contains: first book appearance of "A Nursery Rhyme" (C67), pp. 239–40; "Poetry in a Dry Season" (C69), pp. 629–33. "The Metamorphoses" is reprinted on p. 283.

Publication: published 9 September 1946 at $3.75.

B9   *A SOUTHERN VANGUARD* (1947)

A Southern Vanguard | THE JOHN PEALE BISHOP | MEMORIAL VOLUME | *Edited by* ALLEN TATE | PRENTICE-HALL, INC. | *New York*

Copyright Page: '*Copyright*, 1947, *by* | PRENTICE-HALL, INC.'

Binding and Dust Jacket: rust cloth boards measure $8^{1}/_{4}$ × $5^{1}/_{2}$ in. (211 × 140 mm.). Stamped in green; front: '[within four curved swelled rules] [script] *A Southern* | [roman] VANGUARD'; spine: '[reversed out in rust against a green panel, vert.] A SOUTHERN VANGUARD | [horiz., at base] PRENTICE | HALL'. All edges trimmed, top edges stained grayish green; yellowish white wove endpapers. Brownish orange dust jacket printed in black and white.

Contains: "The Märchen" (C169), pp. 153–55.

Publication: published in August 1947 at $4.50.

B10 *SPEARHEAD* (1947)

[Left side, reproduction of a pen-and-ink drawing of an upturned spearhead] [reproduced from artist's pen-and-ink original] Spearhead | [remainder in roman] 10 YEARS' EXPERIMENTAL | WRITING IN AMERICA | A NEW DIRECTIONS BOOK

Copyright Page: 'COPYRIGHT 1947 BY NEW DIRECTIONS'.

Binding and Dust Jacket: grayish tan boards measure $9\frac{3}{16}$ × $6\frac{3}{16}$ in. (232 × 156 mm.). Spine stamped in black with a vert. spearheadlike design with 'SPEARHEAD' reproduced from artist's design reversed out in grayish tan. All edges cut, unstained; yellowish white wove endpapers. Light gray dust jacket printed in black, white, and yellow.

Contains: first book appearance of "The Place of Death" (C179), pp. 250–51; "A Camp in the Prussian Forest" (C175), pp. 251–52; "Burning the Letters" (C159), pp. 252–54; "Pilots, Man Your Planes" (C162), pp. 256–58. "Siegfried" is reprinted on pp. 254–56.

Publication: published 10 November 1947 at $5.00; 4,965 copies printed, of which 999 were distributed in England by the Falcon Press.

Note: The table of contents notes incorrectly that these poems were taken from *Little Friend, Little Friend*; in fact, all but "Siegfried" were first collected in *Losses*.

B11 *THE GHETTO AND THE JEWS OF ROME* (1948)

FERDINAND GREGOROVIUS | The Ghetto and the Jews of Rome | SCHOCKEN BOOKS / NEW YORK

Copyright: 'COPYRIGHT 1948 BY SCHOCKEN BOOKS INC.'

Binding and Dust Jacket: pale gray cloth boards measure $7\frac{11}{16}$ × $4\frac{3}{4}$ in. (196 × 121 mm.). Stamped in gold; front: 'GHETTO & JEWS | OF ROME'; spine: '[vert.] GREGOROVIUS: GHETTO & JEWS OF ROME'. All edges cut, unstained; yellowish white wove endpapers. Dark yellowish brown dust jacket printed in dark yellowish brown and white.

Contains: RJ's translation of "Lament of the Children of Israel in Rome" (C200), pp. 11–16.

Publication: published in April 1948 as Schocken Library 12, at $1.50. Reissued in 1966 as Schocken Paperbacks Edition SB137 at $1.75; printed pictorial wrappers.

B12 *SELECTED POEMS,* by William Carlos Williams (1949)

WILLIAM CARLOS | WILLIAMS | SELECTED POEMS | *with an introduction by Randall Jarrell* | *The New Classics Series*

Copyright Page: no statement of first edition.

Binding and Dust Jacket: light gray cloth boards measure 7³⁄₁₆ × 4⅞ in. (183 × 124 mm.). Spine stamped in brown: '[vert.] SELECTED POEMS   W. C. WILLIAMS'. All edges trimmed, unstained; tan wove endpapers. Pale brownish orange and black dust jacket printed in black and white.

Contains: RJ's "Introduction," pp. ix-xix.

Publication: published in March 1949 at $1.50; 3,591 copies printed, of which 1,997 were bound on 31 March 1949 and 1,594 copies on 31 January 1950. A second impression of 4,000 copies was issued in the spring of 1950, at $1.75; all identical to the first issue except the endpapers, which are white instead of tan, and the NBA for Poetry notice that has been added to the jacket. A third printing (first paperback issue) was published in January 1963 at $1.50; 6,751 copies printed; there were four subsequent paperback issues between March 1964 and June 1967.

> *First Appearance:* RJ's "Introduction"   PA. Reprinted in *Literature in America: An Anthology of Literary Criticism,* ed. Philip Rahv (New York: Meriden Books, 1957), pp. 342–49.
>
> *RJ to WCW, December 1946:* I'd like to do the introduction [to your *Selected Poems*]. Shall I write to Laughlin about when, how long, and how much? And I'd love to make some offhand suggestions about things to include—but not *entirely* offhand; I'd want to read everything over and think a while. . . . Writing this introduction makes me feel rather like Little Lord Fauntleroy introducing Henry Wadsworth Longfellow into Heaven; but I'm very much pleased to be asked.
>
> *RJ to ND (JL), January 1947:* [William Carlos] Williams mentioned the introduction to me; I'd like to do it, I think. I'll need to take some space—so let me do the one at $100, not the short one at $50. How

long is long? And when does it *really* need to be finished? (I'm busy until April 1.) Will you send me all of Williams' poems that New Directions has printed? And does anyone have a list of poems published by other publishers or only in magazines?

RJ to EE, Fall 1948: I am miserably writing away at the Williams piece I put off doing all summer—I have it half-done. I wish my "good, prose style" were fast asleep in Barbarossa's cave in the mountain, or grinding salt at the bottom of the sea, or doing anything but making *me* write it. I used to think when I grew up prose would get easier and easier for me to write: but really I have to write it more and more. (Someday) I will live like the immortal gods and write nothing but poetry: I suppose they write nothing else, at least I'm sure they don't write critical prose. Writing criticism is too much like raining into the ocean: you're wasted, and the ocean's as salt[y] as ever. Well, this isn't quite true, but it's entirely too near to being true. . . . I think that later I'll write a different sort of criticism more like notes or letters, just to please myself: but mostly it's better, really, to make things oneself, not to write about what others make—if you *can* make anything yourself.

RJ to ND (JL), 7 October 1948: I can do nothing but apologize about the introduction, and say that—now that I'm back in this country—I'll get it to you in a couple of weeks.

RJ to ND (JL), 7 November 1948: Here is the introduction, along with even more apologies than there were in my last letter: I'm *extremely* sorry to be so late with it. I've worked hard on it and hope it's some good. For some reason I could never get going on it, it hung over me like a nightmare, and I'd—ah well, it's over now.

RJ to ND (JL), 18 November 1948: I believe I'd rather keep the last paragraph; when you consider that only a hundred or so people have ever written good poems in English, it's not much of an anticlimax. I think Williams likes it just as it is, too. [¶] I don't think an introduction a good place for metrical analysis; besides, nobody's ever invented any system for scansion that differentiates good "free verse" from bad, and it would take much work, much space, and God from heaven as an assistant. I can understand why you're so much interested, because you got your own scansion from a kind of Williams free verse that amounts to a simple accentual verse—simple because there are so few stresses to the line; but this is a specialized interest that very few readers would share. . . . [¶] Seventy-five dollars is quite enough. I didn't do it for the money, and four or five hundred wouldn't equal the amount (quite unnecessary god knows *why* it was) trouble it was to me. . . . [¶] Will you be sure and send me proof of the introduction? It's easy for bad errors to slip in, and I'd hate that.

RJ to RL, 5 December 1948: I finally finished the Williams [introduction]—it's O.K. but not too good; Laughlin liked it all right, but was disappointed that I didn't have a lot of metrical analysis—he said that the interest of Williams' poetry is "mainly metrical".

RJ to WCW, 10 December 1948: Your letter about the introduction made me very happy. I can't tell you how glad I am that you liked it that well. I'd had such an awful time putting off writing it and slowly writing it—why I don't know—that I almost cried tears of joy at the happy ending of the whole thing, your letter. [¶] What you said in the middle two paragraphs is all true, and I was much impressed with your seeing it so plainly. The attitude behind most contemporary writing scares and horrifies me, and I was writing about you (and the others I mentioned or didn't mention) most of all as people who didn't have it, who had just the opposite attitude.

RJ to RL, May 1949: Have you seen my Williams introduction? I at last got it done, in November. But mostly, all winter, I read anthropology and psychoanalysis in the greatest quantities.

B13 *TRANSITION WORKSHOP* (1949)

[Vert. from bottom to top] *The Vanguard Press, Inc.* | [horiz.] transition workshop | [vert. from bottom to top] *New York* | [horiz.] edited by *Eugene Jolas* | [device consisting of a circle and vert. arrow of dots with a solid point that separates 'edited by' and '*Eugene Jolas*']

Copyright Page: 'Copyright, 1949, by the Vanguard Press, Inc.'.

Binding and Dust Jacket: black, gray, and white pictorial cloth boards measure 9½ × 6⅜ in. (240 × 163 mm.). Stamped in black; front: '[right side, against gray-and-white cloudy sky design] [top] *Eugene Jolas* | [left side, printed downward] *Vanguard* | [left side in black, against a white panel that extends across spine] workshop'; spine: '[against white panel] transition'. All edges trimmed, top edge stained pink; black wove endpapers. Black-and-red dust jacket printed in black and white.

Contains: first book appearance of "Enormous love, it's no use asking" (C41), pp. 235–36; reprinting of "Because of me, because of you" (C40), p. 235.

Publication: published 29 November 1949 at $6.00; 3,500 copies printed.

B14 *MODERN AMERICAN POETRY* (1950)

[Script] Modern | American Poetry | [remainder in roman] MID-CENTURY EDITION | [reprod. of Greek medallion] | EDITED BY

LOUIS UNTERMEYER | [swelled rule, 101 mm.] | HARCOURT, BRACE AND COMPANY · NEW YORK

Copyright Page: 'COPYRIGHT 1919, 1921, 1925, 1930, 1936, 1942, 1950, BY HARCOURT, BRACE AND COMPANY, INC. | ... | [a·11·49]'.

Contains: first book appearance of "Hope" (C214), p. 685. Also reprints "A Camp in the Prussian Forest," p. 678, "Pilots, Man Your Planes," pp. 679–80, "The Death of the Ball Turret Gunner," p. 681, "Burning the Letters," pp. 681–82, "Jews at Haifa," p. 683, "A Country Life," pp. 683–84, and "The Refugees," pp. 685–86.

Binding and Dust Jacket: brown, blue, or green cloth boards noted, 9¼ × 6⅜ in. (234 × 162 mm.). Spine stamped in gold: '[horiz.] LOUIS | UNTERMEYER | [fancy rule] | *Modern | American | Poetry* | [fancy rule] | Harcourt, Brace | and Company'. All edges trimmed, top edges stained gray, blue, green, or unstained; yellowish white wove endpapers. Dust jacket not seen.

Publication: publication information unknown.

> *Note:* RJ revised "The Refugees" for inclusion in Untermeyer's *Modern American Poetry*. Although this version would seem to indicate his final intentions, it is the original version from BFS that is collected in CP. Untermeyer included the revised "The Refugees" in his *Modern American and Modern British Poetry*, rev. shorter ed. (New York: Harcourt, Brace, 1955). The authorial changes listed here are from BFS to *Modern American Poetry*.
>
> 3   Sprawls] Sits
> 4   Is their calm extravagant?]   But how shall I escape?
> 5   They had faces and lives like you.]   These had lives like mine
> 7   The dried blood sparkles]   There is blood, dried now,
> 11–12   silently. The faces are vacant. | Have none of them found the cost extravagant?]   silently, the vacant | Breath rises, vanishes—Escape, escape!
> 13   How could they? They gave what they possessed.]   One pays, for this freedom, all that one possessed;
> 15–18   And what else could satisfy the extravagant | Tears and wish of the child but this? | Impose its cancelling terrible mask | On the days and faces and lives they waste?]   Sleep; and the emptying hearts escape | Even their own wish—turn back to this | Nothing that hides, with its calm cancelling mask, | The days and the faces: the world they waste.
> 22   Is it really extravagant]   *For I too shall escape,*
> 23   To read in their faces: and what is there that]   We read in the faces; and what is there

RJ to LU, Spring 1949: Here's *The Refugees* in the best shape I've ever managed to get it in; I'm sure I'll be able to change it some more, though—I kept at it a few days trying. . . . How late in the fall will the anthology come out? It will be fun to see?

RJ to LU, December 1949: I just received a copy of the anthology from Harcourt Brace, and I want to thank you for it and to say what a pleasure it was to read what you wrote about my poems. Poets are usually criticized as if they were jugglers—it's wonderful to have the critic interested in what the poems are about, in what they feel like and mean, and not just in the performance.

RJ to MJ, 10 December 1951: The Untermeyer [anthology] has a great big and really well selected bunch of my poems, and the Oxford Book of American Verse has a big and abominably selected bunch—old [F. O.] Matthiessen didn't even know that I'd written *Losses*, everything's from the first two [books].

B15 *MID-CENTURY AMERICAN POETS* (1950)

[All within a double-rule frame] EDITED *by* JOHN CIARDI | Mid-Century | American | Poets | · | [rule, 92 mm.] | *Twayne Publishers, Inc. New York 4*

Copyright Page: 'Copyright 1950 by John Ciardi'.

Binding and Dust Jacket: light blue cloth boards measure 8¹¹⁄₁₆ × 5⅝ in. (220 × 143 mm.). Stamped in pale blue; front: 'MID-CENTURY | AMERICAN | POETS'; spine: '[vert.] MID-CENTURY AMERICAN POETS'. All edges cut, unstained; yellowish white wove endpapers. Grayish pink dust jacket printed in bright blue and grayish pink.

Contains: first appearance of "Answers to Questions," pp. 182–84, in which RJ responds to editor John Ciardi's questionnaire concerning specific points about his work as a poet. First book appearance of "Robert Lowell's Poetry" (originally published as "From the Kingdom of Necessity," (C182), pp. 158–67, and "A Game at Salzburg" (C217), pp. 191–92. Reprints "The State," p. 185, "A Camp in the Prussian Forest," pp. 185–86, "Port of Embarcation," p. 187, "The Dead Wingman," pp. 187–88, "Eighth Air Force," p. 188, "Siegfried," pp. 189–90, "Variations," pp. 192–93, "Burning the Letters," pp. 194–96, "The Dead in Melanesia," p. 196, "A Country Life," pp. 197–98, "The Death of the Ball Turret Gunner," p. 198, and "Lady Bates," pp. 199–201.

Publication: published in April 1950 at $4.00; 2,000 copies printed.

First Appearance: "Answers to Questions"   KA.

RJ to JC, Spring 1949: I'd like to be in the anthology; the only difficulty I can see is that most of my best poems are fairly long ones. On the other hand, my introduction would be 3 typewritten pages, not 15. If you could just give one a certain amount of space to be divided between the poems and the prose, that would be a lot better for me. I don't want to leave out *Burning the Letters,* for instance, if the group is supposed to be the best poems I've written—but it would take up half the number of lines all by itself.

RJ to JC, Summer 1949: Here are my poems—just under 500 lines of them—and my answers to the questionnaire. I just made a final version, for a book, of the long Lowell review; I'd added a few sentences from my earlier review of him, and made an occasional change. I'm quite willing for you to use it in this form—I shouldn't like to have much left out, though, and I'd want to know before hand which parts are to be left out. If you'll send it back to me with these parts indicated, I'll send it right back; if there's something I very much want to keep, I'll suggest an alternative omission. [¶] I've numbered my poems to show the order I'd prefer to have them printed in.

RJ to JC, Fall 1949: Would you just call my section *Answers to Questions?* I believe I'd rather have a gruff factual title, though yours is prettier.

RJ to JC, Fall 1949: It is quite all right to put the comma in the sentence you asked about. I'd taken it out so there wouldn't be three short phrases in succession set off by commas. Logically, *that old closed system Grandfather Winslow* later in the sentence, and if you need a comma in one you do in the other; but we are much more used to leaving it out in the short phrases, and it might look awkward to people in the long, though it's done sometimes. [¶] In the next to the last paragraph of the Lowell review will you please cut out one poem-title—*Christmas Eve Under Hooker's Statue?*

RJ to JC, Fall 1949: It ought to be a nice book; with good luck it might well sell fairly well, since there isn't anything that much resembles it. Also, it's the first use of the term *Mid-Century*; who knows, maybe Eliot and Auden and everybody will now be considered Early Twentieth Century Poetry, and Amy Lowell will stop being a daring contemporary poet.

B16   *THE KENYON CRITICS* (1951)

[Swelled rule, 102 mm.] | The Kenyon Critics | STUDIES IN MODERN LITERATURE FROM | THE Kenyon Review EDITED BY | *John Crowe Ransom* | [rule, 102 mm.] | [publisher's device] | *The World*

Publishing Company | CLEVELAND AND NEW YORK | [swelled rule, 102 mm.]

Copyright Page: 'First Edition . . . | Copyright 1951 by the *Kenyon Review*'.

Binding and Dust Jacket: black cloth boards measure 8½ × 5¹³⁄₁₆ in. (216 × 149 mm.). Stamped in silver; front: '[33 lines in roman, list of contributors]'; spine: '[framed by horiz. and vert. rules, vert.] THE KENYON CRITICS   JOHN CROWE RANSOM'. Top and bottom edges trimmed, fore-edges untrimmed; yellowish white wove endpapers. Yellowish green dust jacket printed in black and white.

Contains: "The Humble Animal" (C107), pp. 277–80.

Publication: published 23 February 1951 at $4.00.

B17   *LITERARY OPINION IN AMERICA* (1951)

LITERARY OPINION | IN AMERICA | [ornamental rule, 114 mm.] | *Essays Illustrating the Status, Methods* | *and Problems of Criticism in the* | *United States in the Twentieth Century* | [ornamental rule, 114 mm.] | *EDITED BY* | MORTON DAUWEN ZABEL | REVISED EDITION | [publisher's device] | HARPER & BROTHERS | *New York*

Copyright Page: 'REVISED EDITION | *Copyright, 1937, 1951, by Harper & Brothers* | . . . | B–A'.

Binding and Dust Jacket: deep red cloth boards measure 9½ × 6⁵⁄₁₆ in. (242 × 161 mm.). Stamped in gold; front: 'LITERARY | OPINION | IN AMERICA | [ornament] | MORTON DAUWEN ZABEL'; spine: '[horiz.] LITERARY | OPINION | IN | AMERICA | [ornament] | ZABEL | REVISED EDITION'. All edges trimmed, unstained; yellowish white wove endpapers. Light olive and reddish brown dust jacket printed in reddish brown and white.

Contains: "The End of the Line" (C101), pp. 742–48.

Publication: published in 1951 at $6.00.

B18   *POETRY AWARDS 1952*

[Type ornament, left] [type ornament, right] | *Poetry* | *Awards* | *1952* | [ornamental rule] | A COMPILATION OF ORIGINAL POETRY |

PUBLISHED IN MAGAZINES OF THE | ENGLISH-SPEAKING WORLD | IN 1951 | [publisher's device] | PHILADELPHIA | UNIVERSITY OF PENNSYLVANIA PRESS | 1952

Copyright Page: 'Copyright 1952'.

Binding and Dust Jacket: reddish purple cloth boards measure 8¾ × 5⁹⁄₁₆ in. (224 × 143 mm.). Spine stamped in white: '[vert.] [fancy ornament] [fancy type] *POETRY AWARDS* 1952'. All edges trimmed; yellowish white wove endpapers. Pink dust jacket printed in red.

Contains: "The Black Swan" (C246), p. 4.

Publication: published in December 1952 at $2.50; 1,500 copies printed.

> *Note:* RJ shared "Second Prize Tie" with Dorian Cooke.

B19   *BEST ARTICLES 1953*

[Two pages] [rule crossing both pages] [left, 8 lines in roman, listing authors included] | [rule like first]   [right] *BEST ARTICLES* | *1953* | 25 MOST MEMORABLE ARTICLES OF THE YEAR | [rule] SELECTED BY | *Rudolph Flesch* | [rule] | HERMITAGE HOUSE: NEW YORK 1953

Copyright Page: 'Copyright, 1953, Rudolf Flesch | . . . | First Edition'.

Binding and Dust Jacket: blue quarter-cloth and red paper-covered boards measure 8³⁄₁₆ × 5½ in. (208 × 140 mm.). Spine stamped in silver and red: '[horiz., in silver, fancy] *Best Articles* | [fancy rule] | *1953* | [fancy rule] | [script] *Rudolf Flesch* | [in red, decorative ornament] | [in silver, fancy] *Heritage*'. All edges trimmed, unstained; yellowish white wove endpapers. Red, gold, blue, and white printed dust jacket.

Contains: "The Age of Criticism" (C256), pp. 203–22.

Publication: published in 1953 at $3.50.

B20   *BORESTONE MOUNTAIN POETRY AWARDS* (1953)

BORESTONE MOUNTAIN | *Poetry Awards* | *1953* | [ornament] | *A Compilation of Original Poetry* | *published in* | *Magazines of the En-*

*glish-speaking World | in 1952 | 1953 | PHILADELPHIA | UNIVER-SITY OF PENNSYLVANIA

Copyright Page: '*Copyright 1953*'.

Binding and Dust Jacket: dark blue cloth boards measure 8¾ × 5⅝ in. (223 × 142 mm.). Spine stamped in whitish-silver: '[vert.] [ornament] Borestone Mountain POETRY AWARDS · Pennsylvania [ornament]'. All edges trimmed; yellowish white wove endpapers. Medium grayish blue dust jacket printed in dark blue.

Contains: "The Survivor among Graves" (C260), pp. 43–44.

Publication: published in December 1953 at $2.50; 1,500 copies printed.

B21   *ESSAYS TODAY 2* (1956)

ESSAYS | *Today* | [numeral the height of the first two lines] 2 | *Editor,* RICHARD M. LUDWIG | PRINCETON UNIVERSITY | *NEW YORK* | [vert. rule] | HARCOURT, BRACE AND COMPANY

Copyright Page: 'COPYRIGHT, © 1956, BY HARCOURT, BRACE AND COMPANY, INC. | . . . | [a · 2 · 56] | . . . '.

Paper Binding: deep red and gold paper wrapper, 8½ × 5½ in. (216 × 141 mm.), printed in white, deep red, and gold.

Contains: "The Intellectual in America" (C286), pp. 129–34.

Publication: published in February 1956 at $.95.

B22   *WRITING FROM EXPERIENCE* (1957)

[Two pages] [left]. Raymond C. Palmer | . James A. Lowrie | .John F. Speer | Department of English and Speech | Iowa State College | [publisher's device left of double rule and place of publication] [double rule that extends across both pages] | Published at Ames, Iowa, U.S.A., | [right] *Writing | From | Experience* | [continuation of double rule] | By the Iowa State College Press

Copyright Page: '© by The Iowa State College Press'.

Binding and Dust Jacket: tannish gray and red cloth boards 9⁄16 × 6 in. (234 × 153 mm.), stamped in black on front and spine: front, '[each of the first three lines against a red panel] [in semi-script] *Writing* | *From* | *Experience* | PALMER . . . LOWRIE . . . SPEER'; spine, '[horiz., reversed out in tannish gray against a red panel] PALMER | [rule] | LOWRIE | [rule] | SPEER | [below panel, vert. in black semi-script] *Writing from Experience* | [horiz., against red panel like first, reversed out in tannish gray] IOWA | STATE | COLLEGE | PRESS'. All edges trimmed; yellowish white wove endpapers. Dust jacket not seen.

Contains: "The Schools of Yesteryear: A One-Sided Dialogue" (C303), pp. 78–89.

Publication: published in 1957.

B23   *THE ANCHOR BOOK OF STORIES* (1958)

THE ANCHOR BOOK OF | STORIES | SELECTED AND WITH AN INTRODUCTION | BY RANDALL JARRELL | DOUBLEDAY AN-CHOR BOOKS | DOUBLEDAY & COMPANY, INC., GARDEN CITY, NEW YORK | 1958

Title Page: 7⅛ × 4 in. (181 × 103 mm.).

Copyright Page: 'First Edition'.

Paper Binding: perfect bound in strong yellow wrapper, 7⅛ × 4 in. (181 × 103 mm.), printed in black and white with black-and-white photograph of Romanesque sculpture on front.

Contains: RJ's "Introduction," pp. ix-xxii.

Publication: published in 1958 at $1.25. A later issue of the first printing contains a white price-change label printed in black, "$1.45," pasted over the printed price in the upper right corner of the front of the wrapper.

> *First Appearance:* RJ's "Introduction"   SHS (as "Stories").
>
> *RJ to AB (JE), December 1956:* Could we use the same type you use in Bentley's first anthology (the one with *Electra*) so as to get as many words a page as possible? and hold the front matter down to a minimum? I think the introduction needs to be longer than I believed—by quoting some very short narratives of one kind or another in the introduction I can give the book a much more representative feeling. I've got rid of all the really long things like *Bartleby*.
>
> *RJ to AB (JE), c. February 1957:* I realized that I had too long a list; I've been cutting, and *The Prussian Officer* was one of the first things

to go. Tell me exactly how many words I can have, will you? . . . I have taken or am taking a lot of trouble on the selections, and am working hard on a good, careful introduction; if the book isn't popular I don't mind making next to nothing, but if it is popular I want to have the possibility of making more [than $1,500, less permissions (about $1,000), plus a 5% royalty].

RJ to AB (JE), March 1957: Here is the contract and here is a list of stories, a little different from which it will finally be but closer than the old list. . . . I've been working on the introduction; I mean to use a number of (what seem to me) interesting short quotations, and the kind of thing I want to say is pretty different from ordinary writing about short stories, so perhaps the whole thing will be interesting—

RJ to AB (JE), June 1957: I think I'll be able to have the book for you about the 12th or 15th of July. I've written about all the permissions letters, and I've been copying stories, buying books and cutting the pages out, and so forth. I have the notes for the introduction and mean to write it as soon as I get up to Cape Cod. . . .

RJ to AB (JE), July 1957: I'm afraid I won't have the anthology ready for a couple of weeks—I'm having a hard time with permissions. . . . I'm hopeful that everything will come through inside the next two weeks.

RJ to AB (JE), mid-October 1957: I expect to have the manuscript ready for you by November 15.

RJ to AB (JE), mid-November 1957: Here are the stories and the introduction. . . . I've enclosed the permissions and a couple of letters. . . . All the other stories are in the public domain, I'm pretty sure. . . . [¶] Have you any plans for the cover? I liked Auerbach's *Mimesis* very much—the book of course, but I mean the cover; might I pick some favorite and appropriate Romanesque sculpture, or some other work of art? . . . In any case I'd really like to have some hand in choosing the cover.

RJ to AB (JE), December 1957: I was waiting until you'd decided what you felt about the cover. I quite agree with what you say about the title: *Wish and Truth* is too abstract, and *The Anchor Book of Stories* or a similar title is better. What you say about the picture's being abstract doesn't convince me at all. After going over your sentences carefully, and thinking about them, I've decided that your response isn't an objective commercial response (whether the picture will make the book sell less) but a personal response to an overbearing work of art, the picture. Judging from the responses of a number of people, a fairly random sample, who've seen the cover, I'd say that the picture will make more people pick up the book and buy it. And, too, as you said in your first letter, it is my book, and I very much want the picture used. The book has been a great deal of work, I'm paying for the permissions myself, and I'd like the pleasure of having that highly relevant picture on the cover. . . . [¶] Let me summarize about the cover: your title and your lay-out or arrangement are quite all right with me, but I want the photograph used as it is.

RJ to Dou (PJ), c. Spring 1962: Thanks so much for your nice letter about *The Anchor Book of Stories*. Naturally, I'm disappointed; I liked using the book with classes and will be sorry to have it go out of existence. But I wanted to make a bigger anthology of stories—with this one gone I can take the best stories from it to be part of the new larger anthology. I'm going to call it *The World's Stories*, and it will be big enough so that people won't call it "special" as easily.

B24 *AN ANTHOLOGY OF GERMAN POETRY* (1960)

An Anthology of German | *Poetry from Hölderlin* | *to Rilke in English* | EDITED BY ANGEL FLORES | [rule, 42 mm.] | ANCHOR BOOKS | DOUBLEDAY & COMPANY, INC. | GARDEN CITY, NEW YORK | 1960

Copyright Page: 'Copyright © 1960 by Angel Flores | . . . | First Edition'.

Paper Binding: perfect bound in gray pictorial wrapper, 7¹⁄₁₆ × 4³⁄₁₆ in. (180 × 106 mm.), printed in black, white, and pink.

Contains: first appearance of RJ's Rilke translation, "Evening," p. 386; first book appearance of RJ's Rilke translations, "Lament" (C310), p. 386; "Childhood" (C316), pp. 395–96; "The Grown-Up" (C296), p. 397; "Washing the Corpse" (C319), pp. 404–5; "The Child" (C318), p. 407; "The Great Night" (C312), p. 420; "Death" (C311), p. 423; "Requiem—For the Death of a Boy" (C265), pp. 424–26.

Publication: published in 1960 as Anchor paperback A197, at $1.45.

First Appearance: RJ's translation of Rilke's "Evening."

Note: reissued in 1965 in red cloth-covered boards by Peter Smith, Gloucester, Mass.

B25 *UNDERSTANDING POETRY* (1960)

Understanding | [open-face type] POETRY | [swelled rule, 98 mm.] | [remainder in roman] *Third Edition* | BY | *CLEANTH BROOKS* | *Yale University* | *ROBERT PENN WARREN* | *Holt, Rinehart and Winston, Inc.* | *New York*

Copyright Page: 'Copyright 1938, 1950, © 1960 by Holt, Rinehart and Winston, Inc.'

Binding and Dust Jacket: light orangish yellow cloth boards measure 8½ × 5⅝ in. (217 × 144 mm.). Stamped in brownish red and black; front: '[in brownish red] Understanding | Poetry | [in black] THIRD EDITION'; spine: '[horiz., in black] THIRD | EDITION | [vert., in brownish red] Understanding Poetry | [horiz., in black] BROOKS | [rule] | WARREN | [at base] HOLT'. All edges cut, unstained; yellowish white wove endpapers. White dust jacket with pink design on front and spine, printed in black.

Contains: RJ's account of how "The Woman at the Washington Zoo" came to be, pp. 531–39. The poem is reprinted on pp. 538–39.

Publication: published in April 1960; 10,000 copies printed. There were twelve additional printings of the third edition, making a total of 153,000 copies.

> *First Appearance:* RJ's account of genesis of "The Woman at the Washington Zoo" SHS (as "The Woman at the Washington Zoo"); reprinted in *The Poet's Work*, ed. Reginald Gibbons (Boston: Houghton Mifflin, 1979), pp. 230–39.
>
> *RJ to RPW, 4 October 1959:* I'd very much like to write the piece for you; I've never written anything of the sort but I'll try—I've been making notes. I wrote two poems when I was in Washington—THE WOMAN AT THE WASHINGTON ZOO and JEROME—and I believe I can write about them together.... [¶] I'm delighted that you want me to write the essay and look forward to seeing the new UNDERSTANDING POETRY.

B26 *WILDERNESS OF LADIES* (1960)

ELEANOR ROSS TAYLOR | *Wilderness of Ladies* | With an Introduction | by RANDALL JARRELL | [publisher's device] | Mc-DOWELL, OBOLENSKY | New York

Copyright Page: 'First Printing'.

Binding and Dust Jacket: dark green cloth (spine and 48 mm. of front and back) and decorated (pale gray and very pale bluish green teardrop design on grayish white) paper boards measure 9¼ × 5¾ in. (235 × 146 mm.). Stamped in gold; front: publisher's device blind-stamped at bottom of cloth edge; spine: '[vert.] TAYLOR *Wilderness of Ladies* [two lines, top] McDOWELL [bottom] OBOLENSKY'. All edges cut, unstained; yellowish white wove endpapers. Grayish white dust jacket printed with same decorated design, lettered in deep bluish green.

Contains: RJ's "Introduction," pp. 5–13.

Publication: published in 1960 at $2.95.

> *First Appearance:* RJ's "Introduction"   SHS. A portion was reprinted in the *Alumni News* (Univ. of N.C. at Greensboro), 49 (Jan. 1961), 9, with a notice of the publication of the book in the "Alumnae Authors" section.
>
> *Note:* RJ was quite enthusiastic about and full of praise for Eleanor Taylor's work, and this book in particular. In his 1961 National Book Award speech Jarrell said: "I cannot help feeling unhappy about the fact that, because this award was given to 'The Woman at the Washington Zoo,' Eleanor Taylor's 'A Wilderness of Ladies' will not be read by people who might have read it if it had been given the award. I assure you that, in heaven or hell or wherever it is that good poets go, Hardy and Emily Dickinson are saying to all the new arrivals: 'Did you really get to see Eleanor Taylor?'—just as Blake and Wordsworth used to say: 'Did you really get to see Hardy and Dickinson?' If you would like to read a true, a unique American poet, read Eleanor Taylor's 'A Wilderness of Ladies.'"

B27   *THE BEST SHORT STORIES OF RUDYARD KIPLING* (1961)

The Best Short Stories of | RUDYARD KIPLING | *Edited by Randall Jarrell* | [swelled rule, 50 mm.] | *HANOVER HOUSE Garden City, New York*

Copyright Page: 'First Edition'.

Binding and Dust Jacket: red (spine and 60 mm. of front and spine) and grayish tan linen-cloth boards measure 8⁷⁄₁₆ × 5⅝ in. (215 × 143 mm.). Spine stamped in gold and black: '[horiz., in black, rule 44 mm.] | [against a black panel, 61 × 44 mm., in gold] The Best | Short Stories | of | RUDYARD KIPLING | [below panel, in black, rule, 44 mm.] | [in gold] *Edited by* | RANDALL | JARRELL | [at base] HANOVER | HOUSE'. All edges cut; top edge stained yellowish pink; yellowish white wove endpapers; white cloth head and tail bands. White dust jacket with elaborate illustration depicting scenes from Kipling's stories, prin. in red, reddish orange, light brown, blue, yellow, and olive green, on front and spine; lettered in black.

Contains: "On Preparing to Read Kipling," pp. vii-xix.

Publication: published in 1961 at $6.95.

> *First Appearance:* "On Preparing to Read Kipling" KA.

B28 *CULTURE FOR THE MILLIONS* (1961)

[Two pages, left] CULTURE | FOR THE | [right] MILLIONS? | MASS MEDIA IN | MODERN SOCIETY | [left] *Edited by* | NORMAN JA-COBS | *With an Introduction by* | PAUL LAZARSFELD | [right] D. VAN NOSTRAND COMPANY, INC. | PRINCETON, NEW JERSEY | Toronto · London · New York

Copyright Page: 'COPYRIGHT 1959 BY | THE AMERICAN ACADEMY OF ARTS AND SCIENCES | COPYRIGHT © 1961 BY | D. VAN NOSTRAND COMPANY, INC.'

Binding and Dust Jacket: grayish green cloth boards measure 9¼ × 6³⁄₁₆ in. (234 × 157 mm.). Stamped in black and white; front: '[left, in black] CULTURE | FOR THE | MILLIONS ["i's" are dotted with solid six-point stars] [right, in white, question mark the height of three lines to left]'; spine: '[horiz., in white] JACOBS | [vert., in black] CULTURE FOR THE MILLIONS | [horiz. at base, in white] VAN | NOSTRAND'. All edges trimmed, unstained; yellowish white wove endpapers. Green and greenish brown dust jacket printed in yellow, white, and brown.

Contains: "A Sad Heart at the Supermarket" (C321), pp. 97–110.

Publication: published in 1961 at $4.95.

B29 *THE ACHIEVEMENT OF WALLACE STEVENS* (1962)

the ACHIEVEMENT of | WALLACE STEVENS | *edited by* ASHLEY BROWN | *and* ROBERT S. HALLER | [publisher's device] | J. B. LIP-PINCOTT · PHILADELPHIA · NEW YORK

Copyright Page: 'FIRST EDITION'.

Binding and Dust Jacket: light grayish green cloth boards measure 8¼ × 5⁹⁄₁₆ in. (210 × 143 mm.). Stamped in blue; front: '[9 lines in roman, list of contributors]'; spine: '[horiz.] THE | ACHIEVE-|MENT | OF | WALLACE | STEVENS | BROWN | & HALLER | LIP-

PINCOTT'. All edges rough trimmed, top edges stained pale green; light green wove endpapers. Dark grayish green, light green, and white dust jacket printed in reddish purple.

Contains: "The Collected Poems of Wallace Stevens" (C287), pp. 179–92.

Publication: published 20 April 1962 at $5.00; 3,500 copies printed.

B30   *THE MOMENT OF POETRY* (1962)

[Left side] The Moment | of | Poetry | [right side] EDITED BY | *Don Cameron Allen* | THE JOHNS HOPKINS PRESS : BALTIMORE

Copyright Page: '© 1962, The Johns Hopkins Press, Baltimore 18, Maryland'.

Binding and Dust Jacket: grayish blue cloth boards measure 8^{7}/₁₆ × 5⅝ in. (215 × 143 mm.). Stamped in silver; front: '*Holmes* | *Sarton* | *Eberhart* | *Wilbur* | *Jarrell*'; spine: '[vert.] ALLEN The Moment of Poetry JOHNS HOPKINS'. All edges trimmed, unstained; yellowish white wove endpapers. White dust jacket containing dark blue and grayish blue design on front and spine, with black-and-white photographs of the five contributors also on front, printed in black, dark blue, and grayish blue.

Contains: "Robert Frost's 'Home Burial,'" pp. 99–132.

Publication: published in June 1962 at $3.50.

> *First Appearance:* "Robert Frost's 'Home Burial'"   TBC. Reprinted in *A Celebration of Poets*, ed. Don Cameron Allen (Baltimore: Johns Hopkins Press, 1967).

> *Note:* "Robert Frost's 'Home Burial'" was presented as one of the Percy Graeme Turnbull Memorial Lectures on Poetry at the Johns Hopkins University, in October 1961. Other lectures included in the series, and in this volume, are by John Holmes, May Sarton, Richard Eberhart, and Richard Wilbur.

B31   *POET'S CHOICE* (1962)

POET'S | CHOICE | [ornamental rule, 46 mm.] | EDITED BY | Paul Engle and Joseph Langland | [publisher's device] | THE DIAL PRESS   New York 1962

Copyright Page: 'Copyright © 1962 *by Paul Engle and Joseph Langland*'.

Binding and Dust Jacket: deep reddish brown cloth boards measure 9⅝ × 6¼ in. (237 × 159 mm.). Spine stamped in gold: '[horiz., ornamental rule] | [vert.] POET'S CHOICE | [horiz.] [ornamental rule like first] | EDITED BY | ENGLE | AND | LANGLAND | [ornament] | [publisher's device] | DIAL'. Top edges trimmed; fore and bottom edges rough trimmed; orange wove endpapers. Tan coated paper dust jacket printed in gold, black, and reddish brown.

Contains: RJ's statement on why he chose "Eighth Air Force" for inclusion in this volume, p. 141; the poem is reprinted on p. 140.

Publication: published on 9 October 1962 at $6.00 (after 31 December 1962, $6.75). Issued in printed paper wrapper 5½ × 8 in., on 22 April 1963, at $1.45; contents identical to cloth issue.

> *First Appearance:* RJ's statement on his choice of "Eighth Air Force" for inclusion in this volume.

B32 *EΣTI: E. E. CUMMINGS AND THE CRITICS* (1962)

EΣTI: | e | e | c | E. E. Cummings and the Critics | Edited, with an Introduction | by | S. V. Baum | MICHIGAN STATE UNIVERSITY PRESS | EAST LANSING, MICHIGAN

Copyright Page: 'Copyright © 1962'.

Binding and Dust Jacket: yellowish brown cloth boards measure 9³⁄₁₆ × 6⅛ in. (233 × 155 mm.). Spine stamped in gold: '[vert.] *S. V. Baum* E. E. Cummings and the Critics *Michigan State*'. All edges trimmed, unstained; yellowish white wove endpapers. Dust jacket not seen.

Contains: "A Poet's Own Way (C284), pp. 191–92.

Publication: publication information unknown.

B33 *SIX RUSSIAN SHORT NOVELS* (1963)

SIX RUSSIAN SHORT NOVELS | *The Overcoat* | *Lady Macbeth of the Mtsensk District* | *A Lear of the Steppes* | *Master and Man* | *The Death of Ivan Ilych* | *Ward No. 6* | SELECTED, WITH AN INTRODUCTION, | BY RANDALL JARRELL | Anchor Books | Doubleday & Company, Inc. | Garden City, New York

Title Page: 7⅛ × 4⅛ in. (181 × 106 mm.).

Copyright Page: 'First Edition'.

Paper Binding: perfect bound in white wrapper, 7⅛ × 4⅛ in. (181 × 106 mm.), printed in black, blue, red, and white.

Contains: RJ's "Introduction," pp. xii-xxxvi.

Publication: published in May 1963 as Doubleday Anchor Original A348, at $1.45.

> *First Appearance:* RJ's "Introduction" TBC. Excerpt first printed as "It's a Gloomy World, Gentlemen," *Atlantic Monthly*, 211 (April 1963), 76–82 (see C337).

> *RJ to An (Miss Ross), August 1958:* I'd like to make the book Leskov's *The Lady Macbeth of the Myinsk* [sic] *District*; Chekhov's *Ward No. 6*; Dostoievsky's *The Eternal Husband*; Turgenev's *A Lear of the Steppes*; and Tolstoy's *The Death of Ivan Ilyich* (though we can't get permission to use Maude's translation, there are others).

> *RJ to An (PJ), 16 February 1959:* After your office found we couldn't get permission—or reasonably inexpensive permission—to use some of the novelettes in the anthology, Jason [Epstein] made what was to me a congenial suggestion, that I have it an anthology of Russian novelettes . . . instead. Three of the selections were already Russian. I've thought a good deal about what to include, and it seems to me that you could make an interesting and representative book out of Leskov's *The Lady Macbeth of the Mzinsk District*, Chekhov's *Ward No. 6*, Turgenev's *A Lear of the Steppes*, Tolstoy's *The Death of Ivan Ilyich* (in another translation since Oxford [Univ. Press] won't permit us to use the Maude), and Gogol's *The Overcoat*. If space permits, we could add a sixth, Dostoievsky's *The Eternal Husband*; or this could be substituted for the Gogol.

> *RJ to An (PJ), April 1960:* Would the first part of October be a good time to get you the manuscript? I'm sure I can have it ready for the fall. . . . I'm trying to get a good substitute for the *Death of Ivan Ilyich*, so the book won't at all resemble the Random [House] book you mentioned.

> *RJ to An (PJ), September 1960:* About the Russian short novels book: do you think it would be possible to use 450 pages for Gogol's *The Overcoat*, Turgenev's *A Lear of the Steppes*, Tolstoy's *Master and Man*, Dostoievsky's *The Eternal Husband*, Chekhov's *Ward No. 6*, and Leskov's *Lady Macbeth of the Minsk District*? This would be, I think, the best collection of Russian novelettes I know; it would be slightly better, slightly (20 pages) longer, and slightly more like other collections if *The*

Death of Ivan Ilyich were substituted for *Master and Man*. Tell me what you think about the size and the selection.

RJ to An (PJ), October 1960: I forgot that *The Eternal Husband* is [in] an Anchor book; I knew that *Notes from the Underground* is. These two, I think, are much Dostoyevsky's best novelettes. I'll try to think of a different selection—without a Dostoyevsky, perhaps.

RJ to An (PJ), February 1962: Just before I got ill [with hepatitis] I read the new Magarshack translation of Leskov's *Lady Macbeth of the Minsk District*, and it is a great deal better than the old one. Do you think we could get permission from him to use his translation?

RJ to An (PJ), 25 March 1962: How does this sound about the Russian stories? I mean to call it *Seven Russian Short Novels*: [list includes the six, with the addition of Chekhov's "A Dreary Story"]. . . . I'll write the introduction for these (if you like the selection) later this spring or early this summer.

RJ to An (PJ), May 1962: Yes, I'm quite satisfied with the [Constance] Garnett translation of *The Overcoat*; for once, I feel, she satisfied herself. . . . I'll start making notes for my introduction as soon as I'm feeling a little better; I'll get the introduction to you before July 1.

RJ to An (PJ), 20 May 1962: I decided *not* to use Chekhov's *A Dreary Story*, so there will only be six selections and only Tolstoy will have more than one. [¶] There is a good translation of *Master and Man* by Nathan Haskell Dole; it's in the public domain. There is a translation of *The Death of Ivan Ilych* by Leo Wiener that's no longer copyright, but it's a very poor and awkward translation. Could we get permission from Oxford Press to use the excellent Maude translation? *or* is there any other reasonably good translation that we could use? Is Garnett's translation of Turgenev's *Lear of the Steppes* now in the public domain? . . . Do we need to get permission to use her translation of Gogol's *The Overcoat*? In what you said about Magarshack's translation you implied that Garnett's was not copyright any longer, but I wanted to be sure. [¶] There is a good translation of Chekhov's *Ward No. 6* (no longer copyright) in that collection I told you about.

RJ to An (PJ), 1 July 1962: Here is the introduction to *Six Russian Short Novels*. . . . [¶] I've worked hard on the introduction and hope that you'll enjoy it. The stories are such masterpieces that they repay a good deal of comment, I think.

RJ to An (PJ), July 1962: I do have too many *but's* in the little fairy tale summary of *The Overcoat*; suppose we change the part you quoted to: *the general wouldn't help, though, but gave him a terrible scolding.* That gets rid of the two that are right together, and if I need to get rid of any other I can do it in proof.

RJ to An (AF), September 1962: What you said about the introductions [including the two Kipling introductions, most likely] really delighted me. Sending them to *Harper's* or to any other magazine your syndicate department thinks of will be just fine. This reminds me that the *Atlantic Monthly* wanted me to send them something, and that I'd like to send them part of my Russian short novels introduction. . . .

RJ to An (PJ), October 1962: The Russian short novels introduction (the parts about Gogol, Turgenev, and Tolstoy—I left out Leskov and Chekhov so it wouldn't be impossibly long) will be published in the February *Atlantic*; I asked them to put *Copyright Randall Jarrell, 1963* on the first page, as you wished me to.

RJ to An (AF), May 1963: Six Russian Short Novels is like having a Russian doll in an embroidered white dress on the coffee-table.

B34   *THE ENGLISH IN ENGLAND* (1963)

The English in England | *SHORT STORIES BY RUDYARD KIP-LING* | *Selected and with an Introduction* | *by Randall Jarrell* | Anchor Books | Doubleday & Company, Inc. | Garden City, New York | 1963

Title Page: 7⅛ × 4¹⁄₁₆ in. (182 × 103 mm.).

Copyright Page: 'The Anchor Books edition | is the first publication of | *The English in England.* | Anchor Books Edition: 1963'.

Paper Binding: perfect bound in yellowish brown and white wrapper, 7⅛ × 4¹⁄₁₆ in. (182 × 103 mm.), printed in black, white, and bluish green.

Contains: RJ's "Introduction," pp. v-xv.

Publication: published as Doubleday Anchor Original A362 in July 1963 at $1.25.

> *First Appearance:* RJ's "Introduction"   TBC, KA (as "The English in England").
>
> *Note:* The Kipling project with Anchor Books started out quite differently from the form the two volumes finally took on. The following letters demonstrate this evolution.
>
> *RJ to An (PJ), May 1960:* I'd be *delighted* to do that with Kipling. Kipling—oddly enough—is one of the three or four writers I know best. He's a very troubling and unsatisfactory writer in some ways, but in other ways he's one of the best writers who ever lived; for imagination, ability to invent something entirely live—just for sheer brute ability to *write*—he's as much of a genius as James said he was. A *great* deal of his best writing isn't much known. . . . [¶] He's a particularly good writer to bring out in the way you suggest. Since he spent three-

quarters of a long industrious life writing short stories, and since he's the sort of writer he is, a volume of *Selected Stories* doesn't do him any real justice. . . . You can [however] make a good *Selected Poems*. I've often compared the *Collected Poems* with [T. S.] Eliot's selection, and liked and been impatient with Eliot's choices. (He has an awfully good feel for Kipling, partially because they're two of the most neurotic writers who ever lived.) The neurotic side of Kipling ought to appeal to many readers, once they realize he's much more like Kafka than like Maugham. [¶] I read all of him every few years—some things much more often; it will be a joy to me to do something for him. . . . And Kipling must be *the* best writer of stories for children, half for grown-ups. I can't think of anyone who's done nearly so many, or such good, truly inspired, ones; it's interesting, too, how they come in big groups, as large-scale subjects. . . . [¶] Well, as you can see, I'm enchanted with your suggestion; this and a real Hardy *Selected Poems* are two things I've always thought particularly needed to be done. You feel about Kipling: if people would only learn what's *really* wrong with him, everything would be fine; he's a warped, self-indulgent, strangely developed writer but he's a real genius and at the same time just unimaginably talented.

RJ to An (PJ), June 1960: I've signed the letter of agreement and returned it. . . . I've got from the library most of Kipling and have reread most of what I got. I have a fairly good rough idea of what to do. In general, I'm pretty sure that the only collection of stories that should be reprinted just as they are are connected ones like *Stalky*, the *Jungle Books*, *Puck of Pook's Hill*, & *Rewards and Fairies*, and so forth; in all other cases the books benefit enormously by having the worst half or two-fifths of the stories left out. I can already think of six or seven plausible groupings of stories for separate books. (For instance, there's one whole volume of practical-joke stories distributed through the various volumes—the last two or three stories are awfully good, but most of them are something only a reader who *loves* Kipling will want to read. *I* love to read them but they're weird affairs, the wish-fantasies of a very strange man, and I don't blame most readers for not caring about them.) [¶] I believe one book that might help the others to be bought (by getting people to want to read more Kipling) would be a sort of *Introduction to Kipling* or *Taste of Kipling*: the very best of the stories and poems, attractively arranged and sympathetically and unconventionally introduced. Any *Selected Kipling's* . . . at present are, at best, Somerset Maugham affairs. . . . I'll go ahead with my reading and list-making and will try to have some definite, fairly detailed plan for you late in August. It's a pleasure to be reading all the books again; with all his faults and strangenesses, he was a truly extraordinary writer, one of the most extraordinary talents that ever existed.

RJ to An (PJ), September 1960: Let me give you a tentative list of suggestions about what we reprint in Anchor: *Kim*; the *Jungle Books* (in one volume, if spatially possible); *Puck of Pook's Hill* and *Rewards and*

Fairies (in one volume, if possible); *The Light That Failed*; a *Complete Stalky and Company*; a Selected Poems (with Eliot's introduction, if possible): six or eight or more volumes of short stories, carefully selected and grouped. Some groupings I've thought of are: *The English in India* (this title explains what the contents would be); *In the Vernacular* (this phrase is Kipling's, that recurs so much, is just right for his stories of natives, I think); a volume of his stories about men's work, jobs, occupations (his own title *The Day's Work* would be perfect for it, and he has a poem about work that would perfectly introduce it); a volume of his stories of Extreme Situations: nightmare, neurosis, torture, ghosts, overwork, plague, famine, etc.; *Stories About Soldiers*; a volume of his humorous or grotesque stories, to include the best of his practical joke stories; *Other Times, Other Places* (or some such title for those stories that primarily create a special age or place—for instance, *The Eye of Allah*, the stories about St. Paul, some of the English countryside stories, etc.); a volume with some title that would indicate it's about *Foster-Children* or Family Romances (in the Freudian sense)—this situation of the being separated from his own family and thrust into an alien world in which he has to find foster-family and the fundamental, final situations for Kipling; a volume called something like *Other Worlds*: his science-fiction stories, machinery stories, bee stories, animal stories, bureaucracy-of-Heaven-and-Hell stories. . . . [¶] One other volume I've thought of is a medium-sized book with such title as *A Taste of Kipling*—a sort of sampler or reader to give people Kipling's poems and stories at their absolute best; such a book might get readers interested in Kipling (in reading these other books) who otherwise wouldn't be.

RJ to An (PJ), January 1961: I believe that the selected Introduction to Kipling (I'll think of a good name)—16 or 18 of the best stories and 12 or 14 of the best poems—might be the best volume to bring out first; then one of the books of short stories. I'm not sure which; then *Kim*. It seems to me that we might (if it's not too expensive) put in his father's illustrations to Kim, those bas reliefs; they're good and charming and of great biographical interest, and would make this edition of *Kim* unique among current ones.

RJ to An (PJ), c. February-March 1961: I've finished the table of contents for *The Best of Kipling* or *Introduction to Kipling* or whatever we want to call it.

RJ to An (PJ), 25 March 1962: Let me talk first about the Kipling and then about the Russian stories. The fifteen stories that I listed, without any additions, ought to be good enough for *The English in England*. As for *The English in India*, it seems to me that I could make better volumes if I didn't divide the Indian stories into two volumes called *In the Vernacular* and *The English in India*, but combined the best of these stories into one volume to be called *In the Vernacular: The English in India*; I'll send it back airmail special delivery the next day.

RJ to An (AF), 10 April 1962: I'm glad you like the idea of combining *In the Vernacular* and *The English in India* into one book. I've been working on the selections for several days, and have decided that I could distribute the best of the stories from *Soldiers and Sailors* among the other books in the same way. This will make four stronger books of selected stories: the one called *The English in England*, one that I'll call *In the Vernacular: The English in India*, one called *Other Worlds* or *Different Worlds* or something of the sort, and one to include most of the stories about ghosts, nightmares, neurosis, revenge, practical jokes, etc. . . . Short of getting sick again or some personal disaster, I'll send you the Kipling introductions during the first two weeks in September.

RJ to An (PJ), June 1962: I've been working on *The English in England* introduction, and have it about done; I'll soon get to work on the introduction to the Indian stories. Doing these introductions is almost amusingly different from doing the Russian introduction.

RJ to An (AF), September 1962: Here are the introductions and the tables of contents for *The English in England* and *In the Vernacular: The English in India*. I made these introductions rather long, since I wanted the reader to know a good deal about Kipling's life before he wrote the Indian stories, and since his late stories are unfamiliar, generally, even to the person who's read a certain amount of Kipling. . . . I really enjoyed writing the introductions and hope they'll be a pleasure to you and later readers.

RJ to AJR, 29 June 1963: I sent your copies of the Kipling books to Westwood yesterday morning.

B35 *IN THE VERNACULAR: THE ENGLISH IN INDIA* (1963)

IN THE VERNACULAR | The English in India | *SHORT STORIES BY RUDYARD KIPLING* | *Selected and with an Introduction* | *by Randall Jarrell* | Anchor Books | Doubleday & Company, Inc. | Garden City, New York | 1963

Title Page: 7⅛ × 4⅟₁₆ in. (181 × 103 mm.).

Copyright Page: 'The Anchor Books edition | is the first publication of | *In the Vernacular: The English in India* | Anchor Books edition: 1963'.

Paper Binding: perfect bound in light grayish green and white wrapper, 7⅛ × 4⅟₁₆ in. (181 × 103 mm.), printed in red, black, and white.

Contains: RJ's "Introduction," pp. v-xix.

Publication: published as Anchor Original A363 in July 1963, at $1.25.

> *First Appearance:* RJ's "Introduction" KA, reduced version, as "In the Vernacular."

> *Note:* See above, **B34**, for a record of RJ's account of the evolution of the Anchor Kipling volumes.

B36 *POESIA AMERICANA DEL '900* (1963)

[Right] *Poesia | americana | del |* '900 | [left] *con testo a fronte | intro-duzioni | e note biobibliografiche a cura di Carlo Izzo |* [right] GUANDA

Copyright Page: 'prima edizione: decembre 1963'.

Binding and Dust Jacket: white pictorial cloth boards measure 8¹⁵⁄₁₆ × 5¹¹⁄₁₆ in. (226 × 146 mm.). Stamped in black; front: '[above illustration in black and red] POESIA AMERICANA | DEL '900 | a cura di CARLO IZZO | [below illustration] GUANDA'; spine: '[vert. from top to bottom] POESIA AMERICANA DEL '900'. All edges trimmed, unstained; white wove endpapers. Dust jacket not seen.

Contains: "The Islands" (C110), pp. 600, 602, with an Italian translation, "Le Isole," on pp. 601, 603.

Publication: published in December 1963 at 5,500 lira.

B37 *JOHN CROWE RANSOM* (1964)

John Crowe Ransom | Gentleman, Teacher, Poet, Editor | Founder of The Kenyon Review | A Tribute from the | Community of Letters | Edited by | D. David Long and Michael R. Burr | [fancy, with '*Kenyon*' imposed against the 'C' of 'Collegian'] The Kenyon [gothic] Collegian | A Supplement of Vol. LXXXX, No. 7 | Gambier, Ohio | 1964

Copyright Page: unprinted.

Paper Binding: one gathering stapled twice in white stiff paper wrapper lettered in gold on front.

Contains: brief statement by RJ (based in part on C207) on p. 30: "John Crowe Ransom is one of the most elegant war correspondents who ever existed of our world's old war between power and love . . . Generations of the future will be reading his poems page by page with Wyatt, Campion, Marvell and Mother Goose."

Publication: published 24 January 1964; 800 copies printed (not for sale). There were two additional printings, one in 1964 (2,000 copies), and the other in 1965 (2,000 copies).

B38 *15 POEMS FOR WILLIAM SHAKESPEARE* (1964)

[All within double-rule frame] 15 *Poems* | *for* William | *Shakespeare* | [rule, 88 mm.] | *edited by* Eric W. White | *with an introduction by* | Patrick Garland | John Lehmann & | William Plomer | [thin rule, 88 mm.] | 1964 : *Stratford-upon-Avon* | The Trustees & Guardians | of Shakespeare's Birthplace

Copyright Page: no statement of first edition.

Binding: Trade Issue: one gathering sewn in tan paper wrapper, 10 × 6 in. (255 × 153 mm.), printed on front in dark green and black: '[within frame of dark green ornamental rules] [in black, decorative type] 15 | POEMS | [remainder in roman] *for* William | *Shakespeare* | [below frame] Edmund Blunden   Dom Moraes | Charles Causley   Peter Porter | Roy Fuller   W. J. Snodgrass | Thom Gunn   Stephen Spender | Randall Jarrell   Derek Walcott | Thomas Kinsella   Vernon Watkins | Laurie Lee   David Wright | Hugh McDiarmid | [thick ornamental rule in dark green]'. *Limited Issue:* bound in paper vellum covered boards, 9¾ × 5⅞ in. (274 × 149 mm.), printed in gold on front: '[portrait of Shakespeare surrounded by a rule and then surrounded by] ∧ WILLIAM SHAKESPEARE ∧ STRATFORD UPON AVON | 1564 1964 | 15 POEMS | *for* William Shakespeare'. All edges trimmed, unstained; white wove endpapers. No dust jacket.

Contains: "Gleaning," p. 17.

Publication: published in June 1964 at 3s. 6d. (trade issue), or 10s. 6d. (limited issue); 1,000 copies in wrappers, 100 copies in paper vellum covered boards.

> *First Appearance:* "Gleaning" CP. Reprinted in *Virginia Quarterly Review*, 41 (Spring 1965), 234–35, and in *Poems from the* Virginia Quarterly Review, *1925–1967*, ed. Charlotte Kohler (Charlottesville, Va.: Univ. Press of Virginia, 1969), p. 159.

> *Note:* Page 9 contains a corrigendum slip attached below the poem.

B39 *NATIONAL POETRY FESTIVAL* (1964)

National | Poetry | Festival | HELD IN THE LIBRARY OF CON-GRESS | OCTOBER 22–24, 1962 | *PROCEEDINGS* | [seal of the Library of Congress] | GENERAL REFERENCE AND BIBLIOGRA-PHY DIVISION | REFERENCE DEPARTMENT | WASHINGTON : 1964

Copyright Page: '[within a single-rule frame] L. C. card 64–60048'.

Paper Binding: black and white paper wrapper, 9⅛ × 5¹¹⁄₁₆ in. (231 × 147 mm.), printed in black and white.

Contains: first appearance of "Fifty Years of American Poetry," pp. 113–38; reprints, with RJ's introductory comments: "The Blind Man's Song," pp. 309–10, "Losses," pp. 310–11, "Eighth Air Force," p. 311, "Cinderella," pp. 312–13, and "The Woman at the Washington Zoo," pp. 313–14.

Publication: published in July 1964 at $1.50.

> *First Appearance:* "Fifty Years of American Poetry" TBC. Polish translation by Halina Carroll, *Tematy* (Perspectives in Culture), 3, no. 9 (1964), pp. 7–36. Excerpts published in *Time*, 80 (9 Nov. 1962), 100, 102.
>
> Note: The proceedings of the National Poetry Festival were taped by the Library of Congress. "Fifty Years of American Poetry" is on T 3868–3, and his reading is on T 3870–2 and 3; see below, G12.

B40 *THE MAN WHO LOVED CHILDREN* (1965)

Christina Stead / The | Man Who Loved Children | Introduction by Randall Jarrell | Holt, Rinehart and Winston | New York Chicago   San Francisco

Copyright Page: 'First Edition'.

Binding and Dust Jacket: tannish white cloth boards measure 8⁷⁄₁₆ × 5¹¹⁄₁₆ in. (214 × 145 mm.). Stamped in brown and bright blue; front: contains an abstract design in brown; spine: '[vert., in two lines] [top, in bright blue] Christina Stead [in brown] The [bottom line] Man Who Loved Children [three lines at base, in bright blue] [top] HOLT [middle] RINEHART [bottom] WINSTON'. All edges trimmed, top edges stained brown; yellowish white wove endpapers. White dust jacket contains an illustration of Sam Pollit and his children in brown and light blue and is lettered in light blue, reddish purple, and brown.

Contains: RJ's introduction, "An Unread Book," on pp. v–xli.

Publication: published in April 1965 at $5.95. Reprinted in paperback as Avon Library N59, in March 1966, at 95¢; RJ's "An Unread Book" appears as the "Afterword," on pp. 492–504.

> *First Appearance:* "An Unread Book" TBC. Excerpt, titled "The Man Who Loved Children," published in The *Atlantic*, 215 (March 1965), 166–71.
>
> *Note:* Christina Stead's *The Man Who Loved Children* was first published in 1940 by Simon and Schuster.
>
> *RJ to MLJ, October 1943:* I started on the Christina Stead last night and haven't read much; gee, it's good. Better than the first time, even. Read it again when I sent it home.
>
> *RJ to MLJ, 2 November 1943: The Man Who Loved Children* really is one of the best novels I've ever read. It's much better on second reading—you see that some of the things you thought extreme aren't really, and you don't have the feeling of dread and complete personal involvement that actually made me rush over some parts the first time.
>
> *RJ to SBQ, c. Spring 1951:* And, since I'm recommending books, let me tell you about a wonderful book that nobody else knows about (except a hundred people I've got to read it), *The Man Who Loved Children*, by Christina Stead; it really is one of the best novels in English, I think.
>
> *RJ to MDC, October 1964:* I just finished the long (45 pages long) piece about *The Man Who Loved Children*.
>
> *RJ to MDC, October 1964:* I've cut my Stead piece in two (literally—from 46 pages to 24) to go in the *New York Review*, possibly. I've been so good I've worked hard on a lot of things are have made plans for more.

B41 *THE DISTINCTIVE VOICE* (1966)

[In script] *the distinctive voice* | [remainder in roman] TWENTIETH CENTURY AMERICAN POETRY | WILLIAM J. MARTZ · RIPON COLLEGE | [rule, 92 mm.] | SCOTT, FORESMAN AND COMPANY

Copyright Page: 'Copyright © 1966 by Scott, Foresman and Company, Glenview, Illinois, 60025'.

Paper Binding: brownish gold printed pictorial wrapper, 9 × 6 in. (228 × 153 mm.), lettering reversed out in white, against a reproduction of a photograph of a rural scene showing a tree and piece of farm equipment.

Contains: "The Player Piano" (C360), pp. 189–90.

Publication: published in 1966 at $3.95.

B42   *HOW TO EAT A POEM* (1967)

[Two pages, left, below illustration in gray and yellow] *Illustrated by Peggy Wilson / Pantheon Books* [right, and right of illustration] *How to Eat a Poem | & Other Morsels* | FOOD POEMS FOR CHILDREN | [rule, 86 mm.] | Selected by Rose H. Agree

Copyright Page: '©, 1967, by Rose Agree.'

Binding: pictorial printed tan boards measure 9¹⁄₁₆ × 6⅝ in. (229 × 168 mm.). Front contains illustration of table setting in pink, light orange, and black, '[upper left corner, in black, within a circle] T T | [all within a frame of black single rules, 80 × 132 mm., the bottom of which is broken by a glass in the table setting] [in black] *How to Eat a Poem* | [in orange, the height of the next two lines] & [in black] *Other Morsels* | FOOD POEMS FOR CHILDREN | [rule, 95 mm.] | Selected by Rose H. Agree'; spine: '[vert., in black] HOW TO EAT A POEM AND OTHER MORSELS · AGREE'. All edges trimmed, unstained; white wove endpapers.

Contains: "My aunt kept turnips in a flock—", p. 21.

Publication: published in April 1967 at $3.50.

> *First Appearance:* "My aunt kept turnips in a flock—" CP. Reprinted in *What a Wonderful Bird the Frog Are*, ed. Myra Cohn Livingston (New York: Harcourt, Brace, Jovanovich, 1973).

B43   *RANDALL JARRELL 1914–1965* (1967)

Randall Jarrell | [rule, 85 mm.] | 1914–1965 | EDITED BY | Robert Lowell, Peter Taylor, | & Robert Penn Warren | [publisher's device] | *Farrar, Straus & Giroux* | NEW YORK

Copyright Page: 'First printing, 1967'.

Binding and Dust Jacket: brown cloth boards measure 8¼ × 5⁹⁄₁₆ in. (210 × 142 mm.). Front blindstamped: '*Randall Jarrell* | [swelled rule, 92 mm.] | 1914–1965'; spine stamped in gold: '[horiz.] *Randall*

| *Jarrell* | [rule, 28 mm.] | 1914– | 1965 | [rule, 28 mm.] | LOWELL, | TAYLOR, | & | WARREN | [rule, 28 mm.] | [publisher's device] | *Farrar, | Straus & | Giroux'*. All edges trimmed, top edge stained pale yellow; yellow wove, unwatermarked endpapers. Black and orange dust jacket printed in black, white, and orange.

Contains: "A Man Meets a Woman in the Street" (C363), pp. 299–302.

Publication: published 29 August 1967 at $6.50; 6,500 copies printed. First paperback edition by photo-offset published 15 April 1968; 3,000 copies.

B44 *MODERN POETRY: ESSAYS IN CRITICISM* (1968)

MODERN POETRY | Essays in Criticism | EDITED BY | JOHN HOLLANDER | OXFORD UNIVERSITY PRESS | London Oxford New York

Copyright Page: 'First published by Oxford University Press, New York, 1968'.

Paper Binding: light olive brown wrapper, $7^{15}/_{16} \times 5^{5}/_{16}$ in. (202 × 135 mm.), printed in purple and white.

Contains: "Texts from Housman" (C64), pp. 140–49.

Publication: published in 1968 as Oxford University Press paperback GB 227, at $2.95.

C

Contributions to Periodicals

C1 "An Interview with Charles Hudson" (in "Our Monthly Interview" column). *Hume-Fogg Echo* (Hume-Fogg High School, Nashville, Tenn., monthly student magazine), 28 (Feb. 1929), 22–23. Facetious "interview" with Hume-Fogg senior Charles Hudson, editor-in-chief of the *Echo*. Signed "Randall Jarrell."

> *Note:* RJ was a student at Hume-Fogg High School from 1928–31. This interview, written during his sophomore year, appears to be RJ's debut in print. The "Noteworthy Contributions" column of the December 1928 *Echo*, p. 28, mentions "A Christmas Dialogue" by RJ, but it apparently was not published.
>
> The headnote that precedes this interview, possibly written by RJ as well, reads: "This is a new feature which we hope to continue permanently and which we hope you will like. In it we propose to obtain for our readers interviews with the famous men of the past, present, and future. We will spare no expense to satisfy Echo readers, and the conductor of the department [RJ] has already set off on an extensive tour. While on his journey he will procure for the Echo exclusive interviews with famous men. Everyone should at once renew their subscriptions so that they may read about the haps and mishaps of a reporter's life."

C2 "An Interview with Mark Twain" (in "Our Monthly Interview" column). *Hume-Fogg Echo*, 28 (March 1929), 16–19. Signed "Randall Jarrell."

C3 "My Family Tree" by Jack Derryberry (in "Our Monthly Interview" column). *Hume-Fogg Echo*, 28 (April 1929), 25–27. Signed "Randall Jarrell."

C4 "How to Approach a Teacher When Unprepared for a Lesson" (in "Our Monthly Interview" column). *Hume-Fogg Echo*, 28 (May 1929), 22–24. Humorous essay; unsigned.

> *Note:* According to this issue of the *Echo*, RJ had submitted an untitled one-act play to the drama club, but his and two others were passed over for performance the next fall for "Jack Derryberry's 'The Intellectual Fool'" (see above, C3).

C5 "The Thanksgiving Miracle." *Hume-Fogg Echo*, 29 (Nov. 1929), 8–9. Story.

> *Note:* RJ served as a literary editor of the *Echo* during his junior year.

C6 "A Doll's House." *Hume-Fogg Echo*, 29 (Dec. 1929), 11–12. Story.

C7 "Liliom" (in "Dramatics" column). *Hume-Fogg Echo*, 29 (Dec. 1929), 17–18, 28. Review of the Nashville Little Theatre production of Franz Molnar's *Liliom*. Signed "Randall Jarrell."

C8 "Rollo and the Spirit of Valentine." *Hume-Fogg Echo*, 29 (Feb. 1930), 7–10. Story.

C9 "Shakespeare versus Ibsen" (in "Dramatics" column). *Hume-Fogg Echo*, 29 (March 1930), 16–20. Review of the Sir Ben Greet Players' Nashville productions of *Hamlet* and *Twelfth Night* and the Little Theatre's production of Ibsen's *The Wild Duck*.

C10 "Candida." *Hume-Fogg Echo*, 29 (April 1930), 23–27, 30. Unsigned review of the Nashville Little Theatre's production of George Bernard Shaw's *Candida*.

> *Note:* Aside from the style of this review, which identifies it (although unsigned) clearly as RJ's, there are a number of references to his earlier attendance at and criticism of the Little Theatre's production of *Liliom* (see **C7**).

C11 "Senior Prophecy (Expurgated Edition)." *The 1931 Echo* (Hume-Fogg High School yearbook), pp. 46–51. Unsigned.

> *Note:* Although the Class of 1931 prophecy is unsigned, internal evidence suggests that it was written by RJ. RJ's authorship of the prophecy is further corroborated by Robert McGaw, of Nashville, class president and member of the *Echo* staff. See Charles Adams, "Excursion to Nashville," *Alumni News* (Univ. of North Carolina at Greensboro), 57 (Spring 1969), 23–25 (expanded version, "A Bibliographical Excursion with Some Biographical Footnotes on Randall Jarrell," published in *Bulletin of Bibliography*, 28 [July–Sept. 1971], 79–81).
>
> RJ was staff correspondent for the *Hume-Fogg Echo* during his senior year, but he submitted no signed contributions to the magazine.

C12 Untitled review of José Iturbi's 1932 Nashville, Tenn., piano recital. *Hume-Fogg Echo*, 31 (May 1932), 29.

C13 "Exchanges" (column). *Vanderbilt Masquerader* (Vanderbilt Univ., Nashville, Tenn., student humor magazine), 9 (Oct. 1932), 27. Contained are two quips signed "Rammer Jammer" which probably were contributed by RJ.

> *Note:* There is no longer a complete file of the *Vanderbilt Masquerader* available for examination at the Vanderbilt University Libraries. Charles Adams apparently had access to a complete file in the late 1960s when he made his "bibliographical excursion" to Nashville, but he located no other signed contributions than those listed below; he made no postulations as to unsigned material. However, it is likely that the listings herein may be incomplete for the period of RJ's undergraduate years, 1931–35.

C14 "Exchanges" (column). *Vanderbilt Masquerader*, 9 (Feb. 1933), 4. Quip signed "Rammer Jammer," which was probably contributed by RJ.

C15 "The Rover Boys at Vanderbilt" (Part I). *Vanderbilt Masquerader*, 10 (Oct. 1933), 10–11. Story; first of two parts.

> *Note:* Both pages of this story contain an illustration which may have been drawn by RJ, a member of the magazine's art board. He drew the cover portrait of Sylvia Frank published in the February 1934 issue of the *Masquerader*.

C16 "The Big Game" (part II of "The Rover Boys at Vanderbilt"). *Vanderbilt Masquerader*, 10 (Nov. 1933), 20–21. See C15.

> *Note:* Page 20 contains a drawing illustrating this story which may have been prepared by RJ.

C17 "Fear." *American Review*, 3 (May 1934), 228–29 ("I" of "Five Poems" by RJ). BFS, CP.

> 1–4 In their thin eyes the sheeting of your name, | The blood's rippling change casts in the form | Of empty wakings and the vacant streets | The lamentable processions of their hell,—] *stanza omitted* BFS⁺*Hereafter, for convenience, the first line of the second stanza will be counted as line 1.*
> 1 that] their BFS⁺
> 6 stage,] ~ˏ BFS⁺

11 That girl told in indifference and courtesy.] She herself tells
carelessly, BFS⁺

12 that] this BFS⁺

16 breast] ∼. BFS⁺

19–20 The dead world outside, its mind | Softened, pitying, confused
with snow—] Whisper: "Child, what you and your kind | Have
accomplished is nothing. But like us, absolute." BFS⁺

21–24 *not in original version*] Yet doubt ends the metaphysician,
and darkness | Prepares in its labyrinth the iron kiss | That persuaded
the heroes: does love lie | Indeed, for the hunter, in that final
pit? BFS⁺

Note: This poem and the four that follow mark Jarrell's professional
debut in print. He had just completed his junior year at Vanderbilt
when these poems were published. Robert Penn Warren, who taught
the advanced sophomore English course at Vanderbilt, which Jarrell, as
a freshman, attended in September 1931, recalled that already "it was
clear that he was a real poet." "In fact," Warren has written, "some of
his best poems were written during his period as an undergraduate"
(ltr., Robert Penn Warren, 1 Sept. 1981).

Allen Tate and Warren guest-coedited the special poetry supplement
in which Jarrell's five poems appear in this issue of the *American Review*.

C18 "O weary mariners, here shaded, fed." *American Review*, 3
(May 1934), 229 ("II" of "Five Poems"). CP.

C19 "The man with the axe stands profound and termless." *American Review*, 3 (May 1934), 229–30 ("III" of "Five Poems"). CP.

C20 "Above the waters in their toil." *American Review*, 3 (May
1934), 230 ("IV" of "Five Poems"). CP.

C21 "The cow wandering in the bare field." *American Review*, 3
(May 1934), 230–31 ("V" of "Five Poems"). BFS, CP.

14 snow,] ∼— BFS⁺

15 snow,] ∼— BFS⁺

18 them then once more from memory] ∼, ∼, from the old
darkness BFS⁺

20 charm,] ∼ˏ BFS⁺

24 blessedness,] ∼: BFS⁺

Reprinted in *Modern Verse in English, 1900–1950*, ed. David Cecil and
Allen Tate (New York: Macmillan, 1958), pp. 583–84; and *Alumni*

News (Univ. of N.C. at Greensboro), special Randall Jarrell issue, 54 (Spring 1966), 23.

Note: Robert Penn Warren recollected that this poem was written during Jarrell's sophomore year at Vanderbilt (1932–33). *Alumni News,* 54 (Spring 1966), 23.

RJ to AT, January 1941: I left out [of RFLP] *The Cow Wandering* because for a long time I've been trying to change part that I think bad. I don't mean to give the impression that I think I can write lots better poetry now; I can't write as exciting language, even, but I can construct lots better and say what I mean more clearly; and say more.

C22 "Editorial." *Vanderbilt Masquerader,* 11 (Oct. 1934), 10. Unsigned editorial in which RJ comments on school spirit.

> *Note:* RJ was editor-in-chief of the *Masquerader* for the school year 1934–35, vol. 11, nos. 1–6.

C23 "Editorials." *Vanderbilt Masquerader,* 11 (Nov. 1934), 10–11. Unsigned editorial commentary in which RJ disagrees with the opinion of some faculty members that the *Masquerader* should be a "serious literary magazine."

C24 "Editorials." *Vanderbilt Masquerader,* 11 (Dec. 1934), 8. RJ again humorously comments on the purpose of the *Masquerader.*

C25 "Zeno." *New Republic,* 81 (26 Dec. 1934), 184–85. CP.

C26 "Poem" (later titled "Jack"). *Westminster Magazine,* 23 (Jan.–March 1935), 254–55. BFS, CP.
    Poem] Jack BFS+
  3 bean-stalk] beanstalk BFS+
  5 split] spilt BFS+
  8 puzzle, that] ~ˌ~, BFS+
  9 barley's] rotting BFS+
 12 As worn figures in a dream] Shameless as someone else's dream BFS+
 14 hair,] ~ . . . BFS+
 16 aghast.] ~, BFS+
 18 wife,] ~ˌ BFS+
 19 Came] Come BFS+
 20 never could comprehend;] could never~, BFS+

Reprinted as "Jack" in *Hero's Way: Contemporary Poems in the Mythic Tradition*, ed. John A. Allen (Englewood Cliffs, N.J.: Prentice-Hall, 1971), pp. 41–42.

C27 "Editorials." *Vanderbilt Masquerader*, 11 (Feb. 1935), 10. RJ comments briefly on this special "co-ed" issue guest-edited by Elizabeth Pitway.

C28 "Editorials." *Vanderbilt Masquerader*, 11 (April 1935), 10. RJ comments on this special "Exchange Number," which he describes as a "sensational agglomeration of side-splitting satire."

C29 "Editorials." *Vanderbilt Masquerader*, 11 (May 1935), 11. RJ writes: "On this happy occasion the editor feels very much like Eurydice; but he is not going to make the mistake of turning his head. So, no editorial."

C30 "And did she dwell in innocence and joy." *Southern Review*, 1 (July 1935), 84–85. CP.

> *RJ to SR (RPW), May 1935:* Here are the poems. I'd have sent them before now except they weren't fixed before.... They haven't any titles—just call any A POEM like that. The more you use the better— I'll have plenty for the group.

C31 "Looking back in my mind I can see" (later titled "The Elementary Scene"). *Southern Review*, 1 (July 1935), 85–86. WWZ, CP.

> *Untitled* The Elementary Scene WWZ⁺
>
> 9 Even now, the air seems to shake] The dead land waking sadly to my life— WWZ⁺
>
> 10 With that violence, that senseless despair.] Stir, and curl deeper in the eyes of time. WWZ⁺
>
> 13–21 Still . . . nails.] *completely rewritten* WWZ⁺
>
> Reprinted as "The Elementary Scene" in *Chief Modern Poets of Britain and America*, ed. Gerald DeWitt Sanders et al., 5th ed. (New York: Macmillan, 1970); *Sounds and Silences: Poetry for Now*, ed. Richard Peck (New York: Dell, 1970); *Silences*, ed. Richard Peck (New York: Delacorte, 1970), p. 161; *The Poem: An Anthology*, 2d ed., ed. Stanley B. Greenfield and A. Kingsley Weatherhead (New York: Appleton-Century-Crofts, 1972), pp. 468–69. *Exploring Poetry*, ed. M. L. Rosenthal and A. J. M. Smith, 2d ed. (New York: Macmillan, 1973).

C32 "Ten Books." *Southern Review*, 1 (Autumn 1935), 397–410. Book review of Ellen Glasgow, *Vein of Iron*; Erskine Caldwell, *Kneel to the Rising Sun*; Stark Young, *Feliciana*; James Hanley, *The Furys*; Jule Brousseau, *A Preface to Maturity*; Gale Wilhelm, *We Too Are Drifting*; Tess Slinger, *Time: The Present*; Willa Cather, *Lucy Gayheart*; Rachel Field, *Time Out of Mind*; Raymond Holden, *Chance Has a Whip*. KA.

> *RJ to SR (CB), August 1935:* I'll be delighted to do the fiction review; if you'll send me the list of novels—and the novels for that matter—I'll start on it immediately—

> *RJ to SR (RPW and CB), September 1935:* I'm sorry I couldn't finish sooner. You can call the review "Twelve Books" [*sic*], if you need a name. . . . Just run in all the reviews together when you print them— that is, don't have any Roman numerals or space but make it one continuous mass of print. . . . *I generally tempered justice with mercy.*

> *RJ to SR (RPW), October 1935:* Was the review all right? If I'd had a few decent books I could have been more constructive, but less entertaining. You know, I'm really very old-fashioned when it comes to reviews, the majority of my tendencies are not at all [T. S.] Eliot-ish and didactic. (Can you recite a review from memory when you finish it? I was astonished to find that I could.)

C33 "A man sick with whirling" (later titled "1789–1939"). *Southern Review*, 2 (Autumn 1936), 373. RFLP, BFS, CP.

Untitled] 1789–1939 RFLP⁺
16 blood—] ~, RFLP⁺

> *RJ to SR (RPW and CB), 27 July 1939:* Here are the poems I am entering for your [*Southern Review*] poetry prize . . . and this is the signed statement entering them in the contest.

> *RJ to SR (AE), early September 1936:* Here are the proofs; there were no errors. I've made one change in the wording. If you will, print A POEM over each of the untitled poems—I've tried to get names, but I can't.

> *RJ to SR (AE), mid-September 1936:* I wish you'd do something for me; that is break up the poems from page to page as little as possible— don't print half of one poem on the top of a page, half of another on the bottom, except when you can't possibly help it. If you want to change the order of the poems to avoid this, that's quite all right with me. If you won't leave an enormous space under my name, you can get the poem that begins "A man sick with whirling" on the first page. Then you could put the Confederate Soldiers poem beginning at the top of the next page, and you could fill out the third page with one of the

two shortest poems—"Old Poem" if 14 lines is too much; "The Indian" if ten lines would be better. Put "Kiriloff" [*sic*] on the fourth page, "An Old Song" on the fifth. . . . Then, on six put the poem that begins "Fat, aging, the child clinging to her hand"—it will continue over to seven; and [you] can fill out with the short poem you haven't already used.

C34 "A Description of Some Confederate Soldiers." *Southern Review*, 2 (Autumn 1936), 374–75. RFLP, BFS, CP.

    11   wax-works]   waxworks   RFLP⁺
    27   arrogance . . .]   ~. . . .   BFS⁺

RJ to AT, January 1941: You know, you said the *Description of Some Confederate Soldiers* is quite as good as *A Little Poem.* Boy, I think so too; better, in lots of ways. But it . . . was absolutely the best poem I could write then (1936).

C35 "The Indian." *Southern Review*, 2 (Autumn 1936), 375. CP.

C36 "A Poem" ("Fat, aging, the child clinging to her hand"). *Southern Review*, 2 (Autumn 1936), 376–77. BFS, CP.

    A Poem]   Fat, Aging, the Child Clinging to Her Hand . . .   BFS⁺
    5   smile,]   ~   BFS₊
    9   up]   ~:   BFS⁺
    12   face . . .]   ~ . . . .   BFS⁺

C37 "Old Poems." *Southern Review*, 2 (Autumn 1936), 377. CP.

C38 "Kirilov on a Skyscraper." *Southern Review*, 2 (Autumn 1936), 378. BFS, CP.

C39 "An Old Song." *Southern Review*, 2 (Autumn 1936), 379. CP.

C40 "Because of me, because of you." *Transition*, 26 (Winter 1937), 15 ("I" of "Two Poems"). RFLP, BFS, CP.

    3   distention,]   ~ₐ   RFLP   ~,   BFS⁺
    13   actuaries' end—]   actuaries~;   RFLP   ~'~   BFS⁺
    Reprinted in *Transition Workshop*, ed. Eugene Jolas (New York: Vanguard, 1949), pp. 235–36.

RJ to SR (RPW), March 1937: I gave "Enormous Love" and the other ["Because of me, because of you"] to *transition* just by accident; [Eugene] Jolas wrote and asked Mr. Ransom to send him something, and Mr. Ransom asked me to give him something to send instead . . . and Jolas liked them.

C41 "Enormous love, it's no good asking." *Transition*, 26 (Winter 1937), 15–16 ("II" of "Two Poems"). CP.

C42 "The Automaton," *Southern Review*, 3 (Autumn 1937), 392–93. RFLP, BFS, CP.

RJ to SR (RPW), March 1937: I'll send on to *Poetry* the [poems] you don't like so well—"Automaton: Mechanical Man" and the one that starts "Where the oil . . ." [apparently unpublished]. The reason is a real simple silly one: I want the money. . . . On second thought, I won't send any to *Poetry* now; I'll send you all and take your pick from the whole bunch. . . . I'll send the ones you don't want to *Poetry*.

RJ to SR (RPW), late March 1937: You may be right about the "sick wind" in "The Automaton"; it's a phrase I just glide over when I'm reading it and hardly notice it at all, for better or worse. As for "discoloured by the gibbous moon"—*gibbous* is a perfectly neutral, scientific, colorless term to me; a descriptive name for the shapeless sort of moon between half- and full; so at least to me, it would be at the other extreme from the *sick*. I'll change the *sick* for a more colorless word ["faint;"], and get my readers to glide over that one (gibbous) as I do over *sick*.

RJ to SR (CB and AE), 14 July 1937: Red [Warren] wrote me and told me when he was here [Nashville] that I'd get paid for my Fall poems on July 1; since I haven't heard from you, I'm writing. . . . Will you send me the money if the [Louisiana State] University comes through with it, or a gentle note to soothe my grief, if it didn't?

C43 "A Poem" ("When Achilles fought and fell"). *Southern Review*, 3 (Autumn 1937), 393. CP.

C44 "A Poem" ("Love, in its separate being . . ."). *Southern Review*, 3 (Autumn 1937), 394–95. RFLP, BFS, CP.

A Poem] Love, in Its Separate Being . . . RFLP+
10 gray] grey RFLP+
18 fields] shires RFLP+

RJ to SR (RPW), October 1937: I'm extremely sorry about these poems—I hadn't managed to finish them and assumed you just wouldn't use them. Here is "Love in its separate being" finished, and one to use in the place of the other if you need an extra one ["The Hanged Man on the Gallows"].

C45 "A Poem" ("The hanged man on the gallows"). *Southern Review*, 3 (Autumn 1937), 395. BFS, CP.

A POEM] The Hanged Man on the Gallows . . . BFS⁺
7 doubted—] ~: BFS⁺

C46 "A Poem" ("O the dummies in the windows"; later titled "Dummies"). *Southern Review*, 3 (Autumn 1937), 396. BFS, CP.

A POEM] Dummies BFS⁺
stanza break between lines 11–12] no stanza break BFS⁺
Reprinted in *Hero's Way: Contemporary Poems in the Mythic Tradition*, ed. Allen (1971), p. 184.

C47 "A Poem" ("Falling in love is never as simple"). *Southern Review*, 3 (Autumn 1937), 396–98. CP.

A POEM] *untitled* CP

C48 "A Dialogue between the Soul and Body." *Southern Review*, 3 (Autumn 1937), 398–99. CP.

RJ to SR (RPW), March 1937: I almost didn't send "Dialogue Between Soul and Body" (though I'm personally fond of it), so I was pleased at your liking it so well.

RJ to SR (AE), October 1937: If you can print "Soul and Body" the way I show [in the proofs] and put "A Poem" over the nameless ones instead of "Poem," I'll be grateful.

C49 "The Machine Gun," *Southern Review*, 3 (Autumn 1937), 399. RFLP, BFS, CP.

THE MACHINE GUN] *THE MACHINE-GUN* RFLP⁺
4 smoldered] smouldered BFS⁺
Reprinted in *The United States in Literature*, ed. James E. Miller, Jr., et al. (Evanston, Ill.: Scott, Foresman, 1973), p. M244.

RJ to SR (RPW), March 1937: You say that you like "The Machine Gun," and "Achilles" and "Orpheus" best; well suppose I save them for you, and send you to go with them six or seven more I've written in the last two or three months, and have finished or almost finished. Some of them are pretty much in the tone of the ones you like.

C50 "Housman." *Pursuit* (Vanderbilt Univ. student literary magazine), 1 (Late Winter [1938]), 19. The first of "two parodies" by Jarrell.

C51 "Auden's Popular Song Style." *Pursuit*, 1 (Late Winter [1938]), 19. The second of "two parodies" by Jarrell.

C52 "The Winter's Tale" ("The storm rehearses through the bewildered fields"). *Kenyon Review*, 1 (Winter 1939), 57–59. RFLP, BFS, CP.

> 22   excess—]   ~, RFLP+
> 61   centrcs]   centers BFS+
> 68   galaxies—]   ~, RFLP+
> Reprinted in *The Achievement of Randall Jarrell*, ed. Frederick J. Hoffman (Glenview, Ill.: Scott, Foresman, 1970), pp. 29–31.

C53 "On the Railway Platform." *Southern Review*, 4 (Winter 1939), 574–75. RFLP, BFS, CP.

> 12   traveler]   traveller BFS+
> Reprinted in Joseph Warren Beach, *Obsessive Images: Symbolism in the Poetry of the 1930's and 1940's*, ed. William Van O'Connor (Minneapolis: University of Minnesota Press, 1960), pp. 178–79.

> *RJ to AB, November 1942:* What you say about *On the Railway Platform* and about what it meant about us and Kenyon [College], is all so; and though I guess nobody else would know, *A Story* [C37] is autobiography."

C54 "A Poem" ("Over the florid capitals . . ."). *Southern Review*, 4 (Winter 1939), 575. BFS, CP.

> A POEM]   Over the Florid Capitals . . . BFS; *untitled* CP
> 1   capitols]   capitals BFS+
> 11   And nothingness and love]   And love and nothingness BFS+

RJ to SR (RPW), October 1938: . . . call the short one "Night" ["Over the florid capitals"]; that's the only "descriptive" title I could think of. When are you printing them, fall or winter?

C55 "A Poem" (later titled "A Picture in the Paper"). *Southern Review*, 4 (Winter 1939), 576–77. BFS, CP.

> A POEM] A Picture in the Paper BFS⁺
> *Variants appear in the headnote to this poem.*
> *headnote all in italics]* headnote all in roman BFS⁺
> got] had BFS⁺
> papers] newspaper BFS⁺
> *The matches were played in a small brightly lighted]* The tournament
>   was held in a brightly lighted gymnasium BFS⁺
> Reprinted as "A Poem" in *New Poems, 1942: An Anthology of British
> and American Verse*, ed. Oscar Williams (Mount Vernon, N.Y.: Peter
> Pauper Press, 1942), pp. 116–17.

C56 "A Poem" ("Up in the sky the star is waiting"). *Southern Review*, 4 (Winter 1939), 577. BFS, CP.

> A POEM] Up in the Sky . . . BFS; *untitled* CP.

C57 "A Poem" ("When you and I were all"). *Southern Review*, 4 (Winter 1939), 578–79. RFLP, BFS, CP.

> A POEM] *WHEN YOU AND I WERE ALL . . .* RFLP, BFS;
>   *untitled* CP
> 38 mend,] ~ᶺ RFLP⁺
> 50 untendered; we] ~. We RFLP⁺

RJ to SR (RPW), October 1938: Here are some poems to pick the rest of my bunch from. I couldn't manage any changes for the long one you're printing ["When you and I were all"].

RJ to SR (RPW), March 1939: Thanks for your nice letter about the poems, especially for the suggestions. I'll try to get a title; the rhythm of "When you and I were all" was purposely broken and stammering in parts, but probably is wrong, and I'll do what I can with it, if I can, that is; *the drumsticks to an orphan's jaw* I thought good, since spryly is just the way they would creak to the hungry orphan gobbling them, and it shows strongly the paradoxical naturalness and innocence the bad world had for the bad *you and I*.

C58 "1938: The Spring Dances." *Southern Review*, 4 (Winter 1939), 580. BFS, CP.

C59 "The Morality of Mr. Winters." *Kenyon Review*, 1 (Spring 1939), 211–15. Book review of Yvor Winters, *Maule's Curse*. KA.

C60 "The Poet at Home." *Hika* (Kenyon College, Gambier, Ohio, student literary magazine), 6 (June 1939), 22. Humorous article based on a self-interview; unsigned.

> *Note:* This article and the two poems that follow, C61 and C62, were written as spoofs of Robert Frost, who had visited the Kenyon campus during the 1938–39 school year.

C61 "The Ballad of the Butcher." *Hika*, 6 (June 1939), 23. See C60.

C62 "Rachel." *Hika*, 6 (June 1939), 23. See C60.

C63 "A Story." *Partisan Review*, 6 (Summer 1939), 19–20. RFLP, BFS, SP55, SP2, CP.

> 1 empty] ~. RFLP[+]
> 7 thought—] ~: SP55[+]
> 23 empty,"] empty SP55[+]
> 31 I] I SP55[+]
> 32 don't."] ~, RFLP[+]
> 36 my] *my* SP55[+]
> Reprinted in *Alumni News* (Univ. of N.C. at Greensboro), 54 (Spring 1966), 42–43.

> *RJ to SR (CB), September 1939:* It's very funny, *The Partisan Review* takes the poems you and Red [Robert Penn Warren] don't wan't; for instance, "A Story," "Nursery Rhyme," and "The Refugees." They say differences of opinion make horse races; well, they'd make my future except that *Partisan Review* pays so little I have an impulse to give them the poems, and maintain my amateur standing.

> *RJ to AB, November 1942:* I guess nobody else but you would know *A Story* is autobiography. I wrote it with "I" meaning "we" for a couple of stanzas before I thought out the story, and then the emotion was certainly mine.

C64 "Texts from Housman." *Kenyon Review*, 1 (Summer 1939), 260–71. KA.

> Reprinted in *Modern Poetry: Essays in Criticism*, ed. John Hollander (London and New York: Oxford Univ. Press, 1968), pp. 140–49.

> *RJ to AT, March 1939:* I've been finishing my thesis ["Implicit Generalization in Housman"] and magazine article ["Texts from Housman"], and, what with classes and coaching tennis every afternoon and writing and typing at night, I've been nuts.

C65 "The Ways and the Peoples." *Poetry*, 54 (July 1939), 187. RFLP, BFS, CP.

> Reprinted in *Poetry*, 121 (Oct. 1972), 15 (60th Anniversary Issue).

> *RJ to AT, March 1939:* I've had a letter to [Delmore] Schwartz written for three weeks, but *Poetry* has had the five or six best poems, I have (with characteristic perspicuity they wanted only the worst), the ones I wanted to send to Schwartz, and I just got them back. I sent them to him yesterday.

C66 "From That Island." *Kenyon Review*, 1 (Autumn 1939), 468–71. Book review of Louis MacNeice, *Modern Poetry: A Personal Appraisal*. KA.

C67 "A Nursery Rhyme." *Partisan Review*, 7 (Jan.–Feb. 1940), 19–20. CP.

> Reprinted in *The Partisan Reader: Ten Years of the* Partisan Review, *1934–44: An Anthology*, ed. William Phillips and Philip Rahv (New York: Dial, 1946), pp. 239–40.

C68 "The Refugees." *Partisan Review*, 7 (Jan.–Feb. 1940), 20–21. RFLP, BFS, CP.

> 5 possessed] ~, RFLP⁺
> 10 through] into RFLP⁺
> Reprinted in *New York Times Book Review*, 1 Nov. 1942, p. 8; *Modern American Poetry* (combined mid-century edition), ed. Louis Untermeyer (New York: Harcourt Brace, 1950), pp. 685–86, and the enlarged edition (1962), pp. 651–52; *Modern American & Modern British Poetry*, ed. Louis Untermeyer, in consultation with Karl Shapiro and Richard Wilbur (New York: Harcourt Brace, 1955), p. 378; *Liter-*

ature for Writing, ed. Martin Steinmann and Gerald Willen 2nd ed. (Belmont, Ca: Wadsworth, 1967), p. 682.

Note: For RJ's further revisions to this poem, see above, B15.

C69 "Poetry in a Dry Season." *Partisan Review*, 7 (March–April 1940), 164–67. Book review of William Baker Evans, *Chorus of Bird Voices, Sonnets, Battle-Dore, Unconventional Verse, etc.*; Florence Becker, *Farewell to Walden*; Reuel Denny, *The Connecticut River and Other Poems*; Kenneth Patchen, *First Will and Testament*; Robert Graves, *Collected Poems*; Muriel Rukeyser, *A Turning Wind*; Dylan Thomas, *The World I Breathe*; W. H. Auden, *Another Time*. KA.

Reprinted in *The Partisan Reader*, ed. Phillips and Rahv (1946), pp. 629–33.

RJ to ND (JL), February 1940: I just reviewed one of your books, among a million others, for *Partisan Review*. I said that no one could afford not to get the Dylan Thomas [New Directions, 1939], or to get the Kenneth Patchen [also New Directions, 1939]. More or less.

C70 "For an Emigrant" (later titled "To the New World (For an emigrant of 1939)"). *Kenyon Review*, 2 (Spring 1940), 190–94. RFLP, BFS, SP55, SP2, CP.

> FOR AN EMIGRANT] TO THE NEW WORLD (For an emigrant
>   of 1939) SP55$^+$
> poem divided into two numbered sections, I and II] one unnumbered
>   section only; section II omitted entirely from this version SP55$^+$
> 8 crying] weeping SP55$^+$
> 9 grew;] ~, SP55$^+$
> 11 window-sill] windowsill RFLP; window-sill
>   BFS; windowsill SP55$^+$
> 12 return;] ~. BFS$^+$
> 13 And] But your SP55$^+$
>   Prague;] ~ BFS$^+$
> 16 But] for SP55$^+$
> 19 Man's strength] An old wish SP55$^+$
> 29 friends;] ~— RFLP$^+$
> 30 life.] ~ ... SP55$^+$
> 34 next."] ~!" RFLP$^+$
> 36 your life] you— SP55$^+$
> 37 tongue] speech SP55$^+$
> 40 lawn; the] ~. The SP55$^+$
> 41 you:] ~‸ RFLP$^+$
>   —superb,] ‸Superb, SP55$^+$

44 gay.] ~ ... SP55⁺
47 great sound] sound SP55⁺
49 you;] ~, SP55⁺
50–55 Free—to be homeless, to be friendless, to be nameless, | To stammer the hard words in the foreign night, | To remember; and free also, child, | To love and be loved, | To see in one face the land, the tongue, the time—| Blind with your joy, to whisper: Happiness | Is possible and difficult: to learn at last | New words and a new country, a new love.] Past the statue there is summer, and the summer smiles | The smile of justice or injustice: blind, | Comfortable, including. Here are the lives | And their old world; | Far off, inside you, a conclusive face | Watches in accusation, in acceptance. It is He. | You escaped from nothing: the westering soul | Finds Europe waiting for it over every sea. SP55⁺
(IN AUGMENTATION)] (in augmentation) RFLP; (In augmentation) BFS; *section II omitted from this version* SP55⁺
64 dew] ~, RFLP⁺
67 ....] ... RFLP; .... BFS⁺
95–96 *stanza break*] *no stanza break* RFLP⁺
99 ....] ... RFLP; .... BFS⁺
    That] *That* BFS⁺
112 can: when] can: BFS⁺
113 they kill you] when ~ BFS⁺
Reprinted in *A Vanderbilt Miscellany, 1919–1944*, ed. Richmond Croom Beatty (Nashville: Vanderbilt Univ. Press, 1944), pp. 358–61; *The Oxford Book of American Verse*, ed. Francis Otto Matthiessen (New York: Oxford Univ. Press, 1950), pp. 1084–88; *The Literature of the South*, ed. Richmond C. Beatty et al. (Chicago: Scott, Foresman, 1952), pp. 770–73; shorter version in rev. ed. (1968), pp. 812–15; as "To the New World" in *To Be an American*, ed. Frank F. Bright and Ralph Potter (Philadelphia: Lippincott, 1957), pp. 54–55; *The Achievement of Randall Jarrell*, ed. Hoffman, (1970), pp. 26–27.

C71 "A Job Lot of Poetry." *New Republic*, 103 (11 Nov. 1940), 667–68. Book review of Joyce Kilmer, *Poems, Essays, Letters*; Sydney Salt, *New Journey*; J. Calder Joseph, *Narration with a Red Piano*; Elder Olson, *The Cock of Heaven*. KA.

RJ to AT, January 1941: Don't worry. I'm peculiarly interested in pleasing you with the reviews. I know what you mean about the Kilmer. I meant to dispose of it in a couple of sentences, but it was so really nasty—so *Catholic* in the absolutely insupportable sense of the word— that it could have goaded me into about anything.

C72 "Poets: Old, New and Aging." *New Republic*, 103 (9 Dec. 1940), 797–800. Book review of Leonard Bacon, *Sunderland Capture* *and Other Poems*; Witter Bynner, *Against the Cold*; Ezra Pound, *Cantos LII–LXXI*; Frederic Prokosch, *Death at Sea*. KA.

> *RJ to AT, January 1941:* I too thought the Pound review so much better: I was disappointed with the other after it was too late to do anything about it.

C73 "Kafka's Tragi-Comedy." *Kenyon Review*, 3 (Winter 1941), 116–20. Book review of Franz Kafka, *Amerika*. KA.

> *RJ to NR (EW), January 1941:* As for the two new ones [reviews, C72, C73]—they aren't really below the level of what I have been reviewing, [and] the big one ["Kafka's Tragi-Comedy"] has a sort of gaseous merit.

C74 "The Rhetoricians." *New Republic*, 104 (17 Feb. 1941), 221–22. Book review of Conrad Aiken, *And in the Human Heart*, and Raymond Holden, *The Arrow at the Heel*. KA.

> *RJ to EW, January 1941:* I sent the Aiken-Holden review to the New Republic yesterday. . . . I'd like awfully to have a good book to review, and be able to make some favorable judgments; the books I've reviewed have been so bad I'm afraid the readers will start thinking, "O, *him*. He doesn't like anything."

C75 "Mr. Jarrell Replies." *New Republic*, 104 (17 March 1941), 374–75. Letter in response to Malcolm Cowley's "Poets as Reviewers," which appeared in the *New Republic*, 24 Feb. 1941.

> *RJ to EW, March 1941:* It's really extraordinarily kind of you to have gone to so much trouble over my letters. . . . *The New Republic* had told me nothing about any such letter from Healey; Nigel Dennis thanked me for my letter . . . and said that the next few correspondence columns would be fun for me to read. . . . If I'd known about all the denunciation I'd have written differently—the books were bad, I said so, and I'm glad, is the way I feel. The last paragraph was pure irony, of course, and rather nasty under the surface; but coming after a letter like Healey's it would have looked awful, as if I were more or less apologizing, something I shouldn't ever dream of, of course.

> *RJ to EB, 25 March 1941:* I felt rather shy about pulling your name into my letter; but your review was implicated in the point I wanted to make, and your review had been condemned even as mine, though hardly so spectacularly. . . . It was awfully kind of you to tell me not to mind the unkind remarks; and to tell the truth, I couldn't; in real life I know I'm normally sensitive to disapproval, but in the disreputable

Limbo of magazines I simply manage to take the things said as anything more than queer and wonderfully funny. (Of course I do take them seriously as signs of the usual bad state of taste, poetry, criticism—and why should I leave out Life?—are in.) Somebody ought to write about the way most poetry *is* reviewed; the formula, the amount of comprehension, etc.

C76 "New Year Letter." *Nation,* 152 (12 April 1941), 440–41. Book review of W. H. Auden, *The Double Man.* KA.

> *RJ to EW, March 1941:* I've just finished a review of Auden for *The Nation.* . . . (If this letter sounds pretty dopey it's the review—*staying up* finishing it, that is.)

C77 "London." *New Republic,* 104 (21 April 1941), 574 (first poem of "The World and Its Life Are Her Dream"). CP.

> *RJ to AT, January 1941:* I've been finishing poems all fall; one of the poems in the New Republic ["London"] has the first eight lines of accentual verse I ever wrote.

C78 "Variations." *New Republic,* 104 (21 April 1941), 574–75 (second poem of "The World and Its Life Are Her Dream"). BFS, SP55, SP2, CP.

```
 1   Judy.]    ~,   BFS+
 7   softly;]   ~.  BFS+
10   O]  But   SP55+
     thread]  rope  SP55+
12   Heaven,]  ~.   SP55+
20   winter—]   ~,  BFS+
25   chamber,]  ~ˌ  BFS+
40   said,]    ~ˌ  SP55+
```
Reprinted in *Mid-Century American Poets,* ed. John Ciardi (New York: Twayne, 1950), pp. 192–93; *The Voice That Is Great within Us,* ed. Hayden Carruth (New York: Bantam, 1970), pp. 400–401; *Possibilities of Poetry: An Anthology of American Contemporaries,* ed. Richard Kostelanetz (New York: Dell, 1970), pp. 49–50.

> *RJ to AT, c. January 1941:* My *Variations* is a result of all the late Beethoven I've got; the variation form is too good not to steal.

> *RJ to MLJ, 21 March 1943:* The *Time* review [of BFS] has had the effect of making me repeat *Variations* to myself many times (while walking to play ping-pong; it's hard, now that I'm old and silly, to say poetry to myself in bed).

C79 "90 North." *New Republic*, 104 (21 April 1941), 575 (third poem of "The World and Its Life Are Her Dream"). BFS, SP55, SP2, CP.

7 sign—] ~; SP55[+]
  huddling,] ~; BFS ~, SP55[+]
9 Here] —~ SP55[+]
10 And I] I SP55[+]
12/12–[13] At the North Pole. And now what? Why, go back.] At the North Pole . . . | And now what? Why, go back. SP55[+]
19 suffer till death] ~ for the end SP55[+]
20–21 *no stanza break*] *stanza break* BFS[+]
26 Death] death BFS[+]
27 Crowd to] Crowd SP55[+]
  darkness—] ~, BFS[+]

Reprinted in *New Poems, 1942*, ed. Williams (1942), pp. 117–18; *Horizon*, 9 (Feb. 1944), 88; *Modern Poetry, American and British*, ed. Kimon Friar and John Malcolm Brinnin (New York: Appleton-Century-Crofts, 1951), p. 386; *Modern American Poetry*, ed. Untermeyer, rev. shorter ed. (1955), p. 379; *Fifteen Modern American Poets*, ed. George P. Elliott, Rinehart Edition 79 (New York: Rinehart, 1956), p. 55; *A Quarto of Modern Literature*, ed. Leonard Brown and Porter G. Perrin, 4th ed. (New York: Scribner's, 1957), p. 426, and in the 5th ed., ed. Brown (1964), p. 470; *Adventures in American Literature*, ed. John Gehlmann and Mary Rives Bowman (New York: Harcourt, Brace, 1958), pp. 330–31; *Modern Verse in English*, ed. Cecil and Tate (1958), pp. 582–83; *A College Book of Modern Verse*, ed. James K. Robinson and Walter B. Rideout (Evanston, Ill.: Row, Peterson, 1958), pp. 426–27; *Modern American Poetry*, ed. Thomas Corbett (New York: Macmillan, 1961), pp. 138–39, and in the rev. ed., with William C. Boldt (1965), pp. 134–35; *Introduction to Literature: Poems*, ed. Lynn Altenbernd and Leslie L. Lewis, 2d ed. (New York: Macmillan, 1963), p. 487; *American Poetry*, ed. Gay Wilson Allen et al. (New York: Harper & Row, 1965), pp. 973–74; *The Contemporary American Poets: American Poetry since 1940*, ed. Mark Strand (New York and Cleveland: World, 1969), pp. 139–40; *50 Modern American and British Poets, 1920–1970*, ed. Louis Untermeyer (New York: David McKay, 1973), pp. 94–95; *The Norton Anthology of Modern Poetry*, ed. Ellmann and O'Clair (New York: Norton, 1973), p. 879; *The New Oxford Book of American Verse*, ed. Ellmann (New York: Oxford University Press, 1976), pp. 770–71; *Contemporary Poetry of North Carolina*, ed. Guy Owen and Mary C. Williams (Winston-Salem, N.C.: John F. Blair, 1977), pp. 65–66; *The Treasury of American Poetry*, ed. Sullivan (New York: Doubleday, 1978), pp. 555–56; *Adventures in American Literature*, ed. Francis Hodgins and Kenneth Silverman (New York: Harcourt, Brace, Jovanovich, 1980), p. 710.

RJ to AT, c. January 1941: I appreciate your advice about *90 North* and feel bad about not being able to show my gratitude by taking it.

But if the [fifth] stanza is removed the first line of the next becomes nonsense (says the opposite of what it now does) and an essential part of the argument is lost. The poem may very well be too long and the stanza may be bad; but it's impossible just to remove it. When you see the poem again see if you don't think so.

RJ to NR (EW), January 1941: I'm glad you're printing the poems. I don't think Allen [Tate] had read *90 North* very carefully when he suggested leaving out the fifth stanza. To do so would make the first line of the 6th stanza nonsense (it would say the precise opposite of what it does); and the stanza is an essential part of the argument, which compares the imaginary conclusive death at the Pole, in the child's warm bed, to the life, the inconclusive going-away, at the real Pole. (This is all just on a metaphorical level, of course.) I suppose anyone who writes such a pessimistic poem ought just to nod with gloomy satisfaction at seeing it spoiled; but I have no heroic consistency at all and would be sorry to see it removed. Read it with the stanza left out and see if it doesn't do what I say.

C80 "Song: Not There." *Partisan Review*, 8 (May–June 1941), 233. BFS, SP55, SP2, CP.

> 2 "O, it's not here!"] *O it's not there!* SP55+
> 10 "To find it, O, I will look anywhere."] *To find it, O, I will look anywhere.* SP55+
> 11 "Anywhere, Anywhere"—"Look anywhere,"] *Anywhere, Anywhere . . .* SP55+
> 12 "Yes,] "yes, BFS+
> 17 "O where is my salvation?"] *O where is my salvation?* SP55+
> 18 anywhere;] ~. SP55+

C81 "The Iceberg." *Southern Review*, 7 (Summer 1941), 106–7. BFS, CP.

> *RJ to SR (CB), January 1941:* Here are some late poems I didn't send; "the *Iceberg*" seems to me a particularly good one.

C82 "January 1938." *Southern Review*, 7 (Summer 1941), 107–8. CP.

C83 "An Essay on the Human Will." *Southern Review*, 7 (Summer 1941), 108–9. BFS, CP.

> 10 Esquimaux,] ~ˌ BFS+

C84 "Contemporary Poetry Criticism." *New Republic,* 105 (21 July 1941), 88–90. Essay. KA.

> *RJ to EW, 8 May 1941:* I'm writing an article for the N[ew] R[epublic] about modern criticism of poetry and I've started it with a part on ordinary commercial criticism, its functions and the conditions it is produced under. I try to show that anything but bad or mediocre criticism (in the ordinary commercial magazines and newspapers) is commercially impossible, because of the nature of publishers' (advertisers') and public's demands. Do you think that's a good idea? Somebody here [Univ. of Texas, Austin] said it was true but too obvious, that sensible people all knew that. Do you think that? *I thought it needed saying.*
>
> *RJ to EW, April 1942:* First of all, I agree [with you] about modern critics of poetry; what I said about them in that *New Republic* article was just for a certain audience and a certain purpose, and if I'd talked at length about all their faults it would have helped make them more unread than they are, while what I wanted to do was get them read now. I think that extensively they're misguided or crazy . . . but intensively they're (2 or 3 of them) the best who have existed.

C85 "Tate versus History." *Nation,* 153 (26 July 1941), 75. Book review of Allen Tate, *Reason and Madness.* KA.

> *RJ to AT, early September 1941:* I got pretty sick . . . but couldn't afford to be, since I had to finish a long *New Republic* article [C89] for a deadline. . . . That and the review of you helped make my June a productive and wretched one.
>
> *RJ to AT, mid-September 1941:* Did you like the review of *Reason and Madness?* . . . I'd made notes for and written part of a long review and at the last moment, owing to the War, I was cut to 750 words; I had an awful time making that.

C86 "Town Mouse, Country Mouse." *Nation,* 153 (20 Sept. 1941), 257–58. Book review of Marya Zaturenska, *The Listening Landscape,* and Horace Gregory, *Poems 1930–1940.* KA.

> *RJ to EW, August 1941:* I've just finished a review of *Zaturenska and Gregory* for the Nation that ought to be printed in a few days.
>
> *RJ to EW, October 1941:* I'm afraid the criticism of [Zaturenska and Gregory] is just; when I start talking about the virtues of so-so people my style collapses, I hardly know how to say the things I feel obliged to say—certainly saying them well or wittily is beyond me. I guess I'll have to practice—seriously, I've thought of doing that; being able to is practically a necessity for the Perfect Reviewer. The *deserves one's grat-*

itude or awe was a little ambiguous stylistic grace that evidently doesn't get over. I agree with you, entirely, about the Gregory family. It amused me to think of their reading the review.

C87 "Changes of Attitude and Rhetoric in Auden's Poetry." *Southern Review*, 7 (Autumn 1941), 326–49. Essay. TBC.

> *RJ to SR (RPW), May 1935:* If you want the Milay or the Auden article for the second issue I can have it all ready; I've been working since I got home on the Auden one. I think it's probably the more interesting. I really know Auden's poetry pretty well.

> *RJ to SR (CB), January 1941:* I will send you the Auden article by the first week in August. It'll be long I know, and good I hope and trust.

> *RJ to EW, August 1941:* Just now I'm half way through an interminable Auden article and very tired of it.

> *RJ to AT, September 1941:* The Auden article which is in the Fall *Southern Review*: do tell me what you think of it, won't you? When I finished it seemed to me better than anything of the sort I've done. Anyway, I'm finally learning to write prose a little faster.

C88 "The Head of Wisdom," *Atlantic Monthly*, 168 (Oct. 1941), 456–57. BFS, CP.

> *Written for Katherine Louise Lyle Starr, born May 16, 1940. The head is Beethoven's.*] (This poem is written for Katherine Louise Lyle Starr, who was born May 16, 1940. The head is Beethoven's.) BFS[+]
> 12 'Do, do,'] "Do, do," BFS[+]
> 19 'Obey,] "~, BFS[+]
>   yours,']~," BFS[+]
> Reprinted in *American Anthology*, ed. Tom Boggs (Prairie City, Illinois: Press of James A. Decker, 1942), pp. 49–50; *A Vanderbilt Miscellany*, ed. Beatty (1944), pp. 356–57; *The Literature of the South*, ed. Beatty et al. (1952), pp. 811–12.

> *RJ to EW, March 1941:* I sent a big bunch of poems to the *Atlantic Monthly*; it was awfully kind of you to recommend them.

> *RJ to AT, September 1941:* I am having two poems [*sic*] printed in the *Atlantic Monthly*. I feel like Jesse Stuart.

> *RJ to AT, October 1941:* How right you were about the disgrace of being in the *Atlantic Monthly*! They put my poem in the middle of pieces most freshmen would be ashamed to write; and in the contributor's column they said that R.J. "writes criticism and poetry when the spirit moves him". . . . But I felt lucky when I saw that the poet above me had "elemental love of the soil." [¶] If you see the poem will you tell

me how you like it?—The first and last, that is—I know the middle is too abstract.

RJ to LD, March 1942: I got a letter from somebody who signed herself Olive O. Lightfoot, Sophomore of Home Economics. She said *The Head of Wisdom* was a wicked defeatest poem. The same week three anthologies wrote asking to reprint it; which made me believe, almost, that she was right.

C89 "Critical Scholars." *New Republic,* 105 (6 Oct. 1941), 439. Letter in which RJ comments on David Daiches's response (19 Aug. 1941) to his essay, "Contemporary Poetry Criticism" (**C84**).

C90 "And His Reply." *Nation,* 153 (8 Nov. 1941), 468. Letter in which RJ comments on Rebecca Pitts's "On Mr. Jarrell as Critic," concerning his review of Zaturenska and Gregory (**C86**).

RJ to AT, November 1941: [David] Daiches wrote a letter to the *New Republic* about me—rather angrier than his letter about you; I answered mildly; see if you like the tone. He called me a good many things, *ignorant* was the mildest.

C91 "Children Selecting Books in a Library." *New Republic,* 105 (8 Dec. 1941), 790. BFS; new version in SP55, SP2, CP.

18   things.]   ~. . . .   BFS
Note: RJ's completely revised version of this poem was first published in the *New Republic,* 132 (21 Feb. 1955), 23, and was reprinted in that form in *New York Times Book Review,* 3 April 1955, p. 2; *Randall Jarrell, 1914–1965,* ed. Robert Lowell, Peter Taylor, and Robert Penn Warren (New York: Farrar, Straus & Giroux, 1967), pp. 193–94, with an illustration by Maurice Sendak drawn especially for this book (p. 192); *The Achievement of Randall Jarrell,* ed. Hoffman (1970), pp. 21–22.

C92 "The Christmas Roses." *New Republic,* 105 (8 Dec. 1941), 790. BFS, CP.

9   footnote]   foot-note   BFS+
20   I'm]   I am   BFS+
25   me.]   ~,   BFS+
29   anything . . .]   ~.   BFS+
31   dying]   ~;   BFS+
38   nuisance.]   ~,   BFS+

RJ to AT, November 1939: The *Christmas Roses* is supposed to be *said* (like a speech from a play) with expression, emotion, and long pauses). It of course needs a girl to do it. I can do it pretty well myself, to anybody I get embarrassed. I'd like to hear it done really nicely by somebody like Bette Davis.

C93 "The Difficult Resolution." *New Republic*, 105 (8 Dec. 1941), 790–91. LFLF, CP.

```
 6   dream]   dreams  LFLF+
14   loving]   love  LFLF+
18   unknown]   ~;  LFLF+
19   world's]   ~,  LFLF+
31   the]   The  LFLF+
37   night!]   ~?  LFLF+
43   kind?...]   ~?  LFLF+
45   "That]   ˌ~  LFLF+
49   death:]   ~.  LFLF+
61   pieces]   ~ˏ  LFLF+
```
Reprinted in *New Poems, 1942*, ed. Williams, pp. 120–22; *Possibilities of Poetry*, ed. Kostelanetz (1970), pp. 45–46.

C94 "The Blind Sheep." *New Yorker*, 17 (13 Dec. 1941), 47. BFS, SP55, SP2, CP.

```
10   is]   Is  BFS+
13   well,]   ~;  BFS+
14   friend,]   ~—  BFS+
15   blankly,]   ~:  BFS+
17   fee,]   ~—  BFS+
```
Reprinted in *The New Yorker Book of Poems* (New York: Viking, 1969), p. 72; *The Oxford Book of American Light Verse*, ed. William Harmon (New York: Oxford Univ. Press, 1979), p. 461.

RJ to AT, 26 February 1941: The *New Yorker* tried to print a very short poem of mine with nine changes in the punctuation!

RJ to EW, December 1942: The nearest thing to couplets I've ever managed to do (except in comic verse, where I can do them till the cows come home) is stuff like *For the Madrid Road* or *The Blind Sheep.*

C95 "The Development of Yeats's Sense of Reality." *Southern Review*, 7 (Winter 1941 [1942]), 653–66. Essay. KA.

RJ to AT, February 1941: Red [Robert Penn Warren] asked me for a Yeats article, as I assume he did you (quite an honor for me). I'm doing the periods, language-change. The rewritten poems, and some value-judgments. Yeats' letters made me remember my old attachment very vividly. He's certainly a writer I'm grateful to.

RJ to SR (CB), September 1941: About the Yeats piece: I've got only part way through & I'm in a swamp half of puzzling messes and half of wonderful ideas (according to me) that need ever so much thinking about and working out. Could you . . . not use my piece in your next issue? I'd much prefer this. I'm sure I can make an enormous and I think good piece if I work a lot—and I'm not at all sure I can finish a decent short quick one.

RJ to AT, October 1941: How's your Yeats [essay] coming along? I'm tired of writing and can barely force myself to work on mine.

RJ to SR (CB), October or November 1941: I'll get you the Yeats article on the 6th, as you ask.

C96 "The Long Vacation" (later titled "A Utopian Journey"). *Kenyon Review*, 4 (Winter 1942), 45–46. BFS, SP55, SP2, CP.

The Long Vacation] *A UTOPIAN JOURNEY* BFS⁺
5 unanswerable] natural BFS⁺
10 Dilemma] Intention BFS⁺
11 last;] ~ͅ BFS⁺
18 withering like the state,] withering, BFS⁺
19 mechanical] inconclusive BFS⁺
20–25/20–26 Conclusive rudeness of Authority: poor Innocent, | [*stanza break*] When you go drugged to death—no, ignorantly recover, | Is there anything that has changed for you? Nothing. | You learned nothing, of your life, of your death—| You have been preserved intact for the maze | From which you had found, in your way, the only exit.] Evasive silence—remembers, silently, a sweet, | [*stanza break*] Evasive, and conclusive speech . . . Goes back to his living, | Day and Night, ask, *Child, have you learned anything?* | He answers, *Nothing*—walled in these live ends, | In these blind blossoming alleys of the maze | That lead, through a thousand leaves, to the beginning | [*stanza break*] Of that lead at last into—dark, leaved—a door. BFS⁺

Reprinted in *New Poems, 1942*, ed. Williams, pp. 119–20; as "A Utopian Journey" in *Fifteen Modern American Poets*, ed. Elliott (1956), p. 54; *Modern American Poetry*, ed. Corbett (1961), p. 139–40, and in rev. ed., with Boldt (1965), p. 133; *A College Book of Verse*, ed. C. F. Main (Belmont, Calif.: Wadsworth, 1970), p.258.

C97 "The Skaters." *Kenyon Review*, 4 (Winter 1942), 46–47. BFS, SP55, SP2, CP.

       2   staff]   ~.   SP55⁺
       5   like]   as   SP55⁺
       8   flocks.]   flock.   SP55⁺
       9   sped]   moved   SP55⁺
      10   lands—]   ~,   SP55⁺
      11   Love]   Lust   SP55⁺
      13   Up]   North   SP55⁺
      15   faces]   glances   SP55⁺
      24   night]   Way   SP55⁺
      25   mark,]   ~ˌ   SP55⁺
      34   assent]   ~ˌ   SP55⁺

RJ to NR (EW), March 1941: I thought I'd enclose one of the poems I was typing, to see if you like it; it's got the *90 North milieu* pretty much.

C98 "The Country Was." *Partisan Review*, 9 (Jan.–Feb. 1942), 58–60. CP.

Note: This poem is a parody of Marianne Moore.

C99 "The Nightmare." *View*, 1 (Feb.–March 1942), 6.

C100 "1938: Tales from the Vienna Woods." *Chimera*, 1 (Spring 1942), 5. BFS, CP.

C101 "The End of the Line." *Nation*, 154 (21 Feb. 1942), 222, 224, 226, 228. Essay. KA.

Reprinted in *Literary Opinion in America*, ed. M. D. Zabel, rev. ed. (New York: Harper's, 1951), pp. 742–48 (B17); *Literary Modernism*, ed. Irving Howe (Greenwich, Conn.: Fawcett, 1967), pp. 158–66 (paperback original).

RJ to AT, October 1941: My last week's been spent miserably and busily, in doing the *Nation* piece.

RJ to EW, October 1941: I've just had a very hard week's work ... doing an article on modern poetry for the *Nation*. I wish I'd done up my theory better (I'm going to, alter, at very great length). . . . I was so pressed for space that I had to cut out long, already-written paragraphs and replace them with sentences: the ones I regret most are ones on Imagisim, another movement, and the singular movement of modern music, which I cut entirely. Anyway, make allowances for that . . . and see how you like the theory. I've been working on it for years and have waste baskets full of notes.

C102 "The Lost Love." *Atlantic Monthly*, 169 (April 1942), 493. BFS, CP.

6   'Your]   "~   BFS[+]
7   you.']   ~."   BFS[+]
8   'Yes.']   "~."   BFS[+]
9   'Your]   "~   BFS[+]
    weeping,']   ~,"   BFS[+]
13   'O my poor love—']   "O my poor love—"   BFS[+]
15   'I am dreaming.']   "I am dreaming."   BFS[+]

RJ to EW, August 1941: I just got a letter from Edward Weeks saying the *Atlantic Monthly* was using two of my poems, so I thought I'd write and thank you for it.

RJ to EW, April 1942: Thanks to your getting me in the *Atlantic Monthly*, I've received several wonderful letters; the best was from a girl who signed herself *Olive Lightfoot, Sophomore* in *Home Economics*; she said that I was a defeatist. I told her that when she woke up some morning transfixed with a meat skewer she'd see whether or not I was a defeatist. [¶] As a matter of fact, being in the *AM* got me something better than that. A full professor [at the University of Texas, where RJ was then teaching], a large white-haired man who lisps badly, congratulated me on an elevator; he said, "I always say there are two sorts of poets: Those who have been published in the *Atlantic Monthly* and those who aren't good enough to be."

C103 "Aesthetic Theories: Art as Expression." *Poetry*, 60 (May 1942), 72–73. BFS, CP.

AESTHETIC]   ESTHETIC   BFS[+]
9   Dr.--------]   Dr.---   BFS[+]
21   dessication]   desiccation   BFS[+]
22   coveralls]   sterile coveralls   BFS[+]
23   *Ubermensch]*   *Übermensch*   BFS[+]

RJ to AT, February 1940: I've been writing stuff that flows glibly off, without emotion but wittingly, I hope, anyways—why it comes out I've no notion, it's certainly not anything I've ever done or meant to do. I am looking at it askance as 1740 and waiting for a Romantic Revival about next fall. To quote the modern poet [RJ, "Aesthetic Theories: Art as Expression"]: Poems like lives, are doing what we can / And very different from what we know. / They start surprisingly, like blood in bones; / The unlucky wake up bleeding at the nose.

C104 "Time and the Thing-in-Itself in a Textbook." *Poetry*, 60 (May 1942), 73–74. CP.

C105 "Man." *Poetry*, 60 (May 1942), 74–75. CP.

C106 "In All Directions." *Partisan Review*, 9 (July–Aug. 1942), 345–47. Book review of *New Directions, 1941.* KA.

C107 "The Humble Animal." *Kenyon Review*, 4 (Autumn 1942), 408–11. Essay-review of Marianne Moore, *What Are Years.* PA.

> Reprinted in *The Kenyon Critics: Studies in Modern Literature from the* Kenyon Review, ed. John Crowe Ransom (Cleveland: World Publishing, 1951), pp. 277–80.

C108 "Questions about Surrealism." *View*, 2d ser., no. 3, Oct. 1942, 30. Letter in "View Listens" column; signed "Randall Jarrell."

> *RJ to ND (JL), March 1943:* You remember my review of *New Directions* [C106] (incidentally, thank you for the kind postcard about it) so you can easily guess what my opinion of *View* is. . . . I'm perfectly willing to answer God for anything I've said about anybody. I'm willing to bet that my judgments [about surrealism] will resemble those of 1960, say, more than those of more favorable critics will.

C109 "Pictures from a World: Orestes at Tauris" (later titled "Orestes at Tauris"). *Kenyon Review*, 5 (Winter 1943), 1–11. Los, CP.

> Pictures from a World: Orestes at Tauris]   Orestes at Tauris   CP
> 2   oil,]   ~.   Los$^+$
> 3   breast,]   ~—   Los$^+$
> 4   (The]   ˏ~   Los$^+$
> 5   rode)]   rode—   Los$^+$
> 8   them]   Them   Los$^+$
> 14   face—]   ~;   Los$^+$
> 42   hardest]   harshest   Los$^+$
> 44   face—]   ~;   Los$^+$
> 45   heads]   head   Los$^+$
> 82   cries.]   ~:   Los$^+$
> 86   blue]   spiked   Los$^+$
> 87   Them]   Some   Los$^+$
> 109   strides]   stride   Los$^+$
> 123   their]   Their   Los$^+$

126 they] They Los^{+}
128 their hands.] Their hands. . . . Los^{+}
169 or eyes nor mouth:] at all: Los^{+}
173 breasts,] ~— Los^{+}
204 head fall and your lids] life halt, your weak Los^{+}
214 isles,] ~‸ Los^{+}
237 move—you could not move—] move, you could not move. Los^{+}
240 foreign] endless Los^{+}
248 fell;] ~. Los^{+}
253 turned] moved Los^{+}
262 living;] ~. Los^{+}
272 it and lean on it longingly] ~, and . . . longingly, Los^{+}
273 firelight,] ~‸ Los^{+}
291 Scyros] ~, Los^{+}
Lemnos] ~, Los^{+}
293 wheat] seed Los^{+}
298 Euxine, and then bore] Euxine and, worn, wandering Los^{+}
299 seemed] seems Los^{+}
301 To gain] He gains Los^{+}
302 Went] Goes Los^{+}
and silently,] silent, Los^{+}
304 went] bears Los^{+}
306 And misshaped and night-balanced flowers—swam sometimes] And night-blanched and misshappen flowers—swims Los^{+}
308 And saw past sodden and ropy locks] Dappled with stars and, at the western brim, Los^{+}
315/316 *stanza break*] *no stanza break* Los^{+}
316 take] ~— Los^{+}
317 it,] ~‸ Los^{+}
319 there] ~— Los^{+}

Reprinted in *New Poems, 1943: An Anthology of British and American Verse*, ed. Oscar Williams (New York: Howell, Soskin, 1943), 53–63.

Note: An explanatory note by RJ about this poem is in *Losses*, p. 68; it is not reprinted in *The Complete Poems.*

C110 "The Islands." *View*, 3 (April 1943), 22. CP.

Reprinted in *English and American Surrealist Poetry*, ed. Edward B. Germaine (Harmondsworth: Penguin, 1978).

RJ to MLJ, 13 May 1943: I got $5.50 from View for my poem; I enclose the check endorsed.

C111 "The November Ghosts." *Sewanee Review*, 51 (April–June 1943), 252. CP.

C112 "The Laboratory." *Sewanee Review*, 51 (April–June 1943), 253. CP.

C113 "The Fall of the City." *Sewanee Review*, 51 (April–June 1943), 267–80. Review of Archibald MacLeish, *The Fall of the City*. KA.

C114 "Absent with Official Leave." *Poetry*, 62 (Aug. 1943), 262–63. LFLF, SP55, SP2, CP.

    3   an instant] a moment SP55$^+$
   10 nothing. . . .] ~ . . . SP55$^+$
   16 light,] ~$_\wedge$ LFLF$^+$
   22 snow. . . .] ~ . . . SP55$^+$
   25 Causes] causes LFLF$^+$
   29 child] man SP55$^+$
   30 silent—] ~, SP55$^+$

RJ to MLJ, 18 February 1943: I don't think I'll be able to do any writing much [while I am in the army]—your whole tendency is to leave after dinner and read or listen to music; and since you get up so early you have to go to bed early too.

RJ to MLJ, 16 July 1943: I got proof from *Poetry*—the poems look lovely, and are in the nicest order, too.

C115 "Port of Embarcation." *Poetry*, 62 (Aug. 1943), 263. LFLF, SP55, SP2, CP.

Reprinted in *Mid-Century American Poets*, ed. Ciardi (1950), p. 187.

RJ to MLJ, 18 June 1943: Isn't the end of *Port of Embarcation* swell? It sounds positively magical to me. Say yes.

C116 "Come to the Stone. . . ." *Poetry*, 62 (Aug. 1943), 264. LFLF, SP55, SP2, CP.

   9   angry,] ~$_\wedge$ SP55$^+$
   12 world;]~, SP55$^+$
   14 (except his death)] —except his death— SP55$^+$
Reprinted in *The Voice That Is Great within Us*, ed. Carruth (1970), p. 399.

RJ to MLJ, 24 June 1943: I'm writing about a child making a journey along a bombed road, in my childish not-at-all terrible style; I have about a dozen goodish lines but I want to fix it up nicely at the end.

RJ to MLJ, 25 June 1943: I'm awfully glad you like *Come to the Stone* so well—I'm charmed by it about as you are, more by the charmingness than its goodness. *The people are punishing the people—why?* is just the child's thought (a natural one I think) and he immediately answers his own question without any trouble—so I don't think it's Hardyish. The child would naturally still believe in angels, especially in dreams (he probably knows that rhyme about the angels guarding the bed he lies on); but *angels* are the symbols for the supernatural anthropomorphic Causes that he puts in his version of what's happening and why; they *sway about his story like balloons* seems to me such a good ambiguity because you can't tell whether like the barrage balloons he sees (grim) or like the toy balloons he used to be bought in clusters (non-grim). And *story* is ambiguous because you can't tell whether it refers to his story, explanation of what's happening (this is the primary meaning) or to his own real story, the things he's going through. I'm *awfully* glad *Come to the Stone and tell me why I died* gets over well with you—this is what I was most anxious about, since it's a very strange device.

C117   "The Emancipators." *Poetry,* 62 (Aug. 1943), 264–65. LFLF, SP55, SP2, CP.

```
13   The]    ~—    SP55⁺
16   chains;]    ~ˬ    LFLF⁺
     yet]   and   SP55⁺
```

Reprinted in *War Poets: An Anthology of the War Poetry of the 20th Century,* ed. Oscar Williams (New York: John Day Company, 1945), p. 157; *The Growth of American Literature,* ed. E. H. Cady et al. (New York: American Book Company, 1956), v. II, p. 696; *Explicator,* 16 (Feb. 1958), p. 26; *Ideas in Poetry,* ed. Oscar Fidell (Englewood Cliffs, N.J.: Prentice-Hall, 1965), pp. 134–35; *The Achievement of Randall Jarrell,* ed. Hoffman (1970), p. 32.

Note: An explanatory note by RJ about this poem is in *SP55* and *SP2* on p. viii and in *CP* on p. 8.

RJ to MLJ, 19 or 20 April 1943: I've started (just barely) one that begins with a surrealist, rather, address to the scientists of old; I don't know how it will grow.

RJ to MLJ, 13 May 1943: I'm so glad you like my scientists poem so much. I agree about the last line—I'll try to change it and the last stanza when I've time.

RJ to MLJ, 24 June 1943: I'm awfully glad you like the new end of the *Emancipators* better than the old; I was so sure myself it was better that I was surprised when you didn't think so. (The *factories* was just a copyright mistake for tenements [line 14], as you guessed.) I think the suppressed parodies on Rousseau and Marx in the first and last lines of the stanza are good. The poem is certainly full of references, isn't it?

C118 "The Soldier Walks under the Trees of the University." *Nation*, 157 (14 Aug. 1943), 186. LFLF, CP.

6   stone.)]   ~‚)   LFLF⁺

Reprinted in *New Poems, 1944*, ed. Oscar Williams (New York: Howell, Soskin, 1944), p. 161; *A New Anthology of Modern Poetry*, ed. Selden Rodman, rev. ed. (New York: Modern Library, 1946), pp. 387–88; *Oxford Book of American Verse*, ed. Matthiessen (1950), pp. 1088–89; *Poetry for Pleasure*, sel. by the editors of Hallmark Cards (Garden City, N.Y.: Doubleday, 1960), pp. 296–97; *The Achievement of Randall Jarrell*, ed. Hoffman (1970), p. 39.

RJ to MLJ, 29 May 1943: What an injustice to call me the Laureate of Libraries on the strength of my last poem, which is not about libraries but a University, and a capitalist one at that. (I think I'll call it *The Soldier Walks Under the Trees of the University*.)

RJ to MLJ, 25 June 1943: Guess what! Margaret Marshall's publishing the *Soldier Walks under the Trees*. I enclose her sweet letter. Isn't that swell?

C119 "Soldier (T. P.)." *New Republic*, 109 (23 Aug. 1943), 249. LFLF, CP.

(T. P.)¹]   [~]*   LFLF⁺
20   traveling]   travelling   LFLF⁺
21   relief map]   relief-map   LFLF⁺
     parade ground]   parade-ground   LFLF⁺
28   sir . . .]   ~. . . .   LFLF⁺
30   *live* . . .]   ~. . . .   LFLF⁺
32   is—]   ~‚   LFLF⁺

Reprinted in *War Poets*, ed. Williams (1945), p. 162.

RJ to MLJ, 14 April 1943: My poem's about the army, and will not endear me or the army to anybody. . . . Gee, my poem's going beautifully. . . . I've been working all evening on [it], and feel tired but thrilled.

RJ to MLJ, 24 June 1943: I believe I like Soldier: TP better than it ["The Emancipators"], too—it's a heavier thicker poem, etc. . . . I've been saying my World War I poem to myself all day. I'm certainly charmed with it.

C120 "The Carnegie Library: Juvenile Division." *Kenyon Review*, 6 (Winter 1944), 64–65. LFLF, SP55, SP2, CP.

> 6 on] no LFLF+
> 27 That owned him] He owned once; LFLF+
> thalers] thaler LFLF+
> 28 a] the LFLF+
> 32 learns] finds SP55+
> 48 books'. . . .] ~'. LFLF+
> Reprinted in *The Achievement of Randall Jarrell*, ed. Hoffman (1970), pp. 64–65.

RJ to MLJ, 18 or 19 April 1943: I've worked some on the *Carnegie Library*, and send it; I've tried but not done much to my army one.

RJ to MLJ, 29 April 1943: The last hours on the train I worked on my *Carnegie Library* and got a few new lines.

RJ to MLJ, 9 May 1943: Clever me—it's 6, and I've been finishing my *Carnegie Library* poem all afternoon; it's almost done.

RJ to MLJ, 29 May 1943: But you are right just the same, and here is the end of my *Carnegie Library* to prove it. Incidentally, about *Of that deep string, half music and half pain:* when notes get down below a certain pitch, they are apprehended by the ear not as sound but as pain—that's the ground for the metaphor. [¶] I worked finishing (the part before the last six lines) the *C. Library* last night. . . .

C121 "The Soldier." *Partisan Review*, 11 (Winter 1944), 98. LFLF, CP.

> 15 learned] guessed LFLF+

RJ to MLJ, 13 May 1943: Here's the middle stanza and another part of my World War poem; I think you'll love it. . . . I'll call the poem *The Soldier*, eh?

RJ to MLJ, 19 May 1943: I wrote poetry night before last—*Dogs at Shepherd Field*—but did only a little; I've got a line or two more for the World War I one.

RJ to MLJ, 25 May 1943: Here's my *The Soldier*, to compete with [Rupert] Brooks'; I've worked on it tonight. O me! You can tell from my gay tone what I've been doing; poetry's the only thing in camp that makes me feel so.

RJ to MLJ, 29 May 1943: I've made the sixth line of *The Soldier*[:] *His joys, his reason, and his blood;. . . .*

C122 "The Boyg, Peer Gynt, the One Only One." *Partisan Review*, 11 (Winter 1944), 98–99. LFLF, SP55, SP2, CP.

15 Nothing? . . .] ~? . . . . LFLF; ~? . . . SP55⁺

C123 "Scherzo." *Partisan Review*, 11 (Winter 1944), 99. CP.

C124 "A Lullaby." *Poetry*, 64 (Aug. 1944), 265. LFLF, SP55, SP2, CP.

Reprinted in *Fifteen Modern American Poets*, ed. Elliott (1956), pp. 57–58; *Possibilities of Poetry*, ed. Kostelanetz (1970), p. 38; *A Reading Apprenticeship: Literature*, ed. Norman A. Brittin (New York: Holt, Rinehart and Winston, 1971), pp. 428–29.

C125 "A Front." *Poetry*, 64 (Aug. 1944), 265–66. LFLF, SP55, SP2, CP.

13 closed . . .] ~. . . . LFLF⁺
Reprinted in *The Voice That Is Great within Us*, ed. Carruth (1970), pp. 399–400.

Note: An explanatory note by RJ concerning this poem is in SP55 and SP2 on p. xvi and in CP on p. 10.

C126 "Losses." *Poetry*, 64 (Aug. 1944), 266–67. LFLF, SP55, SP2, CP.

10 aunts] ants LFLF; aunts SP55⁺
Reprinted in *War Poets*, ed. Williams (1945), p. 163; *Oxford Book of American Verse*, ed. Matthiessen (1950), pp. 1091–92; *Understanding Poetry*, ed. Cleanth Brooks and Robert Penn Warren (New York: Holt, 1952), p. 456, and in the 3d ed. (1960), pp. 401–2; *Anthologie de la Poésie Américaine*, ed. Alain Bosquet (Paris: Librairie Stock, 1956), p. 240, with a French translation by Bosquet, "Pertes," on p. 241; *The Growth of American Literature*, ed. Cady et al. (1956), pp. 695–96; *A College Book of Modern Verse*, ed. Robinson and Rideout (1958), p. 429; *Modern Verse in English*, ed. Cecil and Tate (1958), pp. 584–85; *American Poetry*, ed. Karl Shapiro (New York: Crowell, 1960), pp. 223–24; *Discovering Modern Poetry*, ed. Elizabeth Drew and George Connor (New York: Holt, Rinehart, and Winston, 1961), pp. 278–79; *Literary Types and Themes*, ed. Maurice B. McNamee et al. (New York: Holt, Rinehart, and Winston, 1961), p. 620; *American Literature Survey: The Twentieth Century*, ed. Milton R. Stern and Seymour L. Gross

(New York: Viking, 1962), pp. 576–77, and in 2d ed. (1968), pp. 604–5; *National Poetry Festival, October 22–24, 1962* (Washington, D.C.: Library of Congress, 1964), pp. 310–11, with RJ's brief introductory comments on p. 310; *Introduction to the Poem*, ed. Robert W. Boynton and Maynard Mack (Rochelle Park, N.J.: Hayden Book Co., 1965), pp. 128–29, and in 2d ed. (1973); *Alumni News* (Univ. of N.C. at Greensboro), 54 (Spring 1966), 43; *Literature for Writing*, ed. Steinmann and Willen, 2d ed. (1967), p. 683; *53 American Poets Today*, ed. Ruth Witt-Diamant and Rikutaro Fukuda (Tokyo: Kenkyusha, 1968), pp. 59–61; *The Survival Years*, ed. Sach Salzman (New York: Pegasus, 1969), pp. 88–89; *A Little Treasury of American Poetry, English and American*, ed. Oscar Williams, 3d ed. (New York: Scribner's, 1970), p. 562; *The Achievement of Randall Jarrell*, ed. Hoffman (1970), p. 33; *Possibilities of Poetry*, ed. Kostelanetz (1970), p. 35; *Mirrors: An Introduction to Literature*, ed. John R. Knott and Christopher Reaske, 2d ed. (San Francisco: Canfield Press, 1975), p. 254; *Treasury of American Poetry*, ed. Sullivan (1978), pp. 554–55.

C127 "The Angels at Hamburg." *Poetry*, 64 (Aug. 1944), 267–68. LFLF, SP55, SP2, CP.

16   —the strongest]   he whispers   SP55⁺
17   Stammers, "My burden]   ~ˌ "~ punishment   SP55⁺
18   good]   ~,   SP55⁺
21   loving or]   ~, nor   SP55⁺

C128 "The Sick Nought." *Poetry*, 64 (Aug. 1944), 268–69. LFLF, SP55, SP2, CP.

1   traveling]   travelling   LFLF⁺
20   States]   states   LFLF⁺
21   but]   yours   SP55⁺
22–24   To sell the lives we were too poor to use, | To lose the lives we were too weak to keep— | This was our peace, this was our war]   *deleted*   SP55⁺

RJ to MLJ, 23 July 1943: About *The Sick Nought:* I hadn't noticed the damping-out effect of *pony* or *puppy* because I wrote them at different times and never joined them in my head. (The *simple neglect* is so true.) Do you not like *coughing* because it seems sentimental or what? I just meant to make it a stray animal, sick like the soldier. The *ticket puppy* sentence is followed by a colon to connect it with *you have lost even the right to be condemned* (because you're like a mere unlucky ticket or stray animal). I think you're right about the puppy phrase and we'll try to change it, also the *how can I care about you much* which has a mild mannered insincerity. But I'm going to keep *pick you out / from all the other people / and sent away to die for them*—that seems to me good and effective.

C129 "An Officers' Prison Camp Seen from a Troop-Train," *Partisan Review*, 11 (Fall 1944), 432–33. LFLF, CP.

Reprinted in *War Poets*, ed. Williams (1945), p. 160.

RJ to MLJ, 26 April 1943: (Incidentally, I saw, night before last, a concentration camp for German prisoners; it was some small agricultural college or something of the sort, surrounded by floodlights, guard towers, and electrified fence.)

RJ to MLJ, 26–29 June 1943: When I got home last night, about 11:00—I'd been writing a poem about a German prison camp I saw coming here on the train—I thought from the street outside, "How queer for the barracks to look so deserted." I don't know why it looked so deserted, but it did; and it was—everybody had moved across the street. . . . I've worked some more on my German prisoner poem—I've about eighteen or twenty pretty good lines.

RJ to MLJ, 30 June 1943: I wrote about three lines on my prison camp [poem] during the day, but at night I was too tired and sleepy, and listened to a wretched classical program on the grass for a little, and went home to bed.

C130 "Prisoners." *Partisan Review*, 11 (Fall 1944), 433. LFLF, SP55, SP2, CP.

2 ball] P SP55⁺
Reprinted in *War Poets*, ed. Williams (1945), p. 158; *The Oxford Book of American Verse*, ed. Matthiessen (1950), pp. 1090–91.

Note: A note by RJ about this poem appears in *SP55* and *SP2* on p. xv and in *CP* on p. 9.

RJ to MLJ, 9 August 1945: Gee, I'm pleased with *Prisoners*. I never want to change a word, no matter how often I say it. Shall I send it to the *New Yorker*?

C131 "The Metamorphoses." *Partisan Review*, 11 (Fall 1944), 434. LFLF, SP55, SP2, CP.

Reprinted in *The Partisan Reader*, ed. Phillips and Rahv (1946), p. 283; *Fifteen Modern American Poets*, ed. Elliott (1956), p. 60: *To Play Man Number One: Poems of Modern Man*, ed. Sara Hannum and John

Terry Chase (New York: Atheneum, 1969), p. 87; *The Achievement of Randall Jarrell*, ed. Hoffman (1970), p.38.

C132   "Mother, Said the Child." *Partisan Review*, 11 (Fall 1944), 434. LFLF, CP.

    4   silently...]   ~....   LFLF⁺
    8   life...]   ~....   LFLF⁺
    11   could]   can   LFLF⁺
    12   sleeping...]   ~....   LFLF⁺

C133   "Second Air Force" (later titled "2nd Air Force"), *Nation* 159 (28 Oct. 1944), 526. LFLF, SP55, SP2, CP.

    Second Air Force]   2nd Air Force   LFLF;   Second Air Force   SP55⁺
    6   (A bird falling to a lobster from a star)]   *omitted*   SP55⁺
    [37] *no line*]   Remembering,   SP55⁺
    38   *friend,*]   ~,   LFLF;   ~!   SP55⁺
    40   Watching]   And sees   SP55⁺
        eat]   ~,   SP55⁺
    42   stream,]   ~ out,   SP55⁺
    43   inextinguishable flames]   flames   SP55⁺
    44   Citizens of everybody's heart, the flames]   *omitted*   SP55⁺
    45/44   That burn like stars above the lands of men.   LFLF⁺
    47/46   section]   squadron   LFLF⁺
    Reprinted in *War Poets*, ed. Williams (1945), pp. 11–12; *Fifteen Modern American Poets*, ed. Elliott (1956), p. 58; *The Sound of Wings: Readings for the Air Age*, ed. Joseph B. Roberts and Paul L. Briand (New York: Henry Holt, 1957), pp. 206–7; *A College Book of Modern Verse*, ed. Robinson and Rideout (1958), pp. 427–28; *American Poetry*, ed. Allen et al. (1965), pp. 974–76; *The Distinctive Voice: Twentieth Century American Poetry*, ed. William J. Martz (Evanston, Ill.: Scott, Foresman, 1966), pp. 183–84; *Reading for Understanding*, ed. Caroline Shrodes et al. (New York: Macmillan, 1968), pp. 686–88; *A Little Treasury of Modern Poetry, English & American*, ed. Williams, 3d ed. (1970), pp. 563–64; *Chief Modern Poets of Britain and America*, ed. Sanders et al., 5th ed. (1970).

    Note: A note by RJ about this poem is in *SP55* and *SP2* on p. xvi and in *CP* on p. 60.

C134   "The Death of the Ball Turret Gunner." *Partisan Review*, 12 (Winter 1945), 60. LFLF, SP55, SP2, CP. Published separately as A24.

    Reprinted in *Horizon*, 11 (April 1945), 224; *War and the Poet*, ed. Richard Eberhart and Selden Rodman (New York: Devin-Adair, 1945),

in Poetry, ed. William J. Martz, 2d ed. (Glenview, Ill.: Scott, Foresman, 1973); Joseph Comprone, *From Experience to Expression* (Dubuque, Iowa: William C. Brown Co., 1974), p. 160; Frank Brady and Martin Price, *Poetry Past and Present* (New York: Harcourt, Brace, Jovanovich, 1974), p. 1; *Introduction to Poetry*, ed. William C. Cavanaugh (Dubuque, Iowa: William C. Brown, 1974), p. 149; John Ciardi and Miller Williams, *How Does a Poem Mean?*, 2d ed. (Boston: Houghton, Mifflin, 1975), p. 264; *Poetry since 1900: An Anthology of British and American Verse in the Twentieth Century*, ed. Colin Falck and Ian Hamilton (London: Macdonald and Jane's, 1975); *The New Oxford Book of American Verse*, ed. Ellmann (1976), p. 771; *Introducing Poems*, ed. Linda W. Wagner and C. David Meads (New York: Harper and Row, 1976); *The United States in Literature*, ed. Miller et al. (1973), p. M244; *Literature: An Introduction to Fiction, Poetry, and Drama*, ed. X. J. Kennedy (Boston: Little, Brown, 1976), p. 841; *Literature: Fiction, Poetry, Drama*, ed. Joseph K. Davis et al. (Glenview, Ill.: Scott, Foresman, 1977), p. 514; *The Penguin Book of American Verse*, ed. Geoffrey Moore (Harmondsworth, Middlesex: Penguin, 1977), p. 444; *The Norton Introduction to Literature*, ed. Carl Bain et al., 2d ed. (New York: Norton, 1977), p. 669; *The Treasury of American Poetry*, ed. Sullivan (1978), p. 555; *Communicative Reading*, ed. Elbert R. Bowen et al. (New York: Macmillan, 1978), p. 63; *Fine Frenzy: Enduring Themes in Poetry*. ed. Robert Baylor and Brenda Stokes, 2d ed. (New York: McGraw-Hill, 1978); *Adventures in American Literature*, ed. Francis Hodgins and Kenneth Silverman (New York: Harcourt, Brace, Jovanovich, 1980), p. 709; *The Practical Imagination*, ed. Northrop Frye et al. (New York: Harper & Row, 1980), p. 822; *Perfected Steel, Terrible Crystal*, ed. Ned O'Gorman (New York: Seabury Press, 1981), pp. 64–65; *Poetry: An Introduction and Anthology*, ed. Edward Proffitt (Boston: Houghton, Mifflin, 1981); *The Harper Anthology of Poetry*, ed. John Frederick Nims (New York: Harper & Row, 1981); *Poetry: An Introduction*, ed. Ruth Miller and Robert A. Greenberg (New York: St. Martins, 1981), p. 287; John Hospers, *Understanding the Arts* (Englewood Cliffs, N.J.: Prentice-Hall, 1982), p. 321; *Poetry: Sights and Insights*, ed. James W. Kirkland and F. David Sanders (New York: Random House, 1982), p. 20.

Note: An explanatory note by RJ about this poem is in SP55 and SP2 on p. xiii and in CP on p. 8.

C135 "Poetry in War and Peace." *Partisan Review*, 12 (Winter 1945), 120–26. Book review of Marianne Moore, *Nevertheless*; William Carlos Williams, *The Wedge*; H. D., *The Walls Do Not Fall*; *Five Young American Poets* (New Directions, 1944); and Robert Lowell, *The Land of Unlikeness*. KA.

Steinmann and Willen, 2d ed. (1967), p. 683; *Literature in Critical Perspectives: An Anthology*, ed. Walter K. Gordon (New York: Appleton-Century-Crofts, 1968), p. 257; *Reading Literature: Stories, Plays, and Poems*, ed. Joseph Satin (Boston: Houghton, Mifflin, 1968), p. 508; *Imaginative Literature*, ed. Alton C. Morris et al. (New York: Harcourt, Brace, Jovanovich, 1968), p. 320; Judson Jerome, *Premeditated Art* (Boston: Houghton, Mifflin, 1968), p. 87; *Where Steel Winds Blow*, ed. Robert Cromie (New York: David McKay, 1968), p. 100; *Poetry: Meaning and Form*, ed. Joseph Schwartz and Robert C. Roby (St. Louis: McGraw-Hill, 1969), p. 192; *The Survival Years*, ed. Salzman (1969), p. 88; *Poems of War Resistance: From 2300 B.C. to the Present*, ed. Scott Bates (New York: Grossman, 1969), p. 186; *A Little Treasury of Modern Poetry*, ed. Williams, 3d ed. (1970), p. 561; *The Achievement of Randall Jarrell*, ed. Hoffman (1970), p. 41; *The Voice That Is Great within Us*, ed. Carruth (1970), p. 400; Laurence Perrine, *Literature: Structure, Sound, and Sense* (New York: Harcourt, Brace, 1970), p. 835; *The Norton Anthology of Poetry*, ed. Arthur M. Eastman et al. (New York: Norton, 1970), p. 1097; *A Book of Modern Poetry*, ed. Jane McDermott and Thomas V. Lowery (New York: Harcourt, Brace, Jovanovich, 1970), p. 226; *Discovery and Response*, ed. Martha Banta and Joseph N. Satterwhite (New York: Macmillan, 1970), p. 412; *Mandala: Literature for Critical Analysis*, ed. Wilfred L. Guerin et al. (New York: Harper & Row, 1970), p. 320; *Possibilities of Poetry*, ed. Kostelanetz (1970), p. 34; *Sounds and Silences*, ed. Peck (1970), p. 161; *A College Book of Verse*, ed. Main (1970), p. 257; *Chief Modern Poets of Britain and America*, ed. Sanders et al., 5th ed. (1970); *Poems and Perspectives*, ed. Robert H. Ross and William E. Stafford (Glenview, Ill.: Scott, Foresman, 1971), p. 171; *The Realities of Literature*, ed. Richard F. Dietrich (Waltham, Mass.: Xerox, 1971), p. 125; *The New Voices: The Poetry of the Present*, ed. Angelo Carli and Theodore Kilman (New York: Scribner's, 1971); *Of Time and Experience: Literary Themes*, ed. Richard H. Dodge and Peter D. Lindblom (Cambridge, Mass.: Winthrop, 1972), p. 554; *The Poem: An Anthology*, ed. Greenfield and Weatherhead, 2d ed. (1972), p. 466; *Words in Flight: An Introduction to Poetry*, ed. Richard Abcarian (Belmont, Calif.: Wadsworth, 1972); *The Modern Age*, ed. Leonard Lief and James F. Light, 2d ed. (New York: Holt, Rinehart and Winston, 1972), p. 624, and 3d ed. (1976), p. 667; *50 Modern American and British Poets, 1920–1970*, ed. Untermeyer (1973), p. 93; *The Norton Anthology of Modern Poetry*, ed. Ellmann and O'Clair (1973), pp. 879–80; *Contemporary Poetry in America*, ed. Miller Williams (New York: Random House, 1973), p. 33; *The Norton Introduction to Literature: Poetry*, ed. J. Paul Hunter (New York: Norton, 1973), p. 24; *American Literature: Themes and Writers*, ed. G. Robert Carlsen, 2d ed. (New York: McGraw-Hill, 1973), p. 371; *College English: The First Year*, ed. Alton C. Morris et al. (New York: Harcourt, Brace, Jovanovich, 1973), p. 611; *Beginnings*

p. 200; *War Poets*, ed. Williams (1945), p. 157; *Modern American Poetry*, ed. Untermeyer (1950), p. 681; and in the enlarged ed. (1962), p. 647; *Mid-Century American Poets*, ed. Ciardi (1950), p. 198; *The Oxford Book of American Verse*, ed. Matthiessen (1950), p. 1091; *A Complete College Reader*, ed. John Holmes and Carroll S. Towle (Boston: Houghton, Mifflin, 1950), p. 889; Brooks and Warren, *Understanding Poetry* (1952), p. 221, and in the 3d ed. (1960), p. 200; Babette Deutsch, *Poetry in Our Time* (New York: Holt, 1952), p. 376; *Golden Horizon*, ed. Cyril Connolly (London: Weidenfeld and Nicolson, 1953), p. 100; *The New Partisan Reader, 1945–53*, ed. William Phillips and Philip Rahv (New York: Harcourt, Brace, 1953), p. 166; *Penguin Book of Modern American Verse*, ed. Geoffrey Moore (London: Penguin Books, 1954), p. 269; *The Case for Poetry: A Critical Anthology*, ed. Frederick L. Gwynn et al. (Englewood Cliffs, N.J.: Prentice-Hall, 1954), and in the 2d ed. (1965), p. 166; James R. Kreutzer, *Elements of Poetry* (New York: Macmillan, 1955), p. 146; *The American Treasury, 1455–1955*, ed. Clifton Fadiman (New York: Harper, 1955), p. 617; *Exploring Poetry*, ed. M. L. Rosenthal and A. J. M. Smith (1955), p. 547, and in subsequent editions; *Fifteen Modern American Poets*, ed. Elliott (1956), p. 56; *The Washington* [D.C.] *Daily News*, 6 Sept. 1956, p. 11; *The Sound of Wings*, ed. Roberts and Briand (1957), p. 201; *A College Book of Modern Verse*, ed. Robinson and Rideout (1958), p. 430; *The Sheldon Book of Verse*, ed. P. G. Smith (Oxford: Oxford Univ. Press, 1959), v. III; *Poetry for Pleasure*, sel. by the editors of Hallmark Cards (1960), p. 113; *Trente-Cinq Jeunes Poètes Américains*, ed. Alain Bosquet (Paris: Gallimard, 1960), p. 234, with Bosquet's translation, "La mort du Mitraillaeur de l'air," on p. 235; *An Introduction to Literature: Fiction Poetry Drama*, ed. Sylvan Barnet et al. (Boston: Little, Brown, 1961), and in four subsequent editions; *Literary Types and Themes*, ed. McNamee et al. (1961), p. 620; *Introduction to Literature: Poems*, ed. Altenbernd and Lewis (1963), p. 488; *Introducing Poetry: An Anthology*, ed. Alice Coleman and John R. Theobald (New York: Holt, Rinehart and Winston, 1964), p. 264; *The Poetry of War, 1939–1945*, ed. Ian Hamilton (London: Alan Ross Ltd., 1965), p. 141; *American Poetry*, ed. Allen et al. (1965), p. 976; *Twentieth Century Writing*, ed. William T. Stafford (New York: Odyssey, 1965), p. 672; *Poems and Poets*, ed. David Aloian (St. Louis: McGraw-Hill, 1965), p. 395; *Modern American Poetry*, ed. Corbett and William J. Boldt, rev. ed. (1965), p. 132; *Coraddi* (Univ. of N.C. at Greensboro student literary magazine), Fall 1965, p. 2; *An Introduction to Poetry*, ed. X. J. Kennedy (Boston: Little, Brown, 1966), p. 319, and in all subsequent editions; *The Province of Poetry*, ed. Edwin B. Benjamin (New York: American Book Co., 1966), p. 288; *The Distinctive Voice*, ed. Martz (1966), p. 184; *Alumni News* (Univ. of N.C. at Greensboro), 54 (Spring 1966), 28, with a facsimile of RJ's holograph of this poem on the same page; *Poems Eight Lines and Under*, ed. William Cole (New York: Macmillan, 1967); *The New Modern Poetry*, ed. M. L. Rosenthal (New York: Macmillan, 1967), p. 100; *Literature for Writing*, ed.

C136   "The Wide Prospect." *Nation*, 160 (24 Feb. 1945), 222. LFLF, SP55, SP2, CP.

> *The Wide Prospect*]   THE WIDE PROSPECT | —saw *the Prospect,*
> *and the Asian fen*—   SP55⁺
> 15   gold!]   ~—   LFLF⁺
> 17   meaningless]   changed   SP55⁺
> 37   sea. . . .]   ~ . . .   SP55⁺
> 40   bones—]   ~;   SP55⁺
> 47   East or West,]   West or West,   LFLF⁺

RJ to MLJ, 13 June 1943: I've already written (last night) a new stanza for the *Wide Prospect.* . . . Here's the new stanza (it's leading up to the bird's eye view of Colonies, meaning everywhere else but Europe): What traffickers, the soldiers! How the merchants war! | Beneath their blood and gilt swim like a shade | Black friars who survey with impartial eyes | The coals where Fathers or the Heathen die, | Who bless alike the Corpses and the Trade. [¶] Pretty soon they'll be calling me the 18th century Marx, eh? Seriously, I can see now that some of the 18th Cent. practices you naturally fall into when you're writing with hatred and generality about politics, the world, and such.

RJ to Na (MM) Summer 1945: I'm glad you like the poem. I've gotten to count on you liking my longish poems; if you ever don't I'll probably break down and write short humorous [ones] for the *Saturday Evening Post*, and consequently get sent to Officer's candidate school.

C137   "An Indian Market in Mexico." *Arizona Quarterly*, 1 (Spring 1945), 19. CP.

RJ to EW, August 1941: Mexico is absolutely covered with very big contented dogs, of no definite breed, often resembling nothing you've ever seen, who lie asleep on the pavements or in the market aisles. If a Mexican dog barks at anyone he is taken to a psychoanalyst. The pet cats are tied on little strings. [¶] The upper classes have an unconscious tight hard look, as if they had got on top and were going to stay there. That's very impressive. The nicest things in Mexico, probably, are all Indian: to judge by a vague impression.

RJ to AT, September 1941: I wrote a lot of poetry this spring and two poems about Mexico this summer. I have the impression that I'm at a sort of dead end; though not when I'm writing; then it comes easily enough, too easily, I guess.

C138   "The Miller." *Arizona Quarterly*, 1 (Spring 1945), 91. CP.

C139 "1914." *Partisan Review*, 12 (Spring 1945), 178–80. LFLF, SP55, SP2, CP.

20/23   states] States LFLF[+]
21/24   It is the world of Bernstein, a universe] It is a universe SP55[+]
47/52   post-office] postoffice LFLF[+]
63/70   ground.] ~.... LFLF; ~ ... SP55[+]
67–69/75–77   his | face—] his trousers, just as his coat and hat | merge imperceptively into his face— LFLF[+]
72/74   hillside—] ~; SP55[+]
86   brought] have~ SP55[+]

C140 "Siegfried." *Nation*, 160 (21 April 1945), 447. LFLF, SP55, SP2, CP.

3   blurs—] ~,— LFLF; ~‸— SP55[+]
30   you:] ~; LFLF[+]
47–48   *no stanza break*] *stanza break* LFLF; *no stanza break* SP55[+]
49–50   *no stanza break*] *stanza break* LFLF; *no stanza break* SP55[+]
52   understand] ~, LFLF[+]
54   sleep ...] ~.... LFLF; ~ ... SP55[+]
62   *(What will you do now? I don't know);*] *(What ... know)*— LFLF; *—What ... know*— SP55[+]
63   It is these, it is these.] It is these. LFLF[+]

Reprinted in *Spearhead: 10 Years' Experimental Writing in America* (New York: New Directions, 1947), pp. 254–56; *Mid-Century American Poets*, ed. Ciardi (1950), pp. 189–90; *Reading Modern Poetry*, ed. Paul Engle and Warren Carrier (Chicago: Scott, Foresman, 1955), pp. 224–26; *The Sound of Wings*, ed. Roberts and Briand (1957), pp. 218–20; *American Literature*, ed. Andrew J. Porter et al. (Boston: Ginn and Co., 1964), pp. 688–89; *The Achievement of Randall Jarrell*, ed. Hoffman (1970), pp. 34–35.

Note: An explanatory note by RJ concerning this poem is in SP55 and SP2 on p. xiv and in CP on p. 9.

RJ to Na (MM), January 1945: I've just finished a poem I've been working on ever since I got in the army ["Siegfried"] and I thought I'd send it to you, mostly because you liked "2nd Air Force" that much.

C141 "Ernie Pyle." *Nation*, 160 (19 May 1945), 573–76. Essay. KA.

C142 "A Pilot from the Carrier." *Poetry*, 86 (June 1945), 117–18. LFLF, SP55, SP2, CP.

> Reprinted in *Modern Poetry, American and British*, ed. Friar and Brinnin (1951), p. 385; *To Play Man Number One*, ed. Hannum and Chase (1969), pp. 79–80; *Designs in Poetry*, ed. Peterson (1974); *Contemporary Poetry of North Carolina*, ed. Owen and Williams (1977), p. 66.
>
> *Note:* A note by RJ concerning this poem is in *SP55* and *SP2* on p. xiv and in *CP* on p. 9.

C143 "The Dream of Waking." *Poetry*, 66 (June 1945), 118–19. LFLF, CP.

> *epigraph all in italic*] *epigraph all in roman*   LFLF+

C144 "Mail Call." *Poetry*, 66 (June 1945), 119. LFLF, SP55, SP2, CP.

> 8   in dreams]   dreams   SP55+
> Reprinted in *New York Times Book Review*, 25 Nov. 1945, p. 2; *The Growth of American Literature*, ed. Cady et al. (1956), v. II, p. 695; *Possibilities of Poetry*, ed. Kostelanetz (1970), p. 37; *The Achievement of Randall Jarrell*, ed. Hoffman (1970), p. 38; *The Lyric Potential*, ed. James E. Miller, Jr., et al. (Glenview, Ill.: Scott Foresman, 1974), p. 286.
>
> *RJ to MLJ, 17 June 1943:* I'm also working on one about mail call and finishing one several years old, about the time of *The Christmas Roses*.

C145 "Gunner." *Poetry*, 66 (June 1945), 119–20. LFLF, SP55, SP2, CP.

> 10   over? How easy it was to die!]   over? ... It was easy as that!   SP55+
> Reprinted in *New York Times Book Review*, 25 Nov. 1945, p. 2; *Trente-Cinq Jeunes Poètes Américains*, ed. Bosquet (1960), p. 236, with a French translation by Bosquet, "Mitrailleur," on p. 237; *Possibilities of Poetry*, ed. Kostelanetz (1970), p. 33; *The Modern Age*, ed. Lief and Light, 2d ed. (1976), p. 671; *O Frabjous Day!*, ed. Myra Cohn Livingston (New York: Atheneum, 1977), p. 95; *Poetry: An Introduction*, ed. Miller and Greenberg (1981), p.25.

C146 "Leave." *Poetry*, 66 (June 1945), 120. LFLF, SP55, SP2, CP.

2 A brown four feet] Four brown feet high SP55[+]
    four feet through] three feet wide SP55[+]
10 into] to his LFLF[+]
11 missing—dead perhaps, perhaps a prisoner.] (dead ... prisoner). SP55[+]
16 water—] ~,— LFLF; ~,— SP55[+]

Note: A note by RJ concerning this poem is in SP55 and SP2 on p. xvi and in CP on p. 10.

C147 "Protocols (Birkenau, Odessa)." *Poetry*, 66 (June 1945), 121. LFLF, SP55, SP2, CP.

(Birkenau, Odessa)] [Birkenau, Odessa] LFLF; *(Birkenau, Odessa; the children speak alternately.)* SP55[+]

C148 "The Learners." *Poetry*, 66 (June 1945), 121–22. LFLF, CP.

C149 "A Ghost, a Real Ghost." *Kenyon Review*, 7 (Summer 1945), 441–42. WWZ, SP2, CP.

12 do,] ~, why, WWZ[+]
22 ghost ...] ~. WWZ[+]
28 Am I dead] —~~~? WWZ[+]

C150 "Losses" (later titled "Loss"). *Kenyon Review*, 7 (Summer 1945), 442. Los, SP55, SP2, CP.

Losses] Loss Los[+]
    3 patter in] ~ to Los[+]
    bone] ~— Los[+]
4 (The] ~ Los[+]
5 wings);] ~,; Los[+]
10 child.] ~.... Los[+]
12 beak] bill Los[+]
15–17 Has no crushed seed, from that stony crop, | Sprung narrowly to life, the world-enfolding tree | Beneath whose boughs the child's ghost sleeps?] *omitted* Los[+]
Reprinted in *Fifteen Modern American Poets*, ed. Elliott (1956), p. 56.

C151 "The Germans Are Lunatics." *Kenyon Review*, 7 (Summer 1945), 443. CP.

> *Note:* RJ included an early draft of this poem in a letter to MLJ, c. mid-May 1943. The only variants between it and the published version are contained in line 8:

> stock, or bomb,] ~‚~~‚

C152 "The Dead in Melanesia." *Partisan Review*, 12 (Summer 1945), 309. Los, SP55, SP2, CP.

> 2 psalm] ~: Los⁺
> Reprinted in *Mid-Century American Poets*, ed. Ciardi (1950), p. 196.

> *Note:* A note by RJ about this poem is in Los on pp. 66–67, in SP55 and SP2 on p. xvii, and in CP on p. 11.

C153 "The Snow-Leopard." *Sewanee Review*, 53 (Summer 1945), 425. LFLF, SP55, SP2, CP.

> 20 desire] ~, LFLF⁺
> 24 tail:] ~; LFLF⁺
> Reprinted in *Modern Poetry, American and British*, ed. Friar and Brinnin (1951), pp. 384–85; *The Modern Poets*, ed. John Malcolm Brinnin and Bill Read (New York: McGraw-Hill, 1963), p. 179, and in the 2d ed., *The Modern Poets: An American-British Anthology* (1970), p. 221; *A Little Treasury of Modern Poetry, English and American*, ed. Williams, 3d ed. (1970), pp. 560–61; *Hero's Way: Contemporary Poems in the Mythic Tradition*, ed. Allen (1971), pp. 163–64; *A Celebration of Cats*, ed. Katherine Burden (New York: Popular Library, 1976), p. 176.

C154 "To the New World" ("The leaves are struck . . ."). *Sewanee Review*, 53 (Summer 1945), 426. CP.

C155 "The State." *Sewanee Review*, 53 (Summer 1945), 427. LFLF, SP55, SP2, CP.

> 2, 4–6, 8, 10–12, 14, 16–18 *indented*] *flush left* LFLF⁺
> Reprinted in *Mid-Century American Poets*, ed. Ciardi (1950), p. 185; *Possibilities of Poetry*, ed. Kostelanetz (1970), p. 36; *The Achievement of Randall Jarrell*, ed. Hoffman (1970), p. 40; *A Little Treasury of Poetry, English and American*, ed. Williams, 3d ed. (1970), pp. 564–65.

RJ to MLJ, 28 April 1943: I thought of writing a poem asking the State (the principal god in my new machinery) why it didn't call up Kitten [RJ's pet cat] and train him to catch mice (in some army warehouse of course); but I don't want to put ideas into the world's mind, especially as they've done worse than that with dogs—their trainers are instructed never to pet them or be kind to them, since this would make them friendly.

C156 "The Street Has Changed." *Sewanee Review,* 53 (Summer 1945), 428. CP.

C157 "News." *Sewanee Review,* 53 (Summer 1945), 429. CP.

C158 "The Dead Wingman." *Nation,* 161 (8 Sept. 1945), 232. Los, SP55, SP2, CP.

> 16 gray] grey Los[+]
> 20 coaled and ashen] embers of Los[+]
> 21 worn] ~, Los[+]
>
> Reprinted in *Mid-Century American Poets,* ed. Ciardi (1950), 187–88; *The Poetry of War,* ed. Hamilton (1965), p. 144; *One Hundred Years of* The Nation*: A Centennial Anthology,* ed. Henry M. Christman (New York: Macmillan, 1965), p. 359; *Alumni News* (Univ. of N.C. at Greensboro), 54 (Spring 1966), 43.
>
> *Note:* A note by RJ about this poem is in Los, p. 65, in SP55 and SP2 on p. xv, and in CP, p. 9.
>
> *RJ to NA (MM), May 1945:* I haven't written any more long poems to send you; here is a short one ["The Dead Wingman"], though—the only one I've written in several months.

C159 "Freud to Paul: The Stages of Auden's Ideology." *Partisan Review,* 12 (Fall 1945), 437–57. Essay. TBC.

> Reprinted in *Harvard Advocate,* 108, no. 2–3 (1973), 12–16, 20–22, 24–25 (special Auden number).

C160 "Burning the Letters." *Nation,* 161 (13 Oct. 1945), 372, 374. Los, SP55, SP2, CP.

> Burning the Letters] *Burning the Letters* | *(The wife of a pilot killed in the Pacific is speaking several* | *years after his death. She was once a Christian, a Protestant.)* Los[+]

Reprinted in *Spearhead* (1947), pp. 252–54; *Mid-Century American Poets*, ed. Ciardi (1950), pp. 194–96; *Modern American Poetry*, ed. Untermeyer (1950), pp. 681–82, in the rev. shorter ed. (1955), p. 375, and in the enlarged ed. (1962), pp. 647–48; Brooks and Warren, *An Approach to Literature* (1952), pp. 365–67, and in the 4th ed. (1964), pp. 358–59, and in the 5th ed. (1975), pp. 354–55; *The Achievement of Randall Jarrell*, ed. Hoffman (1970), pp. 43–45; *Of Time and Experience*, ed. Dodge and Lindblom (1972), pp. 557–59.

RJ to Na (MM), September 1945: Would you like to print this poem ["Burning the Letters"]? It's rather long for you, but I wanted a lot of people to read it and thought the *Nation* might be the best place—putting it all from my point of view . . . [¶] The line about *a bird falling to a lobster from a / star* is truthful; nobody knew *what* it was—somebody thought it was a scorpion, a pair of scissors, a lobster's claws—it turned out not to be any of these, but jesses.

RJ to LU, 7 October 1948: As for the war poems [for inclusion in *Modern American Poetry*]: the best, I am sure—and quite a few people think so—is *Burning the Letters*; on the other hand, it's a harder poem than most of them.

RJ to LU, 2 January 1949: "Burning the Letters" is a lot better poem [than "The Refugees"] (William Carlos Williams and quite a few people think it's my best poem), in the first place; in the second place, I've partially rewritten "The Refugees" [but] haven't finished and would hate to have it in the anthology just as it was.

C161 "These Are Not Psalms." *Commentary*, 1 (Nov. 1945), 88–90. Book review of Abraham M. Klein, *Poems*, KA.

C162 "Pilots, Man Your Planes." *Nation*, 161 (1 Dec. 1945), 581. Los, SP55, SP2, CP.

(A Jill is a Japanese torpedo-plane.)] omitted SP55+
9 Who] That Los+
20–21, 37–38 *no stanza break]* *stanza break* Los+
Reprinted in *Spearhead* (1947), pp. 256–58; *Modern American Poetry*, ed. Untermeyer (1950), pp. 679–80, in rev. shorter ed. (1955), p. 380, and in enlarged ed. (1962), pp. 645–46; *Of Time and Experience*, ed. Dodge and Lindblom (1972), pp. 554–57.

RJ to Na (MM), November 1945: I'll send with this letter my carrier poem ["Pilots, Man Your Planes"]. It might be a good idea for me to put this sentence in parenthesis just under the title: *A Jill is a Japanese torpedo-plane.* I'm coming to think this because I can't find anybody who knows what a jill is.

RJ to LU, 2 January 1949: By the way, since you're using "Pilots, Man Your Planes" [in *Modern American Poetry*], it will amuse you to know that I've met five or six carrier pilots who talked to me about it; they say it really brings back the old days, you can always tell when somebody's really served on a carrier, etc. The funny thing is that I've never even been on one for a minute.

C163 "Verse Chronicle" (column by RJ). *Nation*, 161 (29 Dec. 1945), 741–42. Book review of H. D., *Tribute to the Angels*, and Alex Comfort, *The Song of Lazarus*. "Alex Comfort" in PA, and "H. D." in KA.

C164 "The Lines." *Partisan Review*, 13 (Winter 1946), 67. Los, SP55, SP2, CP.

> 8, 14 states] States Los; states SP55+
> Reprinted in *The Faber Book of Modern American Verse*, ed. W. H. Auden (London: Faber & Faber, 1956), p. 276 (in the United States by Criterion Books as *The Criterion Book of Modern American Verse*, p. 276); *The Achievement of Randall Jarrell*, ed. Hoffman (1970), pp. 42–43.

C165 "Oh, My Name It Is Sam Hall." *Nation*, 162 (19 Jan. 1946), 76. Los, SP55, SP2, CP.

> Oh, My Name It Is Sam Hall] *O My Name It Is Sam Hall* Los+
> 3 ditch.] ~: Los+
> 9 conquered.] ~— Los+

C166 "Verse Chronicle." *Nation*, 162 (2 Feb. 1946), 134–36. Book review of Walter de la Mare, *The Burning-Glass*. PA.

C167 "Verse Chronicle." *Nation*, 162 (23 Feb. 1946), 237–38. Book review of Marsden Hartley, *Selected Poems*; and *War and the Poet*, ed. Richard Eberhart and Selden Rodman. *War and the Poet* in PA as "Anthologies," and "Marsden Hartley" in KA.

RJ to Na (MM), 7 February 1946: I'll send you my verse chronicle and a poem air-mail special delivery. I made this a general one about anthologies because I thought that more palatable to readers than writing specifically about such a nondescript, really quite silly anthology.

C168 "New Georgia." *Nation*, 162 (2 March 1946), 263. Los, SP55, SP2, CP.

9 in] on Los+
Reprinted in *The Realities of Literature*, ed. Dietrich (1971), p. 124.

Note: A note by RJ about this poem is in Los, p. 67; a slightly revised version appears in SP55 and SP2 on p. xvii and in CP on p. 11.

C169 "The Märchen (Grimm's Tales)." *Sewanee Review*, 54 (Spring 1946), 269–72. Los, SP55, SP2, CP.

57 together,] ~— Los+
Reprinted in *A Southern Vanguard: The John Peale Bishop Memorial Volume*, ed. Allen Tate (New York: Prentice-Hall, 1947), pp. 153–55; *Fifteen Modern American Poets*, ed. Elliott (1956), 49–52; *The Achievement of Randall Jarrell*, ed. Hoffman (1970), pp. 46–48.

C170 "The Death of the Gods" (later titled "1945: The Death of the Gods"). *Nation*, 162 (6 April 1946), 402. Los, SP55, SP2, CP.

The Death of the Gods] *1945: The Death of the gods* Los+
10 us,] ~; Los+
12 obedient);] ~)— Los+
24 oecumenical] ecumenical Los+
Note: A French translation by Renaud de Jouvenal, "1945: La Mort des Dieux," appeared in *Europe: Revue Mensuelle*, 37 (Feb.–March 1959), 169.

C171 "The Subway from New Britain to the Bronx." *Nation*, 162 (20 April 1946), 472. Los, SP55, SP2, CP.

14 punishment,] ~— Los+

Note: A note by RJ about this poem is in Los, p. 68; a slightly revised version appears in SP55 and SP2 on p. xvii and in CP on p. 11.

C172 "The Sacred Wood" (later completely rewritten and titled "In the Ward: The Sacred Wood"). *Nation*, 162 (20 April 1946), 472. Rewritten version in Los, SP55, SP2, and CP.

Note: A note by RJ on the rewritten version is in SP55 and SP2 on p. xi and in CP on p. 6.

C173 Unsigned editorial brief beginning "Nettled by the shrill justified yelps." *Nation*, 162 (4 May 1946), 522.

C174 "Verse Chronicle." *Nation*, 162 (25 May 1946), 632–34. Book review of Oscar Williams, *That's All That Matters*; Arnold Stein, *Perilous Balance*; Stanton Coblentz, *The Music Makers*; Ruth Pitter, *The Bridge*. RJ's introductory comments from this essay in PA as "Bad Poets" and conclusion and reviews in KA.

C175 "A Camp in the Prussian Forest." *Nation*, 162 (22 June 1946), 756. In Los, SP55, SP2, CP.

> 3 starving] sodden Los[+]
> 33 chimney . . .] ~. . . . Los[+]
> Reprinted in *Horizon*, 16 (Sept. 1947), 156–57; *Spearhead* (1947), pp. 251–52; *Mid-Century American Poets*, ed. Ciardi (1950), pp. 185–86; *Modern American Poetry*, ed. Untermeyer (1950), p. 678; *Chief Modern Poets of England and America*, ed. Sanders et al., 4th ed. (1962), and in the 5th ed. (1970); *Poetry of War*, ed. Hamilton (1965), pp. 142–43; *Modern American Poetry*, ed. Untermeyer, enlarged ed. (1962), p. 644; *American Poetry*, ed. Allen et al. (1965), pp. 976–77; *100 American Poems of the Twentieth Century*, ed. Laurence Perrine and James M. Reid (New York: Harcourt, Brace, Jovanovich, 1966), pp. 227–28; *Alumni News* (Univ. of N.C. at Greensboro), 54 (Spring 1966), 43; *The New Modern Poetry*, ed. Rosenthal (1967), pp. 100–101; *The Many Worlds of Poetry*, ed. Jacob Drachler and Virginia Terris (New York: Knopf, 1969), p. 117; *The Survival Years*, ed. Salzman (1969), pp. 160–61; *Twentieth Century Poetry*, ed. Carol Marshall (Boston: Houghton, Mifflin, 1971); *The New Voices: The Poetry of the Present*, ed. Carli and Kilman (1971); *Themes in American Literature*, ed. Charles Genthe and George Keithley (Lexington, Mass.: Heath, 1972), pp. 554–55; *The Modern Age*, ed. Lief and Light, 2d ed. (1972), pp. 623–24, and in 3d ed. (1976), p. 665; *Introduction to Poetry*, ed. William C. Cavanaugh (Dubuque, Iowa: William C. Brown, 1974), pp. 377–78.
>
> *Note:* An explanatory note by RJ concerning this poem is in *Losses*, p. 65, and in slightly revised form in SP55 and SP2 on pp. xv–xvi and in CP, on p. 10.

C176 "A Chorus." *Kenyon Review*, 8 (Summer 1946), 428–29.

C177 "The Dead." *Partisan Review*, 13 (Summer 1946), 349–50. CP.

C178 "The Poet and His Public." *Partisan Review*, 13 (Sept.–Oct. 1946), 488–500. Book review of Josephine Miles, *Local Measures*; Adam Drinan, *Women of the Happy Island*; *A Little Treasury of Modern Poetry*, ed. Oscar Williams; Robert Graves, *Poems 1938–45*; Denis Devlin, *Lough Derg*; William Carlos Williams, *Paterson* (Book One); and Elizabeth Bishop, *North and South*. In PA as "Poets."

C179 "The Place of Death." *Nation*, 163 (7 Dec. 1946), 650. Los, SP55, SP2, CP.

> Reprinted in *Spearhead* (1947), pp. 250–51; *Poetry Q*, 9 (Autumn 1947), 165–66; *American Sampler: A Selection of New Poetry*, ed. Francis Coleman Rosenberger (Iowa City: The Prairie Press, 1951), 49–50.

> *Note:* A note by RJ on this poem is in Los on p. 66; it is not reprinted in SP55, SP2, or CP.

> *RJ to RL, May 1946:* I have just finished my Spinoza poem ["The Place of Death"], oh joy!

> *RJ to RL, 10 July 1946:* I've written two poems and finished my Spinoza.

C180 "Eighth Air Force." *Quarterly Review of Literature*, 4, no. 1 (1947), 20. Los, SP55, SP2, CP.

> 4 *Ah*] O Los+
> 9 one; one.] One; One. Los+
> 10 *Ah, Murderers!*] O murderers! Los+
> 17 savior] saviour Los+
> 18 lying? . . .] ~?ᴀ Los+
> Reprinted in *Mid-Century American Poets*, ed. Ciardi (1950), p. 188; *An Approach to Literature*, ed. Cleanth Brooks et al., 3d ed. (New York: Appleton-Century-Crofts, 1952), pp. 397–99, in the 4th ed. (1964), p. 396, in the 5th ed. (1975), p. 440; *Reading Modern Poetry*, ed. Engle and Carrier (1955), p. 223; *Modern Verse in English*, ed. Cecil and Tate (1958), p. 585; *Trente-Cinq Jeunes Poètes Américains*, ed. Bosquet (1960), p. 232, with a French translation by Bosquet, "Huitième Armée de l'Air," on p. 233; *Discovering Modern Poetry*, ed. Drew and Connor (1961), pp. 279–80; *Poet's Choice*, ed. Paul Engle and Joseph Langland (New York: Dial, 1962), p. 140, with a brief comment on the poem by RJ on p. 141, and in the 1966 reissue (Delta Book 6982); *Introduction to Literature*, 2d ed., ed. Altenbernd and Lewis (1963), p. 488, and in the 3d ed. (1975); *National Poetry Festival, October 22–24, 1962* (1964), p. 311, with RJ's brief comment on the poem also on p. 311; *The Many Worlds of Poetry*, ed. Drachler and

Terris (1969), p. 123; *Poetry: Meaning and Form*, ed. Schwartz and Roby (1969), pp. 276–77; *Quarterly Review of Literature*, 14, nos. 1–2 (1969); *The Achievement of Randall Jarrell*, ed. Hoffman (1970), p. 42; *A Book of Modern Poetry*, ed. McDermott and Lowery (1970), p. 227; *The Personal Response to Literature*, ed. Harold DeLisle et al. (Boston: Houghton, Mifflin, 1971), p. 250; *The Poem: An Anthology*, ed. Greenfield and Weatherhead, 2d ed. (1972), p. 467; *The Norton Anthology of Modern Poetry*, ed. Ellmann and O'Clair (1973), p. 880; *The Norton Introduction to Literature: Poetry*, ed. Hunter (1973), pp. 17–18; *Quarterly Review of Literature: 30th Anniversary Poetry Retrospective*, ed. T. Weiss and Renée Weiss (Princeton, N.J.: Quarterly Review of Literature, 1974), p. 80; *The New Oxford Book of American Verse*, ed. Ellmann (1976), p. 772; *Literature: Fiction Poetry Drama*, ed. Davis et al. (1977), pp. 731–32; *Fine Frenzy: Enduring Themes in Poetry*, ed. Baylor and Stokes, 2d ed. (1978).

Note: An explanatory note by RJ concerning this poem is in Los, on p. 66, and in revised and expanded form in SP55 and SP2 on p. xiii and in CP on p. 18.

C181 "A Ghost Story." *Quarterly Review of Literature*, 4, no. 1 (1947), 20–21. CP.

Reprinted in *Quarterly Review of Literature: 30th Anniversary Poetry Retrospective*, ed. Weiss (1974), pp. 80–81.

C182 "From the Kingdom of Necessity." *Nation*, 164 (18 Jan. 1947), 74, 76. Book review of Robert Lowell, *Lord Weary's Castle*, PA.

Reprinted in *Mid-Century American Poets*, ed. Ciardi (1950), pp. 158–67 (as "Robert Lowell's Poetry"); in part as "On Lowell's Where the Rainbow Ends" in *Readings for Liberal Education*, ed. Louis G. Locke et al., rev. ed. (New York: Rinehart, 1954), part II, pp. 279–80; *On Contemporary Literature*, ed. Richard Kostelanetz (New York: Avon, 1964), pp. 404–14; *Robert Lowell: A Collection of Critical Essays*, ed. Thomas Parkinson (Englewood Cliffs, N.J.: Prentice-Hall, 1968), pp. 40–47; *Robert Lowell: A Portrait of the Artist in His Time*, ed. Michael London and Robert Boyers (New York: David Lewis, 1970), pp. 19–27; *Critics on Robert Lowell*, ed. Jonathan Price (Coral Gables, Fla.: Univ. of Miami Press, 1972), pp. 47–52.

C183 "The Rising Sun." *Kenyon Review*, 9 (Spring 1947), 260–61. Los, SP55, SP2, CP.

> 30 school.] ~. . . . Los⁺
>
> 38 way,] ~: Los⁺
>
> Reprinted in *Horizon*, 16 (Sept. 1947), 157–58.

C184 "The Range in the Desert." *Virginia Quarterly Review*, 23 (Spring 1947), 231. Los, SP55, SP2, CP.

> Reprinted in *Poems from the* Virginia Quarterly Review, *1925–1967*, ed. Charlotte Kohler (Charlottesville: University Press of Virginia, 1969), p. 144; *The New Oxford Book of American Verse*, ed. Ellmann (1976), pp. 772–73.

C185 "A Ward in the States." *Virginia Quarterly Review*, 23 (Spring 1947), 232. Los, SP55, SP2, CP.

> Reprinted in *Fifteen Modern American Poets*, ed. Elliott (1956), p. 60; *Poems from the* Virginia Quarterly Review, ed. Kohler (1969), p. 145.
>
> *Note:* A note by RJ on this poem is in Los, p. 68; a slightly revised version appears in SP55 and SP2 on p. xvii and in CP on p. 11.

C186 "Jews at Haifa." *Partisan Review*, 14 (May–June 1947), 295–96. Los, SP55, SP2, CP.

> 30 Ours.] "~." Los⁺
>
> Reprinted in *Modern American Poetry*, ed. Untermeyer (1950), p. 683, and in the enlarged ed. (1962), p. 649; *The New Partisan Reader*, ed. Phillips and Rahv (1953), pp. 164–65.
>
> *Note:* A note by RJ on this poem is in SP55 and SP2 on p. xv and in CP on p. 9.

C187 "Tenderness and Passive Sadness." *New York Times Book Review*, 1 June 1947, p. 4. Book review of Robert Frost, *Steeple Bush*. KA.

C188 "A Field Hospital." *Nation*, 164 (14 June 1947), 714. Los, SP55, SP2, CP.

C189 "Stalag Luft." *Nation*, 164 (28 June 1947), 773. Los, SP55, SP2, CP.

> Reprinted in broadsheet accompanying Library of Congress phonograph album V.P. 24B, *Twentieth Century Poetry in English* (see below, **G4**); and in *The Achievement of Randall Jarrell*, ed. Hoffman (1970), p. 41.

> *Note:* A note by RJ about this poem is in Los on p. 66, in SP55 and SP2 on p. 66, and in CP on p. 9 (with one minor textual variant that carries no authorial authority).

C190 "Corrective for Critics." *New York Times Book Review*, 24 Aug. 1947, p. 4. Book review of Yvor Winters, *In Defense of Reason.* KA.

C191 "Poems by Corbière." *New York Times Book Review*, 28 Sept. 1947, p. 5. Book review of Tristan Corbière, *Poems* (trans. Walter McElroy).

> *Note:* See **C196** for another RJ review of this title.

C192 "The Breath of Night." *Kenyon Review*, 9 (Autumn 1947), 507. Los, SP55, SP2, CP.

> Reprinted in *New York Times Book Review*, 4 April 1948, p. 2; *New York Times Book Review*, 13 March 1955, p. 2; *The Faber Book of Modern American Verse* (also *The Criterion Book of American Verse*), ed. Auden (1956), pp. 276–77; *The United States in Literature*, ed. Walter Blair et al. (Glenview, Ill.: Scott, Foresman, 1963), p. 594.

C193 "The Clock in the Tower of the Church." *Kenyon Review*, 9 (Autumn 1947), 508–9. CP.

> *headnote all in roman*] *headnote all in ital* CP

C194 "Overture: The Hostages." *Kenyon Review*, 9 (Autumn 1947), 509. CP.

C195 "The Child of Courts" (later titled "The Prince"). *Kenyon Review*, 9 (Autumn 1947), 510. Los, SP55, SP2, CP.

> THE CHILD OF COURTS] *The Child of Courts* Los; *THE PRINCE* SP55⁺

C196 "Verse Chronicle." *Nation*, 165 (18 Oct. 1947), 424–25. Book review of W. H. Auden, *The Age of Anxiety*, and Tristan Corbière, *Poems*. "Tristan Corbière" in PA, and "W. H. Auden" in KA.

C197 "In the Camp There Was One Alive." *Nation*, 165 (1 Nov. 1947), 44. Los, CP.

> 14/14–15   In gladness—It is the dead.]   In gladness—| [*indented*] It is the dead.   Los⁺
>
> *Note:* A note by RJ on this poem is in Los on p. 67; it is not reprinted in CP.

C198 "Sears Roebuck," *Nation*, 165 (8 Nov. 1947), 506. Los, SP55, SP2, CP.

> *Note:* A note by RJ on this poem is in SP55 and SP2 on p. xii and in CP on p. 7.

C199 "The Other Robert Frost." *Nation*, 165 (29 Nov. 1947), 588, 590–92. Essay-review of Robert Frost, *A Masque of Mercy*. In PA as the first of "Two Essays on Robert Frost."

> Reprinted in *Alumni News* (Univ. of N.C. at Greensboro), 54 (Spring 1966), 39–41.

C200 "Money." *Partisan Review*, 15 (Jan. 1948), 45–47. Los, SP55, SP2, CP.

> 7   remember;]   ~:   Los⁺
> 31   too.]   ~. . . .   Los⁺
> 51   Harriet have]   Harriet've   Los⁺
>
> *Note:* A note by RJ on this poem is in Los on p. 65; a somewhat longer revised version is in SP55 and SP2 on pp. xii–xiii and in CP, p. 7.
>
> *RJ to SBQ, 2 January 1949:* . . . she didn't understand *Money*; the old man *doesn't* know "how incompletely he satisfies the desires of the

spirit," but dies as he lived, thinking that power is everything—when there's nothing left to buy you can still control people through (tax-exempt) Foundations.

C201 "Lament of the Children of Israel in Rome" (Ferdinand Gregorovius). *Commentary*, 5 (Feb. 1948), 171–72. CP.

Reprinted in Ferdinand Gregorovius, *The Ghetto and the Jews of Rome*, trans. Moses Hadas (New York: Schocken Books, 1948), pp. 11–16.

C202 "Lady Bates." *Nation*, 166 (28 Feb. 1948), 239–40. Los, SP55, SP2, CP.

49 bare-footed] barefooted SP55+
    pig-tailed] pigtailed SP55+
Reprinted in broadsheet accompanying Library of Congress 78–RPM recording P24 (Album V) and in booklet accompanying *Twentieth Century Poetry in English* (1949), LP album P L7 (se below, **G4**); *Mid-Century American Poets*, ed. Ciardi (1950), pp. 199–201; *North Carolina Poetry*, ed. Richard Walser, rev. ed. (Richmond, Va: Garrett & Massie, 1951), p. 163.

Note: An explanatory note by RJ concerning this poem is in SP55 and SP2 on p. ix and in CP on p. 5.

RJ to LU, 7 October 1948: I think that the best of my "civilian" poems to use would be *Lady Bates*; it is, with most people, the most popular poem I've ever written.

RJ to LU, 2 January 1949: "Lady Bates" doesn't seem to me like [John Crowe] Ransom but it is a little like Corbière's "Rondels pour apres"— if you ever come on my translation of them you'll see what I mean.

C203 "Jonah." *Virginia Quarterly Review*, 24 (Spring 1948), 214–15. SLC, SP55, SP2, CP.

16 "But] ˌ~   SLC+
22 die....] ~ ... SLC+
31 "To] ˌ~   SLC+
36 night:] ~. SLC+
Reprinted in *Modern Religious Poems: A Contemporary Anthology*, ed. Jacob Trapp (New York: Harper & Row, 1964); *Poems from the* Virginia Quarterly Review, ed. Kohler (1969), pp. 146–47; *The Achievement of Randall Jarrell*, ed. Hoffman (1970), pp. 55–56; *Contemporary Poetry in America*, ed. Williams (1973), p. 34.

C204 "Verse Chronicle." *Nation,* 166 (27 March 1948), 360–61. Book review of Henry Reed, *A Map of Verona*; Rolfe Humphries, *Forbid Thy Ravens*; John Ciardi, *Other Skies.* KA.

C205 "Verse Chronicle." *Nation,* 166 (24 April 1948), 447–48. Book review of R. P. Blackmur, *The Good Europeans.* In PA as "R. P. Blackmur."

C206 "Verse Chronicle." *Nation,* 166 (8 May 1948), 512–13. Book review of Jean Garrigue, *The Ego and the Centaur*; Conrad Aiken, *The Kid*; Muriel Rukeyser, *The Green Wave.* "Muriel Rukeyser" in PA; "Jean Garrigue" and "Conrad Aiken" in KA.

C207 "John Ransom's Poetry." *Sewanee Review,* 56 (Summer 1948), 378–90. Essay. PA.

> Reprinted in *John Crowe Ransom: Critical Essays and a Bibliography,* ed. Thomas D. Young (Baton Rouge: Louisiana State Univ. Press, 1968), pp. 69–79.

C208 "The 'Serious' Critic." *Nation,* 166 (12 June 1948), 670–72. Letter in which RJ responds to Conrad Aiken's attack on his review of *The Kid* (**C206**).

C209 "Verse Chronicle." *Nation,* 167 (17 July 1948), 80–81. Book review of Karl Shapiro, *Trial of a Poet*; Bertolt Brecht, *Selected Poems*; John Berryman, *The Dispossessed.* KA.

C210 "Terms." *Poetry,* 72 (Sept. 1948), 291–94. SLC, SP55, SP2, CP.

> 14   door and]   door,   SLC$^+$
> 57   awoke;]   ~:   SLC$^+$
> 70   but]   then   SLC$^+$
> Reprinted in *Trente-cinq Jeunes Poètes Américains,* ed. Bosquet (1960), pp. 226, 228, 230, with a French translation by Bosquet, "Termes," on pp. 227, 229, 231.

C211 "The Sleeping Beauty: Variation of the Prince." *Poetry*, 72 (Sept. 1948), 294–95. SLC, SP55, SP2, CP.

2   grey]   gray   SLC⁺
10 uncurl . . .]   ~.   SLC⁺
17 finger—]   ~‸   SLC⁺
19 touch—just]   touch (just   SLC⁺
20 once—]   ~)   SLC⁺
22 Death. . . .]   ~.   SLC⁺
30 found—]   ~;   SLC⁺
Reprinted in *Fifteen Modern American Poets*, ed. Elliott (1956), p. 52; *Hero's Way*, ed. Allen (1971), pp. 353–54.

C212 "The King's Hunt" (later titled "A Hunt in the Black Forest"). *Poetry*, 72 (Sept. 1948), 296–98. LW, CP

The King's Hunt]   A Hunt in the Black Forest   LW⁺
2   I call out,]   He calls out: LW⁺
3   my]   his   LW⁺
4   my]   his   LW⁺
[8] *no line*]   The red dwarf   LW⁺
8   I read]   he reads   LW⁺
11–33 *completely rewritten*   LW⁺
[12] *no line*]   The stag is grazing in the wood.   LW⁺
34 out; and he bares]   out. Bares   LW⁺
35 grins.]   smiles.   LW⁺
36–37 The mute's laugh bubbles like the pot | That stands in the embers; with]   The pot bubbles from the embers in the laugh | The mute laughs. With   LW⁺
39 vacantly.]   ~—   LW⁺
41–42 over—till the king at last | Says no more, but ladles]   over. The hunter ladles   LW⁺
43 oily]   shining   LW⁺
44 silently; the]   ~. The   LW⁺
46 The last, little finger]   The last finger   LW⁺
47 runs]   scuttles   LW⁺
48–61 *completely rewritten*   LW⁺
64 world;]   ~ . . .   LW⁺
65 And, over the set limbs, the Hunter wheels. . . .]   *omitted*   LW⁺
67 hut—]   ~,   LW⁺
70 kettle]   pot laughing   LW⁺
71 kettle]   pot   LW⁺
73 panting: a]   ~. A   LW⁺
74 "Let *me*, let *me*"; and the]   Let *me*! Let *me*! The   LW⁺
75–76 *no stanza break*]   *stanza break*   LW⁺
76–77 They press their noses tight against the pane | And the small one sees. . . .]   *omitted*   LW⁺

79 on] ~, LW⁺
80 wrong] ~. LW⁺

C213 "Afterwards" (four adaptations from Corbière's *Rondels pour après*). *Poetry*, 72 (Sept. 1948), 299–301. SLC, SP55, SP2, CP.

2 —The] ‸~ SLC⁺
   our] Your SLC⁺
9 you,] ~‸ SLC⁺

C214 "Hope" ("The week is dealt out like a hand"). *Nation*, 167 (16 Oct. 1948), 431. SLC, SP55, SP2, CP.

7   catch] crack SLC⁺
11 *Woe's*] *woe's* SLC⁺
17 Impossible] *Impossible* SLC⁺
22 *Due,*] ~— SLC⁺
29 *Woe's*] *woe's* SLC⁺
35 Impossible] *Impossible* SLC⁺
Reprinted in *Modern American Poetry*, ed. Untermeyer (1950), p. 685, and in rev. shorter ed. (1955), p. 377, and enlarged ed. (1962), p. 651; *New York Times Book Review*, 7 Sept. 1952, p. 2; *100 American Poems*, ed. Perrine and Reid (1966), pp. 230–31; *Imaginative Literature*, ed. Morris et al. (1968), pp. 320–21; *Practical English* (Scholastic Teacher Edition), 7 Feb. 1969; *Possibilities of Poetry*, ed. Kostelanetz (1970), pp. 47–48.

RJ to EE, 5 October 1948: I send in this letter a poem ["Hope"] I wrote last spring—it's just printed in a magazine. Postmen here are dressed in grey; and my poem parodies a once famous English line of poetry that goes, "In Folly's cup still laughs the bubble, Joy." And in English we talk about entertaining an angel awares à la Abraham. Also, in old novels, people are often left fortunes by their uncles in Australia, who die.

RJ to LU, 2 January 1949: Several people liked *Hope* as you did— better than I expected it to be liked, really; I guess the mailman is everybody's tutelary deity—the only one left for most or many people. I can never see a mailman without thinking he's mine, or an envelope without thinking "Maybe it's addressed to me."

C215 "The Olive Garden" (Rilke). *Nation*, 167 (18 Dec. 1948), 700. SLC, CP.

Reprinted in *New York Times Book Review*, 19 Sept. 1954, p. 2; *The Achievement of Randall Jarrell*, ed. Hoffman (1970), p. 50.

C216 "The Night before the Night before Christmas." *Kenyon Review*, 11 (Winter 1949), 31–42. SLC, SP55, SP2, CP.

> 1 Apartment] Apartments SLC⁺
> 62, 79, 109, 114, 115, 125, 126, 129, 135, 138, 139, 166, 211, 221,
> 249, 265, 276, 373, 379, 385 ....] ... SLC⁺
> 124 In] in SLC⁺
> 156 SEVenty] SEVen SLC⁺
> 290–91 *stanza break*] *no stanza break* SLC⁺
> 316 great, almost, as] greater, ~, than SLC⁺
> 326 Hansel] Hänsel SLC⁺
> 345 grey] gray SLC⁺
> Reprinted in *Shadowbox*, ed. Kathryn D. McMillan and Joanne Dean
> (New York: Harcourt, Brace, Jovanovich, 1975), p. 75.

> *Note:* A note by RJ on this poem is in SP55 and SP2 on p. x and in CP
> on pp. 5–6.

> *RJ to EB, 30 November 1948:* I wanted to send you the Rilke transla-
> tions I talked about. Also I wanted to send you the poem I told you I'd
> written ["The Night before the Night before Christmas"], but I wish
> you'd send it back when you're through with it. . . . I haven't another
> copy, though it will soon be in *Kenyon*.

C217 "A Game at Salzburg." *Nation*, 168 (1 Jan. 1949), 20. SLC, SP55, SP2, CP.

> 5 is] iss SLC⁺
> 37-38 *no stanza break*] *stanza break* SLC⁺
> 38 Life, life everywhere] *omitted* SLC⁺
> 39/38 acceptance,] ~ ₐ SLC⁺
> Reprinted in *Mid-Century American Poets*, ed. Ciardi (1950), pp. 191–
> 92; *The Norton Anthology of Modern Poetry*, ed. Ellmann and O'Clair
> (1973), pp. 883–84, and in subsequent editions; *American Poetry Re-
> view*, 6 (July–Aug. 1977), 12 (early version with variants).

> *Note:* A note by RJ on this poem is in SP55 and SP2 on p. xi and in CP
> on p. 6.

> *RJ to EE, October 1948:* What you say about "A Game at Salzburg"
> is all true; and some of it—the part about the change between the
> American among the things he just knows by seeing, and the last of the
> poem—I had not realized, at least not that way. The point of the end
> of the poem is that when the world says in anguished longing accept-
> ance *Hier bin i'* there is no answering *Du bist du* ever, though the world
> feels that there is always just about to be. This is meant to express our
> longing, worshipping, painful acceptance of things: a sort of question-
> and-waiting that has its own answer.

RJ to RL, April 1949: I was delighted you liked *A Game at Salzburg* that well. Peter [Taylor] writes that he's sent you *Hohensalzburg* which is *really* full of German scenery—Austrian, I mean.

C218   "Transient Barracks." *Nation*, 168 (26 Feb. 1949), 244. SLC, SP55, SP2, CP.

TRANSIENT BARRACKS]   *Transient Barracks* | (1944)   SLC⁺
24   across to]   to   SLC⁺
26   darkness; his]   ~. His   SLC⁺
28   "The times I've dreamed that I was back . . ."]   *The times I've dreamed that I was back . . .*—SLC⁺
33   thinks, "I'm back for good. The States, the States!"]   thinks: *I'm back for good. The States, The States!*   SLC⁺
Note: An explanatory note by RJ about this poem is in SP55 and SP2 on pp. xiii–xiv and in CP on p. 8.

C219   "A Soul." *Nation*, 168 (5 March 1949), 279. SLC, SP55, SP2, CP.

10   sun,"]   ~."   SLC⁺
     art]   are   SP55⁺
Reprinted in *Chief Modern Poets of Britain and America*, ed. Sanders et al., 5th ed. (1970).

Note: An early version of "A Soul" appears in *American Poetry Review*, 6 (July–Aug. 1977), 12.

C220   "Hohensalzburg" (later titled "Hohensalzburg: Fantastic Variations on a Theme of Romantic Character"). *Poetry*, 74 (April 1949), 1–7. SLC, SP55, SP2, CP.

HOHENSALZBURG]   *Hohensalzburg: Fantastic Variations on a Theme of Romantic Character*   SLC⁺
12   "I am a dweller of the Earth."]   *I am a dweller of the earth.*   SLC⁺
22   "They will do,]   *They will do*   SLC⁺
23   But not forever."]   *But not forever.*   SLC⁺
25   earth]   Earth   SLC⁺
28–29   These, and the light that was caught in the boughs at sunset | And lay sleeping there, all night, beneath the leaves—]   *omitted*   SLC⁺
35/33   "I would be invisible."]   *I would be invisible.*   SLC⁺
37/35   saw]   ~,   SLC⁺

38–39 In the window across the room—| Gray as the gray-green milk of the stream—] *omitted* SLC⁺

40/36 limes:] ~— SLC⁺

50/46 I felt turning above] I felt at SLC⁺

53/49 "Only look."] *Only look.* SLC⁺

55/51 "I am here behind the moonlight."] *I am here behind the moonlight.* SLC⁺

73/69 forever.] ~: SLC⁺

75–76 *stanza break*] *no stanza break* SP55⁺

76 Here in the last, least room] *omitted* SLC⁺

80/75 "I am then not dead?"] *I am then not dead?* SLC⁺

86/81 "You are asleep."] *You are asleep.* SLC⁺

87–92/81–87 *all in roman*] *all in ital* SLC⁺

92/87 asleep] *asleep.* SLC⁺

93 I shall open your lips, sink past them into your dream] *omitted* SLC⁺

94, 96, 98, 100, 102, 103/88, 89, 91, 93, 95, 97 I shall take you and . . ." | "No, no, I shall never." | "You must not know," | "I—I shall kiss your throat." | "There, it is only a dream. | I shall not so—I shall never so."] *quotation marks omitted, and all in ital* SLC⁺

104 I looked at you.] *omitted* SLC⁺

113/105 tree flower] ~-~ SLC⁺

115/107 was—] was the taste of— SLC⁺

119/111 throat:] ~. SLC⁺

121–22/111–12 *stanza break*] *no stanza break* SLC⁺

122–112 I would wake and fall asleep and wake:] I woke and fell asleep and woke: SLC⁺

124/114 light and living,] light, a life SLC⁺

125–26/115 Was pulsing under its flesh. When I saw that it was blood,] Pulsed there. When . . . was my~, SLC⁺

132/121 "You must not so.] *You must not so.* SLC⁺

133–34/122–23 *all in roman*] *all in ital* SLC⁺

135–40/124–26 I grew back, slowly, into a child. | The past is a child that sucks our blood | Back into the earth. . . . I said, "Little Sister, | I know now that you are my life." | You answered | [*indented*] "I am also death."] I said to you, "Before I was a ghost | I was only a—| [*indented*] a ghost wants blood. SLC⁺

140–41/126–27 *stanza break*] *no stanza break* SLC⁺

142 A child in the moonlight of the wood] *omitted* SLC⁺

143/128 night:] ~— SLC⁺

145/130 shine.] ~. . . . SLC⁺

150/135 Then, blanching,] Then SLC⁺

151/136 starry limbs] limbs SLC⁺

153/138 Being] dweller SLC⁺

157/142 deer,] ~; SLC⁺

157–58/142–43 *stanza break*] *no stanza break* SLC⁺

158/143 And making] Make SLC⁺

thalers.] thaler. SLC⁺

158–159/143–144 *stanza break*] *no stanza break* SLC⁺
161/146 *verboten.*] ~." SLC⁺
no line/147 *no line*] Or so it went once: I have forgotten. . . . SLC⁺
162–63/148–49 *stanza break*] *no stanza break* SLC⁺
163/149 "What I wish you to call me I shall never hear."] *What I wish you to call me I shall never hear.* SLC⁺
164/150 change:] ~; SLC⁺
167/153 But not forever:] *But not forever:* SLC⁺
168–173/154–160 Stars fall, the iron is earth; and our castle, earth | At its end, a forest through which the deer | May run on, life on life, beneath the limes | That spring age after age from our great limbs—| Will live, as this wood knows life; | Will breathe, as the wood breathes, years.] *Many a star | Has fallen, many a ghost | Has met, at the path to the wood, a ghost | That has changed at last, in love, to a ghost—| [stanza break] We should always have known. In this wood, on this Earth | Graves open, the dead are wandering: | In the end we wake from everything.* SLC⁺
176/165 understood] ~— SLC⁺
no line/162–63 *no line*] Except one word—| *In the end one wakes from everything.* SLC⁺
178/166 understood] ~— SLC⁺

Note: An early version of "Hohensalzburg" appeared in *American Poetry Review* 6 (July–Aug. 1977), 12–13.

RJ to EE, 3 February 1948: I've just been playing *Don Quixote* on the phonograph, and noticing that its sub-title is *Fantastic Variations on a Theme of Knightly Character.* I'd been correcting proof on *Hohensalzburg* (I'll send it to you in print next month) and I thought, "A good subtitle for it would be Fantastic Variations on a Theme of Romantic Character." I tried to imagine what a reader would make of it who knew nothing about Salzburg or me, and I couldn't; in fact, when I read I think, "What does it *really* mean?" And this I can't answer, though usually I know exactly what my poems mean. It's like a dream that needs analysis to be plain.

RJ to RL, 5 December 1948: Peter [Taylor] has a copy of my long *Hohensalzburg* poem—I haven't, or I'd send one; I'll tell him to send it to you instead of sending it back to me.

RJ to LU, 2 January 1949: I don't suggest any brand new poems [for *Modern American Poetry*] because the best two I have are too long, 200 and 450 lines; the long one, "The Night Before the Night Before Christmas," is in the Winter *Kenyon,* and the other's named *Hohensalzburg* and will be in *Poetry* this spring . I imagine you'll like the second, judging from what you've written about Heine. He's one of my favorite poets—I could recognize the linden trees in Salzburg as lindens just from having read about them in Heine.

RJ to SBQ, 11 May 1949: I'm delighted that you liked *Hohensalzburg* so well. No, there's no reference to Kafka's castle; Hohensalzburg *is* a big castle, the best I ever saw, on the hill above Salzburg—I lived under it all last summer. Germans (some of them) really think that ghosts, if you meet them, change you into something else, just like the *Wizard of Oz. These,* at the end, refers first to "our life, our death, and what came past our life" just before; second, to all the varied and opposed things in the poem, many of which have been mentioned in the ten or fifteen lines before.

RJ to SBQ, 24 November 1951: I wrote it ["Hohensalzburg"] in a very queer way. Schloss Leopoldskron, where I stayed, is a big 18th century chateau with tremendous gardens, statues, [and] a lake (it's rather described in "A Game at Salzburg"). I'd been there a week or so, quite overcome—there were only five or six others there. I began writing it breathlessly sitting on a pedestal that had lost its statue, out by the marsh at the end of the garden; the stone maid was there, stone horses, too. I wrote it all either sitting there on the pedestal or else in bed in the early morning looking out at dawn at Hohensalzburg—and it was all done in three or four mornings—I stayed breathless. Done but not *done*—I couldn't manage to finish it as I wanted it finished until six or eight months later when it came out in *Poetry*—I'd try, no good. I like several of the things left out, but I think the revised version is as easy to believe as such a subject can be made by *me.* Now, one has to consent to 2 or 3 things but, in the other, considerably more. It's easy for you because you're imaginative and love metamorphosis; it's not for The World. I felt about the revised one, *Now it's smooth and really done,* in comparison to the troubled way I'd felt about the old. I like *the past is a child that sucks our blood / Back into the Earth* and I think it's true mostly, *but* I think it comes out and says the moral, more than anything in such a poem should. But "Hohensalzburg" has always puzzled me; I didn't do anything, it just came. And several of the strange sentences in it[,] *I would be invisible . . . They will do, but not forever . . . I am a being of the Earth . . .*[,] were really said by someone.

C221 "A Perfectly Free Association." *Nation,* 168 (30 April 1949), 503. CP.

C222 "The Island." *Partisan Review,* 16 (May 1949), 483–84. SLC, SP55, SP2, CP.

17 sand. . . .] ~ . . . SLC+
18 Till I saw Europe naked in its surf,] I lay with you, Europe, in a net of snows: SLC+
19 Open to my barbed limbs the leagues] And all my trolls—their noses flattened into Lapps' SLC+

20 Of its dark blood, the sweet moon wet with bars]   Against the thin horn of my windows—wept;   SLC[+]

21–25 "The locks that glittered to the sighing wharves, | The snowman kissed my entrails like a wolf. | Along the windows where the puddings blazed | My heart trudged rattling its red beads—| Corn popped, the goose gushed grease; my tears danced down]   "Vole, kobold, the snowshoe-footed hare | —Crowned with the smoke of steamboats, shagg'd with stars—| Whispered to my white mistress: *He is Mars;* | Till I called, laughing: *Friends! subjects! customers!* | And her face was a woman's, theirs were mens.   SLC[+]

26–30 "Like snowflakes to the dreaming town, | The skier plunged at my icy feet. | All this I dreamed in my great ragged bed, | The drifts rolled from my rooftop to the stars,]   *omitted*   SLC[+]

31/36 "And I tossed, sweating, in my wife's thin arms. . . .]   "All this I dreamed in my great ragged bed . . .   SLC[+]

32/27 outranging]   outspeaking   SLC[+]

33/28 märchen's wood,]   Märchen's~;   SLC[+]

46/41 life. . . .]   ~ . . .   SLC[+]

48–49/43 There is no Europe." | The man, the goats, the parrot]   There is no Europe." The man, the goats, the parrot   SLC[+]

C223 "Good-bye, Wendover; Good-bye Mountain Home." *Poetry*, 74 (June 1949), 137. SLC, SP55, SP2, CP.

headnote all in roman]   *headnote all in ital*   SP55[+]

C224 "The Girl Dreams That She Is Giselle." *Nation*, 168 (11 June 1949), 664. WWZ, SP2, CP.

3 enchantress!]   ~ᴧ   WWZ[+]

6 traveling]   travelling   WWZ[+]

9 cave . . .]   ~. . . .   WWZ[+]

10 quiver,]   ~ᴧ   WWZ[+]

12 Crumple;]   ~,   WWZ[+]

15 whirrs]   shirs   WWZ[+]

16–17/16 catch: | [*indented*] life, life! I dance]   Life, life! I dance.   WWZ[+]

Reprinted in *Hero's Way*, ed. Allen (1971), p. 401.

C225 "The Truth." *Sewanee Review*, 57 (Autumn 1949), 654–55. SLC, SP55, SP2, CP.

Reprinted in *Saturday Review*, 55 (7 Oct. 1972), 51; *Echoes 3*, ed. Donna Denison (Toronto: Oxford Univ. Press, 1981), pp. 68–69.

RJ to EE, 20 September 1948: It ["The Truth"] is said by a child most of whose family has been killed in the London air-raids early in the war—she has been evacuated to a sort of institution for children, and hysterically alienated from her mother because of her mother's lies about what has happened. I read a number of such case histories in a book by Anna Freud. One child in the book said, "I'm nobody's nothing."

C226 "La Belle au Bois Dormant." *Sewanee Review*, 57 (Autumn 1949), 656. SLC, SP55, SP2, CP.

Note: An explanatory note by RJ about this poem is in SP5 and SP2 on p. xiii and in CP on p. 8.

C227 "Nollekens." *Virginia Quarterly Review*, 25 (Autumn 1949), 544–46. SLC, SP55, SP2, CP.

headnote all in roman] *headnote all in ital* SP55⁺
35 With which he oiled] He kept to oil SLC⁺
Reprinted in *Poems from the* Virginia Quarterly Review, ed. Kohler (1969), pp. 148–50.

C228 "The Venetian Blind." *Virginia Quarterly Review*, 25 (Autumn 1949), 547–48. SLC, SP55, SP2, CP.

11 dream] dreams SLC⁺
12 Has] Have SLC⁺
Reprinted in *Poems from the* Virginia Quarterly Review, ed. Kohler (1969), pp. 151–52.

C229 "A Sick Child." *Nation*, 169 (15 Oct. 1949), 374. SLC, SP55, SP2, CP.

11 Goodby] Good-bye SLC⁺
17 "Come."] ˄~." SLC⁺
Reprinted in *Invitation to Poetry: A Round of Poems from John Skelton to Dylan Thomas*, ed. Lloyd Frankenberg (New York: Doubleday, 1956), pp. 251–52; *Poets of North Carolina*, ed. Richard Walser (Richmond: Garrett & Massie, 1963), p. 60; *Time for Poetry*, ed. May H. Arbuthnot and S. L. Root, Jr., 3d ed. (Glenview, Ill.: Scott, Foresman, 1968), p. 5; *Three Dimensions of Poetry*, ed. Vincent Stewart (New York: Scribner's, 1969); *The Voice That Is Great within Us*, ed. Carruth (1970), p. 402; *Straight On till Morning: Poems of the Imaginary World*, ed. Helen Hill et al. (New York: Crowell, 1977); *An Introduction to Poetry*, ed. Kennedy, 4th ed. (1978), p. 15.

RJ to EE, 16 February 1949: I'll send two poems ["A Sick Child" and "A Quilt-Pattern"] I've written in the last couple of weeks—my sort of children's poems. I hadn't written any poems for two or three months, and it feels good to have some new ones.

C230 "B. H. Haggin." *Nation,* 169 (17 Dec. 1949), 599–600. Book review of B. H. Haggin. *Music in the Nation.*

RJ to EE, October 1949: I had to interrupt writing *An English Garden* for two days, to write a review of the criticism of Bernard Haggin, a music critic whom I like very much. I'll send you a copy of the review to read—I think it will be fun for you to read, not as though it were something unkind about some bad American poet you don't know.

C231 "Poetry Unlimited." *Partisan Review,* 17 (Feb. 1950), 189–93. Book review of Louis Simpson, *The Arrivistes*; Elizabeth Coatsworth, *The Creaking Stair*; Donald F. Drummond, *No Moat No Castle*; John Williams, *The Broken Landscape*; Theodore Spencer, *An Acre in the Seed*; Harry Brown, *The Beast in His Hunger*; Francis Golffing, *Poems 1943–1949*; and José Garcia Villa, *Volume Two.* KA.

C232 "An English Garden in Austria (Seen after *Der Rosenkavalier*)." *Poetry,* 75 (March 1950), 311–15. SLC, SP55, SP2, CP.

Note: An early version of this poem appears in *American Poetry Review,* 6 (July–Aug. 1977), 16.

An explanatory note by RJ concerning this poem is in SP55 and SP2 on pp. xi–xii and in CP on pp. 6–7.

RJ to EE, October 1949: I've put off writing you for ten days because each day I would think I'd have this poem finished to send. I mean, and I didn't finish it until today. Finishing it made me feel wonderful, the way Goethe felt when he said, "You know, I'm a born writer." I almost never feel like a born writer and I particularly didn't this fall— I hadn't written a poem for six months. . . . Now I'll write some about the poem. Since it's a poem about the "cultural past", so to speak, it has about a million allusions in it; often the allusions are made by faintly parodying, or echoing things people said or wrote. I took "English Gardens" as a symbol of Romanticism spreading across Europe: they were the first big sign—it's wonderful to think of people carefully *building* a Ruin in a garden, and grottoes, and all the rest. Milton called Adam and Eve *our first great parents*; Racine really did write *Athalie* for Madame de Maintenon's convent school. And Strauss called the Baron [Ochs] "a rustic beau of thirty-five or so,"—one who'd have been behind the times and have expected it to be Metastasio when it was really Rousseau. Have you ever read anything about Farinelli? I read a book about him, as is evident. He really did half-cure the King of Spain of his madness, by singing the same four songs to him, every day for ten years; as the books say, he was "prime minister in all but name." All the great writers, composers, singers in Italy belonged to the Arcadian Academy, and had pastoral names; Goethe actually belonged and was called Melalio Melpomeneo. Faustine Hesse and her husband were the other greatest singers of the day and her husband was the compser of the operas Metastasio wrote the libretti for and Farinelli sang in. Then I have all the stuff about Voltaire and Frederick the Great, and the French Revolution, and *Figaro* and Mozart, he did write Mason's Funeral Music. The Revolutionists—to take the place of religion—once had a ceremony in honor of Raison, it being acted by a French actress. Napoleon really did read *Werther* seven times; criticized *Werther*, to Goethe, as being too ambitious (he should have felt only love, according to Napoleon). He did carry *Werther* to Egypt, when he fought the Mamalukes under the pyramids, and told his soldiers that History was looking down upon them; he told them that every French soldier carries his Marshall's baton in his knapsack. He would delight his favorites, show favor to them, by leaning forward and pinching one of their ears, vulgar man! At Jena, of course, he did say *Voila un homme!* to Goethe; and also said to him Politics is Destiny. *Others have understood the world; we change it* is a parody of what Marx said; *Truth is what works* is roughly what the most famous American philosopher of this century said; and *I have seen the future and it works* is what a fairly famous American writer said when he first saw the New Russia. I wanted a collection of statements to express Our Present World. Then, all the stuff at the end is stuff you'll remember from "Der Rosenkavalier". There are really a hundred or two hundred allusions or echoes on the poem. Don't think of it unkindly, even in part, as the work of "the American critic" because it's not that, as you can see from the end. Aren't you surprised at my knowing so many German words? Once I knew none, now I know almost none. Anyway, don't tell me if you don't like the poem, because it will break my heart; I still feel a happy daze from writing it.

RJ to EE, February 1950: Baron Ochs and Rousseau meet not because they have anything to do with each other, but because they are opposites: Ochs, as typical of the 18th century, the *ancien regime*, is walking in the garden when he meets (in the person of Rousseau) the beginning of Romanticism, the 19th century, of everything that is going to destroy the old way of life and feeling. Unless I remember incorrectly, Rousseau *did* make several visits to Vienna—and he recited, with feeling, everywhere he went. I knew, found out later, about having *Götz* wrong and had corrected it: but it's no wonder I got it wrong, since I wrote it from memory and I don't know *any* grammar. [¶] I'll send two poems in this letter: "An English Garden" in a somewhat improved version and a new poem ["Seele im Raum"].

C233 "Seele im Raum." *Poetry*, 75 (March 1950), 316–19. SLC, SP55, SP2, CP.

23–24 *stanza break*] *no stanza break* SLC+
Reprinted in *Fifteen Modern American Poets*, ed. Elliott (1956), p. 45; *College Book of Modern Verse*, ed. Robinson and Rideout (1958), pp. 431–33; *The Achievement of Randall Jarrell*, ed. Hoffman 1970), p. 57; *American Poetry Review*, 6 (July–Aug. 1977), 16–17 (early version).

Note: An explanatory note by RJ about this poem is in SP55 and SP2 on p. x and in CP on p. 5.

C234 "A Quilt-Pattern." *Virginia Quarterly Review*, 26 (Spring 1950), 219–21. SLC, SP55, SP2, CP.

77–78 *no stanza break*] *stanza break* SLC+
78–79 *stanza break*] *no stanza break* SLC+
Reprinted in *Poems from the* Virginia Quarterly Review, ed. Kohler (1969), pp. 153–55.

RJ to RL, May 1949: I haven't written much poetry this spring— mostly one medium-length poem, a child's Hansel-and-Gretel poem ["A Quilt-Pattern"]; but I've improved several old ones.

RJ to Na (MM), Fall 1949: Here are two poems—the long one for the book number, if you like it, and the short one for ordinary life. . . . Tell me how you like [them] and what effect they have. I read them at Detroit last spring (the short one along with *Hope*, and my other postman poem) and they seemed quite to affect the audience, which more or less squirmed or shuddered at the uneasiest part in *A Quilt-Pattern*. It's the only good-sized poem I've written lately.

RJ to Na (MM), October 1949: Here's the proof of Short Poem; about Long Poem—wouldn't you rather have one of reasonable length to take its place? I know how it is about long advertisements and book issues. I have a poem, just about forty lines long, that even has some Austrian scenery in it. . . . Want me to trade it for the *Quilt-Pattern*?

RJ to HA, May 1951: I enclose a poem ["A Quilt-Pattern"]: I won't tell *you* what it's a—so to speak—translation of.

C235 "The Orient Express." *Nation*, 170 (20 May 1950, 475. SLC, SP55, SP2, CP.

15 world . . .] ~. . . . SLC+
28 goodby] good-bye SLC+
Reprinted in *New York Times Book Review*, 15 June 1952, p. 2; *Fifteen*

Modern American Poets, ed. Elliott (1956), p. 48; *College Book of Modern Verse*, ed. Robinson and Rideout (1958), pp. 430–31; *American Poetry*, ed. Shapiro (1960), pp. 224–25; *Modern American Poetry*, ed. Corbett (1961), pp. 140–41, and in the rev. ed. (with Boldt, 1965), pp. 136–37; *American Poetry*, ed. Allen et al. (1965), p. 978; *Twentieth Century Writing*, ed. Stafford (1965), pp. 672–73; Jacob Korg, *The Force of Few Words: An Introduction to Poetry* (New York: Holt, Rinehart, Winston, 1966), pp. 377–78; *The Contemporary American Poets*, ed. Strand (1969), pp. 142–43; *The Achievement of Randall Jarrell*, ed. Hoffman (1970), p. 49; *Possibilities of Poetry*, ed. Kostelanetz (1970), pp. 39–40; *Chief Modern Poets of Britain and America*, ed. Sanders et al., 5th ed. (1970); *The New Oxford Book of American Verse*, ed. Ellmann (1976), pp. 776–77; *Structure and Meaning: An Introduction to Literature*, ed. Anthony Dubé et al. (Boston: Houghton, Mifflin, 1976), pp. 613–14.

Note: An early version of "The Orient Express," titled "It Is Like Any Other," was published in *American Poetry Review*, 6 (July–Aug. 1977), 14.

C236 "The Contrary Poet" (by Tristan Corbière) (later titled "Le Poète Contumace"). *Poetry*, 76 (Aug. 1950), 249–56. SLC, SP55, SP2, CP.

> THE CONTRARY POET *by Tristan Corbière*] *The Contrary Poet* (Tristan Corbière) SLC; LE POÈTE CONTUMACE (*Tristan Corbière*) SP55⁺
>
> 11 memories...] ~.... SLC⁺
> 34 squall...] ~.... SLC⁺
> 38 default...] ~.... SLC⁺
> 50 waiting...] ~.... SLC⁺
> 58 forehead...] ~.... SLC⁺
> 74 Asking...] ~.... SLC⁺
> 75 It] "~ SLC⁺
> 84 know:] ~, SLC⁺
> 85 tweezers...] ~.... SLC⁺
> 90 heaven] ~— SLC⁺
> 91 —what's] ₍~ SLC⁺
> 110 mushrooms...] ~.... SLC⁺
> 118 paradise...] ~.... SLC⁺
> 124 customs-inspector...] ~.... SLC⁺
> 146 *Sierra*...] ~.... SLC⁺
> 153 storm...] ~.... SLC⁺
> 169 itself...] ~.... SLC⁺
> 171 weep...] ~.... SLC⁺
> 172 comical...] ~.... SLC⁺

173 *love . . .*] ~. . . . SLC⁺
177 *] *** SLC⁺

RJ to EE, October 1949: Earlier this fall I finished, really finished after long labors, a translation of Corbière's longest poem ["Le Poète Contumace"].

RJ to RPW, February 1950: I've written medium-long poems and finished a translation of Corbière's longest poem; but I did it during the winter, so I already have an "I don't *do* anything in this world" feeling.

RJ to HA, November 1950: I have [a new book]—of poems—all done; I just wrote two longish ones ["An English Garden in Austria" and "Seele im Raum"], finished a Corbière translation, and worked on some old ones. The new ones were a great joy to me, as I hadn't written a new poem in seven or eight months, and that long a gap always gives you an uneasy feeling that maybe you never will be able to write another.

C237 "The Profession of Poetry." *Partisan Review*, 17 (Sept.–Oct. 1950), 724–31. Book review of Marshall Schacht, *Fingerboard*; John Frederick Nims, *A Fountain in Kentucky*; Howard Nemerov, *Guide to the Ruins*; Alfred Hayes, *Welcome to the Castle*; e. e. cummings, *Kaire*; *The Collected Poetry of Isaac Rosenberg*; Wilfred Owen, *Poems*. KA.

RJ's review of *Kaire* reprinted in *The New Partisan Reader*, ed. Phillips and Rahv (1953), pp.418–21, as part of "Reflections on Wallace Stevens and e. e. cummings."

C238 "The Traveler." *Poetry*, 77 (Dec. 1950), 146–47. WWZ, SP2, CP.

 5 But where] Where WWZ⁺
 9 Shall I spare this city?] *Shall I spare this city?* WWZ⁺
10 Raze it, raze it.] *Raze it, raze it.* WWZ⁺
12 *all in roman*] *all in ital* WWZ⁺
18 As] When WWZ⁺
19 slow,] ~. WWZ⁺
21 money] ~: WWZ⁺
24 money] ~: WWZ⁺
30 Shall I spare this city?] *Shall I spare this city?* WWZ⁺
Reprinted in *L'Ephémère*, no. 14 (1970), pp. 154, 156, with a French translation by Alain Suied, "Celle qui voyage," on pp. 155, 157.

C239 "The Face." *Poetry*, 77 (Dec. 1950), 147–48. SLC, SP55, SP2, CP.

> Reprinted in *Poesia Americana del '900*, ed. Carlo Izzo (Parma: Ugo Guanda Editore, 1963), p. 604, with an Italian translation, "Le Faccia," on p. 605.

> *Note:* An explanatory note by RJ about this poem is in SP55 and SP2 on p. ix and in CP on pp. 4–5.

> *RJ to EE, November 1948:* What makes a sad poem [like "The Face"] convincing and moving is for the sadness to be an unwilling sadness. So many writers *want* to take the *worst* possible view of everything: how can you trust what they say?

> *RJ to HA, November 1949:* Here's the Rilke translation I told you about, and another little poem ["The Face"].

C240 "The Princess Wakes in the Wood." *Poetry*, 77 (Dec. 1950), 148–49. CP.

C241 "Charles Dodgson's Song." *Poetry*, 77 (Dec. 1950), 149–50. WWZ, SP2, CP.

> 12 father] Father WWZ+
> Reprinted in *The Achievement of Randall Jarrell*, ed. Hoffman (1970), p. 66.

C242 "Deutsch durch Freud." *Poetry*, 77 (Dec. 1950), 150–53 WWZ, SP2, CP.

> 1–3/1 I believe—| [*indented*] I do believe, I do believe—| The country I like best of all is German.] I do believe my favorite country's German. WWZ+
> 8/6 *Nachtigallenchor:*] ~: WWZ+
> 10/8 the] *der* WWZ+
> 15/13 Believed that you are—] Wished that you were— WWZ+
> 16/14 enchanting:] ~. WWZ+
> 18/16 black] old WWZ+
> 19/17 home; charcoal-burners] ~. Charcoal-burners WWZ+
> 20/18 all . . .] ~. . . . WWZ+
> 21/19 he only] only he WWZ+
> 25/23 In] —~ WWZ+
> anything] everything WWZ+
> 31/29 fast . . .] ~. . . . WWZ+
> 38/36 What's a teaspoon? What's] what's . . . ? what's WWZ+

42/40 *does*] does WWZ⁺
47/45 Schools'] schools' WWZ⁺
51/49 noble—] ~; WWZ⁺
52/50 Ochs] Leupold WWZ⁺
55/53 (There] ₊~ WWZ⁺
56/54 *Fremde.*)] ~.₊ WWZ⁺
57/55 *traumte*] *träumte* WWZ⁺
60/58 —And] ₊~ WWZ⁺
61/59 Mondenscheine!...] ~!₊ WWZ⁺
68–79/66–67 *no stanza break*] *stanza break* WWZ⁺
73/71 *suit-case*] *suitcase* WWZ⁺
75/73 *Quin-*] "~ WWZ⁺
77/75 German:] ~₊ WWZ⁺
78/76 If] —~ WWZ⁺
　　　German...] ~.... WWZ⁺
81–85 Meanwhile I sit here on the sofa reading Grimm. | Next year I start *Des Knaben Wunderhorn.* | O happiness! The record-player's playing Mahler: | I lean back snugly, like a fly in amber. | I'm what I've wished to be: a perfect fool.] *omitted* WWZ⁺
89/81 prospect] thought WWZ⁺
90–93 You poor Germans: not ever to learn German! | ... It's this that's at the bottom of my Method: | Surely *this* way no one could learn German, | I tell myself; and yet that isn't sure:] *omitted* WWZ⁺
94/84 It's difficult—it is impossible?] [*indented*] It's difficult; is it impossible? WWZ⁺
96/86 certain] ~: WWZ⁺

Reprinted in *The Distinctive Voice*, ed. Martz (1966), pp. 184–86; *Alumni News* (Univ. of N.C. at Greensboro), 54 (Spring 1966), 44; *American Poetry Review*, 6 (July–Aug. 1977), 15 (early version).

RJ to EE, February 1950: The *feel* of German delights me. It has such a folky, old, primitive, poetic feel compared to English: it really is *the* language for fairy tales and folk-poems and all sorts of things. I often wonder what the feel of English is: since it's my own language, I naturally haven't any idea at all. How does it feel to you, compared to German? [¶] I wrote an absurd poem about learning German, full of jokes and German phrases I like and fairy-tale furniture; when I get it really finished I'll send it to you, even though I'm not sure it will be much fun for you to read—since naturally the German things won't seem to you the way they would to an English-speaking reader. The poem is named *Deutsch durch Freud* or *German by the Aesthetic Method.* . . .

C243 "The Obscurity of the Poet." *Partisan Review*, 18 (Jan.–Feb. 1951), 66–81. Essay. PA.

.Reprinted in *Harvard Summer School Conference on the Defense of Poetry* (see below, F1); *Students*, ed. Harlow O. Waite and Benjamin R. Atkinson (New York: Holt, Rinehart, Winston, 1958), pp. 113–25 (also in 2d and 3d eds.); "Şairin Kapaliliği," a Turkish translation by Doğan Hizlan, in *Türk Dili*, 10 (Spring 1961), 256–57; *Discovering Modern Poetry*, ed. Drew and Connor (1961), pp. 344–61.

C244 "All or None." *Kenyon Review*, 13 (Spring 1951), 204. CP.

C245 "The Tower." *Kenyon Review*, 13 (Spring 1951), 205. CP.

C246 "The Black Swan." *Kenyon Review*, 13 (Spring 1951), 206. SLC, SP55, SP2, CP.

   4 open,] ∼ₐ SLC⁺
   19 swans....] ∼ ... SLC⁺
   Reprinted in *Poetry Awards 1952* (Philadelphia: University of Pennsylvania Press, 1952), p. 4; *Fifteen Modern American Poets*, ed. Elliott (1956), p. 47; *The New Modern Poetry*, ed. Rosenthal (1967), p. 102; *The Achievement of Randall Jarrell*, ed. Hoffman (1970), p. 51; *Chief Modern Poets of Britain and America*, ed. Sanders et al., 5th ed. (1970); *Exploring Poetry*, ed. Rosenthal and Smith, 2d ed. (1973).

   Note: An explanatory note by RJ concerning this poem is in SP55 and SP2 on p. x and in CP on p. 6.

C247 "A Conversation with the Devil." *Poetry*, 78 (April 1951), 1–6. SLC, SP55, SP2, CP.

   47 it:] ∼; SLC⁺
   136 he's] He's SLC⁺
   139–40 *no stanza break*] *stanza break* SLC⁺
   153–54 *no stanza break*] *stanza break* SLC⁺
   Reprinted in *Botteghe Oscure*, 7 (1951), 240–45; *Botteghe Oscure Reader*, ed. George Garrett (Middletown, Conn.: Wesleyan Univ. Press, 1974), pp. 27–32.

   Note: An explanatory note by RJ concerning this poem is in SP55 and SP2 on pp. ix–x and in CP on p. 5.

   RJ to SBQ, November 1950: I want to send you, for a Christmas present, these two poems I've just finished. . . . You're in the beginning of one]"A Conversation with the Devil"], as you'll see.

C248 "A Girl in a Library." *Poetry*, 78 (April 1951), 7–11. SLC, SP55, SP2, CP.

> 20 Brunnhilde] Brünnhilde SLC+
> 24 off,] ~, SLC+
> 28–31 *inaccurately transposed to ll. 52–55 by typesetter*] *order correct in* SLC+
> 93 me...] ~.... SLC+
> 109 Goodbye, goodbye] Good-bye, good-bye SLC+

Reprinted in *Botteghe Oscure*, 7 (1951), 237–40; *Penguin Book of Modern American Verse*, ed. Moore (1954), pp. 271–74; *Pine Needles* (Univ. of North Carolina at Greensboro student yearbook), 1956, p. 11; *Fifteen Modern American Poets*, ed. Elliott (1956), p. 42; *Poets of North Carolina*, ed. Walser (1963), pp. 60–63; *The Greensboro Reader*, ed. Robert Watson and Gibbons Ruark (Chapel Hill: Univ. of North Carolina Press, 1968), pp. 57–60; *Possibilities of Poetry*, ed. Kostelanetz (1970), pp. 41–44; *The Achievement of Randall Jarrell*, ed. Hoffman (1970), pp. 52–55; *The Modern Age*, ed. Lief and Light, 2d ed. (1972), pp. 624–27, and 3d ed. (1976), pp. 667–69; *The Norton Anthology of Modern Poetry*, ed. Ellmann and O'Clair (1973), pp. 880–83; *Botteghe Oscure Reader*, ed. Garrett (1974), pp. 24–27; *The New Oxford Book of American Verse*, ed. Ellmann (1976), pp. 773–76; *The Literary South*, ed. Louis D. Rubin (New York: Wiley, 1979), pp. 623–25.

Note: An explanatory note by RJ about this poem is in SP55 and SP2 on pp. viii–ix and in CP on p. 4.

RJ to HA, November 1950: I've meant to write you for a long time, but especially since I finished the poem I send. . . . I got so enchanted with it I sat up day and night writing it, and when it was done I hardly knew what to do with myself, except to read it ["A Girl in a Library"].

RJ to SBQ, c. Spring 1951: I was extremely delighted to have you like *A Girl in a Library* so well, and I certainly wish you would write your impressions about the other [poem]. [¶] *Many a dolphin curved up from necessity* means: many people have, like dolphins, leaped for a moment, from the world of what Leibnitz calls "brute and geometrical necessity," up into the purer world of—oh, art, mysticism, philosophy, love; from actuality to potentiality; but the poor girl sleeps placidly in the trap, and has never even felt the need to escape. [¶] Tatyana is the heroine of Pushkin's *Eugene Onegin*; I'm fond of it and quite fond of the opera.

RJ to Po (KS), c. June–July 1951: . . . five lines in *A Girl in a Library* have strayed thirty lines or so from their proper place; they're at the bottom of [page] 8 instead of top. Say next month that the fire did it. I always felt it was a very live poem and now I'm sure.

C249 "Reflections on Wallace Stevens." *Partisan Review*, 18 (May–June 1951), 335–44. Essay. PA.

> Reprinted as part of "Reflections on Wallace Stevens and e. e. cummings" in *The New Partisan Reader*, ed. Phillips and Rahv (1953), pp. 408–17. A long excerpt from this essay is printed on the back of the jacket of *Letters of Wallace Stevens*, ed. Holly Stevens (New York: Knopf, 1966), and on the back of the jacket of *The Palm at the End of the Mind*, ed. Holly Stevens (New York: Knopf, 1971).

C250 "The Knight, Death, and the Devil." *Nation*, 172 (16 June 1951), 566. SLC, SP55, SP2, CP.

> Reprinted in *Art News*, 50 (Nov. 1951), 36–37; *Penguin Book of Modern American Verse*, ed. Moore (1954), pp. 269–70; *The Faber Book of Modern American Verse* (and *The Criterion Book of Modern Verse*), ed. Auden (1956), pp. 277–78; *Literature as Experience: An Anthology*, ed. Irving Howe et al. (New York: Harcourt, Brace, Jovanovich, 1979), pp. 569–71; *The Literary South*, ed. Rubin (1979), p. 626; *Poetry: Sight and Insight*, ed. Kirkland and Sanders (1982), pp. 302–3.

> *Note:* An explanatory note by RJ concerning this poem is in SP55 and SP2 on p. ix and in CP on p. 4.

> *RJ to HA, March or April 1951:* I enclose a poem of you to use, if you like it; it is a translation (really, I'm not kidding; look and you'll see) of Dürer's *The Knight, Death, and the Devil*.

C251 "A War." *Nation*, 173 (22 Sept. 1951), 242. SP55, SP2, CP.

> 3   *omelette*—]   ~$_\wedge$ SP55$^+$
> 4   That's]   —~   SP55$^+$
> Reprinted in *Don't Forget to Fly*, ed. Paul Janeczko (Scarsale, N.Y. Bradbury Press, 1981), p. 68.

> *RJ to RL, April 1951:* Here's another poem I just wrote:
> A WAR
> There set out, slowly, for a Different World,
> At four, on winter mornings, different legs . . .
> *You can't break eggs without making an omelette—*
> That's what they tell the eggs.

C252 "A View of Three Poets." *Partisan Review*, 18 (Nov.–Dec. 1951), 691–700. Book review of Richard Wilbur, *Ceremony and Other Poems*; Robert Lowell, *The Mills of the Kavanaughs*; William Carlos Williams, *Paterson* (Book Four). In PA as "Three Books."

RJ's review of Robert Lowell, *The Mills of the Kavanaughs*, reprinted in *Robert Lowell: A Collection of Critical Essays*, ed. Parkinson (1968), pp. 99–103 (as "Review of *The Mills of the Kavanaughs*"); *Robert Lowell: A Portrait of the Artist in His Time*, ed. London and Boyers (1970), pp. 38–43 (as "The Mills of the Kavanaughs").

RJ to PR (CC), September 1951: I'll get the piece to you on October 5, Special Delivery; I was just writing to Delmore [Schwartz] last night to make sure that was the date.

RJ to PR (CC), 4 October 1951: So I'm sending you my piece now minus the last four pages on William Carlos Williams, which I still have to correct and type; I'll send them late tonight Special Delivery.

RJ to PR (CC), 5 October 1951: Here's the last section on Williams. Would you please send me two copies of the proof?

C253 "No Love for Eliot." *New York Review of Books*, 18 Nov. 1951, p. 36. Book review of Rossell Hope Robbins, *The T. S. Eliot Myth*. KA.

C254 "To Fill a Wilderness." *Nation*, 173 (29 Dec. 1951), 570. Book review of *A Dictionary of Americanisms*, ed. Mitford M. Matthews, KA.

RJ to Na (MM), March or April 1951: The Dictionary of Americanisms is such a nice crazy idea that I accept with joy; I'll write a Marianne Moore review of it—in my old joke, "quotations and a few conjunctions."

C255 "Walt Whitman: He Had His Nerve." *Kenyon Review*, 14 (Winter 1952), 63–79. Essay. In PA as "Some Lines from Whitman."

Reprinted as "Some Lines from Whitman" in *Perspectives U.S.A.*, no. 2 (Winter 1953), 61–72 (and in French, German, and Italian language editions); *The Art of the Essay*, ed. Leslie Fiedler (New York: Crowell, 1958), pp. 587–98; *Criticism: Some Major American Writers*, ed. Lewis Leary (New York: Holt, Rinehart, Winston, 1971), pp. 117–30.

Note: This essay as originally published was titled "Walt Whitman: He Had His Nerve" by John Crowe Ransom, editor of *Kenyon Review*, without RJ's authority. The title used in the collected and reprinted appearances, "Some Lines from Whitman," was the one chosen by RJ.

C256 "The Age of Criticism." *Partisan Review*, 19 (March–April 1952), 185–201. Essay. PA.

> Reprinted in *Best Articles, 1953*, sel. By Rudolf Flesch (New York: Heritage House, 1953), pp. 203–222 (**B19**); a long excerpt in *American Writers Today*, ed. Alexander Cowie (Stockholm: Radiotjanst, 1956), pp. 198–204. A *Quarto of Modern Literature*, ed. Leonard Brown, 5th ed. (New York: Scribner's, 1964), pp. 546–51.

> *RJ to MJ, 15 February 1952:* This weekend I must start on the undone half of my Auden lectures. How I hope having made myself write "The Age of Criticism" will carry over to making myself write the Auden! Surely the Will gets better with exercise?

C257 "The Forsaken Girl" (Eduard Mörike). *Ladies' Home Journal*, 69 (Sept. 1952), 101. CP.

C258 "To the Laodiceans." *Kenyon Review*, 14 (Autumn 1952), 535–61. Essay. In PA as the second of "Two Essays on Robert Frost."

> Reprinted in part in *Literature: An Introduction to Fiction, Poetry, and Drama*, ed. Kennedy (1976), pp. 740–41 (as "Randall Jarrell: Commentary").

> *RJ to KR (JCR), September 1952:* I'm delighted that you liked the Frost [essay], and was pleased to have it in the magazine; and I *loved* the little typographical error about the spider web, *A sudden passing pullet shook it dry*—it delights me to think of most of the readers laughing and a few knitting their brows.

C259 "The Situation of the Poet." *Perspectives U.S.A.*, no. 1 (Fall 1952), 165–68. Essay-review of William Carlos Williams, *Collected Earlier Poems* and *Collected Later Poems*. PA.

> *Note:* This number was also published in French, German, and Italian language editions.

C260 "The Survivor among Graves." *Poetry*, 81 (Oct. 1952), 42–44. CP.

> Reprinted in *Borestone Mountain Poetry Awards, 1953* (Philadelphia: Univ. of Pennsylvania Press, 1953), pp. 43–44; *Antología de la Poesia Norteamericana Contemporanea*, ed. Eugenio Florit (Washington, D.C.: Pan American Union, 1955), pp. 132–33, with a Spanish translation, "El Vivo entre Tumbas," on pp. 133–34.

C261 "Thoughts about Marianne Moore." *Partisan Review*, 19 (Nov.–Dec. 1952), 687–700. Essay. In PA as the second of "Two Essays on Marianne Moore" (retitled "Her Shield").

> Reprinted in *Marianne Moore: A Collection of Critical Essays*, ed. Charles Tomlinson (Englewood Cliffs, N.J.: Prentice-Hall, 1969), pp. 114–24.
>
> *RJ to PR (CC), 30 September 1952:* Here is the Marianne Moore piece, which I've labored myself dumb over; will you send me two copies of the proof, please?

C262 "Woman." *Botteghe Oscure*, 11 (1953), 382–89.

> *Note:* RJ later completely rewrote this poem. See **C349**.
>
> *RJ to RH, c. Fall 1952:* I do have one thing that I've just finished, after working on it for years off and on; it's a piece about women, in verse, called *Women*. It's not a regular poem, but a sort of verse essay, something people can read even if they can't read poems.

C263 "Pictures from an Institution: Book I." *Kenyon Review*, 15 (Winter 1953), 104–26. PI; see **A6**.

C264 "In Those Days." *Ladies' Home Journal*, 70 (Jan. 1953), 90. WWZ, SP2, CP.

> Reprinted in *The Achievement of Randall Jarrell*, ed. Hoffman (1970), p. 62; *Hero's Way*, ed. Allen (1971), pp. 47–48.
>
> *RJ to EE, November 1948:* I'll send by this letter a poem I wrote a few days ago; it's about somebody older than we are, remembering someone he loved when he was young.

C265 "Requiem for the Death of a Boy" (Rainer Maria Rilke). *Partisan Review*, 20 (March–April 1953), 191–93. WWZ, SP2, CP.

4   too . . .] ~. . . . WWZ⁺

5   [*indented*] Who] What WWZ⁺

6   watermark] water line WWZ⁺

8   One] I WWZ⁺

     one] I WWZ⁺

12 He promises . . .] "~ ~. . . ." WWZ⁺

13 I promised, yes—but what I promised *you*] Yes, I promised. But what I promised you, WWZ⁺

14 Was never] That was never WWZ⁺

19 loved no one.] didn't love anybody. WWZ⁺

20/20–21 Loving was anxiousness, —don't you see,] Loving was misery—| Don't you see, WWZ⁺

22/23 *I was what I was afraid of,*] Then a man, WWZ⁺

24/25 it,] ~. WWZ⁺

26/27 For] Because WWZ⁺ WWZ⁺

together] ~— WWZ⁺

27/28 believe.] believe that. WWZ⁺

32/33 lay.] lay there. WWZ⁺

did me] felt so WWZ⁺

33/34 apple—] ~. WWZ⁺

34/35 moved.] ~— WWZ⁺

35/36 they quieted the year] how peaceful they made the year! WWZ⁺

37/38 by me like the other things, as sure they are] as reliable, almost, as the other, WWZ⁺

38/39 stood, as though half way] stood halfway WWZ⁺

41/42 without a] with only one WWZ⁺

43/44 looked at] saw WWZ⁺

44/45 Since,] Because WWZ⁺

46/47 size:] ~. WWZ⁺

47/48 then] and later on WWZ⁺

50/51 *you*'re] you're WWZ⁺

51/52 legs] ~— WWZ⁺

52/53 (So] ‸~ WWZ⁺

man?)] ~?‸ WWZ⁺

57/58 When] Whenever WWZ⁺

it] ~, WWZ⁺

60/61 sang,] ~‸ WWZ⁺

61/62 forced myself on] made myself at home with WWZ⁺

62/63 And yet] Only WWZ⁺

63/64 grew] got WWZ⁺

63–64/64–65 *indented; no stanza break*] *stanza break* WWZ⁺

64/65 Now I am, all at once, cut off from it.] Now, all at once, we're separated WWZ⁺

66/67 Or shall I] ~, now, ought I to WWZ⁺

67/68 Now, what] What WWZ⁺

70–71 who] *who* WWZ⁺

really] really WWZ⁺

71/72 That, in the forest,] ~‸ . . . ‸ WWZ⁺

76/77 *Well. . .*] ~. . . . WWZ⁺

Reprinted in *An Anthology of German Poetry from Hölderlin to Rilke in English Translation*, ed. Angel Flores (Garden City: Doubleday-Anchor, 1960), pp. 424–26.

C266 "The Sphinx's Riddle to Oedipus." *Accent*, 13 (Summer 1953), 132. WWZ, SP2, CP.

> 5 father—] ~‸ WWZ^{+}
> 6 Is] —~ WWZ^{+}
> 7 seeing:] ~; WWZ^{+}
> Reprinted in *The Charioteer*, 1, no. 3 (1961), 118.

C267 "Reading Poetry." *New York Times Book Review*, 23 Aug. 1953, p. 2. Essay. PA.

C268 "On the Underside of the Stone." *New York Times Book Review*, 23 Aug. 1953, p. 6. Book review of Robert Penn Warren, *Brother to Dragons*. KA.

> Reprinted in *Critical Essays on Robert Penn Warren*, ed. William B. Clark (Boston: G. K. Hall, 1981), pp. 43–44.

C269 "Gertrude and Sidney" (Book V from *Pictures from an Institution*), *Sewanee Review*, 61 (Autumn 1953), 633–57. PI.

> Reprinted in *The Best American Short Stories 1954*, ed. Martha Foley (Boston: Houghton, Mifflin, 1954), pp. 185–205; *A New Southern Harvest*, ed. Robert Penn Warren and Albert Erskine (New York: Bantam, 1957), pp. 147–64.

C270 "Constance and the Rosenbaums" (Book IV of *Pictures from an Institution*). *Accent*, 13 (Autumn 1953), 227–62. PI.

C271 "Writers and Critics." *New York Times Book Review*, 22 Nov. 1953, p. 2. Essay. PA.

C272 "Malraux's Thunder of Silence." *Art News*, 52 (Dec. 1953), 22–24, 54. Book review of André Malraux, *The Voices of Silence*. In SHS, KA as "Malraux and the Statues of Bamberg."

C273 "Pictures from an Institution, Book III: Miss Batterson and Benton." *Kenyon Review*, 16 (Winter 1954), 81–123. PI.

> *RJ to KR (JCR), 12 May 1953:* I've got Book III about done; in a couple of weeks I'll have it all typed and beautiful and will send it so that you can compare it with Book II—I imagine you'll like it better.

RJ to KR (JCR), 28 June 1953: Here is Book III for you to look at. I think that it's the best of all the Books, so far as printing by itself is concerned: if it's too long for one issue perhaps you could split it for two issues.

C274 "Aristotle Alive!" *Saturday Review of Literature,* 37 (3 April 1954), 29. Book review of Ronald S. Crane, *The Language of Criticism and the Structure of Poetry.* KA.

C275 "Pictures from an Institution (epigrams selected from the novel)." *Vogue,* 123 (15 April 1954), 88–89. PI.

C276 "The Lonely Man." *Encounter,* 3 (Aug. 1954), 22. WWZ, SP2, CP.

```
 4  grey]  gray  WWZ⁺
18  one;]   ~:  WWZ⁺
19  uncertainly . . .]   ~. . . .  WWZ⁺
25  humanity:]   ~,  WWZ⁺
27  animal . . .]   ~. . . .  WWZ⁺
28  grey]  gray  WWZ⁺
```

Reprinted in *Poetry,* 84 (Sept. 1954), 311–12; Jacob Korg, *The Force of Few Words* (1966), pp. 378–79; *Man in the Poetic Mood,* ed. Joy Zweigler (Evanston, Ill.: McDougal, Littell, 1970), p. 26; *Modern Poetry,* ed. John Rowe Townsend (Philadelphia: Lippincott, 1971), pp. 85–86.

C277 "Cinderella." *Encounter,* 3 (Aug. 1954), 23. WWZ, SP2, CP.

```
 7  want . . .]   ~. . . .  WWZ⁺
    softly]   ~—  WWZ⁺
 8  —How]   ‸~  WWZ⁺
11  gossip,"]   ~";  WWZ⁺
15  They]  She  WWZ⁺
    knew . . .]   ~. . . .  WWZ⁺
17  gauze:]   ~.  WWZ⁺
    the]  The  WWZ⁺
```

Reprinted in *Art News* (Christmas edition), 53 (Nov. 1954), 86; *National Poetry Festival, October 22–24, 1962* (1964), pp. 312–13, with RJ's brief comment on the poem on p. 312; Judson Jerome, *Poetry: Premeditated Art* (Boston: Houghton, Mifflin, 1968), pp. 419–20; *The Achievement of Randall Jarrell,* ed. Hoffman (1970), pp. 61–62; *Hero's Way,* ed. Allen (1971), pp. 229–30.

C278   " 'The Poet's Store of Grave and Gay.' " *New York Times Book Review*, 15 Aug. 1954, p. 5. Book review of James Stephens, *Collected Poems*. KA.

C279   "The Meteorite." *Poetry*, 84 (Sept. 1954), 313. WWZ, SP2, CP.

   3   One:]   ~;   WWZ⁺

C280   "Windows." *Poetry*, 84 (Sept. 1954), 313–14. WWZ, SP2, CP.

   5   *sentence omitted*]   The lights of others' houses.   WWZ⁺
   6–8   *indented* There is the world—| Storm-windowed, or curtained in the summer wind—| That I have watched and wished to live within.]   *omitted*   WWZ⁺
   12/9   rite, have kept a meaning]   rite—. . . meaning—   WWZ⁺
   13/10–12   That I, that they, knowing nothing of.]   That I, that they know nothing of. What I have never heard | He will read me; what I have never seen | She will show me.   WWZ⁺
   14/13   As dead actors on a rainy afternoon]   *indented* As dead actors, on a rainy afternoon,   WWZ⁺
   15/14   living room]   living-room   WWZ⁺
   16/15   were—]   ~,   WWZ⁺
   17   The looked-at lives, the lives that are not lived,]   *omitted*   WWZ⁺
   19/17   doubt,]   ~ₐ   WWZ⁺
   19–20/17–18   *no stanza break*]   *stanza break*   WWZ⁺
   24/22   lived—|~;   WWZ⁺
   26/24   peace,]   ~. . . .   WWZ⁺
   30–31   [*indented*] Some evening | I will push a window up and step inside]   *omitted*   WWZ⁺
   32–33/27–28   *no stanza break*]   *stanza break*   WWZ⁺
   33/28   Next]   Some   WWZ⁺
   34/29   speechlessly]   ~,   WWZ⁺
   35/30   And shift the plates]   Shifting the plates,   WWZ⁺
   36/31   fire. . . .]   ~.   WWZ⁺
   40–41,   42–43/35–36,   37–38 *no stanza break*]   *stanza break*   WWZ⁺
   Reprinted in *Times Literary Supplement: American Writing Today*, 17 Sept. 1954, p. xvi; *100 Postwar Poems: British and American*, ed. M. L. Rosenthal (New York: Macmillan, 1968), pp. 103–4; *The Achievement of Randall Jarrell*, ed. Hoffman (1970), pp. 63–64.

C281   "Aging." *Poetry*, 84 (Sept. 1954), 315. WWZ, SP2, CP.

   2   sleep . . .]   ~.   WWZ⁺
   3   are]   is   WWZ⁺

```
4   —But]   ...~   WWZ+
7   time—]   ~;   WWZ+
8   desk]   ~,   WWZ+
8–9   no stanza break]   stanza break   WWZ+
10   the]   The   WWZ+
12   skies?]   ~....   WWZ+
```

C282   "The Little Cars." *Vogue*, 124 (15 Sept. 1954), 128–29. Essay. KA.

C283   "The End of the Rainbow." *Kenyon Review*, 16 (Autumn 1954), 600–610. WWZ, SP2, CP.

```
47   through]   out past   WWZ+
107   On out]   Out   WWZ+
334–35   no stanza break]   stanza break   WWZ+
```

C284   "A Poet's Own Way." *New York Times Book Review*, 31 Oct. 1954, p. 6. Book review of E. E. Cummings, *Poems: 1923–1954*. KA.

Reprinted in *EΣTI: eec: E. E. Cummings and the Critics*, ed. Stanley V. Baum (East Lansing: Michigan State Univ. Press, 1962), pp. 191–92.

C285   "The New Books: 'Very Graceful Are the Uses of Culture.'" *Harper's Magazine*, 209 (Nov. 1954), 94, 96, 98, 100, 102–4. Book review of John P. Marquand, *Thirty Years*; Arnold Toynbee, *A Study of History*; Frans G. Bengtsson, *The Long Ships*; Wallace Stevens, *The Collected Poems*; Evelyn Waugh, *Tactical Exercises*; Russell Lynes, *The Tastemakers*; Hamilton Basso, *The View from Pompey's Head*; Wright Morris, *The Huge Season*; Malcolm Cowley, *The Literary Situation*; Shepherd Mead, *The Big Ball of Wax*; Alfred Duggan, *Leopard and Lilies*; *The Youth's Companion*, ed. Lovell Thompson; and *The Saturday Evening Post Treasury*. KA.

C286   "The Intellectual in America." *Mademoiselle*, 40 (Jan. 1955), 121–23. Essay. SHS, KA.

Reprinted in *Essays Today*, 2, ed. Richard M. Ludwig (New York: Harcourt, Brace, 1956), pp. 129–34; *Literary Types and Themes*, ed. McNamee et al. (1961), pp. 275–79.

C287 "The Collected Poems of Wallace Stevens." *Yale Review*, 44 (Spring 1955), 340–53. Essay-review. TBC.

> Reprinted in *The Achievement of Wallace Stevens*, ed. Ashley Brown and Robert S. Haller (Philadelphia: Lippincott, 1962), pp. 179–92.

C288 "A Literary Tornado." *New York Times Book Review*, 17 April 1955, p. 4. Book review of Roy Campbell, *Selected Poems*. KA.

C289 "A Matter of Opinion." *New York Times Book Review*, 29 May 1955, p. 5. Review of Marianne Moore, *Predilections*. KA.

C290 "A Dylan Thomas Collection." *New York Post*, 5 June 1955, p. M–10 ("Weekend Magazine" section). Book review of Dylan Thomas, *Adventures in the Skin Trade*. KA.

C291 "Recent Poetry." *Yale Review*, 44 (Summer 1955), 598–609. Book review of Edith Sitwell, *The Collected Poems of Edith Sitwell*; James Stephens, *Collected Poems*; Christopher Fry, *The Dark Is Light Enough*; James Kirkup, *A Spring Journey and Other Poems*; Mark Van Doren, *Selected Poems*; Elder Olson, *The Scarecrow Christ and Other Poems*; William H. Matchett, *Water Ouzel and Other Poems*; Rolfe Humphries, *Poems: Collected and New*; Constance Carrier, *The Middle Voice*; Archibald MacLeish, *Songs of Eve*; W. H. Auden, *The Shield of Achilles*. KA.

C292 "Speaking of Books." *New York Times Book Review*, 24 July 1955, p. 2. Article about children's books in general and Christina Stead's *The Man Who Loved Children* in particular. RJ's list of recommended books is also included. KA.

C293 "Recent Poetry." *Yale Review*, 45 (Autumn 1955), 122–32. Book review of Isabella Gardner, *Birthdays from the Ocean*; David Ignatow, *The Gentle Weight Lifter*; Lincoln Fitzell, *Selected Poems*; Howard Nemerov, *The Salt Garden*; Ben Belitt, *Wilderness Stair*; Stephen Spender, *Collected Poems*. KA.

C294 "The Year in Poetry." *Harper's Magazine*, 211 (Oct. 1955), 96–101. Brief book notices of Dylan Thomas, *Under Milk Wood*; Wallace Stevens, *Collected Poems*; *The Poems of Emily Dickinson*, ed.

Thomas H. Johnson; Elizabeth Bishop, *Poems*; Robert Graves, *Collected Poems*; Isabella Gardner, *Birthdays from the Ocean*; Louis Simpson, *Good News of Death and Other Poems* (in *Poets of Today II*); Ben Belitt, *Wilderness Stair*; Constance Carrier, *The Middle Voice*; Roy Campbell, *Selected Poems*; David Ignatow, *The Gentle Weight Lifter*. KA.

C295 "Graves and the White Goddess." *Yale Review*, 45 (Winter 1956), 302–14 (first of two parts). Essay-review of Robert Graves, *Collected Poems*; concluded in **C298**. TBC.

C296 "The Grown-Up" (Rainer Maria Rilke). *Prairie Schooner*, 30 (Winter 1956), 351. WWZ, SP2, CP.

> Reprinted in *An Anthology of German Poetry*, ed. Flores (1960), p. 397.

C297 "Love and Poetry." *Mademoiselle*, 42 (Feb. 1956), 123, 223–25. Essay. KA.

C298 "Recent Poetry." *Yale Review*, 45 (Spring 1956), 467–80 (second of two parts). Essay review of Robert Graves, *Collected Poems* (conclusion of **C295**); brief reviews of William Carlos Williams, *Journey to Love*; Louis O. Coxe, *The Second Man*; Robert Conquest, *Poems*; Alan Ross, *Something of the Sea*; John Ciardi, *As If*; Conrad Aiken, *A Letter to Li Po*; P. D. Cummins, *Some Phases of Love*; Adrienne Cecile Rich, *The Diamond Cutters*. "Graves and the White Goddess" in TBC; others in KA.

> "Review of *The Diamond Cutters and Other Poems*" reprinted in *Adrienne Rich's Poetry*, ed. Barbara C. and Albert Gelp (New York: Norton, 1975), pp. 127–29.

C299 "Nestus Gurley." *Virginia Quarterly Review*, 32 (Spring 1956), 201–3. WWZ, SP2, CP.

    11   Who]   That   WWZ+
    35   News]   *News*   WWZ+
    58   in]   ~,   WWZ+
    59   And go]   Go   WWZ+
    63   it:]   ~.   WWZ+
    67   would be a—]   would   WWZ+

79/79–80   Or tune or breath . . . recognizing the breath]   Or tune or
breath | [*indented*] recognizing the breath   WWZ[+]

Reprinted in *High Life* (Greensboro, N.C., Senior High School weekly
student newspaper), 11 May 1956, p. 2; *The Modern Poets*, ed. Brinnin
and Read (1963), pp. 175–77, and in the 2d ed. (1970), pp. 216, 218–
20; *Poems from the* Virginia Quarterly Review, ed. Kohler (1969), pp.
156–58; *The Norton Anthology of Poetry*, ed. Eastman et al. (1970),
pp. 1099–1100.

Note: An article about the "real Nestus Gurley," by Anne White,
"Sounds and Sights," and a photograph appeared in the *Greensboro
Daily News*, 27 April 1953, Sec. 3, p. 1.

C300   "With Berlioz, Once upon a Time. . . ." *New York Times
Book Review*, 15 April 1956, p. 3. Book review of Hector Berlioz,
Evenings with the Orchestra. KA.

C301   "Harmony, Discord and Taste." *New York Times Book Review*, 17 June 1956, p. 7. Book review of Bernard Haggin, *The Listen-
er's Musical Companion*. KA.

C302   "Five Poets." *Yale Review*, 46 (Autumn 1956), 100–110.
Book review of Adrienne Cecile Rich, *The Diamond Cutters*; Ezra
Pound, *Section: Rock Drill. 85–95 Los Cantares*; Rolphe Humphries,
Green Armor on Green Ground; Donald Hall, *Exiles and Marriages*;
Katherine Hoskins, *Villa Narcisse*. KA.

C303   "The Schools of Yesteryear: A One-Sided Dialogue." *New Republic*, 135 (19 Nov. 1956), 13–17. Essay. SHS.

Reprinted in *Writing from Experience*, ed. Raymond C. Palmer et al.
(Ames: Iowa State College Press, 1957), pp. 78–89; *Readings for Opin-
ion*, ed. Earle Davis and William C. Hummel, 2d ed. (Englewood Cliffs,
N.J.: Prentice-Hall, 1960), pp. 219–29; *Harbrace College Reader*, ed.
Mark Schorer et al., 2d ed. (Harcourt, Brace, 1964), pp. 206–18, and
in 5th ed. (1976), pp. 247–58.

C304   "Songs of Rapture, Songs of Death." *New York Times Book
Review*, 25 Nov. 1956, pp. 5, 50. Book review of *Selected Writings of
Jules Laforgue*, ed. and trans. by William Jay Smith. KA.

C305 "In Pursuit of Beauty." *New York Times Book Review,* 10 March 1957, p. 5. Book review of Sidney Cox, *A Swinger of Birches: A Portrait of Robert Frost.* KA.

C306 "Go, Man, Go!" *Mademoiselle,* 45 (May 1957), 98–99. 140–43. Humorous essay about sports cars. KA.

C307 "The Age of the Chimpanzee: A Poet Argues as Devil's Advocate against the Canonization of Abstract-Expressionism." *Art News,* 56 (Summer 1957), 34–36. Essay. In KA as "Against Abstract Expressionism."

C308 "Jamestown." *Virginia Quarterly Review,* 33 (Autumn 1957), 512–13. WWZ, SP2, CP.

> 20 after ...] ~. . . . WWZ+
> Reprinted in *Poems from the* Virginia Quarterly Review, ed. Kohler (1969), pp. 241–42; *The Gift Outright: America to Her Poets,* ed. Helen Plotz (New York: Greenwillow Books, 1977), pp. 39–40.
>
> *RJ to VQR (CK), 23 January 1957:* I like the idea of writing a poem about Jamestown—whether I can really write one I don't know. We'll try to drive to it early this Spring and see what it's like; perhaps seeing it will work. If it does I'll send you the poem before the first of June.
>
> *RJ to EB, March 1957:* I've just written a queer, nay weird, poem and can't resist sending it. I was asked to write a poem about Jamestown (300th anniversary) and said that I doubted I could but if one came it would. I imagine the magazine will turn pale when it sees what came.

C309 "The Bronze David of Donatello." *Art News,* 56 (Oct. 1957), 36–37. WWZ, SP2, CP.

> 11 molded] moulded WWZ+
> 20 The   navel,   nipples,   rib-case] The   rib-case,   navel, nipples WWZ+
> 25 use, take, notice] take, use, notice WWZ+
> 79 Blessèd] Blessed WWZ+
> 80 blessèd] blessed WWZ+
> Reprinted in *The Achievement of Randall Jarrell,* ed. Hoffman (1970), pp. 67–69; *Words in Flight: An Introduction to Poetry,* ed. Abcarian (1972).
>
> *RJ to EB, September 1956:* I haven't written too many poems lately— I wrote a long one about Donatello's *David,* the bronze one, [and] I just

wrote a poem named *The Woman at the Washington Zoo*, and I've done eleven or twelve Rilke translations.

C310 "Lament" (Rainer Maria Rilke). *American Scholar*, 27 (Spring 1958), 166. WWZ, SP2, CP.

    10 striking. . . .] ~ . . . WWZ+
Reprinted in *An Anthology of German Poetry*, ed. Flores (1960), p. 386.

RJ to AS (HH), June 1957: I've been meaning to send you something for the *American Scholar*, and here it is, three Rilke translations: *Lament, Death,* and *The Great Night.*

C311 "Death" (Rainer Maria Rilke). *American Scholar*, 27 (Spring 1958), 167. WWZ, SP2, CP.

     1 Death] death AGP+
     6 And:] ~ ̬ AGP+
    10 Being] being AGP+
    14 Present] present AGP+
    15 Present] present AGP+
        dental-plate] ~ ̬ ~ AGP+
    16 mumble . . .] ~ . . . . WWZ+
Reprinted in *An Anthology of German Poetry*, ed. Flores (1960), p. 423; *The Achievement of Randall Jarrell*, ed. Hoffman (1970), p. 65.

C312 "The Great Night" (Rainer Maria Rilke). *American Scholar*, 27 (Spring 1958), 168. WWZ, SP2, CP.

     6 lamppost] lamp post AGP+
     7 lamplight] lamp light AGP+
     8 —Already] ̬~ AGP+
    10 were] ~, AGP ~— WWZ+
    11 dry.] ~; AGP ~— WWZ+
    12 sang,] ~ ̬ AGP ~, WWZ+
    18 ball,] ~ ̬ AGP+
    20 off,] ~— AGP+
    27 senses:] ~, AGP ~: WWZ+
Reprinted in *An Anthology of German Poetry*, ed. Flores (1960), p. 420.

C313 "Recommended Summer Reading." *American Scholar*, 27 (Summer 1958), 372.

C314 "The Appalling Taste of the Age." *Saturday Evening Post*, 231 (26 July 1958), 18–19, 44–45, 47–48. Essay. In SHS, KA as "The Taste of the Age." Published separately as **A8**.

> Reprinted in *Imagination and Intellect: Readings for Composition*, ed. Edward G. McGehee and Edgar L. McCormick (Englewood Cliffs, N.J.: Prentice Hall, 1962), pp. 367–78.

> *Note:* A French translation by A. Sacriste, "Un Américain fait le procès de ce temps," was published in *Le Figaro Litteraire*, 28 March 1959, pp. i–ii.

C315 "Poets, Critics, and Readers." *American Scholar*, 29 (Summer 1959), 277–92. Essay. SHS, KA.

> Reprinted in *Vanderbilt Alumnus*, 46 (July–Aug. 1961), 10–13, 26–27. See also **F4**.

> *Note:* See below, **C316**, for RJ's response to J. Donald Adams's comments on this essay.

C316 "Childhood" (Rainer Maria Rilke). *Prairie Schooner*, 33 (Fall 1959), 240. WWZ, SP2, CP.

> 3 time . . .] ~. . . . WWZ⁺
> 4 ringing,] ~; AGP ~, WWZ⁺
> 8 gone:] ~. AGP ~, WWZ⁺
> 16 trust:] ~. AGP ~: WWZ⁺
> 22 grown-ups] grownups AGP; grown-ups WWZ⁺
> 24 to:] ~. AGP] ~: WWZ⁺
> 27 grey] gray AGP⁺
> 28 sailboat] sail-boat WWZ⁺
> 32 sinking:] ~. AGP; sl: WWZ⁺
> Reprinted in *An Anthology of German Poetry*, ed. Flores (1960), pp. 395–96.

> *RJ to PS (KS), 5 October 1958:* Here are some Rilke translations and a Goethe translation for the *Prairie Schooner*.

> *RJ to SBQ, 21 November 1960:* "Childhood" I called an adaptation because two additional phrases came to me at one place—perhaps it's rather like adding some instruments in a place where the orchestration's muffled in English.

C317 "The Archangels' Song" (Johann W. von Goethe). *Prairie Schooner*, 33 (Fall 1959), 241. WWZ, SP2, CP.

> 3 thund'rous] thunderous WWZ⁺

C318 "The Child" (Rainer Maria Rilke). *Prairie Schooner*, 33 (Fall 1959), 242. WWZ, SP2, CP.

> *(Translated from Rainer Maria Rilke)*]   *(Rainer Maria Rilke)*   AGP[+]
> 8   endures,]   ~: AGP;   sl, WWZ[+]
> 10   waiting-room]   ~ˌ~ AGP;   waiting-room   WWZ[+]
> Reprinted in *An Anthology of German Poetry*, ed. Flores (1960), p. 407.

C319 "Washing the Corpse" (Rainer Maria Rilke). *Prairie Schooner*, 33 (Fall 1959), 242. WWZ, SP2, CP.

> 5   fate,]   ~. AGP   ~, WWZ[+]
> 10   minute,]   ~ˌ WWZ[+]
> 11   brush;]   ~ˌ WWZ[+]
> 17   net]   ~, AGP   ~ˌ WWZ[+]
> 19   window-frame]   ~ˌ~ AGP;   ~-~ WWZ[+]
> 21   there,]   ~ˌ AGP;   ~, WWZ[+]
> Reprinted in *An Anthology of German Poetry*, ed. Flores (1960), pp. 404–5; *The Achievement of Randall Jarrell*, ed. Hoffman (1970), p. 64.

C320 [Untitled letter] in "The Reader Replies" (column). *American Scholar*, 29 (Winter 1959–60), 136. RJ's reply to J. Donald Adams's comments (in this number) on **C315**.

C321 "A Sad Heart at the Supermarket." *Daedalus*, 89 (Spring 1960), 359–72. Essay. SHS.

> Reprinted in *Culture for the Millions*, ed. Norman Jacobs (Princeton, N.J.: Van Nostrand, 1961), pp. 97–110.

C322 "Brief Comments." *American Scholar*, 29 (Autumn 1960), 576, 578. Review of *The Poem Itself: 45 Modern Poets in a New Presentation*, ed. Stanley Burnshaw.

C323 "Jerome." *Analects* (Univ. of N.C. at Greensboro literary magazine), 1 (Oct. 1960), 25. WWZ, SP2, CP. Published separately as **A25**.

> 12   the]   his   WWZ[+]
> 18   And,]   ~ˌ WWZ[+]
>   time,]   ~ˌ WWZ[+]

19 "I see] *I see* WWZ+
20–28 *all in roman*] *all in ital.* WWZ+
25 "The] *The* WWZ+
27 angel—] *angel:* WWZ+
29 speak . . ."] *speak.* WWZ+
31 slept . . .] ~. . . . WWZ+

Reprinted in *The Distinctive Voice*, ed. Martz (1966), pp. 186–87; *Poetry Past and Present*, ed. Brady and Price (1974), pp. 401–2.

C324 "The Winter's Tale" (Henrikas Radauskas). *Analects*, 1 (Oct. 1960), 26. WWZ, SP2, CP.

Reprinted in *The Contemporary World Poets*, ed. Donald Junkins (New York: Harcourt, Brace, Jovanovich, 1976), pp. 201–2.

C325 "The Woman at the Washington Zoo." *Times Literary Supplement* ("American Imagination" issue), 6 Nov. 1960, p. xx. WWZ, SP2, CP.

Reprinted in Brooks and Warren, *Understanding Poetry*, 3d ed. (1960), pp. 538–39, with RJ's account of how this poem came to be on pp. 531–38; *The Modern Poets*, ed. Brinnin and Read (1963), pp.178–79, and in the 2d ed., pp. 220–21; *National Poetry Festival, October 22–24, 1962* (1964), pp. 313–14, with RJ's brief introductory comment about the poem on p. 313; *American Poetry*, ed. Allen et al. (1965), p. 979; *The New Modern Poetry*, ed. Rosenthal (1967), pp. 102–3; *53 American Poets Today*, ed. Witt-Diamant and Fukuda (1968), pp. 61–62; *The Contemporary American Poets*, ed. Strand (1969), pp. 143–44; *The Achievement of Randall Jarrell*, ed. Hoffman (1970), p. 60; *A Little Treasury of Modern Poetry*, ed. Williams, 3d ed. (1970), pp. 565–66; *Quarterly Journal of the Library of Congress*, 27 (April 1970), 153; *Literature in America: The Modern Age*, ed. Charles Kaplan (New York: Free Press, 1971), pp. 366–67; *The Poem: An Anthology*, ed. Greenfield and Weatherhead, 2d ed. (1972), pp. 467–68; *50 Modern American and British Poets, 1920–1970*, ed. Untermeyer (1973), pp. 96–97; Agnes Stein, *The Uses of Poetry* (New York: Holt, Rinehart and Winston, 1975), pp. 56–57; *Introduction to Literature: Poems*, ed. Altenbernd and Lewis, 3d ed. (1975); *Poems since 1900: An Anthology of British and American Verse in the Twentieth Century*, ed. Falck and Hamilton (1975); *Washington and the Poet*, ed. Francis Coleman Rosenberger (Charlottesville: Univ. Press of Virginia, 1977); *Contemporary Poetry of North Carolina*, ed. Owen and Williams (1977), p. 67; Kennedy, *An Introduction to Poetry*, 4th ed. (1978), pp. 358–59; *The Treasury of American Poetry*, ed. Sullivan (1978), pp. 556–57; *An Introduction to Literature*, ed. Sylvan Barnet et al. (Boston: Little, Brown,

1981), pp. 526–27; *The Harper Anthology of Poetry*, ed. Nims (1981), pp. 667–68.

RJ to EB, September 1956: I haven't written too many poems lately— I wrote a long one about Donatello's *David*, the bronze one, [and] I just wrote a poem named *The Woman at the Washington Zoo*, and I've done eleven or twelve Rilke translations.

C326 "Goethe's 'Faust,' Scene I" ("Night"). *Quarterly Review of Literature*, 11, no. 2/3 (1961), 199–215. *Faust, Part I* (**A28**).

RJ to KS, 5 October 1958: Since last spring I've been translating *Faust*, the first part that is; I'm about a third through and am part happy and part worked to death and generally distracted—it's too hard and too long really, and I'm hopeful that in the end I can get it done.

RJ to Ath (HH), 10 March 1959: The $3500 [for WWZ] will be fine. With that much I can afford to work hard on the *Faust* and not have to write other things to get some extra money. [¶] I've been working hard all the last month and now have the first long scene, ending with the Easter choirs, all done except for the song they sing. And I have the Forest and Cavern scene four-fifths done.

RJ to SBQ, 21 November 1960: I'm about three-quarters through FAUST.

C327 "A Scene from 'Faust, Part I,' translated from the German by Randall Jarrell." *Analects* (Univ. of N.C. at Greensboro literary magazine), 1 (Spring 1961), 29–36. Rev. version in *Faust, Part I* (**A28**).

C328 National Book Award for Poetry Acceptance Speech, *National Book Committee Quarterly*, 5 (Spring–Summer 1961), 2–3. See below, **F5**.

C329 "Randall Jarrell." *American Scholar*, 30 (Summer 1961), 444, 446. Under "Recommended Reading" column is RJ's choice, *Invitation to a Beheading* by Vladimir Nabokov, with a brief note.

C330 "Washing." *American Scholar*, 30 (Summer 1961), 345. LW, CP.

    16 It was dead—nevertheless it moved.] *omitted* LW+
    21/20 But—as old hens like to say—] But, . . . say, LW+
Reprinted in *Three Dimensions of Poetry*, ed. Vincent Stewart (New

York: Scribner's, 1969); *L'Ephémère*, no. 14 (1970), p. 152, with a French translation by Alain Suied, on p. 153.

C331 "Four Shakespeare Plays." *HiFi/Stereo*, 7 (Aug. 1961), 42–44. Review of the Cambridge Univ. Marlowe Society and Professional Players recording of *The Winter's Tale*; *Henry IV, Part One*; *Henry IV, Part Two*; and *The Two Gentlemen of Verona*. KA.

C332 "Hope" ("To prefer the nest in the linden"). *Partisan Review*, 28 (Sept.–Nov. 1961), 594–601. LW, CP.

```
16/16–17   mother squirrel,]   ~ | ~   LW+
56   apple-blossoms]   ~,~   LW+
76   Star-system]   ~,~   LW+
106   moué]   moue   LW+
108   story:]   ~;   LW+
118   us—did   ~. Did   LW+
123   —or else her feet—]   (or . . . feet)   LW+
124   —or else away from it—]   (or . . . it)   LW+
136   them]   ~—   LW+
137   —And]   ,~   LW+
140, 168   street-lamp]   streetlamp   LW+
206–7   no stanza break]   stanza break   LW+
207–8   stanza break]   no stanza break   LW+
212   wife's . . .]   ~.   LW+
218   son't]   son's   LW+
   not;]   ~.   LW+
226/226–27   me—she'll say to me—]   me—| she'll say to me—
227/228   dreaming"—]   dreaming."   LW+
```

C333 "The One Who Was Different." *Poetry*, 101 (Oct.–Nov. 1962), 50–53. LW, CP.

```
44   Wordsworth:]   ~.   LW+
60–61/60   A pair of eyes. | [indented] Too young to have learned
   yet]   A pair of eyes. Too young to have learned yet   LW+
```

C334 "The Blind Man's Song" (Rainer Maria Rilke). *Poetry*, 101 (Oct.–Nov. 1962), 53. CP.

Reprinted in *National Poetry Festival, October 22–24, 1962* (1964), pp. 309–10, with RJ's introductory comments on the poem on p. 309.

Note: This poem was originally titled "The Song of the Blind Man."

See Charles Adams, "A Supplement to Randall Jarrell: A Bibliography," *Analects*, 1 (Spring 1961), 55.

C335 "Field and Forest." *Poetry*, 101 (Oct.–Nov. 1962), 54–55. LW, CP.

Reprinted in *Alumni News* (Univ. of N.C. at Greensboro), 54 (Spring 1966), 46; *The Norton Anthology of Poetry*, ed. Eastman et al. (1970), pp. 1098–99; *The Voice That Is Great within Us*, ed. Carruth (1970), pp. 403–4; *The Modern Age*, ed. Lief and Light, 2d ed. (1972), pp. 628–29; *Contemporary Poetry of North Carolina*, ed. Owen and Williams (1977), pp. 68–69.

RJ to SBQ, 8 November 1962: The *Field and Forest* poem, though it has an easy surface, is a hard poem, I'm afraid; it's about the unconscious and conscious in man—I use the fields to stand for the conscious and the forest to stand for the unconscious.

C336 "Fifty Years of American Poetry." *Prairie Schooner*, 37 (Spring 1963), 1–27. Essay. TBC.

Reprinted in *National Poetry Festival, October 22–24, 1962* (1964), pp. 113–38. A Polish translation by Halina Carroll, "Pięćdziesiąt Lat Poezji Amerikańskiej," was published in *Tematy* (Perspectives in Culture, New York City), 3, no. 9 (1964), 7–36.

C337 "It's a Gloomy World, Gentlemen." *Atlantic Monthly*, 211 (April 1963), 76–82. Excerpt from RJ's forthcoming introduction to *Six Russian Short Novels* (B33). TBC.

C338 "The X-Ray Waiting Room in the Hospital." *New York Review of Books*, 26 Sept. 1963, p. 16. LW, CP.

> *text all in ital]* text all in roman LW+
> 8 forever. . . .] ~ . . . MLW+
> 16 I] *I* LW+
> 21 *mines]* mine LW+
> 25 *dressing-gown]* dressing‸gown LW+

C339 "The Love for One Orange." *New York Review of Books*, 26 Sept. 1963, p. 16. CP.

C340 "Three Bills." *Partisan Review*, 30 (Fall 1963), 387. LW, CP.

12 *St.*] St. LW+

C341 "The Lost World." *Poetry*, 103 (Oct.–Nov. 1963), 37–47. LW, CP.

Note: In three titled parts: "I. Children's Arms"; "II. A Night with Lions"; "III. A Street off Sunset."

I. Children's Arms

6   wind-machines] ~ˬ~ LW+
16 beaverboard] beaver board LW+
31 THIS IS THE GREENWOOD] THIS IS THE GREENWOOD LW+
42 cocoanuts] coconuts LW+
48 enemies. . . .] ~ . . . LW+
61 *Sunday.*] ~! LW+
79 light-bulbs] ~ˬ~ LW+
104 forever. . . .] ~ . . . LW+
127 practising] practicing LW+
135 Lucky. . . .] ~ . . . LW+
145 bud-vases] ~ˬ~ LW+
146 Drawing-room] ~ˬ~ LW+

II. A Night with Lions

12 dewclaw. . . .] ~ . . . LW+

III. A Street off Sunset

58 Training. . . .] ~ . . . LW+
88 cries. . . .] ~ . . . LW+
97 forgiven. . . .] ~ . . . LW+
107 chicken-coop] ~ˬ~ LW+
116 over. . . .] ~ . . . LW+
123 her] ~ . . . LW+
127–28 *stanza break*] *no stanza break* LW+

Part I, "Children's Arms," reprinted in *A Time beyond Us*, ed. Myra Cohn Livingston (New York: Harcourt, Brace, 1968), p. 25, and *The Many Worlds of Poetry*, ed. Drachler and Terris (1969), p. 71; Part III, "A Street off Sunset," reprinted in *The Achievement of Randall Jarrell*, ed. Hoffman (1970), pp. 70–73.

RJ to Po (HR), November–December 1962: I have three new poems that I'd love to give you for *Poetry's* golden anniversary issue. One is a translation of Rilke, but I can't help feeling sentimentally that it would be nice for the anniversary issue to have something connected with Rilke.

RJ to Po (HR), early 1963: I was delighted that you liked *The Lost World*; it will be very pleasant to have it in the double issue.

C342   "In Montecito." *New Yorker*, 39 (5 Oct. 1963), 50. LW, CP.

12   toothbrush,]   ~;   LW⁺
17   night—]   ~:   LW⁺
Reprinted in *The New Yorker Book of Poems* (1969), pp. 332–33; *The Contemporary American Poets*, ed. Strand (1969), p. 144; *The Voice That Is Great within Us*, ed. Carruth (1970), pp. 402–03; *The Norton Anthology of Poetry*, ed. Eastman et al. (1970), p. 1097; *Shake the Kaleidoscope*, ed. Milton Klonsky (New York: Pocket Books, 1973), p. 104; *Messages: A Thematic Anthology of Poetry*, ed. X. J. Kennedy (Boston: Little, Brown, 1973).

C343   "The Mockingbird." *New Yorker*, 39 (2 Nov. 1963), 48. LW, CP.

4   squeak,]   ~:   LW⁺
     here;"]   ~";   LW⁺
10   lawn;]   ~:   LW⁺
20   that,]   ~ˌ   LW⁺
Reprinted in *Alumni News* (Univ. of N.C. at Greensboro), 54 (Spring 1966), 45; *Poems to Remember*, ed. Dorothy Petitt (New York: Macmillan, 1967), pp. 166–67; *A Time Beyond Us*, ed. Livingston (1968), p. 189; *The New Yorker Book of Poems* (1969), pp. 440–41; *Out of the Ark: An Anthology of Animal Verse*, ed. Gwendolyn Reed (New York: Atheneum, 1970), p. 203; on the record sleeve of Bill Crofut's *Poetry in Song*, William Crofut Productions, 1973; *Room for Me and a Mountain Lion*, ed. Nancy Larrick (New York: M. Evans and Co., 1974), p. 146; William Crofut, *The Moon on the One Hand: Poetry in Song* (New York: Atheneum, 1975), p. 33; *Dusk to Dawn: Poems of Night*, ed. Helen Hill et al. (1981).

C344   "Thinking of the Lost World." *Poetry*, 103 (Dec. 1963), 149–51. LW, CP.

An Epilogue to "The Lost World" | *in the last issue of this magazine*]   *omitted*   LW⁺
4   travelled]   traveled   LW⁺
18   down. . . .]   ~ . . .   LW⁺
24–25   *no stanza break*]   *stanza break*   LW⁺
45   *Stories,*]   ~;   LW⁺
59   good. . . .]   ~ . . .   LW⁺
68   Nineties. . . .]   ~ . . .   LW⁺
87–88   *all in small caps*]   *all in caps*   LW⁺
Reprinted in *The Achievement of Randall Jarrell*, ed. Hoffman (1970),

pp. 82–84; *The Norton Anthology of Poetry*, ed. Ellmann and O'Clair (1973), pp. 889–91; *The New Oxford Book of American Verse*, ed. Ellmann (1976), pp. 782–84.

C345 "Next Day." *New Yorker*, 39 (14 Dec. 1963), 58. LW, CP.

34 know....] ~... LW+
48 me,] ~: LW+
Reprinted in *Alumni News* (Univ. of N.C. at Greensboro), 54 (Spring 1966), 47; *The New Yorker Book of Poems* (1969), pp. 482–83; *The Norton Anthology of Modern Poetry*, ed. Ellmann and O'Clair (1973), pp. 884–85; *Poetry: Points of Departure*, ed. Henry Taylor (Cambridge, Mass.: Winthrop, 1974), pp. 71–73; *The Harper Anthology of Poetry*, ed. Nims (1981), pp. 668–69.

C346 "Bats." *Quarterly Review of Literature*, 13, no. 1/2 (1964), 122–23. BP, LW, CP.

Reprinted in *Out of the Ark*, ed. Reed (1968), pp. 10–11; *A Paper Zoo*, ed. Renee Karol Weiss and Ellen Raskin (New York: Macmillan, 1968), p. 22; excerpt in *Wonders and Surprises*, ed. Phyllis McGinley (Philadelphia: Lippincott, 1968); *Modern Poetry*, ed. Townsend (1971), p. 156; *Literature in America*, ed. Kaplan (1971), pp. 367–69; *Round About Eight: Poems for Today*, ed. Geoffrey Palmer and Noel Lloyd (London: Frederick Warne, 1972), pp. 19–20; *Beginnings in Poetry*, ed. Martz, 2d ed. (1973); *Room for Me and a Mountain Lion*, ed. Larrick (1974), pp. 138–39; *Quarterly Review of Literature: 30th Anniversary Poetry Retrospective*, ed. Weiss (1974), pp. 273–74; *To See the World Afresh*, ed. Lillian Moore and Judith Thompson (New York: Atheneum, 1974), pp. 61–62; *Poetry Lives!* (green level), ed. Joy Littell (Evanston, Ill.: McDougall, Littell, 1975), pp. 80–81; Stein, *The Uses of Poetry* (1975), p. 243; *News of the Universe: Poems of Twofold Consciousness*, ed. Robert Bly (San Francisco: Sierra Club Books, 1980); *Poetry: An Introduction*, ed. Miller and Greenberg (1981), pp. 207–8.

C347 "The Bird of Night." *Quarterly Review of Literature*, 13, no. 1/2 (1964), 123. LW, CP. Published separately as A18.

Reprinted in *Poems of the Sixties*, ed. F. E. S. Finn (London: John Murray, 1970), p. 131; *Bird Songs*, ed. Gwendolyn Reed (New York: Atheneum, 1971), p. 45; *Contemporary Poetry in America*, ed. Williams (1973), p. 34; on record sleeve of Bill Crofut's *Poetry in Song*, William Crofut Productions (1973); *Room for Me and a Mountain Lion*, ed.

Larrick (1974), p. 55; *Quarterly Review of Literature: 30th Anniversary Poetry Retrospective*, ed. Weiss (1974), p. 274; *To See the World Afresh*, ed. Moore and Thompson (1974), p. 65; *New Coasts and Strange Harbors*, ed. Helen Hillard and Agnes Perkins (New York: Thomas Y. Crowell, 1974); William Crofut, *The Moon on the One Hand* (1975), p. 43; *Little Creatures*, 1978 Sierra Club Calendar and Almanac for Young People (New York: The Sierra Club and Scribner's, 1977), entry for 29 Oct.; *American Forests*, 86 (March 1980), 24; *Dusk to Dawn*, ed. Hill et al. (1981).

C348   "The House in the Wood." *Quarterly Review of Literature*, 13, no. 1/2 (1964), 123–25. LW, CP.

Reprinted in *Best Poems of 1964: Borestone Mountain Poetry Awards 1965* (Palo Alto, Calif.: Pacific Books, 1965), pp. 55–56; Stein, *The Uses of Poetry* (1975), pp. 267–68.

C349   "Woman." *Kenyon Review*, 26 (Winter 1964), 48–53. LW, CP.

69   equalled]   equaled   LW+
73–74   *stanza break]   no stanza break*   LW+
77   persons]   women   LW+
174–75   *stanza break]   no stanza break*   LW+
Reprinted in *The Achievement of Randall Jarrell*, ed. Hoffman (1970), pp. 75–80; *The Norton Anthology of Modern Poetry*, ed. Ellmann and O'Clair (1973), pp. 886–89; *The New Oxford Book of American Verse*, ed. Ellmann (1976), pp. 777–82.

Note: This poem is a completely rewritten version of **C262**.

C350   "In Galleries." *Atlantic Monthly*, 213 (April 1964), 81. LW, CP.

C351   "Good Fences Make Good Poets." *New York Herald Tribune*, 30 Aug. 1964, pp. 1, 10 ("Book Week" section). Book review of Lawrence Thompson, *Selected Letters of Robert Frost*. KA.

C352   "A Masterpiece." *New York Times*, 29 Nov. 1964, Sec. 2, p. 3. Letter concerning the Jonathan Miller production of Robert Lowell's *The Old Glory*.

C353 "A Well-to-Do Invalid." *Encounter*, 24 (Jan. 1965), 17–18. LW, CP.

Reprinted in *The Distinctive Voice*, ed. Martz (1966), pp. 187–89.

C354 "The Lost Children." *New York Review of Books*, 28 Feb. 1965, p. 7. LW, CP; also published separately (see **A32**).

Reprinted in *Alumni News* (Univ. of N.C. at Greensboro), 54 (Spring 1966), 48; *The Contemporary American Poets*, ed. Strand (1969), pp. 144–46; *The Premier Book of Major Poets: An Anthology*, ed. Anita Dore (New York: Fawcett, 1970); *The Roses Race around Her Name*, ed. Jonathan Cott (New York: Stonehill, 1974), pp. 8–10; *Parnassus*, 5 (Fall–Winter 1976), 225, 227, with Mrs. Randall Jarrell's account of how this poem came to be, on pp. 223–29; *The Treasury of American Poetry*, ed. Sullivan (1978), pp. 557–59; *Always Begin Where You Are: Themes in Poetry and Song*, ed. Walter Lamb (New York: McGraw Hill, 1979), pp. 35–37; *The Practical Imagination*, ed. Frye et al. (1980), pp. 473–75.

C355 "The Man Who Loved Children." *Atlantic Monthly*, 215 (March 1965), 166–71. Excerpt from RJ's forthcoming "An Unread Book," an introduction to the new edition of Christina Stead's *The Man Who Loved Children*. In TBC as "An Unread Book."

Note: See above, **C292**, for other published comments on this book.

C356 "Well Water." *New York Times Review of Books*, 25 March 1965, p. 7. LW, CP.

Reprinted in *Quarterly Journal of the Library of Congress*, 27 (April 1970), 152; *The Norton Anthology of Poetry*, ed. Eastman et al. (1970), pp. 1097–98; *The Voice That Is Great within Us*, ed. Carruth (1970), p. 403; *L'Ephémère*, no. 14 (Spring 1970), 150, with a French translation by Alain Suied, "Eau de puits," on 151; *Poetry: Points of Departure*, ed. Taylor (1974), p. 71; *The New Oxford Book of American Poetry*, ed. Ellmann (1976), p. 777.

C357 "The Fire at the Waxworks" (Henrikas Radauskas). *Literary Review*, 8 (Spring 1965), 323. CP.

Reprinted in *The Contemporary World Poets*, ed. Junkins (1976), p. 202.

C358 "In a Hospital Garden" (Henrikas Radauskas), *Literary Review*, 8 (Spring 1965), 324. CP.

C359 "Outside the City Gate" (section from RJ's trans. of *Faust: Part One*). *Southern Review*, N.S., 1 (July 1965), 574–89. *Faust, Part I* (**A28**).

C360 "The Player Piano." *Greensboro Daily News*, 31 Oct. 1965, Sec. D, p. 3. CP.

> Reprinted in *Alumni News* (Univ. of N.C. at Greensboro), 54 (Spring 1966), 25; *The Distinctive Voice*, ed. Martz (1966), pp. 189–90; *Harper's Magazine*, 234 (Feb. 1967), 72; and *Themes in American Literature*, ed. Genthe and Keithley (1972), pp. 398–99.

C361 "The Augsburg Adoration." *New Yorker*, 41 (11 Dec. 1965), 56. CP.

> Reprinted in *The New Yorker Book of Poems* (1969), p. 39.

> *RJ to MDC, 15 October 1964:* I've written a new poem ["The Augsburg Adoration"] full of European things, that I'll send you with this letter. It's an appropriate poem since we have about twenty sparrows living six inches from us when we sit in the living-room; they have five big straw nests in the ivy, looking made-by-an-idiot-with-a-pitchfork.

C362 "Say Goodbye to Big Daddy." *Atlantic*, 220 (Sept. 1967), 99. CP.

> Reprinted in *A Literature of Sports*, ed. Tom Dodge (Lexington, Mass.: D. C. Heath, 1980), p. 509.

C363 "A Man Meets a Woman in the Street." *Harper's*, 234 (April 1967), 79. CP.

> Reprinted in *Randall Jarrell: 1914–1965*, ed. Robert Lowell et al. (New York: Farrar, Straus, and Giroux, 1968), pp. 299–302; see above, **B43**.

C364 "Fairy Song [Collected at Levanto (La Spezia) Italia]." *Atlantic Monthly*, 222 (Aug. 1968), 66. CP.

C365 "The Birth of Venus." *Mademoiselle*, 68 (Dec. 1968), 78. CP.

C366 "Letters to Maurice Sendak." *Greensboro Review*, no. 10 (Summer 1971), 47–50.

C367 "The Tears at the Movies." *Prairie Schooner*, 47 (Fall 1973), 232–33.

C368 "Sleeping at the Shamrock Hilton." *Prairie Schooner*, 47 (Fall 1973), 233.

C369 "Randall Jarrell: Letters to Vienna." ed. Mary Jarrell. *American Poetry Review*, no. 4 (1977), 11–17. Letters and excerpts from letters to Elisabeth Eisler; reprinted or early versions of the following poems: "A Game at Salzburg," "A Soul," "Hohensalzburg," "It Is Like Any Other," "Deutsch durch Freud," "An English Garden in Austria," and "Seele im Raum."

C370 Untitled tribute to Elizabeth Bishop. *Envoy* (American Academy of Poets), Spring–Summer 1982, pp. 1–2.

> *Note:* This tribute to Elizabeth Bishop was presented at the Guggenheim Museum, in New York City, on 29 Oct. 1964. It was recorded on tape; see below, G13.

D

Interviews and

Published Comments

D1 Untitled notice. *Vanderbilt Hustler* (Vanderbilt Univ., Nashville, Tenn., student newspaper), 9 Nov. 1934, p. 1. Comment upon publication of his first issue of the student humor magazine, the *Vanderbilt Masquerader*, by editor Randall Jarrell.

D2 Evelyn DeWitt, "Faculty Foibles" (column). *The Carolinian* (Woman's College of the Univ. of North Carolina [hereafter referred to as the Univ. of N.C. at Greensboro], weekly student newspaper), 17 Oct. 1947, p. 4. Includes RJ's comments on the ballet, how much he likes Greensboro (he had just joined the Woman's College faculty), and how little he liked living in New York City.

D3 Lewis Nichols, "Talk with Randall Jarrell." *New York Times Book Review*, 2 May 1954, p. 14. Interview that includes RJ's comments on *Pictures from an Institution*; sports cars; teaching and writing poetry; and work in progress (including his translation of Chekhov's *The Three Sisters*).

D4 Joyce Long and Bunny Robeson, "Jarrell Contributes to Forum Success with Lively Comment, Valued Criticism." *The Carolinian*, 23 March 1956, p. 4. Article about a Univ. of North Carolina at Greensboro Arts Festival that includes RJ's paraphrased comments.

D5 "Verse A-La-Canoe Days Gone, Jarrell Reports." *Greensboro* [N.C.] *Daily News*, 6 Sept. 1956, Sec. 1, p. 6. Includes RJ's humorous comments on recorded poetry; on his not knowing "who's reading poetry to girls in canoes these days," and the "last contemporary poet whose poetry was read by boys to girls in canoes was Edna St. Vincent Millay"; his approval of recorded poetry; how poetry is "in a better state that we have any right to expect, seeing as how people are not much interested in poetry"; and the false conception that new poets are wild and wooly.

D6 Milton Berliner, "Poet Sees Literacy in D.C." *Washington Daily News*, 6 Sept. 1956, p. 11. Includes RJ's brief comments on poetry and young poets; Edna St. Vincent Millay and Dylan Thomas; and recreation.

D7 "Future of Poetry Assessed as Dim by Glum Jarrell." *Greensboro Record*, 6 Sept. 1956, p. 12(B). Article based on RJ's humorous comments to reporters.

D8 Bess Furman, "Poetry Rate Hi with Expert's Fi: LP's Will Boom in Library Room." *New York Times*, 6 Sept. 1956, p. 27. Includes RJ's humorous comments on recorded poetry; how new poems also have rhyme and rhythm and are not so "wild and wooly"; his newly grown beard; and how, at a stoplight, out of a group of young boys came "a beautiful voice, deeply poetic," which called: "White Mercedes, have you come for me?" (referring to RJ's 190C convertible).

D9 George Dixon, "Poetry Consultant Will Help Congress." *Columbus* [Ohio] *Evening Dispatch*, 19 Sept. 1956, p. 1. Interview that includes RJ's comments on his beard; how poetry is at a low ebb; how modern poetry is not radical; and how he had found culture in Washington.

D10 "'Ready-Mixed Literature' Appalls Randall Jarrell." *Greensboro Record*, 18 Dec. 1956, p. 6(A). Article that quotes from Jarrell's comments at a 17 December lecture at the Library of Congress.

D11 Evangeline Davis, "Books" (column). *Greensboro Daily News*, 20 Jan. 1957, p. 3 ("Feature" section). Article about RJ's appearance on the "Good Morning" television program with Will Rogers, Jr., and his paraphrased comments on being called a "highbrow."

D12 Frank Van Der Linden, "Poet Jarrell Anticipating Return to Hometown." *Nashville* [Tenn.] *Banner*, 10 May 1957, p. 1. Article that includes RJ's comments about returning to Nashville for a visit; his service in World War II at a celestial navigation tower; how he began writing poetry as a boy in Nashville; his new white Mercedes convertible; his beard; his work on the *Anchor Book of Stories*, then in progress; and his forthcoming lecture at Vanderbilt.

D13 "Professor Is Critical of 'Instant Literature'." *Greensboro Daily News*, 28 July 1958, p. 1(B). Article that includes RJ's comments on "instant literature"; the inherent difficulty of the "truth"; and literature as "the union of a wish and a truth."

D14 Burke Davis, "Randall Jarrell Returns to WC [Woman's College] after Two Years in Washington." *Greensboro Daily News*, 5 Oct. 1958, Sec. 1, pp. 1, 8. Article that includes RJ's comments on his term as Poetry Consultant to the Library of Congress.

D15 "Statement of the Year". *Greensboro Daily News*, 2 Jan. 1959, p. 6(A). Republishes a quote from RJ's NBA speech, "About Popular Culture" (see above, **A31**, and below, **F3**).

D16 Anne White, "He's A Good Picker, Is Poet Jarrell" (in "Sights and Sounds" column). *Greensboro Daily News*, 5 Feb. 1959, p. 4(B). Article that includes RJ's comments or paraphrased comments on picking out clothes for his family; playing tennis; painting and sketching; his record collection; reading; working on his *Faust* translation; Pasternak; his beard; and his family and cat.

D17 "The Rewards of Vice." *Time*, 77 (24 March 1961), 88. Article that includes RJ's brief comments on the poet's relationship to the general public and on receiving the National Book Award.

D18 Nathan Glick, "About American Poetry: An Interview with Randall Jarrell." *Analects* (Univ. of N.C. at Greensboro literary magazine), 1 (Spring 1961), 5–10. Topics include writing poetry in contemporary America; Whitman, Frost, Dickinson, *Moby Dick*; nineteenth-century British and American poetry; Eliot, Pound, Stevens, Williams, Marianne Moore; the profession of letters; trends and styles among young American poets; foreign influences on American poetry; *Leaves of Grass*, "The Wasteland," and Freud.

> *Note:* This interview was originally published in Russian and Polish translations in *Amerika* (U.S.I.A. magazine), no. 38 (1959), 10–12; see below, I24, I28.

D19 "Trade Winds" (column). *Saturday Review*, 44 (1 April 1961), 6. Includes RJ's brief comments on receiving the National Book Award in Poetry and what he plans to do with the money.

D20 James Ross, "Randall Jarrell Discredits Ivory Tower Idea of Poet." *Greensboro Daily News*, 2 April 1961, pp. 1, 3(A). Article based on an interview that includes RJ's comments on writing poetry during his air force days; his interest in sports; how people don't read poetry because they're not exposed to it; his opposition to separating poetry from "the rest of literature"; how, to read poetry, one must have "practice" at it; Eliot, Browning, Wordsworth, Coleridge, Frost, Faulkner; how poetry is more natural to people than prose; dry periods in his poetry writing and how his wife encourages him; his love of ice hockey; *A Sad Heart at the Supermarket*, then in progress; and his belief that "poetry isn't on the way out," as some people have suggested, "unless humanity is on the way out."

D21 Larry Daughtrey, "Ignore Critics, Writers Told: Jarrell, at Literary Symposium, Discusses Author's Artistic Role." *Nashville Tennessean*, 28 April 1961, p. 1. Article about a Vanderbilt Univ. literary conference at which RJ took part in a panel discussion with Katherine Anne Porter, Robert Penn Warren, and Austin Warren (the topic of the discussion was "Art and Reality").

D22 Ida Kay Jordan, "No Sign of the Beatnik behind Poet's Beard" (in "Tarheel of the Week" column). *News and Observer* (Raleigh, N.C.), 11 June 1961, Sec. III, p. 3. Article that includes RJ's comments on teaching; critics; translating; his work on *Faust*; beatnik theory; how he writes from "inspiration of a sort"; his "timeless marriage" with his second wife Mary; his house and the surrounding wildlife; his belief in "art for art's sake"; how works of art "won't conform"; his work on the Kipling anthologies (in progress), and his review of

Shakespeare recordings (C331); his current preoccupation with reading Freud and learning to ice-skate; and how most of the "best" girls he teaches are southern.

D23 Peggy Pegues, "Poet-Professor Likes Rustic Life." *Charlotte* (N.C.) *Observer*, 18 Oct. 1961, p. 7(A). Article based on an interview that includes RJ's comments on his house and the surrounding wildlife; listening to classical music; tennis and professional football; *A Sad Heart at the Supermarket* (in progress); and his interest in World War II.

D24 "Poet Randall Jarrell Honored." *News and Observer* (Raleigh, N.C.), 19 Oct. 1961, p. 3. Article that includes RJ's brief comment about a tribute he received in Greensboro after receiving the National Book Award for Poetry.

D25 James Ross, "Fellow Craftsmen Pay Greensboro Poet Honor." *Greensboro Daily News*, 19 Oct. 1961, Sec. 1, p. 1. Article that includes brief comments by RJ following an affair in his honor after receiving the National Book Award.

D26 "Packed Hall Pays Homage to Poet." *Chapel Hill* (N.C.) *Weekly*, 19 Oct. 1961, p. 1. Article concerning RJ's receiving the National Book Award for Poetry, including brief comments by RJ.

D27 "Beginning—and Changes—Are Recalled." *Greensboro Daily News*, 23 March 1962, p. 1. Article concerning RJ's receiving North Carolina O. Max Gardner Award for excellence in teaching.

D28 "Poetic Justice." *Greensboro Record*, 24 March 1962, p. 4(A). Article that includes brief comments by RJ upon receiving the O. Max Gardner Award for excellence in teaching.

D29 Bill Landau, "Randall Jarrell: Poet Turns Critical of Today's Writers." *Journal-Sentinel* (Winston-Salem, N.C.), 4 Nov. 1962, p. 1(D). Article based on an interview with RJ that includes his comments on recent poetry and novels; *The Gingerbread Rabbit*; and his translation of *Faust*, in progress.

D30 Mary von Schrader Jarrell, "Recipe for a Carolina Christmas." *Greensboro Daily News*, 9 Dec. 1962, pp. 1, 18(C). Article by RJ's wife that includes several quoted comments by RJ.

D31 Larry Queen, "Jarrell Says Frost Was a Poet's Poet." *Journal-Sentinel* (Winston-Salem, N.C.), 8 March 1964, p. 3(D). Article based on an interview with RJ that includes his comments on Frost, Yeats, and Rilke; how he came to be a writer; the poems he published in the *American Review* (C17–C21); the creation of a poem; disillusionment and modern poetry; his current interest in writing about women or doing dramatic monologues "like little plays"; his own poems; the general lack of interest in poetry.

D32 Mortimer Guiney, "Randall Jarrell as Translator: A Previously Unpublished Interview." *Cahiers de l'V.E.R. Centre Universitaire de Valenciennes et du Hainaut*, Autumn 1976, pp. 59–68. Topics include RJ's reasons for translating *Faust*; the lack of a "definite-infinite" in his poetry; how "truthful war poems" are also "truthful peace poems"; childhood; Rilke's view of children; Sartre; Eleanor Ross Taylor's poetry; the general limited audience for poetry; *Pictures from an Institution*; the relation of poetry to prose; and translating Rilke and Goethe's *Faust*.

D33 Mary Jarrell, "Ideas and Poems." *Parnassus*, 5 (Fall/Winter 1976), 213–30. Article about how RJ's poem "The Lost Children" came to be, with many paraphrased comments by RJ throughout (as recollected by Mary Jarrell). The poem is reprinted in pp. 225–27.

E

Blurbs

E1 Blurb for Eleanor Ross Taylor, *Wilderness of Ladies* (New York: McDowell, Obolensky, 1960). Jarrell's blurb, which is actually taken from his introduction to this book, is printed on the back of the dust jacket:

> The taste of someone else's life—and while you are reading these poems you are someone else—is almost too sour to be borne; but sweet, too. The life is that of one woman, one (as the census would say) housewife; but a family and section and century are part of it, so that the poems have the "weight and power, / Power growing under weight" of a world. Some of this world is grotesquely and matter-of-factly funny, some of it is tragic or insanely awful—unbearable, one would say, except that it is being borne. But all of it is *so*, seen as no one else could see it, told as no one else could tell it. . . . The poems come out of the Puritan South. This Scotch Presbyterianism translated into the wilderness is, for her, only the fierce shell of its old self, but it is as forbidding and compulsive as ever: the spirit still makes its unforgiving demands on a flesh that is already too weak to have much chance in the struggle. . . . The world of the poems is as dualistic as that of Freud; everything splits, necessarily, into two warring opposites. This fault along which life divides, along which the earthquakes of existence occur, is for the poet primal—underlies all the gaps, disparities, cleavages, discontinuities that run right through her: she could say with Emerson, "There is a crack in everything God has made."

E2 Blurb for Robert Watson, *A Paper Horse* (New York: Atheneum, 1962). RJ's blurb is printed on the back of the dust jacket:

> The matter-of-fact and macabre world of these poems is one we recognize partly as Robert Watson's and partly as our own; when we read poems of the imaginative and dramatic immediacy of "An Elderly Ghost Has His Say" and "Whore with Trick", we cannot help realizing that we are in the presence of a true poet.

E3 Blurb for Sylvia Wilkinson, *Moss on the North Side* (Boston: Houghton, Mifflin, 1966). RJ's blurb is printed on the back of the dust jacket:

> The best writer of prose fiction that I've ever taught ... At her best she's really an inspired writer [and] has a detailed personal knowledge of the world she writes about.

F

Items Reproduced

by Ditto Process

F1 *Harvard Summer School Conference on the Defense of Poetry* (Cambridge: Harvard Univ., 1951). 166–fol. typescript transcription of the major addresses and discussions held at the conference. In punch-type binder, with cover title printed on thick yWhite (Centroid 92) stock: '[within red triple-rule frame] [in black] HARVARD SUMMER SCHOOL | *Conference on* | THE DEFENSE OF POETRY | AUGUST 14–17 · 1950 | [Harvard emblem] | HARVARD UNIVERSITY | CAMBRIDGE 38 MASSACHUSETTS'. RJ's "The Obscurity of the Poet," which was delivered at the evening session on "The Poem and the Public," 16 August 1950, appears on pp. 77–97. He then participated in a discussion with Robert Lowell, Harry Levin, William Y. Elliott, and John Ciardi, among others; his brief comments are found on pp. 140 and 141.

> *Note:* A complete transcription of this conference is available on phonograph records in the Woodberry Poetry Room of the Lamont Library, Harvard University.

F2 *The Three Sisters: A Drama in Four Acts*, translated from the Russian of Anton Chekhov, by Randall Jarrell, with the assistance of

Peter Kudrick. A 59-fol. acting script, 11 × 8½ in., of the first version of RJ's translation, reproduced on yellowish white wove, unwatermarked paper, by ditto process on rectos only. Bound in black paper clasp binder, with typed title label pasted on front.

> *Note:* This version of RJ's translation of *The Three Sisters* was produced by Giles Playfair at Aycock Auditorium, on the campus of the University of North Carolina at Greensboro (then, Woman's College), 12–13 March 1954. The production was set by Willard Barchenger, with costumes by W. A. Crews and Dee Boquist. Incidental music was composed for this production by Elliott Weisgarber.
> See above **A22**, for the final, heavily revised published version.

F3 *About Popular Culture.* New York, 11 March 1958. The National Book Award Committee distributed this 10-fol. leaflet as a press release. Reproduced from typescript by ditto process on rectos only, on yellowish white wove, unwatermarked paper; stapled in upper left corner; 11 × 8½ in.

> *Note:* See above **A33**, for published version.

F4 *Poets, Critics, and Readers.* [Charlottesville, Va.], 20 March 1959. A 10–fol. leaflet containing Jarrell's address to the Peters Rushton Seminar in Contemporary Prose and Poetry, the University of Virginia. Reproduced from typescript by ditto process, on rectos only, on yellowish white wove paper, watermarked '[open-face] HAMILTON MIMEO'; 22 × 8½ in., stapled in upper left corner.

> *Note:* see above, **C315**, for published version.

F5 *Address of Randall Jarrell, National Book Award.* New York, 14 March 1961. The National Book Award Committee distributed this 4–fol. leaflet as a press release. Reproduced by ditto process on rectos only, on yellowish white, wove, unwatermarked paper, 11 × 8½ in.; stapled in upper left corner.

> *Note:* published in *National Book Committee Quarterly*, 5 (Spring–Summer 1961), 2–3, with introductory material on pp. 1–2 (**C328**).

G

Sound Recordings

G1 *Randall Jarrell Reading His Poems in the Recording Laboratory, 9 June 1947.* Washington, D.C.: Library of Congress, 1947. Magnetic tape. T 6117–28, side B (formerly, LWO 2689, reel 6).

Contains: "Variations [I–IV]," "The Place of Death," "Oh My Name It Is Sam Hall," "New Georgia," "A Camp in the Prussian Forest," "Jews at Haifa," "The Boyg, Peer Gynt, the One Only One," "The Emancipators," "The Death of the Ball Turret Gunner," "The State," "The Snow Leopard," "The Wide Prospect," "Losses," "Eighth Air Force," "A Field Hospital," "Siegfried," "A Pilot from the Carrier," "The Dead Wingman," "New Georgia" (rereading), "Pilots, Man Your Planes," "A Camp in the Prussian Forest" (rereading), "Gunner," "Terms," "A Ward in the States," "The Lines," "The State" (rereading).

G2 *Randall Jarrell Reading His Poems in the Recording Laboratory, 28 November 1947.* Washington, D.C.: Library of Congress, 1947. Magnetic tape. T 6117–29, side A (formerly, LWO 2689, reels 5 and 6).

Contains: "Terms," "Money," "Moving," "Lady Bates," "A Country Life," "The Rising Sun," "The Child of Courts," "The Breath of Night," "Stalag Luft," "Burning the Letters."

G3 *Randall Jarrell Reading His Poems in the Recording Laboratory, 29–30 March 1948.* Washington, D.C.: Library of Congress, 1948. Magnetic tape. T 6117–29, side B (formerly, LWO 2689, reel 6).

Contains: "Losses," "Eighth Air Force," "A Field Hospital," "Stalag Luft," "Siegfried," "A Pilot from the Carrier," "The Dead Wingman," "New Georgia," "Pilots, Man Your Planes," "A Camp in the Prussian Forest," "Gunner," "Terms," "A Ward in the States," "The Lines," "The State."

G4 *Randall Jarrell Reading His Own Poems.* Washington, D.C.: Library of Congress, 1949. 78–rpm phonodisc. Recording Laboratory album P5, record P24. Recorded from magnetic tape of 28 November 1947 (see above, G2).

Contains: "Lady Bates" and "Stalag Luft." Texts included in slipcase.

> *Note:* The poems in this album were reissued as *Poets Reading Their Own Poems.* Washington, D.C.: Library of Congress, 1954. 33⅓-rpm phonodisc. PL 7. Texts contained in accompanying booklet.

G5 *Randall Jarrell Reading His Poems from* The Seven-League Crutches, *at the Home of Donald Stauffer, Princeton, N.J., 28 September 1951.* Washington, D.C.: Library of Congress, 1951. Magnetic tape. T 1963–1 (formerly, LWO 1963, reel 1).

Contains: "Transient Barracks: 1944," "A Game at Salzburg," "A Girl in a Library," "A Conversation with the Devil," "The Truth," "Seele in Raum," "The Night before the Night before Christmas."

G6 *Randall Jarrell Reading "The Taste of the Age."* Washington, D.C.: Library of Congress, 1956. Recorded at the Coolidge Auditorium of the Library of Congress, 17 December 1956. Magnetic tape. T 2516 (formerly, LWO 2516).

G7 *Randall Jarrell Reading "Poets, Critics, and Readers."* Washington, D.C.: Library of Congress, 1957. Recorded in the Coolidge Auditorium of the Library of Congress, 28 October 1957. Magnetic tape. T 2609 (formerly, LWO 2609).

G8 *Richard Wilbur Reading His Poems, with Commentary, in the Recording Laboratory, 2 December 1957, Including a Discussion be-*

tween Wilbur and Randall Jarrell. Washington, D.C.: Library of Congress, 1957. Magnetic tape. T 2623 (formerly, LWO 2623).

G9 *John Crowe Ransom Reading His Poems, and Discussing Them with Randall Jarrell, in the Recording Laboratory, 14 January 1958.* Magnetic tape. T 2628 (formerly, LWO 2628).

G10 *Robert Frost Interviewed by Randall Jarrell, in the Recording Laboratory, 19 May 1959.* Magnetic tape. T 2849 (formerly, LWO 2849).

G11 *Randall Jarrell Reading His Poetry at the Second Johns Hopkins Poetry Festival, 25 October 1961.* Washington, D.C.: Library of Congress, 1961. Magnetic tape. T 3558 (formerly, LWO 3558).

Contains: three Rilke translations, "The Blind Man's Song," "Washing the Corpse," and "Childhood"; and RJ's poems "The Lines," "Eighth Air Force," "Transient Barracks," "The Death of the Ball Turret Gunner," "The Woman at the Washington Zoo," "Cinderella," and "The Bronze David of Donatello."

G12 *National Poetry Festival, 22–24 October 1962.* Washington, D.C.: Library of Congress, 1962. Includes RJ reading "Fifty Years of American Poetry," recorded during the Monday evening session, 22 October 1962, magnetic tape T 3868–3 (formerly, LWO 3868, reel 3), and his Rilke translation, "The Blind Man's Song," and his poems "Eighth Air Force," "Cinderella," and "The Woman at the Washington Zoo," with extensive commentary, at the Wednesday afternoon session, 24 October 1962, magnetic tape T 3870–2 and 3 (formerly LWO 3870, reel 3).

G13 *Randall Jarrell Reading His Poems, and those of Elizabeth Bishop, at the Guggenheim Museum, New York City, 29 October 1964,* as part of a program honoring Miss Bishop. Washington, D.C.: Library of Congress, 1964. Magnetic tape. T 4868 (formerly, LWO 4868).

Contains: Jarrell's introductory remarks, and his reading Bishop's "The Fish," "The Man-moth," "The Prodigal," "Manuelzinho," "Rain towards Morning," "At the Fish House," "The Armadillo," and his own poems "In Montecito," "Next Day," "A Well-to-do Invalid,"

"A Street off Sunset" (with extensive commentary), "Three Bills," "The Player Piano."

    Note: Jarrell is introduced by Robert Lowell.

G14 *Randall Jarrell Interviewed by Edithe Walton on "Speak Up," for broadcast over WNBC Radio, New York City, 4 February 1965.* Washington, D.C.: Library of Congress, 1965. Magnetic tape. T4861 (formerly, LWO 4861).

Topics discussed include RJ's writing habits; themes; his children's books; *The Lost World, Pictures from an Institution,* and *A Sad Heart at the Supermarket;* the Actors Studio production of his translation of Chekhov's *The Three Sisters;* translations he is interested in doing; Russian literature; teaching; his anthologies; his term as Poetry Consultant at the Library of Congress; and his recent work.

G15 *The Spoken Arts Treasury of 100 Modern American Poets Reading Their Poems.* New York: Spoken Arts, 1969. 33⅓-rpm phonodisc. SA 1051, vol. XII, side 1.

Contains: "Cinderella" and "The Woman at the Washington Zoo," with RJ's remarks and comments on the two poems.

G16 *Randall Jarrell Reading* The Gingerbread Rabbit. New York: Caedmon Records, 1971. 33⅓-rpm phonodisc. Caedmon TC 1381. Notes on the slipcase by Mary von S. Jarrell.

Reissued as Caedmon tape cassette CDL 51381; Mrs. Jarrell's notes are contained on the inner sleeve.

G17 *The Bat-Poet Read by the Author.* New York: Caedmon Records, 1972. 33⅓-rpm phonodisc. Caedmon TC 1364. Notes on slipcase by Mary von S. Jarrell.

Reissued as Caedmon tape cassette CDL 51364; Mrs. Jarrell's notes are contained on the inner sleeve.

G18 *Randall Jarrell Reads and Discusses His Poems against War.* New York: Caedmon Records, 1972. 33⅓-rpm phonodisc. Caedmon TC 1363. Recorded on 13 April 1961, at Pfeiffer College, North Carolina. Notes on slipcase by Mary von S. Jarrell.

Contains: "A Lullaby," "Mail Call," "The Lines," "The Death of the Ball Turret Gunner," and "Eighth Air Force," with extensive commentary on the poems.

Reissued as Caedmon tape cassette CDL 51363; Mrs. Jarrell's notes are contained on the inner sleeve.

G19 *Randall Jarrell Reading His Poems at the New York City YM/ YWHA, 28 April 1963*. New York: McGraw-Hill, 1978. Tape cassette C-325. Distributed by Poet's Audio Center, Washington, D.C., as *The Poetry of Randall Jarrell.*

Contains: "The Mockingbird," "The Bird of Night," "Bats," "Next Day," "Three Bills," "Gleaning," "In Montecito," and "The Lost World," with extensive commentary on the poems.

G20 *The Poet's Voice: Poets Reading Aloud and Commenting upon Their Work*, sel, and ed. by Strathis Haviaris (Cambridge, Mass.: Harvard Univ. Press, 1978). Boxed set of twelve unnumbered cassettes which includes "Randall Jarrell" (with "John Berryman" on opposite side). First five selections were recorded for the Poetry Room, Harvard University, December 1946, and the last four poems were recorded at the Guggenheim Museum, New York City, in October 1964 (see above, G13).

Contains: "Gunner," "The Lines," "A Camp in the Prussian Forest," "The Prince," "A Ward in the States," "In Montecito," "Next Day," "Three Bills," and "The Player Piano," with extensive commentary on the poems.

H

Musical Settings

'

H1   Frank Becker, Cantata (1968). Setting for soprano, alto, tenor, and bass voices, flute, oboe, horn, two violins, cello, and viola. In four parts: I. "The State"; II. "Protocols"; III. "The Death of the Ball Turret Gunner"; and IV. "The Truth." Unpublished.

H2   Frank Boehnlein, "The Death of the Ball Turret Gunner." Setting for chorus, orchestra, and theater media. Unpublished. Registered in the name of Frank Boehnlein, under E unpub. 517034, 5 September 1974.

H3   William Crofut, *The Moon on the One Hand* (New York: Atheneum, 1975).

Contains: Crofut's musical settings for voice, with piano or guitar accompaniment, of "The Chipmunk's Day," pp. 30–32 (text of poem printed on p. 29); "The Mockingbird," pp. 34–41 (text of poem printed on p. 33); "The Bird of Night," pp. 44–46 (text of poem printed on p. 43).

> *Note:* William Crofut has recorded these musical settings of Jarrell's poems on Crofut Productions recording CO 6005 A, *Poetry in Song* (1973), side A; the individual texts of the poems are printed on the slipcase.

H4 Edward Johnson, "The Christmas Roses" (c. 1968). Setting for soprano with piano. Unpublished.

H5 Andrew Thomas, "A Bat Is Born" (1974). Setting for soprano with saxophone quartet. Unpublished.

H6 Paul Alan Levi, "The Truth" (New York: American Composer's Alliance, 1975). Setting for treble voice with chamber orchestra.

H7 Edward Johnson, "A Bat Is Born" (New York: Mindover Music, 1979). Setting for tenor with clarinet.

H8 Edward Johnson, "The Death of the Ball Turret Gunner" (New York: Mindover Music, 1980). Reduction for voice and piano from original setting for bass with string quartet.

H9 Edward Johnson, "The Player Piano" (New York: Mindover Music, 1981). Setting for soprano with clarinet.

I

Translations

FRENCH

Books

I1 *Poèmes Choisis*, ed. and trans. Renaud Jouvenel. Paris: Pierre Segher, 1965. Orangish brown and white printed paper boards; dust jacket.

Contains: the English texts and French translations of "A Girl in the Library," "The Face," "The Venetian Blind," "The Wide Prospect," "An English Garden in Austria," "A Utopian Journey," "90 North," "The Emancipators," "Losses," "A Pilot from the Carrier," "Burning the Letters," "The Dead Wingman," "Jews at Haifa," "Absent with Official Leave," "The Sick Nought," "1945: The Death of the Gods," "Come to the Stone," "The Metamorphoses," "The Survivor among Graves."

I2 *Le lapin de pain d'épice*, trans. Dominique Jean. Paris: Fernand Jean, 1979. Pictorial paper wrapper. Translation of *The Gingerbread Rabbit*, with the Garth Williams illustrations.

I3 *La chauve-souris poète*, trans. Catherine Chaine and Bernard Noël. Paris: Renard Poche, 1980. Translation of *The Bat-Poet*, with the Sendak illustrations. Pictorial wrapper.

Anthology

I4 *Anthologie de la Poésie Americaine,* ed. and trans. Alain Bosquet. Paris: Librairie Stock, 1956. Printed wrapper, with glassine jacket.

Contains: Bosquet's translations of "Losses," pp. 240, 241, and "The Sick Nought," pp. 241, 242.

I5 *Trente-Cinq Jeunes Poètes Américains,* ed. Alain Bosquet. Paris: Gallimard, 1960. Printed wrapper.

Contains: the English texts and French translations of "The Death of the Ball Turret Gunner," p. 235; "Gunner," p. 237; "Eighth Air Force," p. 233; and "Terms," pp. 227, 229, 231.

Periodicals

I6 *Perspectives USA* (French language edition), no. 1 (Fall 1952). Not seen.

Contains: translation of "The Situation of the Poet."

I7 *Perspectives USA* (French language edition), no. 2 (Winter 1953). Not seen.

Contains: translation of "Some Lines from Whitman."

I8 *Europe: Revue Mensuelle,* 37, nos. 358–59 (Feb.–March 1959).

Contains: translations of "The Survivor among Graves," pp. 169–71, and "1945: The Death of the Gods," p. 169.

I9 *Le Figaro Litteraire,* 28 March 1959.

Contains: translation of "The Appalling Taste of the Age," by A. Sacriste, pp. i-ii.

I10 *L'Ephémère,* no. 14 (Summer 1970).

Contains: translations by Alain Suied of "Well Water," p. 151, "Washing," p. 153, and "The Traveller," pp. 155, 157.

GERMAN

Book

I11 *Nachtschwärmer*, trans. Hildegard Krahé. Zurich: Diogenes, 1980. Translation of *Fly by Night*, with the Sendak illustrations. Bluish gray cloth boards; printed pictorial dust jacket (design ident. to **A27**).

I12 *Die Tierfamilie*, trans. Barbara Henninges. Zurich: Diogenes, 1984. Translation of *The Animal Family*, with the Sendak illustrations. Light brown pictorial wrapper.

Periodicals

I13 *Perspectives U.S.A.* (German language edition), no. 1 (Fall 1952). Not seen.

Contains: translation of "The Situation of the Poet."

I14 *Perspectives U.S.A.* (German language edition), no. 2 (Winter 1953). Not seen.

Contains: translation of "Some Lines from Whitman."

HUNGARIAN

Book

I15 *Döntés Électre-Halálra*, trans., with an biographical afterword, by Tandori Dezsö. Budapest: Tandori Dezsö Fordítása, 1972. Printed wrapper.

Contains: translations of "A Country Life," "The Orient Express," "The Death of the Ball Turret Gunner," "Burning the Letters," "The Survivor among Graves," "The Woman at the Washington Zoo," "Windows," "The Lonely Man," "The Traveler," "The Lost World," "A Well-to-Do Invalid," "The X-Ray Waiting Room in the Hospital," "In Galleries," "The Lost Children," "Three Bills," "The Old and the New Masters," "Field and Forest," "Thinking of the Lost World," "Gleaning," "A Man Meets a Woman in the Street," "The Player Piano," "Eine Kleine Nachtmusik," "On the Railway Platform," "A

Poem for Someone Killed in Spain," "The Bad Music," "An Essay on the Human Will," "The Christmas Roses," "The Difficult Resolution," "The Street Has Changed," "News," "The Tree," "The Northern Snows," "I Loved You Too," "The Lot Is Vacant Still," "There Was Glass and There Are Stars," "The Birth of Venus," "The Wild Birds," "Women on a Bus," "What Was Longed for and, Once, Certain," "A Prayer at Morning," "The Old Orchard in the Middle of the Forest," "What's the Riddle."

ITALIAN

Books

I16 *La Poesia di un'Epoca*, trans. Donatella Manganotti. Parma: Ugo Guanda, 1956. Printed pictorial wrapper. Translation of *Poetry and the Age*.

I17 *L'Insidiosa Modestia della Corazza*, by Marianne Moore, trans. Giovanni Galtieri. Parma: Ugo Guanda, 1962. Pictorial paper boards.

Contains: introduction by Jarrell, in translation by Galtieri, pp. ix-xxi.

Anthology

I18 *Poesia Americana del '900*, ed. Carlo Izzo. Parma: Guanda, 1963. Pictorial cloth boards.

Contains: translations of "The Islands," pp. 601, 603, and "The Face," p. 605.

Periodicals

I19 *Perspectives U.S.A.* (Italian language edition), no. 1 (Fall 1952). Not seen.

Contains: translation of "The Situation of the Poet."

I20 *Perspectives U.S.A.* (Italian language edition), no. 2 (Winter 1953). Not seen.

Contains: translation of "Some Lines from Whitman."

JAPANESE

Books

I21   *The Gingerbread Rabbit.* Tokyo: Iwanami Shoten, 1979. Pictorial paper boards, with clear plastic wraparound jacket. Contains the Garth Williams illustrations.

I22   *The Animal Family.* Tokyo: Iwanami Shoten, 1981. Pictorial paper boards. Contains the Sendak illustrations.

Periodicals

I23   *Japan-America Forum,* 14 (Dec. 1968).

Contains: an excerpt from "Fifty Years of American Poetry," pp. 76–83.

POLISH

I24   *Amerika,* no. 38 [1959].

Contains: Polish translation of an interview with RJ, by Nathan Glick.

I25   *Tematy,* 3, no. 9 (1964).

Contains: translation of "Fifty Years of American Poetry," pp. 7–36.

SPANISH

I26   *Antologia de la Poesia Norteamericana Contemporanea,* ed. and trans. Eugenio Florit. Washington, D.C.: Pan American Union, 1955. Not seen.

Contains: translation of "The Survivor among Graves," pp. 132–34

TURKISH

Periodical

I27   *Türk Dili,* 10, no. 113 (1961).

Contains: translation, by Doğan Hizlan, of "The Obscurity of the Poet," pp. 256–57.

RUSSIAN

Periodical

I28 *Amerika,* no. 38 [1959].

Contains: interview, "Interv'iu s Randollom Jarrellom," pp. 10–12. Published in Polish translation; see above I23. Also published in English translation; see D18.

J

Published Drawing

J1 *Vanderbilt Masquerader* (Vanderbilt Univ., Nashville, Tenn., student humor magazine), 10 (Feb. 1934). Cover contains a drawing of Sylvia Frank, by Randall Jarrell.

> *Note:* It is likely that Jarrell contributed other drawings, or perhaps cartoons, but none is signed or directly attributable to him.

K

Sound Films

K1 "North Carolina Books and Authors: Mr. Randall Jarrell," no. 5 in the series of "North Carolina Books and Authors," produced by WUNC-TV, Channel 4, University of North Carolina at Chapel Hill, 1960. 1,000-foot reel (30 minutes) which features RJ reading and discussing six of his poems: "A Lullaby," "Mail Call," "The Lines," "Losses," "A Pilot from the Carrier," and "Eighth Air Force."

K2 Walter Kaufman, "Arts Hour," Channel 13, New York City, 10 July 1964. 60 minutes. Topics discussed include the writing and production of RJ's translations of *The Three Sisters* and *Faust*. RJ also read "A Street off Sunset," "Night with Lions," and "The Lost World."

K3 "Randall Jarrell: 1914–1965," produced by WUNC-TV, Channel 4, University of North Carolina at Chapel Hill, 1971. Hour-long sound film tribute to Jarrell which blends his own readings of "In Montecito," "The Mockingbird," "Next Day," "Three Bills," "The Death of the Ball Turret Gunner," and "The Woman at the Washington Zoo," with visualizations from the works of Paul Klee, Maurice Sendak, Amadeo Modigliani, Walter Barker, and Charles Huntley. Jarrell's Princeton friend Edward Cone provided music for the sound track, selections from the piano music of Franz Liszt. Mrs. Randall Jarrell discusses her husband's work and offers possible interpretations.

Index